University of Plymouth Library

Subject to status this item may be renewed
via your Voyager account
http://voyager.plymouth.ac.uk
Tel: (01752) 232323

DEFINING THE HOLY

Defining the Holy
Sacred Space in Medieval and Early Modern Europe

Edited by
ANDREW SPICER
Oxford Brookes University, UK

and

SARAH HAMILTON
University of Exeter, UK

ASHGATE

Published by
Ashgate Publishing Limited
Gower House
Croft Road
Aldershot
Hants GU11 3HR
England

Ashgate Publishing Company
Suite 420
101 Cherry Street
Burlington, VT 05401-4405
USA

Ashgate website: http://www.ashgate.com

British Library Cataloguing in Publication Data
Defining the holy : sacred space in medieval and early modern Europe
   1.Sacred space—Europe—History—To 1500 2.Sacred space—Europe—
   History—16th century 3.Sacred space—Europe—History—17th century
   4.Church buildings—Europe—History—To 1500 5.Church buildings—
   Europe—History—16th century 6.Church buildings—Europe—History—17th
   century
   I.Hamilton, Sarah, 1966– II.Spicer, Andrew
   263'.0424

Library of Congress Cataloging-in-Publication Data
Defining the holy : sacred space in medieval and early modern Europe / edited by
Sarah Hamilton and Andrew Spicer.
   p. cm.
 Includes index.
 ISBN 0-7546-5194-0 (alk. paper)
 1. Sacred space. I. Hamilton, Sarah, 1966- II. Spicer, Andrew.

BL580.D44 2005
263'.0424—dc22

2005012315

Printed and bound in Great Britain by TJI Digital, Padstow, Cornwall

ISBN-10 0 7546 5194 0
ISBN-13 978 0 7546 5194 9

Contents

List of Figures

List of Contributors

Lisa A. Banner is the Samuel H. Kress Curatorial Fellow, the Hispanic Society of America. She is completing her doctoral thesis on 'The Religious Patronage of the Duke of Lerma' with Professor Jonathan Brown, at the Institute of Fine Arts, New York University. She has published articles on the patronage of the Duke of Lerma and Spanish drawings.

Stijn Bossuyt is a Research Assistant at the Catholic University of Leuven where he is completing his Ph.D. thesis on the social structures and devotional practices in Flanders (Lille, Saint-Omer and Bruges) between 1100 and 1350. He has published several articles in connection with his master's thesis on funeral inscriptions and their social meaning in Ypres.

Simon Dixon is currently completing his Ph.D. thesis on 'The Quaker Community in London, c.1667–1714' at Royal Holloway, University of London. His research interests focus on religious nonconformity in the seventeenth and early eighteenth centuries and the history of London.

Claire Gapper completed her Ph.D. thesis at the Courtauld Institute of Art, University of London, and is now an independent architectural historian, publishing and researching into the plasterwork of the Tudor and Stuart periods.

Sarah Hamilton is Lecturer in Medieval History, University of Exeter. She is the author of *The Practice of Penance, 900–1050* (2001) and several articles on penance in its wider context.

Eric Johnson completed his doctorate at the University of California at Los Angeles and is currently a visiting scholar at the UCLA Clark Library and Center for Seventeenth- and Eighteenth-Century Studies.

Caroline Knight is an independent architectural historian, specializing in sixteenth- to eighteenth-century British architecture. She is currently writing a book about the country houses round London.

Cynthia Lawrence was Professor of Art History at Temple University, Philadelphia. Her research has concentrated on art and society in the Low Countries, focusing in particular on patronage, Rubens, religious and sepulchral art. Her publications include, *Flemish Baroque Commemorative Monuments, 1566–1725* (1981), *Gerrit Adriaensz. Berckheyde (1639–98): Haarlem Cityscape Painter* (1991) and she edited *Women and Art in Early Modern Europe. Patrons, Collectors and Connoisseurs* (1997).

Judi Loach is Reader in Architectural History at the Welsh School of Architecture, Cardiff. Her research has primarily focused on seventeenth-century French culture, especially Jesuit patronage. She is the author of numerous articles on this and other topics, and is currently working on a critical edition of Menestrier's *Idée de l'estude d'un honneste home*.

June L. Mecham is Assistant Professor in History at the University of Nebraska at Omaha. Her research interests focus on gender and religious devotion; material culture, space, and performance in Northern Europe, particularly Germany, during the later Middle Ages.

Graeme Murdock is Senior Lecturer in Modern History at the University of Birmingham. His current research interests include the material culture of Reformed religion and the Reformation in Hungary and Transylvania. Recent publications include *Calvinism on the Frontier, 1600–1660. International Calvinism and the Reformed Church in Hungary and Transylvania* (2000), and *Beyond Calvin. The Intellectual, Political and Cultural World of Europe's Reformed Churches* (2004).

Jeanne Nuechterlein is Lecturer in the History of Art at the University of York. Her research interests are in northern European art of the fifteenth and sixteenth centuries. Her monograph *The Essential Image: Holbein's Reformation of Art* is forthcoming with Pennsylvania State Press.

Tim Pestell is Curator of Archaeology at Norwich Castle Museum and an Honorary Research Fellow at the University of East Anglia. He has co-edited *Markets in Early Medieval Europe* (2003) which won the Best Scholarly Book prize in the 2004 British Archaeological Awards. His book *Landscapes of Monastic Foundation* was published in 2004. His research interests include monasticism, medieval landscape history and artefacts studies.

Annabel Ricketts (1945–2003) was the leading authority on Protestant country house chapel after the Reformation, and her doctoral thesis 'The Evolution of the Protestant Country House Chapel, *c.*1500–1700' is being prepared for publication by Spire Books. She lectured at Birkbeck College, University College London, the Courtauld Institute of Art and the Victoria and Albert Museum. From 1995 to 2003 she was head of the Fine and Performing Arts Department at Regent's College, London.

Andrew Spicer is Senior Lecturer in Early Modern European History at Oxford Brookes University. His research explores the socio-cultural impact of the Reformation, in particular the impact that Calvinist ideas had upon church architecture and the beliefs associated with places of worship. He is currently writing a monograph entitled *The Reformed Church: Architecture and Society* for Manchester University Press. He recently co-edited *Society and Culture in the Huguenot World, 1559–1685* (2002) and *Sacred Space in Early Modern Europe* (2005).

Diana Webb is Senior Lecturer in History at King's College London. Her research has focused on medieval social and religious history and city-state Italy. She is the author of *Patrons and Defenders: the Saints in the Italian City States* (1996), *Pilgrims and Pilgrimage in the Medieval West* (1999), *Pilgrimage in Medieval England* (2000) and *Medieval European Pilgrimage* (2002).

Richard L. Williams read Theology before completing a doctorate at the Courtauld Institute of Art on the impact of the Reformation on Tudor visual culture. He is currently associate lecturer at Birkbeck College, University of London and is a lecturer at the National Gallery. He has contributed chapters to several books all of which focus on the Reformation and the visual arts.

Preface

The origins of this volume lie in a conference we organized at the University of Exeter, 10–12 April 2003, on the theme of *Defining the Holy: Sacred Space in Medieval and Early Modern Europe.* The conference was attended by some 125 people from Russia, North America, and Europe as well as the British Isles, and attracted a rich variety of papers. Over seventy-five papers were delivered during the conference and the essays in this volume therefore represent only some of the themes which came to the fore on that occasion. We would like to take this opportunity to thank all those who attended the conference and the Department of History at Exeter for their support.

We would also like to acknowledge the generous support of the Institute for Historical and Cultural Studies, Oxford Brookes University, for providing a substantial grant towards the costs associated with editorial work and publication of this volume. We would also like to thank Alex Walsham for her advice and judicious observations in the course of editing this volume, and Barbara Crostini for her assistance in preparing the text for publication.

Sarah Hamilton
Andrew Spicer

List of Abbreviations

BAR	British Archaeological Reports
BL	British Library
CEPR	*Calendars of Entries in the Papal Registers Relating to Great Britain and Ireland*, ed. W.H. Bliss *et al.* (London, 1893–)
CCCM	Corpus Christianorum, Continuatio Mediaevalis
Coster & Spicer, *Sacred Space*	W. Coster and A. Spicer (eds), *Sacred Space in Early Modern Europe* (Cambridge, 2005)
DSp	M. Viller, F. Cavallera and J. de Guibert (eds), *Dictionnaire de spiritualité ascétique et mystique, doctrine et histoire* (16 vols, Paris, 1932–95)
Eliade, *The Sacred and the Profane*	M. Eliade, *The Sacred and the Profane: the Nature of Religion*, trans. W.R. Trask (New York, 1959); originally published in German in 1957
Gilchrist, *Gender*	R. Gilchrist, *Gender and Material Culture: the Archaelogy of Religious Women* (London, 1994)
HBS	Henry Bradshaw Society
NA	The National Archives (formerly The Public Record Office)
P&P	*Past & Present*
PL	*Patrologia Latinae cursus completus series latinae*, ed. J.P. Migne (221 vols, Turnhout, 1844–64).
PS	Parker Society
SCH	Studies in Church History
SCJ	*Sixteenth-Century Studies Journal*

VCH	*The Victoria County History of the Counties of England*
Wickham Legg, *English Orders*	*English Orders for Consecrating Churches in the Seventeenth Century*, ed. J. Wickham Legg, HBS li (1911)

Chapter 1

Defining the Holy:
the Delineation of Sacred Space

Sarah Hamilton and Andrew Spicer

For any pilgrim who walks along the Via Dolorosa to the church of the Holy Sepulchre today, as in the medieval and early modern periods, the experience combines the sacred with the profane, the public with the personal. On the one hand, pilgrims walk along the route they believed Christ took to the site of his crucifixion, on the other they walk along a street lined with shops to the church of the Holy Sepulchre, built on the site of Calvary, a building made holy not only through being the site of the events central to the Christian faith (a liminal space as the locus for Christ's resurrection), but also through the rite of consecration,[1] and through the liturgical rites conducted there on a daily basis. Both en route and once inside the church the pilgrims may choose to participate in public prayers, that is those of their tour group, and sometimes, as on Good Friday, the liturgies of the Christian churches, or conduct their own private devotions, or to take part in both. Such pilgrimages, by visiting the places of Christ's life, help the participant to come closer to the heavenly Jerusalem; in his early twelfth-century guide to the Holy Places, Rorgo Fretellus urged his audience to 'ponder upon the heavenly city of Jerusalem ... which is an allegory for us of the heavenly paradise'.[2] Inevitably, however, the secular penetrated into such terrestrial paradises, be they twelfth-century Jerusalem or fourteenth-century Rome, where stall holders selling food and

---

[1] Egeria witnessed the feast of the dedication of the Holy Sepulchre on her pilgrimage to the Holy Land 381–4 AD: *The Pilgrimage of Etheria*, trans. M.L. McClure and C.L. Feltoe (London, 1919), pp. 95–6. The Latin church on the site was consecrated on 15 June 1149, on the fiftieth anniversary of the capture of Jerusalem: John of Würzburg, *Descriptio Terrae Sanctae*, ch. xiii, in S. de Sandoli, *Itinera Hierosylmitana Crucesignatorum (saec. xii–xiii)* (3 vols, Jerusalem, 1981–83), II, p. 290.

[2] P.C. Boeren, *Rorgo Fretellus et sa description de la Terre Sainte. Histoire et édition du texte* (Amsterdam, 1980), p. 6: 'considera sanctam Iherusalem, contemplare et ipsam Syon, que celestem paradysum allegorice nobis figurat'; B. Hamilton, 'The Impact of Crusader Jerusalem on Western Christendom', *Catholic Historical Review* 80 (1994), 699.

pilgrimage badges, as well as tooth-pullers and cobblers, are recorded as paying rent for pitches on the steps leading up to and in the atrium of St Peter's basilica itself.[3] The persistence of this Durkheimian juxtaposition between the sacred and the profane therefore points to some of the issues which confront any historian who wishes to study the nature of sacred space in any period, and in particular the problems surrounding how sacred space is defined by Christians whose cosmology regards the whole world as God's creation.[4] To what extent is sacred space constructed or is it innate? How far is sacred space restricted to certain buildings and locations? Is sacred space defined through opposition to that which is not sacred? To what degree is sacred space defined by public or personal devotion? In other words, how is sacred space constructed and defined?

Views of Eliade's Paradigm from Other Disciplines

The nature and meaning of sacred space was considered by Mircea Eliade over forty years ago, when he constructed his paradigm for the nature of religion in *The Sacred and the Profane: the Nature of Religion* (1959). For Eliade the sacred was defined by space, time and cosmology. Although Eliade drew on Émile Durkheim's identification of the bipolar distinction between the sacred and the profane as characteristic of all religious beliefs, it is worth noting that both scholars, in using a distinction derived from the Latin, *sacer* and *profanus*, were using words which originally had a primarily spatial meaning.[5] *Sacer* denoted that which was sacred, and could be used of both objects and places. *Profanus*, on the other hand, referred to the area outside the *sacrum*, the sacred place, that is the temple, but came to mean the opposite to *sacer*, that which was not sacred. *Sacer* should be distinguished from another concept, *fas*, designating in Latin acts which were sanctioned by religious authorities; the *dies fasti* were days on which civil activities were permitted, the *dies nefasti* those on which such activities were forbidden. Whilst *sacer* is associated with both place and authority, the resonances for *profanus* are predominantly spatial. In other words, the concept of sacred space lies at the heart of sociologists' distinction between the sacred and the profane. Moreover, it is worth noting that this verbal dichotomy was in (relatively) common

---

[3] D. Birch, *Pilgrimage to Rome in the Middle Ages: Continuity and Change* (Woodbridge, 1998), pp. 120–21.

[4] É. Durkheim, *The Elementary Forms of the Religious Life*, trans. J.W. Swain (London, 1915), pp. 36–42.

[5] C. Colpe, 'The Sacred and the Profane', in M. Eliade, ed., *The Encyclopedia of Religion* (16 vols, New York, 1987), XII, pp. 513–14.

use by writers from the patristic period onwards, although they commonly employed it in its more general sense, to refer to those things which were, and were not, sacred.[6]

For Eliade the sacred distinguishes itself from the profane, an act he described as hierophany, that is the manifestation of the sacred.[7] He therefore viewed a sacred place as one where the three cosmic levels, earth, heaven and the underworld, at once come into contact with each other, and are represented.[8] Whilst he acknowledged that in many religions the entire living world is sacred, he argued that 'since religious man cannot live except in an atmosphere impregnated with the sacred, we must expect to find a large number of techniques for consecrating space'.[9] At the same time he acknowledged that religious man regarded the entire world as 'the work of the gods' and therefore sacred.[10] For Eliade hierophany represented the centre of consecrated space, and at the edges of the sacred lurked chaos, the unknown, which he described as the profane.

Scholars from the disciplines of sociology, anthropology, and archaeology have been happy to engage with Marcel Eliade's paradigm.[11] Archaeologists of religion, especially those who study prehistory, have been preoccupied with the question as to how one reconstructs the religious practices of societies, including identification of their sacred sites, when many of the religious practices which signify sacredness leave little or no physical trace in the archaeological record. For behaviour, as modern observers have noted, often constitutes an important marker for recognizing the sacred.[12] Building on material from anthropology, it has been observed that 'many of the sites and areas regarded as significant by living peoples are not marked by any human construction or other human activity which would be

---

[6] A search of the term 'sacer et profanus' in the *Patrologia Latina: The Full Text* database (http://pld.chadwyck.co.uk) reveals many references; a search of the term 'sacred and profane' in the *Early English Books On-Line* database (http://eebo.chadwyck.com) similarly provides copious references to the use of the term. On the influence of early modern polemic about idolatry on anthropological distinctions between the sacred and the profane, see J. Sheehan, 'Sacred and Profane: Idolatry, Antiquarianism and the Polemics of Distinction', *P&P* (forthcoming).

[7] Eliade, *Sacred and Profane*, p. 11: 'Man becomes aware of the sacred because it manifests iteself, shows itself, as something wholly different from the profane'.

[8] Ibid., pp. 36 ff.

[9] Ibid., p. 28.

[10] Ibid., p. 64.

[11] See the summary and bibliography in J.P. Brereton, 'Sacred Space', in *The Encyclopedia of Religion*, XII, pp. 525–35.

[12] J. Hubert, 'Sacred Beliefs and Beliefs of Sacredness', in D.L. Carmichael, J. Hubert, B. Reeves, and A. Schanche (eds), *Sacred Sites, Sacred Places* (New York, 1994), pp. 9–19.

recognized through archaeological excavations'.[13] For many peoples the mundane landscape was, and is, interwoven with sacred sites.[14] Grappling with the problems of using the physical record to study how sacred spaces were defined, and religion practised, archaeologists of prehistory have thus pointed to the problems raised by attempts 'to maintain a distinction between sacred or ritual landscapes, and secular or mundane landscapes'.[15] In Timothy Insoll's words, 'the same landscape can mean different things to different people, and can be one and the same, and thus lack any arbitrary division'.[16] Growing awareness of the problems raised by accepting a simple dichotomy between secular or everyday sites (farms, homes, fields) versus sacred ones (ceremonial sites, tombs) has led archaeologists of religion recently to argue that their work should not be focused solely on publicly recognized sacred sites, but rather on their overall context.[17]

This emphasis on the fluidity between boundaries, such as those between the sacred and secular, is an issue which is equally alive in social anthropology. Sacred spaces are interpreted as foci for the religious identities of communities, acting as a 'lens', focusing 'attention on the forms, objects and actions' in it.[18] In a study of how different definitions are attached to two different shrines by the various religiously different communities of Palestinians living in the West Bank in the 1980s, Glenn Bowman emphasized their fluidity, in particular the porous boundaries between those sites which are officially acknowledged as sacred, and those which are not so acknowledged, but nevertheless regarded as 'secret-sacred' by both Christian and Moslem communities.[19]

Scholars from other disciplines have thus considerably refined Eliade's paradigm, emphasizing the importance of behaviour in defining sacred space, the

---

[13] P. Ucko, 'Foreword', in Carmichael *et al.* (eds), *Sacred Sites, Sacred Places*, p. xix. As well as the contributions to this collection, see those in P. Garwood, D. Jennings, R. Skeates and J. Toms (eds), *Sacred and Profane. Proceedings of a Conference on Archaeology, Ritual and Religion, Oxford 1989* (Oxford, 1991), and in A.T. Smith and A. Brookes (eds), *Holy Ground: Theoretical Issues Relating to the Landscape and Material Culture of Ritual Space Objects. Papers from a Session held at the Theological Archaeology Group Conference, Cardiff 1999*, BAR, International Series 956 (2001). For an overview of archaeological approaches to the history of religion see now T. Insoll, *Archaeology, Ritual, Religion* (London, 2004).

[14] O.V. Ovsyannikov and N.M. Terebikhin, 'Sacred Space in the Culture of the Arctic Regions', in Carmichael *et al.* (eds), *Sacred Sites, Sacred Places*, pp. 44–81.

[15] B. Bender, S. Hamilton and C. Tilley, 'Leskernick: Stone Worlds; Alternative Narratives; Nested Landscapes', *Proceedings of the Prehistoric Society* 63 (1997), 149.

[16] Insoll, *Archaeology*, p. 88.

[17] Ibid., p. 89.

[18] Brereton, 'Sacred Space', p. 526.

[19] G. Bowman, 'Nationalizing the Sacred: Shrines and Shifting Identities in the Israeli-Occupied Territories', *Man* 28 (1993), 431–60.

problems raised by attempts to maintain too strict a dichotomy between the sacred and the profane, the significance of personal as well as public sacred space, and the fluidity of boundaries between the sacred and other space. In contrast to this body of work on current behaviour and past physical remains, historians have been slow to attribute the topic of sacred space with importance, and have only recently begun to explore in depth the rich textual evidence in order to answer questions about how people in this period understood, and defined, sacred space.[20] These *lacunae* are in part because the subject has been perceived as the preserve of ecclesiologists and antiquarians rather than historians. Furthermore, until recently, historians have tended to accept the rhetoric of the Reformation concerning sacred space and the post-Enlightenment rationalist approach to sanctity, which was later encapsulated in Weber's concept of the 'disenchantment of the world'.

Sacred and Profane: Defining Sacred Space Through Context

Historians of the medieval and early modern periods have, for the most part, up to now preferred to study the law, geography and architecture of sacred spaces rather than how they were defined. Studies have thus focused not on rites and the practice of prayer, nor on informal 'secret-sacred' spaces, but rather on ecclesiastical buildings and shrines.[21] In the early Church, saints' tombs became the setting for ecclesiastical buildings, which in turn acquired sanctity by association. As these sites became the foci for pilgrimages, the routes to them became sanctified, and the chapels along the route also came to be regarded as sacred.[22] This paradigm holds equally true for sites established in the Middle Ages, such as the pilgrimage routes to the shrine of St James at Compostella.[23] At the same time recent work has demonstrated that medieval ideas about protected space and legal sanctuary were not so much a consequence of ideas of zones of holiness radiating out from a shrine, although these too played a part, but rather the result of dynamic and

---

[20] For references to work on the ancient world and America, see the review of literature in W. Coster and A. Spicer, 'The Dimensions of Sacred Space in Reformation Europe', in Coster and Spicer (eds), *Sacred Space*, p.1, n. 1.

[21] Except for B.Z. Kedar and R.J. Zwi Werblowsky (eds), *Sacred Space: Shrine, City, Land. Proceedings of the International Conference in Memory of Joshua Prawer* (Basingstoke, 1998). See also M. Kaplan (ed.), *Le Sacré et son inscription dans l'espace à Byzance et en Occident* (Paris, 2001).

[22] P.L.R. Brown, *The Cult of the Saints: its Rise and Function in Latin Christianity* (Chicago, 1981).

[23] R.B. Tate, *Pilgrimages to St James of Compostella from the British Isles during the Middle Ages* (Liverpool, 1990).

constructive relationships between individual institutions and royal authority, between churchmen and kings.[24]

Despite the preoccupations of modern historians, the evidence from the twelfth century onwards for territorial sanctuaries, like those around Hexham, Beverley and Durham in the north of England, taken together with the composition of liturgies for the consecration of both churches and, from the tenth century onwards, for cemeteries suggests that medieval people, both clerical and lay, attached great importance to the act of definition when demarcating space.[25] Nevertheless, whilst bishops believed that it was dedication ceremonies which made churches sacred, it was not only ritual which helped to mark out places as holy. Both a church's external appearance, and its place in the landscape, often helped distinguish it from the surrounding buildings and pointed to its status as a sacred site. The wooden chapels of the early period probably differed little in their external appearance from the lords' halls nearby. It was only in the tenth and eleventh centuries, when there was, seemingly, an expansion in local church building, and these churches were built or rebuilt in stone, that ecclesiastical buildings began to make an impact on the landscape, described by Rodulfus Glaber as 'a white mantle of churches' spreading over the earth.[26] This central medieval building programme thus helped distinguish the church from its surroundings, and to link these different sacred spaces into a truly Christian landscape.[27] Such spaces comprised not only the

---

[24] B.H. Rosenwein, *Negotiating Space. Power, Restraint and Privileges of Immunity in Early Medieval Europe* (Manchester, 1999): on the ban, see pp. 1–3, 156–83. See also W. Davies, '"Protected Space" in Britain and Ireland in the Middle Ages', in B.E. Crawford (ed.), *Scotland in Dark Age Britain* (Aberdeen, 1996), pp. 1–19, and her 'Adding Insult to Injury: Power, Property and Immunities in Early Medieval Wales', in W. Davies and P. Fouracre (eds), *Property and Power in the Early Middle Ages* (Cambridge, 1995), pp. 137–64.

[25] On Beverley, see J.C. Cox, *Sanctuaries and Sanctuary Seekers* (London, 1911), pp. 126–30. On Hexham and Durham, see D. Hall, 'The Sanctuary of St Cuthbert', in Gerald Bonner, D. Rollason and C. Stancliffe (eds), *St Cuthbert, His Cult and His Community to AD 1200* (Woodbridge, 1989), pp. 425–36. On early medieval church consecration rites, see H. Gittos, *Sacred Space in Anglo-Saxon England: Liturgy, Architecture and Place* (Oxford, forthcoming), ch. 5; on the evolution of cemetery consecration rites, see her 'Creating the Sacred: Anglo-Saxon Rites for Consecrating Cemeteries', in S. Lucy and A. Reynolds (eds), *Burial in Early Medieval England and Wales* (London, 2002), pp. 195–208.

[26] Rodulfus Glaber, *Historiarum Libri Quinque*, ed. and trans. J. France (Oxford, 1989), III, iv and vi, pp. 114–17, 126–27. William of Malmesbury observed a similar pattern in early twelfth-century England: *Gesta regum anglorum*, ed. W. Stubbs (2 vols, Rolls Series 90, London, 1888), II, p. 306.

[27] On this point see J. Howe, 'Creating Symbolic Landscapes: Medieval Development of Sacred Space', in J. Howe and M. Wolfe (eds), *Inventing Medieval Landscapes: Senses of Place in Western Europe* (Gainesville, FL, 2002), p. 215; T. Pestell, *Landscapes of*

churches, but from the tenth century onwards bounded cemeteries also were built around them, and, by the twelfth century, formal, marked sanctuaries stretching up to a mile around the church, as at Hexham, or a mile and a half at Beverley, had been established at certain sites. Protection was granted to fugitives who entered the sanctuary, and graded penalties for violation of this sanctuary were imposed which increased the nearer the violation occurred to the church. In both churches there were thus six boundaries: the first zone began a mile, or a mile and a half, away from the shrine, and was marked by four crosses; the second was inside the town; the third was inside the walls of the church precincts (described as the walls of the *atrium*, or porch, by Richard of Hexham); the fourth in the nave of the church; the fifth at the entrance to the choir; the sixth in the chancel.[28]

Churches, and the sacred spaces around them, were not only distinguished from the surrounding physical landscape, but also by more sensory distinctions. The ringing of church bells echoed across the landscape, calling the faithful to prayer, not just to the Mass but, at least in the medieval period, to the canonical hours eight times a day.[29] Although intended to regulate the time of prayer, such bells could be intrusive, denoting the lordship and domination of a particular house over its territory.[30] The Carolingian monk Walahfrid Strabo compared the bells which called the faithful to prayer to the 'bronze and silver trumpets' of the Old Testament: 'because the prophet orders that the "voice" of teaching can be lifted up "like a trumpet", we properly use these vessels to call the faithful together'.[31] Other sensory distinctions also emerged during the Middle Ages between churches and the secular world, which came increasingly across the period to be associated with the celebration of the Mass. The burning of incense, for example, set the divine apart from the smells of the world. According to St Thomas Aquinas, incense was used 'out of reverence for the sacrament [the Holy Eucharist], in order that any disagreeable smell (arising from the number of persons gathered together) in the building, that could cause annoyance, might be dispelled by its fragrancy. Secondly, to symbolize the effect of grace, of which Christ was full, as of a good

---

Monastic Foundation: the Establishment of Religious Houses in East Anglia, c.650–1200 (Woodbridge, 2004); R. Morris, *Churches in the Landscape* (London, 1989), p. 147.

[28] On Beverley, see Cox, *Sanctuaries*, pp. 126–30. On Hexham, see Hall, 'The Sanctuary of St Cuthbert', pp. 426–7. On the dating of evidence for cemetery boundaries see Gittos, 'Creating the Sacred', pp. 202–4.

[29] *Walahfrid Strabo's Libellus de exordiis et sacramentis quarundam in observationibus ecclesiasticis rerum*, trans. with commentary by A.L. Harting-Correa (Leiden, 1996), ch. 5, pp. 62–3: 'Bells ... ring the hours for celebrating the liturgy in the house of God'.

[30] M. Brand Honneur, 'La Motte et le clocher: l'affrontement des symboles?', *Cahiers de civilisation médiévale* 43 (2000), 3–31.

[31] *Walahfrid Strabo's Libellus*, ch. 5, pp. 62–3.

odour'. Incense was also viewed as a sacrificial offering, a means of driving away evil spirits as well as the setting apart of objects for holy use.[32] Church bells were popularly regarded as having the power to banish evil spirits and subdue storms, but they also served to define the sacred audibly. They announced particular moments of sanctity; the ringing of the *sanctus* bell defined the start of the canon as well as being rung again at the holiest part of the Mass, the elevation of the host. Lights served similar purposes.[33] The placing of candles on the altar signified a saint's feast day; the custom of lighting a candle at the *Sanctus*, and leaving it lit until after Communion, originated in the later medieval period, and helped mark out a sacred point in the Mass.[34] Light also played an important role in the medieval church dedication rite. At the beginning, according to one of the earliest detailed accounts, that in the mid-tenth-century Romano-German pontifical from Mainz, twelve candles were lit to illuminate the episcopal procession around the outside of the church, before the bishop entered the building to dedicate the church and consecrate the altar. These candles were interpreted as representing the light brought by Christ's teaching to the world.[35]

To a degree these sensory definitions of the sacred were rejected during the Reformation as part of a reaction against the material culture of holiness with which late medieval Catholicism and its rituals were embued. The priest no longer made Christ metaphysically present through transubstantiation, and the cult of saints was rejected by the Reformers. Incense, lights and bells as signals of the sacred became redundant. Nonetheless Protestant places of worship evoked their own sensory definition of the sacred which signalled their particular place in the landscape. The sound of psalm-singing marked Huguenot temples from the

---

[32] E.G.C.F. Atchley, *A History of the Use of Incense in Divine Worship* (London, 1909), pp. 117, 128, 132–3, 204–5. Unfortunately we were not able to consult the more recent work of C. Gauthier, *L'Encens dans le haut Moyen Age occidental. Son utilisation dans la liturgie* (Brussels, 2001).

[33] D.R. Dendy, *The Use of Lights in Christian Worship* (Alcuin Club Collections 41, London, 1959). On the burning of lights in Merovingian and Carolingian churches throughout the night, and the origins of this practice in Old Testament precepts, see P. Fouracre, 'Eternal Light and Earthly Needs: Practical Aspects of the Development of Frankish Immunities', in Davies and Fouracre (eds), *Property and Power*, pp. 68–9.

[34] F.L. Cross and E. Livingstone (eds), *The Oxford Dictionary of the Christian Church* (Oxford, 1997), p. 1452. For altar candles on a saint's feast, see Dendy, *Use of Lights*, pp. 108–19, and S. Bossuyt, pp 200–201 below. The cathedral church at Le Mans in the mid-ninth century burnt thirty lamps and five candles on ordinary Sundays, but ninety lamps and ten candles on feast days: Fouracre, 'Eternal Light', p. 72, fn. 57.

[35] 'XXXIII: Ordo romanus ad dedicandam ecclesiam', 3b, and 'XXXV: Quid significent duodecim candelae', in *Le Pontifical romano-germanique du dixième siècle*, ed. C. Vogel and R. Elze (3 vols, Studi e Testi 226, 227, 269, Vatican City, 1963–72), I, pp. 82, 90–121.

Catholic churches, for example.[36] Bells continued to sound out across the landscape to call Protestants to worship just as they did for their Catholic counterparts.[37] For the Calvinists and Zwinglians in particular the luminosity and pure white light that resulted from the clear glass windows and whitewashed walls was regarded as making a place of worship visually distinctive.[38]

Churches were however more than distinctive buildings in the landscape, they stood as beacons of order against the chaos of the world through determining human relations between the sacred and the profane.[39] In practical terms, this 'cosmic order' was achieved through the regulation of daily life by the measuring and ordering of time.[40] Time-keeping instruments, that is sundials, and, from the late thirteenth century, mechanical clocks broadcast the passing of sacred time both within and outside the church. Anglo-Saxon sundials are usually found above the south door, as at Great Edstone in North Yorkshire, where the sundial was marked out to distinguish the five (canonical) hours of the day: Prime, Terce, Sex, None, Vespers.[41] An inscription described it as a 'wayfarer's clock', perhaps suggesting it was also intended for use by travellers passing by the church, or for all Christians passing through the world.[42] Mechanical clocks were similarly concerned to mark liturgical time; early clocks like that at Wells cathedral lacked faces, striking the hours, sounding the trumpets throughout the church. Such timepieces, once secular clocks were introduced, helped ensure that the sacred time of the church was

---

[36] The 'disturbance' caused by psalm-singing could be sufficient grounds to justify the demolition of a temple: A. Spicer, '"Qui est de Dieu oit la parole de Dieu": the Huguenots and their Temples', in R.A. Mentzer and A. Spicer (eds), *Society and Culture in the Huguenot World, 1559–1685* (Cambridge, 2002), p. 190.

[37] R.A. Mentzer, 'The Reformed Churches of France and the Visual Arts', in P. Corby Finney (ed.), *Seeing beyond the Word. Visual Arts and the Calvinist Tradition* (Grand Rapids, 1999), pp. 218–19; M. Todd, *The Culture of Protestantism in Early Modern Scotland* (New Haven, 2002), pp. 28–30.

[38] L.P. Wandel, 'Revelation and Nature: Light in Reformed Churches', unpublished paper delivered at 'L'Architecture des temples réformés (XVIe–XVIIe siècles) en Europe et notamment en France', Faculté de théologie protestante de Montpellier, May 2003. Compare with Lateran IV (1215), c.19: 'We command also that the aforesaid churches, vessels, corporals and vestments be kept clean and bright. For it is absurd to tolerate in sacred things a filthiness that is unbecoming even in profane things', *Decrees of the Ecumenical Councils*, ed. N.P. Tanner (2 vols, London, 1990), I, p. 244.

[39] Eliade, *The Sacred and the Profane*, pp. 58–65.

[40] R.W. Scribner, 'Cosmic Order and Daily Life: Sacred and Secular in Pre-Industrial German Society', in his *Popular Culture and Popular Movements in Reformation Germany* (London, 1987), pp. 1–16.

[41] J. Wall, 'Anglo-Saxon Sundials in Ryedale', *Yorkshire Archaeological Journal* 69 (1997), 93–117, at 96, 100, 105; A.R. Green, *Sundials, Incised Dials or Mass-Clocks* (London, 1926).

[42] '+ORLOGIVM VIATORVM': Wall, 'Anglo-Saxon Sundials', 104–5.

distinguished from that of world.[43] The measurement of time, not only daily, but yearly, was a matter of concern to churchmen, anxious to calculate accurately the date of Easter. Thus, in the early modern period, some cathedrals in fact became observatories for studying the heavens and in particular the solar cycle. The construction of *meridiana* turned the cathedrals into *camera obscura*, plotting the course of the noon-day sun as it moved along a line marked on the floor. From the mid-seventeenth to the mid-eighteenth century, four Catholic churches were the principal solar observatories in Europe.[44]

It was very difficult for Reformed Protestants to break this close association between a place of worship and time. The New England Puritans rejected the liturgical calendar, regarding no time as more sacred than another, and ensured that Christmas Day was treated as a normal working day. But the retention of Sunday as an obligatory day of worship and the necessity of assembling in a meeting house for communal worship on that day were problems which caused a degree of angst for a community which rejected ideas of sacred space and time.[45]

Church buildings thus encapsulated sacred time, literally, whilst the liturgy translated them into a metaphor for the heavenly Jerusalem. But how was sacred space defined, and differentiated, within the church building itself? For the mundane often permeated these sacred spaces, both in terms of decorative schema and physical activities, and in doing so helped to articulate their holiness. *Atria*, in particular, acquired importance as intermediary spaces between the church and the street: Caesarius of Arles complained about them being used for public business as early as the sixth century and by the fourteenth century that in St Peter's, Rome, had seemingly become the site of a market.[46] Ecclesiastical courts were often held in, or at the entrance to, great churches; Fulbert of Chartres, writing in the early eleventh century, described episcopal courts as *atria*, petitioning the bishop of

---

[43] J. LeGoff, 'Au Moyen Age: temps de l'église et temps du marchand', in his *Pour un autre Moyen Age. Temps, travail et culture en occident* (Paris, 1978), pp. 46–65. See the corrective to LeGoff's views provided by C. Humphrey, 'Time and Urban Culture in Late Medieval England', in C. Humphrey and W.M. Ormrod (eds), *Time in the Medieval World* (York, 2001), pp. 105–17.

[44] See H. Heilbron, *The Sun in the Church. Cathedrals as Solar Observatories* (Cambridge, MA, 1999).

[45] J.P. Walsh, 'Holy Time and Sacred Space in Puritan New England', *American Quarterly* 32 (1980), 79–95. See also M. Todd, *The Culture of Protestantism in Early Modern Scotland* (New Haven, 2002), pp. 341–52; E. Muir, *Ritual in Early Modern Europe* (Cambridge, 1997), p. 77.

[46] Nancy Gauthier, 'Atria et portiques dans les églises de Gaule d'après les sources textuelles', in Christian Sapin (ed.), *Avant-nefs et espaces d'accueil dans l'église entre le IVe et le XIIe siècle* (Paris, 2002), pp. 30–36; Birch, *Pilgrimage to Rome*, pp. 120–21.

Paris for justice as regards the laws of our courts, *'de legibus atriorum'*.[47] *Atria* were thus liminal spaces, and their place in the transition from the profane to the sacred space, entrance into a divine world defined by sound, smell and light, was emphasized by both their architecture and role in the liturgy.[48] Burial in the *atrium*, that is at the entrance to the church, came to have great prestige: Pippin, the father of Charlemagne, was buried in the porch of Saint-Denis in the eighth century, Bruno, archbishop of Cologne and duke of Lotharingia, enjoyed a similarly prestigious burial in the tenth century. Burial *ante limina ecclesiae* articulated in physical form the metaphor of the soul awaiting judgement before entrance into paradise; it was thus a form of *humiliatio-exaltatio* for great men.[49] Although such acts suggest that medieval clergy had a heightened sense of awareness of the boundaries between these worlds, nevertheless the evidence of actual practice suggests the boundaries between sacred and secular space were thus often blurred in the Middle Ages.

The secular world could, and often did, especially in the case of pilgrimage churches, penetrate the church building itself. Such problems persisted throughout the period despite the efforts of those present at the Merovingian council of Chalon (647–53), which railed against men and women who celebrated feasts, including dedications, by coming into church and singing filthy songs, and decreed 'it is right that the priests of those places ought to keep and fence off those people from the enclosures and the porticos of their basilicas and even from the atria', and excommunicate those who would not submit to their authority.[50] In the central Middle Ages hagiographical writings mention pilgrims sleeping overnight in the church and the sick lying in the sanctuary itself. The choir of Chartres cathedral included five rooms in which some of the church officers slept, including the cook who had to light the candles, and the sacristan who guarded the relics from theft at night, whilst the cathedral's crypt functioned as a hospital for a community of

---

[47] *The Letters and Poems of Fulbert of Chartres*, ed. and trans. F. Behrends (Oxford, 1976), Ep. 9, p. 20.

[48] On their role in the liturgy, see Gittos, *Sacred Space in Anglo-Saxon England*, ch. 6; N. Spatz, 'Church Porches and the Liturgy in Twelfth-Century Rome', in T.J. Heffernan and E. Ann Matter (eds), *The Liturgy of the Medieval Church* (Kalamazoo, MI, 2001), pp. 327–67.

[49] A. Dierkens, 'Avant-corps, galilées, massifs occidentaux: quelques remarques méthodologiques en guise de conclusions', in Sapin (ed.), *Avant-nefs*, pp. 495–503; P. Ariès, *Western Attitudes towards Death from the Middle Ages to the Present* (London, 1974), pp. 15–20.

[50] Rosenwein, *Negotiating space*, p. 77, citing Council of Chalon, c.19: *Concilia Galliae A. 511–A. 695*, ed. C. De Clercq (Corpus Christianorum, Series Latina 148A, Turnhout, 1963), p. 307.

nursing sisters.[51] The nature of secular penetration was different in lesser churches. Prohibitions on using churches as storage depots are a constant refrain of church councils from the early Middle Ages onwards. Even in the seventeenth century, the Calvinist visitors complained about the smell caused by the storage of meat and the mice found in grain stored in some churches.[52] In many communities the parish church was the principal or only sizeable public building and so it became the venue for civic meetings as well as more raucous village festivities; even after the Reformation, newly built Huguenot temples were sometimes used as a meeting place by town councils.[53] Churches and cemeteries were often the focus for trade and business; this was particularly true of cemeteries, which as legally protected spaces became the sites for markets.[54] This could lead to them being regarded more as public space than consecrated ground.[55]

[51] On sleeping in the sanctuary, see L. Hicks, 'The Laity and Sacred Space in Normandy *c*.1050–1300', unpublished paper delivered to the *Defining the Holy* conference; on Chartres, see D.M. Hayes, *Body and Sacred Place in Medieval Europe 1100–1389* (New York, 2003), p. 54.

[52] E.g. Lateran IV, c.19, *Decrees of the Ecumenical Councils*, ed. Tanner, I, p. 244; G. Murdock, *Calvinism on the Frontier 1600–1660. International Calvinism and the Reformed Church in Hungary and Transylvania* (Oxford, 2000), p. 216.

[53] B. Kümin, *The Shaping of a Community. The Rise and Reformation of the English Parish c.1400–1560* (Aldershot, 1996), pp. 53, 57; D. Gentilcore, *From Bishop to Witch. The System of the Sacred in Early Modern Terra d'Otranto* (Manchester, 1992), p. 60; Mentzer, 'The Reformed Churches of France and the Visual Arts', pp. 209–10; see also p. 285 below.

[54] H. Guillotel, 'Du Rôle des cimetières en Bretagne dans le renouveau du XIe et de la première moitié du XIIe siècle', *Mémoires de la Société d'histoire et d'archéologie de Bretagne* 52 (1972–4), 5–26; Julia Barrow, 'Urban Cemetery Location in the High Middle Ages', in S. Bassett (ed.), *Death in Towns. Urban Responses to the Dying and the Dead, 100–1600* (Leicester, 1992), pp. 78–100; Rosenwein, *Negotiating Space*, p. 179, discusses how in the eleventh century consecrated Catalan cemeteries became sanctuaries, and, as protected spaces, were soon filled with houses, cattlesheds and barns, becoming the focus for new settlements; V. Harding, *The Dead and the Living in Paris and London, 1500–1670* (Cambridge, 2002), pp. 53, 73–4. During the 1630s specific steps were taken to remove shops and buildings which abutted onto English churches and cathedrals, see *The Works of the Most Reverend Father in God, William Laud D.D.*, ed. W. Scott and J. Bliss (7 vols, Oxford, 1853), V, pp. 480–81, 482, 491, 494, 498–9; S. Lehmberg, *Cathedrals under Siege: Cathedrals in English Society, 1600–1700* (Philadelphia, 1996), pp. 11–13; A. Spicer, 'Laudianism in Scotland? St Giles' Cathedral, Edinburgh, 1633–39 – A Reappraisal', *Architectural History* 46 (2003), 101, 105. A similar move was attempted in the early eleventh century: Council of Seligenstadt (1022), c.12, PL 142, cols 1060–61.

[55] See A. Maslakovic, 'Time, Profit and Devotion: Rethinking the Nature of Public Space in Renaissance Lyon', *P&P* (forthcoming).

Attempts were made, periodically, to purify churches and their precincts of more secular activities. Strenuous efforts were made by both Catholic and Protestant Churches to prevent the commercial and popular use of churchyards, with as little success as their medieval predecessors.[56] In the precincts of English cathedrals in the later Middle Ages the clergy tried to restrict the tenancy of houses in the close to those in clerical orders. Even as late as 1576 the Bishop of Rochester ordered 'that none shall inhabit, have or enjoy within the precinct of this Church any house or part of house etc., except he be a member of the said Church or servant to the dean or one of the canons and licensed thereunto by the dean and chapter'.[57] In the later Middle Ages passages were built, as at Wells and Chartres, which connected the church with the chapter's meeting house, palace and close: efforts, in other words, were being made to isolate the sacred space of the cathedral church and its environs from the secular world.[58] Do these efforts to counteract or prevent secular intrusion into the cemeteries and cloisters suggest that they were deemed to be less sacred than other parts of the ecclesiastical complex? Here the work of archaeologists, such as Roberta Gilchrist's analysis of the way the iconography of the corbels was used to delineate different spaces at Lacock abbey, proves helpful in examining the different shades of sacred space within ecclesiastical complexes.[59]

Efforts were made to cleanse not only the church precincts, but the church itself. In the 1230s, for example, Pope Gregory IX (1227–41) argued that judicial trials for blood crimes should not be heard in churches or cemeteries (both consecrated spaces) because 'the church of God should be a house of prayer, not a den of thieves or a blood court'.[60] Nonetheless churches continued to be the venue for ecclesiastical courts even after the Reformation. The former Lady Chapel at Chester Cathedral was used until 1635 when the consistory court was moved to the

---

[56] D. Dymond, 'God's Disputed Acre', *Journal of Ecclesiastical History* 50 (1999), 464–97; Todd, *The Culture of Protestantism in Early Modern Scotland*, p. 332; K.P. Luria, 'Separated by Death? Burial, Cemeteries, and Confessional Boundaries in Seventeenth-Century France', *French Historical Studies* 24 (2001), 210. As Luria points out, the burial of Huguenots within Catholic cemeteries provided a further source of profanation.

[57] W.P.M. Kennedy (ed.), *Elizabethan Episcopal Administration. An Essay in Sociology and Politics* (3 vols, Alcuin Club 27, London, 1924), II, p. 35.

[58] On passages at Chartres, see D.M. Hayes, 'From Boundaries Blurred to Boundaries Defined: Clerical Emphases on the Limits of Sacred Space in England and France during the Later Middle Ages', in Smith and Brookes (eds), *Holy Ground*, p. 88.

[59] Gilchrist, *Gender*, pp. 152–60; see also her 'Reading Sacred and Secular Space in English Monasticism: the Changing Spaces of Norwich Cathedral', unpublished paper delivered to the *Defining the Holy* conference, and the work of Tim Pestell, pp. 167–95 below.

[60] Gregory IX, *Decretals*, Lib III. tit. XLIX, c.V, cited by Hayes, 'From Boundaries Blurred', p. 87.

south-west tower; Huguenot temples similarly provided the venue for meetings of the consistory which dispensed religious discipline.[61] This penetration of the secular world into the sacred is well known; but modern commentators, like their medieval predecessors, have concentrated rather more on the scandal than on what such acts tell us about how sacred space was perceived.

Entering through the *atrium* into the church itself, historians have long been aware of how internal church decoration helped to define spaces within the church as holy and link the space to the celestial heavens. In the words of the twelfth-century monk Theophilus, the decoration of 'the ceilings and walls with varied work in different colours have, in some measure, shown to beholders the paradise of God'.[62] The concern of art historians has been primarily with the iconography, that is, the religious and historical context of church decorations; their role in shaping space has been subordinated to a study of the paintings or other decorations themselves.[63] Nevertheless case studies of individual churches have helped, implicitly, to further the understanding of how architecture and decorative programmes combined to define sacred spaces within the building.[64] More explicit in its treatment of sacred space is the recent case study by Dawn Marie Hayes of Chartres cathedral, which she uses to survey medieval ideas about, and treatment of, sacred space. She investigates the consequences of Harold W. Turner's views that the New Testament introduced the body as 'a competing focus' to the temple for the location of the sacred, through the study of the building, whose floor plan, like other cruciform churches, reflected not just the body of Christ on the cross, but also symbolized the body of the whole Christian Church.[65] She argues that the body-church metaphor declined in popularity at the same time as the boundaries between clerical and non-clerical sacred space became more rigidly defined in the later Middle Ages.[66] It was, however, Christopher Brooke who first highlighted the pattern of ebb and flow in church design, pointing out the multiple foci on the

---

[61] R.V.H. Burne, *Chester Cathedral: from its Founding by Henry VIII to the Accession of Queen Victoria* (London, 1958), pp. 118–19. The move to the liminal space of the *atrium* was part of a more widespread 'Laudian' effort within England to remove secular activities from ecclesiastical spaces. Mentzer, 'The Reformed Churches of France', pp. 209–10.

[62] *Theophilus, De Diversis Artibus*, ed. C.R. Dodwell (London, 1961), pp. 63–4.

[63] On the devotional function of murals and their place within romanesque churches see T.E.A. Dale and J. Mitchell (eds), *Shaping Sacred Space and Institutional Identity in Romanesque Mural Painting* (London, 2004).

[64] For example, K. van der Ploeg, *Art, Architecture and Liturgy: Siena Cathedral in the Middle* Ages (Groningen, 1993); J. Elliott and C. Warr, *The Church of Santa Maria Donna Regina: Art, Iconography and Patronage in Fourteenth-Century Naples* (Aldershot, 2004).

[65] Hayes, *Body*, p. xxi; H.W. Turner, *From Temple to Meeting House: the Phenomenology and Theology of Places of Worship* (The Hague, 1979).

[66] Hayes, *Body*, p. 99; see also her 'From Boundaries Blurred'.

sacred in the early Middle Ages (the eighth to tenth centuries), when major churches either had several, competing altars, as in the ninth-century plan of St Gall, or were made up of complexes of smaller churches, held together by a processional liturgy.[67] The focus changed in the eleventh and twelfth centuries when rebuilt cathedrals became long, open spaces which focused the eye of members of the congregation on the high altar, and again in the later twelfth and thirteenth centuries when competing foci were re-introduced: screens were built which blocked the view of the altar, as at Winchester, saints' altars were built close to the bishop's throne, as at Canterbury, reredos were constructed behind the altar. All these developments served to cut the choir and high altar off from the surrounding church. Brooke traced these changes to the development of devotion to the real presence in the Eucharist; efforts were made to isolate the altar and thus protect the sacrament.[68] It has thus been argued that in the later Middle Ages the clergy made increasing efforts to define their sacred spaces from their more profane surroundings, erecting barriers around the high altar within the church.[69] It was a practice which continued with construction of *jubés* in the classical style in the cathedrals of France and the Southern Netherlands into the early seventeenth century, in spite of the post-Tridentine efforts to increase the visibility of the Mass. Interestingly in her 1559 Religious Settlement Elizabeth I required the removal of rood lofts but sought to retain the screen or a partition between the choir and the nave. The choir screen erected by Inigo Jones at Winchester Cathedral perhaps should be considered in the same tradition as the continental *jubés* although it did come in the wake of the 1630s 'Laudian' policy of erecting rails around altars.[70] The Laudian refurbishment of churches came after a series of building programmes which reflected more parochial or communal pride.[71] By removing the seating

---

[67] C.N.L. Brooke, 'Religious Sentiment and Church Design in the Late Middle Ages', in his *Medieval Church and Society* (London, 1971), pp. 162–82.

[68] Ibid., pp. 177–81.

[69] For the argument that Gregorian reformers' attempts to professionalize the clergy in the eleventh century led to a renewed emphasis on the bishop's palace in north Italian cities, as bishops sought to distinguish clerical space from its secular surroundings, see M.C. Miller, *The Bishop's Palace: Architecture and Authority in Medieval Italy* (Ithaca, NY, 2000).

[70] B. Jestaz, 'Le Jubé comme organe de diffusion des formes classiques', in J. Guillaume (ed.), *L'Eglise dans l'architecture de la Renaissance* (Paris, 1995), pp. 181–94; J. Dupertius Bangs, *Church Art and Architecture in the Low Countries before 1566* (Kirksville, MO, 1997), pp. 44–63; J. Harris and G. Higgott (eds), *Inigo Jones. Complete Architectural Drawings* (New York, 1989), pp. 248–50; K. Fincham, 'The Restoration of Altars in the 1630s', *Historical Journal* 44 (2001), 919–40. For opposition to altar rails, see D. Cressy, 'The Battle of the Altars: Turning the Tables and Breaking the Rails', in D. Cressy (ed.), *Travesties and Transgressions in Tudor and Stuart England* (Oxford, 2000), pp. 186–212.

[71] See H. Colvin, 'Church Building in Devon in the Sixteenth Century', in H. Colvin (ed.), *Essays in English Architectural History* (London, 1999), pp. 22–51; N. Mole, 'Church-

occupied by civic corporations, clergy wives and prominent townsmen from cathedral choirs, the clergy were able to reclaim this space as their own.[72] Nonetheless, can we, as one recent study has done, argue that the erection of defined barriers to sacred space represents a withdrawal of the clergy into a specialist sphere, a move which suggested, in Mary Douglas's view, a transition from the primitive to the modern?[73] While the early Reformation initially advanced the doctrine of the priesthood of all believers and saw artisans abandoning their trades to become popular preachers, this was exceptional, as the second generation Protestant clergy were educated and trained for their role. The early modern period therefore witnessed the professionalization of the clergy, emphasizing their sacramental duties and setting them apart from the local community.[74] Ironically amongst Protestants this created a neo-clericalism amongst both the Lutheran and Reformed Churches. Calvinist ministers were seen as having a special calling as the interpreters of the Word of God and through their preaching as His mouthpiece. The recognition of the clergy's special relationship with God heightened the sense of their sacerdotal role, and contributed to the increasing significance of benediction and services, such as consecration, which distinguished between the sacred and the profane.[75]

Material remains, however, provide only a partial answer as to how the holy was defined in the medieval and early modern periods. As we noted earlier, anthropologists have emphasized the importance of behaviour in signifying the sacred, and it is clear that throughout the period covered by this volume the Churches struggled to maintain an air of reverence. In the late fourteenth century, John Myrc's *Instructions for Parish Priests* urged:

Building and Popular Piety in Early Seventeenth-Century Exeter', *Southern History* 25 (2003), 8–38; J.F. Merritt, 'Puritans, Laudians, and the Phenomenon of Church-Building in Jacobean London', *Historical Journal* 41 (1998), 935–60.

[72] Lehmberg, *Cathedrals under Siege*, pp. 14–15.

[73] Hayes, 'From Boundaries Blurred', p. 89; M. Douglas, *Purity and Danger: an Analysis of Concepts of Pollution and Taboo* (London, 1966), pp. 94–5.

[74] M.R. Forster, *Catholic Revival in the Age of the Baroque. Religious Identity in Southwest Germany, 1550–1750* (Cambridge, 2001), pp. 167–83; A. Pettegree, 'The Clergy and the Reformation: from "Devilish Priesthood" to New Professional Elite', in A. Pettegree (ed.), *The Reformation of the Parishes. The Ministry and the Reformation in Town and Country* (Manchester, 1993), pp. 1–21. See also C. Scott Dixon and L. Schorn-Schütte, *The Protestant Clergy of Early Modern Europe* (Basingstoke, 2003).

[75] P. Benedict, *Christ's Churches Purely Reformed. A Social History of Calvinism* (New Haven, 2002), pp. 437–8; T.H.L. Parker, *Calvin's Preaching* (Edinburgh, 1992), pp. 35–47; J. Davies, *The Caroline Captivity of the Church. Charles I and the Remoulding of Anglicanism 1625–1641* (Oxford, 1992), p. 54; R.W. Scribner, 'The Impact of the Reformation on Daily Life', in *Mensch und Objekt im Mittelalter und in der Frühen Neuzeit: Leben – Alltag – Kultur* (Vienna, 1990), pp. 327–8.

... within church and churchyard
Do exactly as I say to you;
Singing and shouting and such activity,
You will not hesitate to stop;
Throwing of axle-tree [cart axle] and also of stone,
Let them practise none there.
Ball and bares [an outdoor game] and such sport,
Put away out of the churchyard;
Sessions of court and such kinds of dispute,
You must put out of the sanctuary;
For Christ Himself teaches us
That the holy church is His house,
That is made for nothing else
Except to pray in, as the book [Bible] prescribes;
The people shall gather therein
To pray and also to weep for their sins.[76]

Strikingly similar sentiments were expressed two centuries later by the Council of Trent, which required bishops to

banish from the churches all such music, whether by the organ or in the singing, [which] contains things that are lascivious or impure; likewise all worldly conduct, vain and profane conversations, wandering around, noise and clamour, so that the house of God may be seen to be and may truly be called a house of prayer.[77]

Protestants were also concerned 'whether there be any that use to go out of the church; or to sleep, talk, walk, or use any other unseemly or unreverent behaviour at the times of prayer, preaching, catechizing or administration of the sacraments'.[78] These oft repeated measures reflected a perennial concern (not solely a post-Reformation one) to ensure an appropriate setting for worship, but at the same time established certain behavioural requirements or expectations that set the church building apart from the secular world.

From at least the twelfth century onwards, however, objects and images with secular associations 'invaded' churches. The funeral monuments of founders were

---

[76] G.E. Bryant and V.M. Hunter, *'How Thow Schalt Thy Paresche Preche'. John Myrc's Instructions for Parish Priests* (Barton-on-Humber, 1999), p. 59; John Myrc, *Instructions for Parish Priests*, ed. E. Peacock (Early English Text Society, Original Series XXXI, rev. edn, London, 1902), p. 11 (ll. 330–45).

[77] *The Canons and Decrees of the Council of Trent*, ed. H.J. Schroeder (Rockford, IL, 1978), p. 151. See also Forster, *Catholic Revival in the Age of the Baroque*, p. 125.

[78] W.P.M. Kennedy (ed.), *Elizabethan Episcopal Administration. An Essay in Sociology and Politics* (3 vols, Alcuin Club 27, London, 1924), III, p. 261. See also A. Spicer, '"Accommodating of Thame Selfis to Heir the Word": Preaching, Pews and Reformed Worship in Scotland, 1560–1638', *History* 88 (2003), 409–10.

erected in the middle of choirs, founders and their coats of arms commemorated in stained glass windows, the relics of secular heroes, like Ogier the Dane, displayed in churches.[79] In the Netherlands the tomb of William of Orange, erected in 1612, occupying the choir of the Grote Kerk in Delft, was only the first of a series of monuments to national heroes.[80] Even newly-built post-Reformation churches were decorated with coats of arms and emblems of the secular authorities.[81] The placing of tombs in the choir in founder's churches in the later Middle Ages, and the continued location of burials in the chancels of ruined monastic churches after the Reformation reflects a continued belief in their sanctity.[82]

Decoration remains a useful guide as to how particular areas of the church were regarded as holier than others. The decoration of the mosaic floors was sometimes used to mark off the presbytery from the choir and nave. The twelfth-century presbyteries of several north Italian churches were distinguished by floor mosaics which contained personifications of the four rivers of Paradise issuing forth to the four corners of the earth mentioned in Genesis. One, predominant, exegesis interpreted these four rivers as the four Gospels, spreading Christ's message throughout the world. This reading was echoed in the contemporary dedication rite, in which the bishop wrote two alphabets, one in Latin, one in Greek, across the body of the church, interpreted as the Old and New Testament respectively, the Gentiles and the Jews. Such floors, in other words, supported the dedication rite's concern with spreading salvation from the church throughout the world. A separate iconography in the floor thus helped to mark the sanctuary off as the preserve of the pastors charged with spreading Christ's word.[83]

It should be remembered therefore that architecture and iconography were not the only means for distinguishing sacred space in this period: rite and prayer also played an important role. How far did these physical, and ritual, markers of the

---

[79] Andrew Martindale, 'Patrons and Minders: the Intrusion of the Secular into Sacred Spaces in the Late Middle Ages', in D. Wood (ed.), *The Church and the Arts* (SCH 28, Oxford, 1995), pp. 143–78; quote at p. 143.

[80] J. Pollmann, 'The Cleansing of the Temple. Church Space and its Meanings in the Dutch Republic', in J.P. Paiva (ed.), *Religious Ceremonials and Images: Power and Social Meaning (1400–1750)* (Coimbra, 2002), p. 184.

[81] Mentzer, 'The Reformed Churches of France and the Visual Arts', p. 218.

[82] M. Crăciun, '*Apud Ecclesia*: Church Burial and the Development of Funerary Rooms in Moldavia', in Coster and Spicer (eds), *Sacred Space*, pp. 144–66; A. Spicer, '"Defyle not Christ's Kirke with your Carrion": Burial and the Development of Burial Aisles in Post-Reformation Scotland', in P. Marshall and B. Gordon (eds), *The Place of the Dead. Death and Remembrance in Late Medieval and Early Modern Europe* (Cambridge, 2000), pp. 149–69.

[83] L. Donkin, '"Unto the Uttermost Ends of the Earth": Mapping Salvation on the Decorated Floor', unpublished paper delivered to the *Defining the Holy* conference.

sacred change with the Reformation? Recent research has fundamentally challenged the Weberian hypothesis that the Reformation was responsible for the 'disenchantment of the world'. Bob Scribner, in particular, criticized the nineteenth-century construction of the Reformation which had been shaped by the concerns of that era and had viewed it as a logical step on the path to modernization. In challenging the Weberian rationalization of the world, Scribner drew not upon the theological principles and ideals of the Reformers themselves, but upon the actual religious practice of ordinary people, thereby writing a social history of the Reformation.[84] He argued that 'the world of Luther and the Reformation was a world of highly charged sacrality' and that 'Protestantism did not represent, for the popular mind at least, a major dramatic and paradigm shift from a sacramental to a secularised world'.[85]

Although the leading Reformers of the sixteenth century dismissed the belief that one place was holier than another, recent research has shown how sacred space was created and re-created during the early modern period, exploring the degree of change wrought in reality by the religious beliefs of the period.[86] Actual religious practice, in fact, demonstrated considerable continuities in the perception of sacred space in the post-Reformation era. Burials continued to be located both within church buildings, and in surrounding churchyards, reflecting the fact that Protestant believers, like their medieval counterparts, regarded the dead as part of a community with the living, and sought to bury the dead in sites regarded as holy in the late Middle Ages.[87] In doing so, scholars have investigated the changes which took place not only in attitudes towards religious buildings themselves but also to

---

[84] See R.W. Scribner, 'The Reformation, Popular Magic, and the "Disenchantment of the World"', *Journal of Interdisciplinary History* 23 (1993), 475–94; Scribner, *Popular Culture and Popular Movements in Reformation Germany*, pp. xii–xiv.

[85] Scribner, 'The Reformation, Popular Magic, and the "Disenchantment of the World"', 483; B. Scribner, 'Reformation and Desacralisation: from Sacramental World to Moralised Universe', in R. Po-Chia Hsia and R.W. Scribner (eds), *Problems in the Historical Anthropology of Early Modern Europe* (Wiesbaden, 1997), pp. 77–8. See also J. Bossy, 'Holiness and Society', *P&P* 75 (1977), 129–37.

[86] What follows is deeply indebted to the more extensive review of the literature in Coster and Spicer, 'The Dimensions of Sacred Space'.

[87] W. Coster, 'A Microcosm of Community: Burial, Space and Society in Chester 1598 to 1633', in Coster and Spicer (eds), *Sacred Space*, pp. 124–43; H. Colvin, *Architecture and the After-Life* (New Haven, 1991), esp. pp. 253–82, 295–326; Harding, *The Dead and the Living*, chs 5 and 6; A. Spicer, '"Rest of Their Bones": Fear of Death and Reformed Burial Practices', in P. Roberts and W.G. Naphy (eds), *Fear in Early Modern Society* (Manchester, 1997), pp. 167–83; Spicer, '"Defyle not Christ's Kirke with your Carrion"'; see also M. Engammarre, 'L'Inhumation de Calvin et des pasteurs genevois de 1540 à 1620', in J. Balsamo (ed.), *Les Funérailles à la Renaissance* (Geneva, 2002), pp. 271–93.

the wider landscape.[88] Other historians, led by Margaret Aston, have demonstrated the way in which sacred space continued to be defined by social divisions; seating within church, for example, echoed the predominant social structures as well as the survival of popular beliefs associated with parts of the building.[89] Patterns of seating also represented the continued gendering of sacred space during the early modern period; Cardinal Borromeo called for wooden partitions to be erected down the middle of the nave to separate men from women.[90] Gender concerns about holy space were expressed even more starkly in architectural terms with the renewed emphasis on the claustration of female religious orders, for example, following the Council of Trent.[91] Furthermore the boundaries of parochial jurisdiction, both religious and civic, continued to be defined by the Church after the Reformation with Rogationtide processions. Although shorn of much of their medieval ritual, the custom retained its liturgical character with the singing of psalms, saying of prayers and the delivery of a sermon by a minister wearing a surplice.[92] Such continuities in the use, perception and ordering of sacred space did

---

[88] C. Zika, 'Hosts, Processions and Pilgrimage: Controlling the Sacred in Fifteenth-Century Germany', *P&P* 181 (1988), 25–64; K.R. Stow, 'Holy Body, Holy Society: Medieval Structural Conceptions', in Kedar and Weblowsky (eds), *Sacred Space*, pp. 151–71; L. McClain, 'Without Church, Cathedral or Shrine: the Search for Religious Space among Catholics in England, 1550–1625', *SCJ* 33 (2002), 381–99; F.E. Dolan, 'Gender and the "Lost" Spaces of Catholicism', *Journal of Interdisciplinary History* 32 (2002), 641–60; P. Roberts, 'The Most Crucial Battle of the Wars of Religion? The Conflict over Sites for Reformed Worship in Sixteenth-Century France', *Archiv für Reformationsgeschichte* 89 (1998), 247–66. See also the contributions in Coster and Spicer (eds), *Sacred Space*.

[89] M. Aston, 'Segregation in Church', in D. Webb (ed.), *Women in the Church* (SCH 27, Oxford, 1990), pp. 237–94; C. Marsh, 'Sacred Space in England, 1560–1640: the View from the Pew', *Journal of Ecclesiastical History* 53 (2002), 286–311; Spicer, '"Accommodating of Thame Selfis to Heir the Word"', 405–22.

[90] E.C. Voelker, 'Borromeo's Influence on Sacred Art and Architecture', in J.M. Headley and J.B. Tomaro (eds), *San Carlo Borromeo. Catholic Reform and Ecclesiastical Politics in the Second Half of the Sixteenth Century* (Washington, 1988), p. 179.

[91] U. Strasser, 'Bones of Contention: Cloistered Nuns, Decorated Relics, and the Contest over Women's Place in the Public Sphere of Counter-Reformation Munich', *Archiv für Reformationsgeschichte* 90 (1999), 255–88; L. Lux-Stemitt, 'Between the Cloister and the World: the Successful Compromise of the Ursulines of Toulouse, 1604–1616', *French History* 16 (2002), 247–68. In particular, see H. Hills (ed.), *Architecture and the Politics of Gender in Early Modern Europe* (Aldershot, 2003), pp. 115–30, 131–50, 151–76.

[92] E. Duffy, *The Stripping of the Altars. Traditional Religion in England, 1400–1580* (London, 1992), pp. 136–9, 578–9; A. Walsham, 'The Reformation of the Landscape', unpublished paper delivered to the Reformation Studies Colloquium, University of Birmingham, in April 2004, pp. 44–5; K. Thomas, *Religion and the Decline of Magic*, pp. 71–4; R. Hutton, *The Stations of the Sun: a History of the Ritual Year in Britain* (Oxford, 1996), ch. 26. We are grateful to Alex Walsham for access to her unpublished paper. See also Scribner, 'The Impact of the Reformation on Daily Life', pp. 321–2.

not go unchallenged by the first generation of Reformers who regarded such practices as superstitious.

Nonetheless sacred space in the early modern period should not be regarded solely as a survival of pre-Reformation traditions, for during the later sixteenth and early seventeenth centuries there was a resurgence in interest in defining the holy. Sacred space was constructed anew or redefined. A Protestant ritual of consecration developed, for example, through which cemeteries, church buildings, and their fittings – altars, pulpits, organs and fonts – were separated from the profane secular world. Even though this had been rejected by the first generation of Reformers, the practice of consecration was again firmly established in the evangelical churches by 1700.[93] There was a redefining of sacrilege, the profaning of sacred space, during the early seventeenth century. Some came to view the destruction of religious buildings during the Dissolution of the Monasteries as a desecration which had blighted the history of the Reformation. Authors such as Robert Pont and Sir Henry Spelman regarded the appropriation of church lands as being sacrilegious, because they had been set aside for holy use. This was an opinion which could also be extended to those who possessed former monastic lands.[94] One new area of research has shown the interest there was during the early modern period for sacred geography, in which cartographic and documentary techniques were employed in mapping the sacred space of the Holy Land.[95] Ironically, while the Puritans of New England in mapping the landscape tried to avoid place names which suggested that these localities were sacred spaces, at the same time they attempted to build towns following biblical accounts of the Temple of Solomon.[96] Although the resurgence of sacred space during the second generation of the Reformation still remains to be fully explored, these examples

---

[93] Ibid., pp. 327–8; Scribner, 'The Reformation, Popular Magic, and the "Disenchantment of the World"', p. 483. For examples of consecrations of Calvinist churches, see A. Spicer, '"What Kinde of House a Kirk is": Conventicles, Consecrations and the Concept of Sacred Space in Post-Reformation Scotland', in Coster and Spicer (eds), *Sacred Space*, pp. 99–102, and Murdock, pp. 241–60 below.

[94] Robert Pont, *Against Sacrilege. Three Sermons Preached by Maister Robert Pont* (Edinburgh, 1599); Henry Spelman, *De non temerandis ecclesiis. A Tracte of the Rights and Respect Due vnto Churches* (London, 1613); M. Aston, 'English Ruins and English History: the Dissolution and the Sense of the Past', *Journal of the Warburg and Courtauld Institutes* 36 (1973), 235–7; I. Atherton, 'Viscount Scudamore's "Laudianism": the First Religious Practices of the First Viscount Scudamore', *Historical Journal* 34 (1991), 571.

[95] See C. Delano Smith, 'Maps as Art and Science: Maps in Sixteenth-Century Bibles', *Imago Mundi* 42 (1990), 65–83; Z. Shalev, '*Geographia Sacra*: Cartography, Religion and Scholarship in the Sixteenth and Seventeenth Centuries' (unpublished Ph.D. thesis, Princeton University, 2004). I am grateful to Dr Shalev for giving me access to his thesis.

[96] Walsh, 'Holy Time and Sacred Space', 85, 90; J. Archer, 'Puritan Town Planning in New Haven', *Journal of the Society of Architectural Historians*, 34 (1975), 140–49.

demonstrate that while continued perceptions of sacred space were important, new definitions also developed.

The Way Forward

In general, the work of both medieval and early modern historians of sacred space has therefore largely focused on attitudes to public spaces: places of public worship, be they shrines, chapels, churches or landscapes, or even cemeteries or sanctuaries. Their studies have been much more concerned to investigate the context for sacred space rather than to ask questions about how it was defined and constructed both by personal experience and communal practice. Concentration on physical monuments has thus left little room for the consideration of 'secret-sacred' spaces, which have not been the focus of the same intense study. In exploring the spatial boundaries between the ecclesiastical and domestic realms, the personal piety of the home versus the public liturgy of the church, several of the contributors to this volume therefore bring a new dimension to bear on the study of sacred space.[97] At the same time, the work of early modern historians has suggested that, as in the Middle Ages, the boundaries between sacred and secular space were often blurred. Like the archaeologists of prehistory, Bob Scribner rejected the futility of 'the radical division of reality into two clearly identifiable realms, the sacred and the profane', because 'the sacred is always experienced from within the profane'.[98] The pattern across the whole period covered by this volume therefore seems to be one of continuity rather than change. The aim of this volume, covering as it does the period from the late Middle Ages to the end of the *ancien régime*, is to investigate continuities and redefinitions in attitudes to sacred space across this divide, and to ask how it was constructed both by personal experience and communal practice.

The fifteen essays in this volume therefore illustrate both continuities and changes in attitudes and practices with regard to defining the holy and demarcating sacred space in both the medieval and early modern period. As editors it was also our intention that the collection would reflect the interdisciplinary character of research in this field; contributions from archaeologists, art historians, architectural historians, liturgists and historians illustrate different approaches to the subject and

---

[97] See the contributions by D. Webb, J. Nuechterlein, L. Banner and R. Williams, pp. 27–116 below.

[98] Scribner, 'Cosmic Order and Daily Life', pp. 1–2. See also B.L. Brown, 'Between the Sacred and the Profane', in B.L. Brown (ed.), *The Genius of Rome, 1592–1623* (London, 2001), pp. 276–303.

broaden our understanding of sacred space. With this in mind, the intention of this volume is not to examine sacred space *per se*, but to consider the way in which it was delineated, evoked and perceived in a wide variety of different contexts.

The essays are divided into two parts. In the first, the existence of sacred space within a domestic context is explored. Private, often solitary, devotion within the home often had a spatial dimension, and these essays explore from different perspectives some of the ways in which sacred space could be established and defined within the secular world of the domestic household. Whether worship took place within a private chapel or within the bedchamber, efforts were made to distinguish the sacred (albeit often temporarily) from the profane.

The definition of sacred space in the public realm is explored in Part II. Buildings were set apart from the world through liturgical rites, while the use of particular places and religious iconography were also intended to re-create and evoke the sanctity associated with the Holy City of Jerusalem, Rome or the Christian past.[99] Several essays reflect the interaction and interplay between the sacred and the profane, through exploring the secular penetration of monastic houses, but also how processions brought the holy into the secular realm, establishing a sacred presence which was defined not only spatially, but also in temporal terms.[100] A final strand that can be identified in this section is the extent to which defining sacred space was exploited by the authorities as a means of reinforcing their own position and political ideologies.[101] These essays therefore reflect the complexities in defining the sacred as well as echoing Scribner's sentiments that the sacred is indeed experienced from within the profane.

---

[99] See especially the contributions by J. Mecham, S. Bossuyt, C. Lawrence and J. Loach, pp. 143–66, 197–216, 261–313 below.
[100] See especially the contributions by T. Pestell, S. Bossuyt, J. Loach, and E. Johnson, pp. 167–216, 291–313, 333–50 below.
[101] See the contributions by G. Murdock, J. Loach and S. Dixon, pp. 241–60, 291–332 below.

PART 1

Chapter 2

Domestic Space and Devotion in the Middle Ages

Diana Webb

The relationship and the frontier between public and private religious activities, and between public and private religious spaces, have varied in different religious cultures and also within the history of Christianity. The Athenian busybody and would-be legislator in Plato's *Laws* would have forbidden the possession of domestic shrines on the grounds that they encouraged faulty ideas about the gods.[1] He was well aware that his ideas were very much at variance with the common practice of his society, as indeed they were with the common practice of Mediterranean antiquity in general. There were temples built and maintained by the 'state' and cults which exacted participation from the citizen, but at home his ancestors and household gods demanded attention, as the spirits of grove, field and spring might also do. The Roman state possessed its own religious spaces and made its religious stipulations, but these did not have a monopoly. What additional pious impulses you might feel were largely your own affair. Born into this world, Christianity came to present an interestingly different spectacle.

For very good reasons, Christians met and worshipped privately in the earliest days. Sometimes, at least, their activities were clandestine. Much Christian worship took place in a domestic setting, as Jewish worship also did, in the houses of adherents and sympathizers; but the drive to adapt these settings to the specific needs of the congregation and to appropriate buildings to that sole purpose was manifested from an early date and famously exemplified in the third century at Dura Europos in Syria (where there was also a notable synagogue).[2] With the Peace of the Church in the fourth century came the multiplication of purpose-built churches and the adaptation of the essentially public basilica form to Christian uses.

---

[1] Plato, *The Laws*, trans. T.J. Saunders (Harmondsworth, 1970), X, pp. 446–7.
[2] For brief accounts and further references see E. Ferguson (ed.), *Encyclopedia of Early Christianity* (New York, 1999), pp. 352–3, 546–7.

From a situation in which it was difficult for Christianity to wear a public face, it first became possible and permissible for it to do so, and finally compulsory. Christians had to conform their observances strictly to authoritative, publicly established norms. In the later medieval period, the focus of the present discussion, meetings held for religious purposes in private premises might well once again be regarded as clandestine and suspect, not, now, by a hostile secular state, but by the religious authorities themselves. What legitimate place did the private space and what went on in it, occupy in a world of compulsory public Christianity?

Different religious activities were of course controlled and officially monopolized to different degrees and this had certain implications for the location in which they might take place. As far as the sacraments were concerned, the first and twenty-first canons of the Fourth Lateran Council in 1215 established a broad disciplinary framework for western Christendom.[3] The first canon declared that the performance of the eucharistic miracle was reserved to the ordained clergy. This did not necessarily confine it to public spaces, but the tendency of earlier legislation had been to insist that Mass should be celebrated only in a properly consecrated church.[4] The requirement in c.21 that every adult Christian should make his or her confession to the parish priest and receive communion once a year also implied a public, not private, demonstration of compliance at the parish church, the more public because the confessional box lay in the future. This was a minimum requirement. The desire of the devout lay person to hear Mass, make confession and receive communion more frequently, which manifested itself during the later middle ages, had manifold effects: on the one hand, the promotion of a more intimate and active relationship between the laity and local churches; on the other, the importation into the homes of those who were able to do so of some part of the paraphernalia of public religion.

In theological terms, baptism was a different matter, although this sacrament too was normally administered by a priest and in church. Baptism was indispensable for salvation as the Eucharist was not, and c.1 of the Lateran Council reminded its audience that it could be performed in case of necessity by anyone whatsoever,

---

[3] J. Alberigo, G. Dossetti, P.-P. Joannou, C. Leonardi and P. Prodi (eds), *Conciliorum Oecumenicorum Decreta* (Bologna, 1973), pp. 230–31, 245.

[4] The principle was enunciated *c.*802 in the Capitulary of Aachen (c.9: 'Ut nullus sacerdos in domibus vel in aliis locis, nisi in ecclesiis dedicatis, celebrare missas audeat') which was also echoed in early English legislation: D. Whitelock, M. Brett and C.N.L. Brooke (eds), *Councils & Synods with Other Documents Relating to the English Church I, A.D. 871–1204* (2 vols, Oxford, 1981), I, pp. 210 & fn. 1, 258, 324, 456, 575. Ælfric, Pastoral Letter for Wulfsige II, Bishop of Sherborne, c.70, and the Canons of pseudo-Edgar, c.30, permit exceptions in case of 'grave necessity if anyone is ill'.

provided that water and the correct form of words were used. The midwife or other responsible bystander might have to do duty if an infant seemed unlikely to live. Similar considerations applied at the other end of life. A priest was indispensable for the administration of the last rites, but confession at the point of death could be heard by any Christian if no priest was available. When death was predictable, the professionals entered the domestic space to perform their allotted functions, but untimely death might occur anywhere: the Sieur de Joinville memorably records hearing (but not remembering) the confession of Guy d'Ibelin, constable of Cyprus, on board ship when they thought they were about to be slaughtered by the Saracens. Joinville replied to his confession with the words 'I absolve you with such power as God has given me'.[5]

In their most basic form, these rites of passage did not require specialized personnel or equipment, but it is important to note that there was conformity, not contradiction, between what was done in church – the public sphere of Christianity – and what was done in other settings, the home among them. This conformity was demonstrated, as we shall see, by the adaptation and equipping of the domestic space to accommodate worship, but it also found expression in ritual gestures. Until very recently, kneeling has been regarded by many people as the proper and all but obligatory attitude for prayer, even for prayer offered in total privacy by one's bedside. The early thirteenth-century guidebook *Ancrene Wisse* directed the anchoress, immediately upon awaking, to say the *Veni Creator Spiritus* kneeling on her bed. She should conclude her early morning devotions by saluting her image of the Virgin and then 'bow or kneel to the other images and to your relics'.[6] Gestures which in other contexts visually demonstrated submission to a lord were thus carried out, in complete solitude, in the space which served the anchoress for sleep and prayer alike.

The bedchamber (at least for those who had the luxury of such an apartment) was the probable location of much informal religious practice. In his good conduct manual for his daughters, written towards the end of the fourteenth century, the Chevalier de la Tour Landry gives priority to prayers on awaking and before sleeping. He does not prescribe a place or a posture for them, but they clearly belonged to the bedchamber. Everyone 'as soone as he awaketh ... ought to nowleche [God] for his lord and maker and hym self to be his creature'. At the other end of the day,

---

[5] *Histoire de Saint Louis*, ed. N. de Wailly (Paris, 1868), ch. LXX, pp. 125–6.
[6] *Anchoritic Spirituality: Ancrene Wisse and Associated Works*, trans. A. Savage and N. Watson (New York, 1991), pp. 53–4.

we ought to praye for them that ben dede to fore we goo to slepe … And also forgete not
the blessid and swete Vyrgyne Marye whiche nyght and day prayeth for us; And also to
recommaunde yow to the hooly sayntes of heuen, and when this uis done thenne maye
ye well goo slepe, For this ought to be done as ofte as ye awake.

The Knight tells a cautionary tale of two sisters – daughters of an emperor of
Constantinople, as it happened – who 'lay bothe in one bedde'. The younger was
assiduous in her prayers, the elder was not, and scolded her sister for keeping her
awake by praying. She rapidly came to a bad end.[7] In another of the Chevalier's
tales, a devout daughter 'never wold ete till that she had said all her houres and
herd all the Masses that she myght here'.[8] At a very similar date, the Menagier de
Paris also insisted on the complementary performance of public and private
religious duty. He thoughtfully provided prayers in both Latin and French for the
use of his young wife, to be said 'either at the hour of matins, or on awaking in the
morning, or both, or while you are getting up and dressing, and after you dress; all
are good, as long as you are still fasting and before you do any other duty'.[9] Here
again domestic devotion is validated by being carried out according to the rules,
although the Menagier does not prescribe a posture for prayer and was also
insistent on the necessity of fervour.

Already in the ninth century the Lady Dhuoda, counselling her son William,
envisaged that his private prayers would be nourished by reading.[10] A host of later
medieval writers, the Menagier and Christine de Pizan among them, saw such
reading as an important part of private religious formation. The Menagier
possessed the Bible, the Golden Legend, the Apocalypse and the Life of the Fathers
in French and offered free use of them to his wife.[11] We are accustomed to the
notion that monastic reading was contemplative and prayerful, rather than
recreational or scholarly in character; in the domestic setting too it is hard to
establish a dividing line between pious reading and the prayer which it fertilized.
We cannot know down to the last detail what the private prayers of medieval
people consisted of, but they were not typically extemporized. The selection
contained in a particular Book of Hours might be of the individual worshipper's

---

[7] William Caxton, *The Book of the Knight of the Tower*, ed. M.Y. Offord (Early English
Text Society, Supplementary Series 2, London, 1971), pp. 14–16.
[8] Ibid., pp. 17–18.
[9] *Le Menagier de Paris*, ed. G. Brereton and J. Ferrier (Oxford, 1981), pp. 6–9.
[10] *Dhuoda, Handbook for Her Warrior Son: Liber Manualis*, trans. and ed. M. Thiébaux
(Cambridge, 1998).
[11] *Le Menagier*, p. 46. For Christine, see *The Treasure of the City of Ladies*, trans. S.
Lawson (Harmondsworth, 1985), pp. 68, 161.

choosing, but severally the prayers were common property.[12] The act and the content of private prayer, and to a very large degree its timing, expressed the individual's participation in a shared spiritual culture. Even now it is very often formulaic in character; comfort is derived from familiar words and rhythms which are assumed to be especially acceptable to God: to take the most obvious example of all, the Lord's Prayer. The medieval version of this common culture centred upon the Psalms;[13] and the key to participation was literacy, even if oral repetition of the memorized text was a more prominent feature than we might now expect. The sale of books of prayers for all occasions still perhaps reveals not merely a feeling of difficulty or inadequacy in addressing God in our own words but a positive desire to establish links with what others are feeling and saying.

Printing and other forms of reproduction have now made images and music, as well as texts, much more generally available, while the mass manufacture of devotional objects and the diffusion of literacy and modest spending power which puts all these things within reach have transformed the capacity of ordinary people to create a devout visual and even aural environment in their own homes, should they wish to do so. In later medieval Europe these opportunities were obviously more restricted, but they were beginning to extend, to a not insignificant degree, beyond the confines of the very highest social classes. The spread of private book ownership must be among the most familiar features of later medieval cultural history, and a high proportion of the subject-matter was devotional if not theological in the strict sense. In town and country alike, many people were occupying a more substantial and diversified living space than their forefathers had done, and there was a limited extension of the enabling factors: literacy, purchasing power and the production of goods, from books to furniture. There was no single location for reading, any more than there was for prayer, but the possession of 'a room of one's own' would clearly be helpful.

Time and space, then, were found for religious exercises in the domestic environment but, to any medieval spiritual adviser, no amount of private prayer and devotion would have compensated for the failure to attend church dutifully. There was, and is, more to the ecclesiastical space than its official character. Still today we observe people going into a church to pray privately or just to sit and think. This clearly is a space which for many people has a quality that is to be found only there, whether because of the fact of consecration, the presence of relics or of the reserved sacrament, or simply the accumulated spiritual potency of the past prayers

---

[12] On Books of Hours in general, see J. Harthan, *Books of Hours* (London, 1977); R. Wieck, *The Book of Hours in Medieval Art and Life* (London, 1988).

[13] N. van Deusen (ed.), *The Place of the Psalms in the Intellectual Culture of the Middle Ages* (New York, 1999).

of a multitude of worshippers lingering in the air. That God is more likely to be
found in certain locations than in others remains a deeply felt and widely held
conviction, despite the asseverations of a multitude of preachers – not to say Christ
himself, according to St John (4:21–24) – to the contrary. This is not a
phenomenon peculiar to Christianity, as the universality of belief in holy places and
therefore of pilgrimage indicates. The presence of the holy is signposted by
commonly understood exterior signs, the church and its furnishings among the most
obvious.

This had its impact on private religious practice in the medieval period. When
the domestic space was (so to speak) customized for religious purposes, an effort
was made to impart something of this visible sacral character to it. Its furniture and
fittings, such as carved or painted altarpieces, replicated in miniature those of
public ecclesiastical buildings. Medieval houses were not over-burdened with
furniture and their several apartments were readily adaptable for different purposes.
Usually no special word distinguished a bedchamber, even if it was habitually used
for sleeping. Such chambers could further display their adaptability by taking on
the qualities of an oratory – a word which means simply a place for prayer.
Sometimes an anchorite possessed an 'oratory' which was distinct from his sleeping
space, but, as we have seen, the inner chamber in which the anchoress of *Ancrene
Wisse* slept also contained her altar and her images.

When we consider domestic religion in the narrow and most obvious sense –
that is, as the complex of devotions performed by laypeople in their own homes – it
is worth remembering that there were men and women all over Christian Europe
who were leading the religious life outside the cloister: hermits, anchorites and
anchoresses, beguines and tertiaries of all descriptions. Some of these were
celebrated individuals, many thousands more, whose names are unknown to us,
must have been well-known in their localities. That the anchoress should be
genuinely enclosed and not pass her time in chatting to the neighbours was the
constant theme of their counsellors, for a ground-floor window could be the
gateway to temptation. The salient point is that devout laymen and women did not
lack handy models for the religious use of everyday spaces. I have chosen one
example out of many of a holy woman who lived her life in a domestic setting.

Umiliana de' Cerchi of Florence died in May 1246 at the age of 27. In her short
life she moved from the status of wife and mother to that of widowed apprentice
saint, leading a life of monastic austerity in a room of her father's tower-house in
the middle of Florence. Umiliana became a protégée of the Franciscans and it was a

Franciscan, Vito da Cortona, who wrote her *Life* shortly after her death.[14] It is not necessary here to describe how she lived in her husband's household, where her religiosity expressed itself in active charity and church-going. On her return to her father's house as a widow, she continued for a time in this mode of life but came under increasing pressure to enter into a second marriage. One day, she betook herself to her room and prayed before an image of our Lady, receiving divine reinforcement of her determination never to remarry. We are not told anything further, at this moment, about the space she was using for prayer, but we do learn something about one of its all-important accessories, the portable religious image, which appears again in her story.[15]

Enraged by her obstinacy, Umiliana's father now defrauded her of her dowry and thus deprived her of the means of doing the practical works of charity she so much loved. She thereupon resolved to lead the religious life in the unpropitious setting of her hostile parental home. As a propagandist for the opportunities that the mendicants were now helping to fashion for the laity, brother Vito explains that Umiliana had in fact wished to become an enclosed nun, but God had other plans for her. She was 'this wondrous foundress of a new way of holy life'. Vito underlines the point by effecting a subtle verbal transformation of what Umiliana's family probably called her *camera*. She went every morning to hear the office, that is to church, and then returned, not to her room but 'into her cell' (*in cellam suam*), where she divided her time between prayer and fasting, sleeping very little.

> What did she lack of the monastic life, who lived in such continuous silence and observance? What less did she possess than the holy hermits, who found herself a solitude in the midst of the city and converted her bedchamber into a prison cell (*thalamum in carcerem commutavit*)?

There are further transformations a little later. 'This little cell, or better the prison, located in her father's tower, she changed, so far as was possible, into an oratory'. *Cella* remains Vito's preferred word for the room. He is not particularly interested in describing it for us, for it is important only as a setting for the extraordinary spiritual life that Umiliana was leading within it. Of course it had a door, which was sometimes locked, and windows. At one moment, Umiliana expressed the wish that

---

[14] The text of the *Vita* is in *Acta Sanctorum*, ed. J. Bollandus *et al.* (70 vols, Antwerp, 1643–1940; vols 1–61 repr. Brussels 1965–70), Maii 4, cols 385–418. The present writer hopes to publish an English translation of this work, together with other thirteenth-century Italian *Lives*.

[15] H. Maginnis, 'Images, Devotion and the Beata Umiliana de' Cerchi', in A. Ladis and S. Zuraw (eds), *Visions of Holiness: Art and Devotion in Renaissance Italy* (Athens, GA, 2001), pp. 13–20. I am grateful to Joanna Cannon for this reference.

it had neither: 'Would that my father would shut me up in this tower, with no door or window in it, for Christ's sake'. The devil sometimes tempted Umiliana to look out of the window at the mundane sights of the city and he even invaded it in the form of a serpent; on one occasion she bodily flung him out of it. Once she went to the window of her own accord to watch her maidservant drawing water from the well; she was suspicious of the water because it had a tendency to turn into wine. The room had a bed to which, however, Umiliana preferred a bag of straw. It had beams; one night when Umiliana's lamp went out while she was meditating on the Lord's Prayer a white dove flew into the cell and perched on one of them. Umiliana somewhat obtusely failed to recognize the dove for what it was, although its radiance illuminated the whole room, and she tried to catch it for her little nephew, whereupon it landed next to her panel of the Virgin and miraculously merged into it. Of all the physical fittings of the chamber, this image, which was drawn either on parchment or on paper, is by far the most important to Umiliana's story. We are told that she kept it covered with a cloth which one night seemed to her to catch fire, only for her to discover that these were not material flames.

If saints inspired by mendicant spirituality were going to be recruited from among the laity and to remain in 'the world', their physical environment would be something like this. Umiliana's father wanted to move her out of the tower-house, so that her cousin Galgano could occupy her room with his wife, but she refused to go. A century later, Catherine of Siena grew up in a house in Siena (now transformed into a shrine) where her father kept his dyeing shop on the ground floor. As a girl she had her own bedroom, until her parents realized that she was using it for prayer and thus fortifying herself in her determination never to get married. Her bedroom was taken from her and she was forbidden ever to be in a room with the door shut. Her response was, 'with holy cunning', to appropriate her brother's bedroom when he was out during the day and even to pray in it while he was asleep. When eventually her father was convinced of her vocation, she got her bedroom back and proceeded to transform it, as Umiliana had done, into the 'cell' appropriate to one who had embraced a quasi-monastic vocation.[16]

These were not typical Italian townswomen, but their stories demonstrate the possible uses of a room with a door that could be shut. Spiritual counsellors of later generations – the Dominicans Giovanni Dominici and later Savonarola, the Franciscan Bernardino da Siena – suggested ways of sanctifying the household more generally. Around 1400 Giovanni Dominici had the spiritual upbringing of

---

[16] These particulars of Catherine's domestic background are given in the *Vita Prima* by her confessor Raymond of Capua; see *The Life of St Catherine of Siena*, trans. G. Lamb (London, 1960), especially pp. 42–6. The Latin text is in *Acta Sanctorum*, Aprilis 3, cols 853–959.

children particularly in mind. He not only recommended the use of images, which should be constantly before the eyes of children from their babyhood, but advocated that altars should be set up in the home which boys could tend like little acolytes, dressing up in vestments and playing at celebrating Mass and preaching in imitation of what they saw at church. The message that what was done in private must conform to what was done in public was thus reinforced, albeit playfully. If boys were to be encouraged to see themselves in images of the Baptist, the needs of women and girls could be met by the use of images of the Holy Virgin and of religious dolls representing the Christ-child on and around these 'toy' altars.[17] At the end of the fifteenth century, Savonarola advised 'sex separation during prayer, avoidance of polluted areas like bedrooms and the use of public times for private prayer'. Avoidance of the bedroom seems to go beyond previous recommendations, but for Richard Trexler all these counsels have to be seen in a context in which Florentines tended to agree that religious practice ideally belonged in the public setting that was provided for them 'by the church, commune and honorable men'.[18]

It is against this background, and partly in stark contrast to it, that Trexler also describes the inner agony of the merchant and diarist Giovanni di Pagolo Morelli, who wrestled in solitude with the grief caused by the death of his young son Alberto in 1406.[19] A year after the event, Morelli was tormented by the memory that he had withheld the ceremonial and sacramental comforts from Alberto, because he was unable to accept that he was going to die. He tried now to put this right, in private, in his chamber: barefoot, in a nightgown, with a halter round his neck, he prayed before a painted image of the Crucified Christ, addressing himself in turn to the Crucified One, to Mary and to St John. In so doing he used (and then apologized for) 'rough speech' (*rozzo parlare*), seemingly worried by the fear that it might make his anguished petitions less acceptable to God. This ritual was followed, when Morelli had kissed the image, undressed and made the sign of the cross, by a sleepless, tormented night in which he reviewed his life. Falling asleep at last he experienced a vision of his favourite saint, Catherine of Alexandria, who brought him into contact with the soul of his son and thus effected a resolution. It is an altogether exceptional story, not perhaps because nothing like it ever happened to anyone else at the same period but because no one else wrote about it.

It was clearly acceptable, and perhaps not uncommon, for a Florentine to equip his bedchamber, as Morelli had done, with religious imagery. It would probably not have occurred to him to aspire to possess a private chapel, licensed for the

---

[17] C. Klapisch-Züber, *Women, Family and Ritual in Renaissance Italy* (Chicago, 1985), pp. 114–15, 310–29.
[18] R. Trexler, *Public Life in Renaissance Florence* (Ithaca, NY, 1991), p. 160.
[19] Ibid., pp. 174–85.

performance of the Eucharist, with a consecrated altar. Private chapels were not features of the early Florentine *palazzo*, by marked contrast with the numerous chapels bearing family names which adorn the city's churches.[20] The art tourist may instantly think of a conspicuous exception: the gorgeously frescoed chapel of the Medici palace, built probably just before 1450. This was, however, 'almost the first chapel to be constructed for a private palace in Florence',[21] and later in the century Florentine patricians continued to invest heavily in chapels in favoured churches rather than in their *palazzi*.[22] In some other societies, England among them, the dissemination of private chapels among the laity was evidently more precocious and widespread, although this by no means precluded continued and increasing investment in the public ecclesiastical sphere.

The greatest men had had private chapels from early times. Charlemagne's palatine chapel at Aachen or Louis IX's Sainte Chapelle might be regarded as lying outside the present remit, but there were less exalted examples in noble residences which were clearly intended to serve the needs of the household. At the end of the twelfth century Lambert of Ardres describes the chapels at the castle of Guines and, somewhat earlier, at Ardres itself, both of which he grandly likened to Solomon's Temple for the splendour of their decoration. At Ardres the chapel was in an elevated position on the eastern side of the house.[23] From the thirteenth century, private chapels, like so much else, were beginning to spread down the social scale, a process partly reflected in the more and more frequent grants that the popes were making for the possession of portable altars.

Again, these were hardly new. Missionaries and great men, ecclesiastical and lay, who were often on the road between different residences had always had a need for them, but now the less great and less peripatetic were entering the arena. Once again it is worth remembering the recluse, who often had an altar within the anchorhold, even if he or she was able to view the high altar of the adjacent church

---

[20] R. Goldthwaite, *The Building of Renaissance Florence* (Baltimore, 1980), pp. 12–13, 99–102.

[21] D. Kent, *Cosimo de' Medici and the Florentine Renaissance* (New Haven, 2000), p. 306. Oliviero de' Cerchi (a member of Umiliana's family as well as a contemporary of Dante) mentions a chapel in his palace in his will dated 30 August 1291 and Cosimo's father Giovanni di Bicci may also have possessed one: D. Cohl Ahl, *Benozzo Gozzoli* (New Haven, 1996), p. 294, fn. 28.

[22] F.W. Kent, *Household and Lineage in Renaissance Florence* (Princeton, 1977), pp. 100–106, 263–70. From the eleventh century onwards it had become more common for bishops to have chapels in their palaces, see M.C. Miller, *The Bishop's Palace: Architecture and Authority in Medieval Italy* (Ithaca, NY, 2000), pp.105–107, 216–52.

[23] *The History of the Counts of Guines and Lords of Ardres*, trans. L. Shopkow (Philadelphia, 2001), pp. 110–11, 161.

through a squint. These altars, like those which Florentine householders were later encouraged to have, sometimes had a purely devotional rather than liturgical function, establishing a religious décor with the assistance of a crucifix and other images. The anchoress of *Ancrene Wisse* was to revere 'the saints to whom you have dedicated your altars out of love', especially 'if any of them has been consecrated'.[24] The celebration of Mass of course required a consecrated altar, and this was the ambition of an increasing number of prosperous householders.

In the ten years of his pontificate (1342–52) Pope Clement VI granted licences for the possession of portable altars to some hundred and fifty individuals in England alone. These people ranged in rank from the king himself and the highest nobility (such as Henry, count and later duke of Lancaster) and ecclesiastical dignitaries (such as the abbot of Bury), through royal career clerks and parish priests to lay individuals and married couples of the rank of knight, squire or citizen of London or Lincoln. A few of these grantees (including Henry of Lancaster) were also licensed to hear Mass before daybreak or to have it celebrated privately in places under interdict, but this was much less usual, if only because probably less frequently requested. Only occasionally was it specified where the altar was to be used. In November 1343 three West-Country petitioners were licensed to use portable altars in eleven named manors in Devon and Somerset.[25] It seems unlikely that there was a specially-built chapel, as distinct from a chamber habitually used for that purpose, in every one of these houses. The 1452 inventory of the possessions of a prosperous ecclesiastic, William Duffield, canon residentiary of York, Southwell and Beverley, suggests that he had chapels in his houses at York and Beverley, but not at Cawood, where there was a table with high trestles 'for the celebration of Masses'; presumably Duffield used a portable altar on this table.[26] His contemporary John Dawtre, a pious lawyer of York, evidently used a 'low chamber' or parlour as his oratory, for he refers in his will (proved in August 1459) to 'a chest in the *bassa camera* on which I have made my altar' and later to 'the altar *in bassa camera*'.[27]

In July 1351 the widow Joan Bouford, of the diocese of Salisbury, was granted the use of a portable altar 'in consideration of her being more than seventy years of

[24] *Anchoritic Spirituality*, p. 54.

[25] *CEPR*, II, p. 113. The petitioners were the knights John de Moulton and Richard de Stapeldon, and the 'donsel' John de Prodhomme.

[26] *Testamenta Eboracensia*, ed. J. Raine (6 vols, Surtees Society iv, xxx, xlv, liii, lxxix, cvi, Durham, 1836–1902), III, p. 139. In his chapel at Beverley, Duffield had 'a table of wainscotting with a chest underneath, in the style of an altar' (p. 138).

[27] Ibid., II, pp. 232–3.

age'.[28] It was often on similar pleas that episcopal licences for private chapels were sought and granted. In England as elsewhere individuals and families were eager to leave their mark on the public religious space, as Nigel Saul's recent study of the activities of the Cobham family, and more generally the host of chantry chapels to be seen in churches all over the country, amply demonstrate.[29] Yet chapels were increasingly numerous in English late medieval private houses and they represented something rather different from the customized bedroom.[30] They had to be officially licensed and there were limitations on what was permitted to take place in them. In 1268, c.16 of the legatine council held at London by Cardinal Ottobuono stated that offerings collected in a chapel that had no parishioners of its own (for example, a chapel of ease) must go to the rector of the mother church; it was made clear that this applied also to offerings made in any *capella propria* possessed by a *privata persona*.[31] In 1287 the synodal statutes of the bishop of Exeter (c.9) reaffirmed this principle, adding that no private or other non-parochial chapel might possess a baptismal font or the privilege of celebrating nuptials or other *divina*, unless that had been allowed for in the act of foundation. Everyone aged fourteen or more had to make his or her offering at the mother church at Christmas, Easter and on other stipulated festivals. The burden of repairing and maintaining private chapels fell on the proprietors.[32]

In the nearly twenty years that he was bishop of Lincoln (1280–99), Oliver Sutton licensed a number of persons of quality to possess chapels.[33] The petitioners normally adduced the distance of the parish church from their places of residence (sometimes as little as one mile, but often more) and the difficulty or even danger of the road, especially in winter. These problems might be aggravated by the physical condition of the petitioner or another member of his family: gout, pregnancies, unspecified infirmities, and in one memorable instance the fact that the petitioner's mother was extremely old and his wife extremely fat.[34] A sub-group of Sutton's suppliants could not plead distance from a parish church: certain Oxford masters, including the future archbishop of York, William Greenfield,

---

[28] *CEPR*, II, p. 456.

[29] N. Saul, *Death, Art and Memory in Medieval England: the Cobham Family and their Monuments 1300–1500* (Oxford, 2001).

[30] See M. Wood, *The English Mediaeval House* (London, 1965), pp. 227–46.

[31] F.M. Powicke and C.R. Cheney, *Councils & Synods with Other Documents Relating to the English Church, II, A.D. 1205–1313* (2 vols, Oxford, 1964), II, p. 766.

[32] Ibid., p. 1003.

[33] *The Rolls and Registers of Bishop Oliver Sutton 1280–1299*, ed. R.M.T. Hill (8 vols, Lincoln Record Society 39, 43, 48, 52, 60, 69, 76, Hereford, 1948–86), III, pp. l–lii, offers an excellent summary of the norms governing private chapels.

[34] Ibid., IV, pp. 46–7.

obtained licences for chapels in their lodgings.[35] The Master and Fellows of Balliol managed to convince Sutton that they were too constantly absorbed in the pursuit of knowledge to be required to go to the parish church, but they let him down by celebrating publicly on the feast of All Saints and entertaining members of other colleges at their services.[36] This contravened the most basic of the bishop's requirements, that the services held in private chapels should be for the benefit only of the petitioner and his immediate household, not for fellow-parishioners or dwellers nearby. Sutton insisted that all household members must not only fulfil their Easter duty at the parish church but attend there at other major festivals, especially in the summer, when the condition of the roads was presumed to improve. Most important of all, at no time were the sacraments to be administered to those present by the clergy who served these chapels. A clear distinction was therefore drawn between the Mass as devout spectacle, the *divina* which petitioners often said they were eager to hear as often as possible and which were thus licensed for performance in the domestic setting, and the actual reception of the Eucharist. All oblations were to go to the rector of the parish.

Sutton does not have much to say about the physical characteristics of these chapels. They had to be suitable (*decens*), and there is occasional reference to the fact that a chapel would be inspected before the licence was granted, or that it had already been inspected. How this fitness was assessed is not further specified, but there are some negatives. Although the bishop has nothing to say about modes of access, he makes it clear that chapels were not to draw attention to themselves. Several petitioners were forbidden to erect a bell tower, to hold processions or (in one case) to ring bells *pubblice*; John, lord of Orby, was told that he was not to display *insignia* (not further described) detrimental to the rights of the parish church.[37] The bishop occasionally had to intervene when private chapels were misused. The case of the scholars of Balliol has been mentioned. Another involved one of the greatest men in England, the king's cousin, Edmund, earl of Cornwall. In 1296 reports reached the bishop that people were flocking to the chapel in the earl's manor of Hambleden in Buckinghamshire and that healing miracles were being done there. Sutton personally investigated and verified these allegations. He imposed a ban on the use of the chapel and only permitted the earl to use it again when all popular recourse to it was at an end.[38]

---

[35] Ibid., V, p. 108.

[36] Ibid., III, p. 95; IV, pp. 132–3.

[37] Ibid., VI, pp. 61–2. For examples of prohibitions on bell towers etc., see ibid., V, pp. 212–13, 215–16.

[38] Ibid., V, pp. 143–4, 176, 212.

A striking tension is revealed here. Miracles could legitimately take place anywhere. Curative miracles frequently took place in the home; there was no ecclesiastical objection when God intervened to rescue shipwrecked mariners, children buried in the ruins of a fallen building or householders threatened by fire. At Hambleden, however, a vicious circle had been set up. Miracles had begun because people who should not have obtained access to the chapel had done so, and the miracles were now attracting further people who should not have been there. Now unlicensed Masses were being celebrated. 'They have presumed without legitimate authority openly to celebrate the divine office, illicitly venerating a place altogether profane as if it were hallowed'.[39] That this was a *locus omnino prophanus* disqualified it not as a site for miracles but as a place where persons other than members of the earl's household were permitted to attend Mass. What Sutton either did not know, or more likely did not want to say, was that the earl of Cornwall was an enthusiast for the memory of Thomas Cantilupe of Hereford, soon but not yet to be the subject of a formal canonization process, and these miracles were almost certainly associated with his cult.[40]

Sutton used similar phraseology two years later when denouncing 'presumptuous priests' who had dared to celebrate in the newly-built chapel, which had not been licensed, in Joyce of Haigh's house in the parish of Pinchbeck. The guilty priests had been unmindful 'that it was prohibited to celebrate Mass except in places consecrated by a bishop or where he has given permission'.[41] This *oratorium* was, once again, 'altogether profane' and the priests had in effect been celebrating in a private house. The use of the term 'oratory' here may be intended to underline the informal character of a space which might legitimately be used for prayer (which could of course take place anywhere) but had not yet received episcopal licence. The necessity for such licence and the restriction of the congregation to the immediate household continued to be upheld, but in other respects licences became more permissive with the passage of time, as we shall see.

What were such chapels like and how were they experienced as part of the domestic environment? In about 1290, far to the south of Sutton's extensive diocese, members of a Kentish gentry family, probably the Culpepers, built themselves a stone annex to what was almost certainly a timber-framed hall block, at Old Soar in the depths of the countryside between the North Downs and the

---

[39] Ibid., V, p. 143.
[40] For a summary of these events, see D. Webb, *Pilgrimage in Medieval England* (London, 2000), p. 146.
[41] *Rolls and Registers*, VI, pp. 112–13.

Weald, some four miles from the parish church of Wrotham.[42] The hall has been replaced by an eighteenth-century house which preserves at one end traces of the aisled structure of its predecessor and of the raised dais on which the high table would have been placed. In accordance with a growing trend for gentry families to acquire amenities previously associated with the very rich, the new stone annex contained not only a fine upstairs chamber with kingpost roof, chimneyed fireplace, window-seats of polished marble and an adjacent garderobe block, but also a chapel. The present aspect of the chapel is in several respects misleading. Access to it is now obtained directly from the solar, through a rather rough doorway made in the eighteenth century when it was used as a grain-store, but originally it was reached by an external staircase to a doorway in the angle between chapel and solar. There are a few vestiges of its once churchly aspect: a piscina and a decorated corbel on which a candle or perhaps an image once stood. It has been suggested that here as elsewhere the master of the household may have used the chapel for non-religious purposes, as a study or for confidential meetings.

This multi-functionality also characterized the very much more sumptuous chapel built a century and half later by Cosimo de' Medici in his Florentine palace. In 1422, over twenty years before work began on the palace, Cosimo and his wife Contessina de' Bardi received from Pope Martin V the licence to have a portable altar.[43] It is hard to think that they would have had any more difficulty than other Florentines in getting to a parish church, even in winter. Devout persons of rank clearly wanted, as Oliver Sutton's clients had wanted, to have the comforts of religion more or less constantly on tap. It was one thing to have a holy image in one's bedroom which could be used as the focus of an entirely personal and private ritual, as in Giovanni Morelli's agonized improvisation, another to possess a properly constituted chapel with its altar, other apparatus and clerical personnel. Cosimo's chapel was used, however, for a variety of purposes, from his private meditations on death and the afterlife to audiences and the reception of

---

[42] There is a plan in Wood, *English Mediaeval House*, p. 69, and for further references see the index. For the chapel, see also N. Lloyd, *A History of the English House* (London 1985), pp. 180–81.

[43] This privilege is printed in H. Saalman and P. Mattox, 'The First Medici Palace', *Journal of the Society of Architectural Historians* 44 (1985), 343. Cosimo's father Giovanni and his wife had received the same privilege in the previous year. For Cosimo's chapel see Kent, *Cosimo de' Medici*, pp. 305–28, and also R. Hatfield, 'Cosimo de' Medici and the Chapel of his Palace', in F. Ames-Lewis (ed.), *Cosimo 'il Vecchio' de' Medici, 1389–1464* (Oxford, 1992), pp. 221–44. Interestingly in view of the numbers of licences granted to English petitioners by Clement VI in the middle of the preceding century, Kent regards the privilege granted to Cosimo as very rare.

distinguished guests and delegations, and its existence did not exclude the presence of religious imagery elsewhere in the palace, notably in Cosimo's own *camera*.[44]

In the long and elaborate will made by John Baret of Bury St Edmunds in 1463 there is an oblique glimpse of the chapel of a somewhat less rich and powerful merchant. Baret was a great frequenter of churches and clergy, a friend of the monks of Bury, including John Lydgate, and a benefactor to the parish church of St Mary where his tomb is still to be seen.[45] He envisaged that his niece Jenette Whitwelle would continue to live in his principal house and he wished her to have her choice of chambers and adjacent withdrawing rooms. Were she to choose the chamber above the kitchen, not the one she had hitherto occupied, 'I will she have hire liberte at alle lefull tymes to go in to the chapell to seye hire devocyons'.[46] This suggests that, as was normal, the chapel was on the upper floor.

Custom-built accommodation would be used for prayer if it was available, but religion penetrated the other rooms of the houses of the devout. The devotions of Cecily, duchess of York, mother to Edward IV and Richard III, were divided between her chapel and her chamber, where she heard Low Mass before breakfast and where she prayed at other times. Her dining-table too was sanctified by holy reading.[47] In John Baret's house as in the Medici palace, hangings decorated with religious subjects, books and other objects of varying degrees of portability created a devout atmosphere elsewhere than in the chapel. Among the most portable of Baret's possessions were numerous sets of beads, one of which was bequeathed to the abbot of Bury. One of the monks was to have 'my smale tablets of ivory gravyn with ymages wiche were the pryour hooly John of Bridlington'. Baret's numerous bequests to Jenette Whitwell included a 'steynyd clooth of the Coronacion of oure lady'. He left what he called 'my crucifix' to Dame Margaret Spurdaunce of Norwich; it was to be found in his 'white chamber', and it seems it had a cloth covering, with 'a valaunce of scripture abowte the image'. This covering was not to go to Dame Margaret; another crucifix was to be made for the white chamber, at the expense of the estate, to replace the one bequeathed to her, and presumably this was to be covered with the same cloth, as if to say that *a* crucifix was an

---

[44] Ibid., p. 247.

[45] For the Barets, see R. Gottfried, *Bury St Edmunds and the Urban Crisis: 1290–1539* (Princeton, 1982), pp. 153–9; G. Gibson, *The Theater of Devotion* (Chicago, 1989), pp. 72–9. His will is published in *Wills and Inventories from the Registers of the Commissary of Bury St Edmunds and the Archdeacon of Sudbury*, ed. S. Tymms (Camden 1st Series xlix, London, 1850), pp. 15–44.

[46] Ibid., p. 22.

[47] C.A.J. Armstrong, 'The Piety of Cicely, Duchess of York: a Study in Late Mediaeval Culture', in C.A.J. Armstrong, *England, France and Burgundy in the Fifteenth Century* (London, 1983), pp. 141–3.

indispensable feature of this chamber.[48] We do not know exactly where in his house Baret kept or read his 'book of ynglysch and latyn with diverse matters of good exortacions' or his 'book called *Disce mori*' or, for that matter, his copy of his friend Lydgate's *Siege of Thebes*. The evidence of numerous other English wills of the period is that where chapels existed books were often kept in them; but (like his contemporary John Dawtre of York) Baret possessed a 'study', which may have served him either as an all-purpose private sanctum or simply as a writing-office.[49]

By this period, Baret and others like him were able to obtain more extensive privileges for their private chapels than Oliver Sutton's clientele had done. Already in 1352 Clement VI conceded to Henry, duke of Lancaster and his wife that their chaplains might administer the sacraments of baptism and the Eucharist to them, their children and household, and also give nuptial blessings.[50] In 1444 John Baret, a lesser man, received a very similar indult from Eugenius IV, except that there is no mention of nuptial blessings.[51] This omission was consistent with the drive against clandestine marriage: special licence could be obtained to celebrate a marriage in a domestic chapel after the banns had been published in the parish church.[52] A Suffolk gentleman was now able to receive the Eucharist and to have baptism administered in his private chapel by his own or any other fit priest. It is unlikely that Baret could have guaranteed a permanent chaplain the kind of living that the conspicuously devout Henry of Lancaster had been able to guarantee his,[53] and equally unlikely that he would have been able to commission decorations for his chapel of a quality comparable to those which Cosimo de' Medici could purchase for his: Cosimo's altarpiece (now replaced by a copy) was Filippo Lippi's so-called *Adoration in the Woods*.[54]

The *disjecta membra* of medieval private devotion, by no means all of high aesthetic quality, are now scattered among the world's museums. Apart from prayer books, they include images in all media, from crucifixes and free-standing

---

[48] *Wills and Inventories*, p. 36.

[49] Ibid., p. 33; *Testamenta Eboracensia*, II, p. 232.

[50] *CEPR*, II, p. 50 (repeated pp. 166, 459).

[51] Ibid., IX, p. 365. The privilege is identical with one previously granted to the earl of Buckingham and his wife. Baret is described as 'nobleman, esquire and lord in part of the town of Fronham (*sic*) All Saints' in the diocese of Norwich. Fornham All Saints is just north of Bury.

[52] Numerous such licences are listed in *Testamenta Eboracensia*, III, pp. 311–75.

[53] In 1353 the duke had three chaplains at Pontefract Castle, one of them designated dean and another sub-dean; their benefices were described as 'fat and well-endowed' (*CEPR*, II, p. 515). In 1344 Henry's chief chaplain had been licensed by the pope to retain the oblations made in his chapel (ibid., p. 458).

[54] Kent, *Cosimo de' Medici*, pp. 322–8.

sculptures to small altarpieces.[55] All were in some degree intended to stimulate the devout imagination; some may even be described as embodying images of the devotion they were designed to nurture. In 1487 the 23-year-old Martinus van Nieuwenhove of Bruges commissioned from Hans Memling a diptych which may have remained in the possession of his family until the later seventeenth century.[56] It shows him adoring the Virgin Mary in a fictive domestic apartment, as if she and the Christ Child were present there with him (they are all reflected together in the mirror which we see behind her on the window-shutter). This picture of himself with the Virgin was clearly to be an aid and inspiration in his devotions. Where was it kept? Did one put such a picture of oneself on an altar in a private chapel? Or was the diptych lodged in Martin's bedchamber?

Flemish fifteenth-century art abounds in images which seem thus to open a window on to the world of private devotion. Manuscript illuminations show affluent donors kneeling at their prayer-desks in both ecclesiastical and domestic surroundings. The Vienna Master of Mary of Burgundy depicts such a lady, perhaps Mary herself, seated by a window reading her prayer-book with her beads to hand; the window overlooks a church in which her repeated figure is to be seen kneeling before the Virgin and Child.[57] This is a visionary image, but such windows on to the ecclesiastical space were available, if only to an elite. Mary's tomb-monument is now to be seen in the choir of the church of Our Lady in Bruges, overlooked by the little barrel-vaulted chapel, with its window-seat, which Louis de Gruuthuse was in 1472 authorized to construct in his adjacent mansion.[58]

Since the twelfth century, the Virgin of the Annunciation had typically been shown reading at the moment of Gabriel's arrival. Flemish artists often located this scene in a domestic interior.[59] It might be rash to take such depictions as simple factual records of the prosperous young bourgeoise reading her prayer-book in the well-appointed sitting-room of her home; for much of the plausible mundane detail may carry other meanings. In a panel now in Brussels, one follower of Robert Campin imitated an Annunciation by the master, with alterations and additions including a woodcut of St Christopher on the wall above the fireplace behind the

---

[55] H. van Os, *The Art of Devotion in the Late Middle Ages in Europe, 1300–1500*, trans. M. Hoyle (London, 1994).

[56] D. de Vos, *Hans Memling: the Complete Works* (London, 1994), pp. 278–83.

[57] For illustration and discussion of this miniature, with further references, see T. Kren and S. McKendrick, *Illuminating the Renaissance: the Triumph of Flemish Manuscript Painting in Europe* (London and Los Angeles, 2003), pp. 140, 229 (figure 65).

[58] See Figure 3.8 below.

[59] D. Robb, 'The Iconography of the Annunciation in the Fourteenth and Fifteenth Centuries', *Art Bulletin* 18 (1936), 480–526.

reading Virgin.[60] This may be intended as a symbol of Mary herself as Christ-bearer, but similar relatively cheap religious images might well in fact have been on show in such a household. In a portrait of an unknown young man by Petrus Christus in London's National Gallery, a manuscript page fixed to the wall behind him shows the Veronica, the image of Christ's face that was venerated by pilgrims to St Peter's in Rome, with the text of the hymn *Salva sancta facies* ('Hail, Holy Face') beneath it. Perhaps the young man (who holds a prayer-book) is to be imagined reciting prayers in the hope of obtaining the indulgences which were offered in connection with the Veronica as with other religious images; but the abbreviated form of Christ's name, 'xpi', in the text of the hymn is also the artist's usual way of signing his pictures.[61] Patrons both lay and ecclesiastical certainly commissioned images for domestic use which were framed or captioned by prayer and indulgence texts. In the Wallraff-Richartz Museum at Cologne there is a fourteenth-century Umbrian panel of the Man of Sorrows with the text of an indulgence underneath it, while in the Musée des Beaux Arts at Tournai a portable altarpiece, once attributed to the son of Rogier van der Weyden, shows the Virgin and Child in a domestic setting with the *Salve Regina* inscribed on the frame. Isolated on the gallery wall, such images cannot now tell us in what physical setting they were originally located or used, or indeed by whom.

Religious visualization could be stimulated by the written word as well as by the image. The Pseudo-Bonaventuran *Meditations on the Life of Christ*, written in the late thirteenth century for the use of a Franciscan nun, and enormously popular later with a wider audience, encouraged the detailed mental recreation of the incidents of the life of Christ in their mundane setting.[62] The reader, for example, was to imagine Christ as a child setting the table and bringing in the water. This did not sacralize domestic space as such but used everyday reality to evoke the reality of the incarnate Christ's earthly life. Holy Land pilgrims took another route to this goal, but armchair pilgrimage with the aid of books was a possibility. An anonymous fourteenth-century Tuscan account of the Holy Places is prefaced by the following rubric: 'These are the journeys which the pilgrims who go overseas must perform to save their souls and which every person can do standing in their

---

[60] F. Thürlemann, *Robert Campin: a Monographic Study with Critical Catalogue* (Munich, 2002), pp. 74–5. The artist is named as the Master of the Hortus Conclusus and the panel is dated 1425–30.

[61] M. Ainsworth, *Petrus Christus, Renaissance Master of Bruges* (New York, 1994), pp. 54, 60, 61.

[62] I. Ragusa and R. Green, *Meditations on the Life of Christ: an Illustrated Manuscript of the Fourteenth Century* (Princeton, 1961). The illustration of the manuscript translated here was never completed; many more manuscripts were not illustrated at all.

house, thinking in every place which is written below and saying in every holy place a Paternoster and an Avemaria'.[63]

It was probably unnecessary to specify where in one's house one was to stand while performing this imaginative exercise. Chapels were possessed by relatively few. The bedchamber was the all-purpose space which offered the individual the best possibility of seclusion within the household, but there were others. One was the garden. For the educated devout the garden may have derived a certain resonance from scriptural imagery; the enclosed garden was a favourite symbol of the purity of the Virgin. On another level, the utility of real gardens, not only as the source of herbs and flowers, but as places of refreshment and tranquillity for the spirit, had long been familiar to monks and others. In the late fourteenth-century Middle English romance *Sir Cleges* the eponymous knight, down on his luck, goes into his garden after Mass one Christmas morning and kneels to pray beneath a cherry tree, which he then realizes is in leaf and laden with fruit.[64] Cherry-trees fruiting in December may have been fictional fancy, but that prayer in the garden after Mass was not as indicated by a letter written by that keen observer and vivid word-painter Agnes Paston. In July 1453 she informed her son John that 'on Tuesday, Sir John Heveningham went to his church and heard three Masses and came home again never merrier, and said to his wife that he would go say a little devotion in his garden; and forthwith he felt a fainting in his leg and slid down. This was at nine of the clock and he was dead ere noon'.[65]

Poor Sir John; but his sad death illuminates for us a corner of late medieval religion. It has sometimes been said that in the century before the Reformation the devout were turning away from the official church towards a world of private devotion. Sir John's movements, like John Baret's will, suggest that the world of private devotion was indeed flourishing, but it represented not an alternative to the public sphere, but an extension of it in which the words and gestures of public worship were reflected rather than contradicted. The late medieval trend towards a more differentiated and well-appointed domestic space had implications for lay spirituality as well as for other aspects of social and cultural life. If the devout desired to explore the possibilities of private prayer and spiritual reading, the houses in which they lived increasingly afforded them opportunities, to the measure of their status and their income, to do so. For many Christians, spaces which at

---

[63] A. Lanza and M. Troncarelli (eds), *Pellegrini scrittori: viaggiatori toscani del Trecento in Terrasanta* (Florence, 1990), p. 315.

[64] 'Sir Cleges', in *The Middle English Breton Lays*, ed. A. Laskaya and E. Salisbury (Kalamazoo, 1995), ll. 193–201. I am most grateful to Ad Putter of Bristol University for drawing my attention to this work.

[65] *The Paston Letters*, ed. J. Gairdner (6 vols, London, 1904), II, p. 286.

other times served them for the enjoyment of worldly leisure and personal privacy could serve also for approaches to God.

Chapter 3

The Domesticity of Sacred Space in the Fifteenth-Century Netherlands

Jeanne Nuechterlein

When we think of 'sacred space' in the late medieval/early modern period, we tend to imagine a place – whether an entire building, a room within a building, or a section of a room – marked out by its layout and furnishings as intended for religious purposes. Within domestic households, sacred space might consist of a private chapel or oratory, or a small shrine area where devotional images and other religious paraphernalia were grouped together. Most castles or palaces included their own chapel served by household chaplains, often with adjacent oratories (non-consecrated religious spaces) where the owners could watch Masses in private, for example in the Burgundian ducal palaces of Rihour in Lille, whose chapel and adjacent oratory are the only parts of the complex still standing, and Germolles in Burgundy, where the ruins of the chapel and great hall stand adjacent to the surviving residential building.[1] Such domestic religious spaces were not reserved to the nobility or extremely wealthy alone: although chapels, whose consecration required ecclesiastical permission, were a sign of prestige, individuals in more modest households might use a section of another room for private devotions. Compared with palatine chapels, however, there is comparatively little evidence about exactly how such domestic spaces were utilized for sacred purposes. Many small religious objects (whose size implies that they were used privately by individuals rather than as a focus of collective worship) survive from this period, including prints, single panels, statuettes, and small diptychs and triptychs, usually portraying saints or emotionally-charged scenes relating to

---

[1] O. Canneva-Tétu et al., Le Palais Rihour et ses vitraux (Lille, 1999), pp. 1, 12–15; P.Beck (ed.), Vie de cour en Bourgogne à la fin du Moyen Age (Saint-Cyr-sur-Loire, 2002), pp. 57–66; Art from the Court of Burgundy: the Patronage of Philip the Bold and John the Fearless, 1364–1419 (Paris, 2004), pp. 137–41. Although few Burgundian examples survive, we can better understand their architectural structure by studying their French precedents, see E. Taburet-Delayahe (ed.), Paris 1400: les arts sous Charles VI (Paris, 2004), pp. 68–71.

Christ's infancy and passion. The wide range of artistic quality and material prestige of such objects suggests that a broad cross-section of society used them, and while many would have been owned by nuns and other religious, others were commissioned and used by the laity.[2] In this paper I will examine a few such images that were painted on panel, which became a popular independent medium in the fifteenth-century Netherlands, in order to explore what they reveal about private devotional experience and the spaces in which it could occur. In particular, I will focus on the rise in the fifteenth-century Netherlands of a new visual iconography, that of the Virgin in a fully-developed domestic interior, which appeared in many small devotional works as well as in some larger altarpieces and in illuminated manuscripts. These images help us understand the spaces of private devotion in part because they sometimes include representations of private devotional objects; but more fundamentally, this iconography gives us insight into the potential 'sacredness' of domestic spaces by choosing to place the Virgin within the home rather than in the church, pointing towards an underlying attitude that the sacred might easily and appropriately enter into the secular domestic world. This paper will suggest that these scenes of the Madonna reading, praying, or sitting with the Christ Child in a bedroom or sitting room responded to the practices of those who owned such works: people who, while not rejecting the church and its fixed sacred spaces, did not see them as the only place for religious experience.

It is important to emphasize that this new iconography of the Virgin in a domestic interior, which seems to have originated in scenes of the Annunciation, developed alongside a slightly older one depicting the Annunciate Virgin within or against a church or chapel-like space, often reading at a scholarly lectern. Examples of this type can be found throughout fifteenth-century Netherlandish painting, such as Jan van Eyck's *Annunciation* in the National Gallery in Washington, an *Annunciation* from the Robert Campin circle in the Prado in Madrid, and a similar image with slightly different subject matter, Van Eyck's *c.1435 Madonna in a Church* now in Berlin, which was faithfully copied some seven decades later by Jan Gossaert as well as The Master of 1499 (Figure 3.1).[3]

---

[2] For an overview see H. van Os, *The Art of Devotion in the Late Middle Ages in Europe, 1300–1500* (Amsterdam, 1994).

[3] For discussions of these works, see E.M. Gifford, 'Assessing the Evolution of van Eyck's Iconography through Technical Study of the Washington Annunciation, I', in S. Foister, S.Jones, and D. Cool (eds), *Investigating Jan van Eyck* (Turnhout, 2000), pp. 59–66; F.Thürlemann, *Robert Campin: a Monographic Study with Critical Catalogue* (Munich, 2002), cat. III.D.1; N. Zenker, *Jan van Eyck: Die Madonna in der Kirche* (Berlin, 2001).

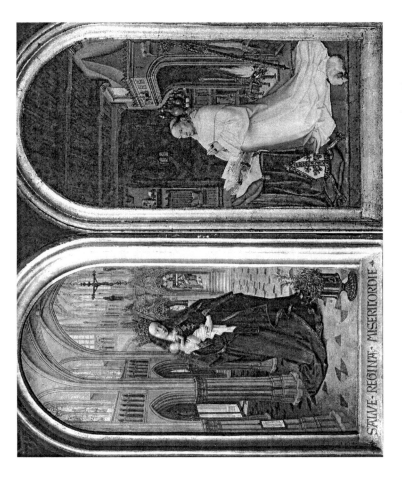

Figure 3.1 Master of 1499 (copy after Jan van Eyck), *Christiaan de Hondt Diptych*, 1499, Antwerp, Koninklijk Museum voor Schone Kunsten; photo copyright: IRPA-KIK, Brussels.

In these examples and many others, the Virgin stands or sits in a church nave as she receives Gabriel's message or holds the Christ Child, showing that the Annunciate Virgin could easily be identified with the institutional Church. The Eyckian *Madonna in a Church* appears on first glance as if it could record more or less faithfully a scene from real life, although that impression is countered by the fact that the Virgin towers up into the triforium, and closer inspection reveals that the tiny figures in the choir are angels rather than human clerics.[4] Therefore, although the represented church interior seems derived from direct observation of actual architecture, there can be little doubt that we are still meant to perceive the spatial setting as symbolic and/or visionary. This is not a literal rendition of a contemporary church scene but a constructed image pointing to the significance of the Virgin, though its realism also tells us that actual church interiors were spaces where the faithful might easily imagine the Virgin making an appearance.[5] The Virgin in such images is usually placed not in the choir but in the nave, the space used predominantly by the laity, although in the case of the Master of 1499's diptych this nave-Virgin has been paired with a Cistercian donor shown kneeling in a domestic interior.

While such scenes of the Madonna in a church continued to be produced, another iconography developed alongside it in the fifteenth-century Low Countries, apparently originating in the circle of the painter Robert Campin in Tournai. The exact attribution of many of these works – whether to Robert Campin himself (or his pseudonym the Master of Flémalle) or his workshop or followers – has been debated,[6] but here I am less interested in the exact identity of the artist(s) than in the sudden popularity of this type of image starting in the early or mid-1420s. In these works the Annunciation takes place not in a church but in a pointedly domestic room. One of the key archetypes is the composition best known from the central panel of the *Mérode Triptych* (Figure 3.2), which was repeated in many variations, including one in Brussels that some researchers think may in fact have been the 'original' version.[7]

---

[4] E. Panofsky, *Early Netherlandish Painting, its Origins and Character* (Cambridge, MA, 1953), p. 147.

[5] C. Harbison, 'Miracles Happen: Image and Experience in Jan van Eyck's *Madonna in a Church*', in B. Cassidy (ed.), *Iconography at the Crossroads* (Princeton, 1993), pp. 157–66.

[6] J. Nuechterlein, 'In Search of Artistic Personality: the Case of Robert Campin', *Art History* 29 (2004), 312–20.

[7] J. Dijkstra, 'The Brussels and the Mérode *Annunciation* Reconsidered', in S. Foister and S. Nash (eds), *Robert Campin: New Directions in Scholarship* (Turnhout, 1996), pp. 95–104.

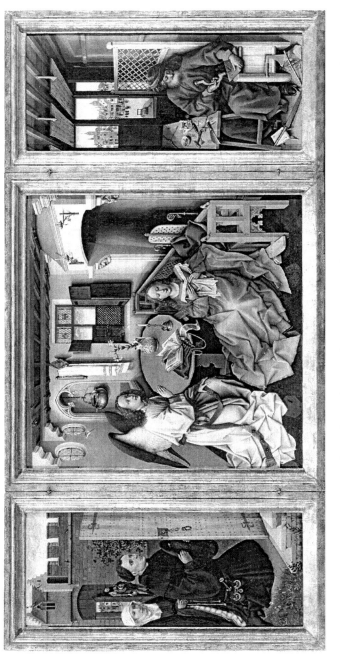

Figure 3.2 Workshop/circle of Robert Campin, *Mérode Triptych*, c.1425. New York, Metropolitan Museum of Modern Art.

Again, identifying the first model is of less concern for the present argument than the fact that the general composition became exceptionally popular, repeated not only in painted panels but in miniatures and even relief sculptures throughout the fifteenth and into the early sixteenth century.[8] In the *Mérode* panel, the Virgin sits on the floor in front of a long bench inside a room with a fireplace in the right wall, a window and a niche with a lavabo and towel on the back wall, and a barely-visible doorway at the left edge. Prominent in the middle of the room is a table on which lies an open book, a carrying bag, a scroll, a candle whose flame has just been extinguished, and a vase of flowers. The angel Gabriel raises his hand in blessing towards the Virgin, who remains attentive to the book she holds while a golden ray with a small figure of the Christ Child emanates towards her from a small circular window. The two side wings were probably added slightly later,[9] turning the painting into a small triptych and extending the domesticity of the setting by showing on the left wing the exterior of the room/house, with the donors kneeling at the bottom of the steps, and on the right Joseph's carpentry workshop.

The artist(s) who first designed this image, and/or the patron(s) who bought it, surely made a deliberate decision in placing the Annunciation not in a church or against a neutral background but in a fully-developed domestic interior. Although the biblical narrative implies that the Annunciation took place indoors (since Gabriel made his announcement upon 'entering', *ingressus*),[10] there is no further explanation of the setting. The late thirteenth-century *Legenda aurea* (*Golden Legend*) by Jacobus de Voragine is slightly more specific, implying that the Virgin was at her parents' home in Nazareth.[11] The Protevangelium of James and the Gospel of Pseudo-Matthew, the apocryphal texts that provided the most detail about the life of the Virgin, both state (in chapters 11 and 9 respectively) that Mary was at home spinning thread for the temple when Gabriel entered, though few Annunciation images depicted this detail.[12] The great majority of medieval imagery

---

[8] Ibid., pp. 99–102, and L. Campbell, 'Robert Campin, the Master of Flémalle and the Master of Mérode', *Burlington Magazine* 116 (1974), 643–4, fn. 78, 79.

[9] M.W. Ainsworth and K. Christiansen (eds), *From van Eyck to Bruegel: Early Netherlandish Painting in the Metropolitan Museum of Art* (New York, 1998), pp. 92, 95–6.

[10] Lk. 1: 26–28 (Clementine Vulgate): 'In mense autem sexto, missus est angelus Gabriel a Deo in civitatem Galilaeae, cui nomen Nazareth, ad virginem desponsatam viro, cui nomen erat Ioseph, de domo David: et nomen virginis Maria. Et ingressus angelus ad eam dixit: Ave gratia plena: Dominus tecum: benedicta tu in mulieribus'.

[11] Jacobus de Voragine, *The Golden Legend: Readings on the Saints*, trans. W. Granger Ryan (2 vols, Princeton, 1993), I, p. 197.

[12] One exception is the Annunciation scene on Melchior Broederlam's altarpiece wings in Dijon, discussed in Panofsky, *Early Netherlandish Painting*, p. 131, though Panofsky, who was probably working from a black-and-white photograph, fails to note that her skein is yellow/gold rather than the purple recounted in the texts.

instead represented the scene through the two figures alone with little indication of their surroundings, other than perhaps a vase of lilies on the floor or a lectern. Fifteenth-century artists and viewers, however, apparently expected a fuller setting. While the church-type Annunciation visualizes this space symbolically, conceptualizing Mary as Ecclesia, the domestic imagery instead turns her into a pious housewife, reading quietly at home when Gabriel appears to her. These images may have taken inspiration from the late thirteenth- or early fourteenth-century *Meditationes vitae Christi* (*Meditations on the Life of Christ*), which state that the Virgin was 'in the bedroom of her little house' when Gabriel appeared; shortly before, the author had commented that according to Jerome, Mary spent her time alternating between praying and weaving.[13] The Carthusian Nicholas Love's early fifteenth-century adaptation of the *Meditationes* into Middle English, *The Mirrour of the Blessed Lyf of Jesu Christ*, says that Mary 'was in hire priue chambre that tyme closed and in here prayeres or in here meditaciouns/ perauenture redynge the prophecie of ysaie touchynge the Incarnacioun'.[14] Love's interpretation perhaps reflects a more widespread assumption in the early fifteenth century about what the Virgin was doing when Gabriel arrived, and several Netherlandish images, such as the *Annunciation* on the left wing of the *Columba Altarpiece* by Campin's associate Rogier van der Weyden, place the scene in a bedroom.

This version of the Annunciation became virtually ubiquitous in later fifteenth-century Netherlandish painting, so much so that it can be difficult to remember that the iconography was a relatively recent invention. We also see artists creatively adapting the idea to a range of other subjects. Two small panels depicting the Madonna preparing to bathe the Christ Child in front of a fireplace survive from the Campin circle, one in the National Gallery, London, and the other in the Hermitage, St Petersburg (Figure 3.3).

[13] F.X. Taney *et al.* (eds), *Meditations on the Life of Christ* (Asheville, NC, 2000), pp. 11, 13.
[14] N. Love, *The Mirrour of the Blessed Lyf of Jesu Christ* (2 vols, Salzburg, 1989), I, pp.24–5.

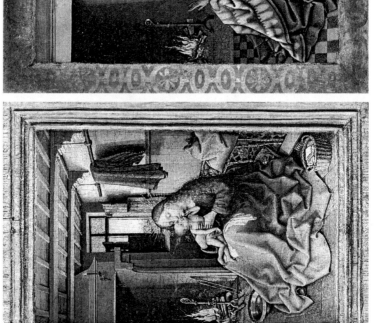

Figure 3.3 Workshop/circle of Robert Campin, *Virgin and Child in an Interior*. Left: before 1432(?), London, National Gallery. Right: c.1433–35 (?), The State Hermitage Museum, St Petersburg. Note that the London panel is about two thirds the size of the other.

In both images the Virgin sits on the floor holding the naked Christ Child in front of a fireplace with a basin nearby, in the National Gallery version with linens and towels also at the ready. Faint haloes indicate the identity of the mother and child here, but otherwise there is little to differentiate the subject from a purely domestic scene. A similar domestic interior appears in the right wing of the Campin-circle *Werl Altarpiece Wings* (Figure 3.4), an altarpiece rather than devotional work, which uses a similar setting as the *Mérode Annunciation* but this time for St Barbara, who reads on a bench in front of the fire while her tower is constructed in the distant landscape outside the window.

Another Campin-circle work, the *Madonna and Child before a Firescreen* in the National Gallery, London, shows the Virgin about to breastfeed the Christ Child while sitting in front of the ubiquitous fireplace, this time shown frontally rather than from a side angle.[15] Petrus Christus' *Holy Family* in Kansas City shows Joseph in the background carrying a rosary as he enters the house while the Virgin sits in the foreground with the Christ Child next to an open book, an unusual composition that has been interpreted as emphasizing the sacred nature of marriage and the family.[16] Domestic Holy Family scenes also became popular in German works in the Rhineland around the mid-fifteenth century, many of them apparently influenced by the Campin circle.[17] By the turn of the sixteenth century in Bruges the domestic Madonna tradition culminated in Gerard David's *Virgin and Child with the Milk Soup* (Figure 3.5), showing the Virgin feeding the Christ Child not with her own breast – which carried theological implications of her right of intercession with Christ on humanity's behalf – but with a bowl and spoon, hardly even identifiable as sacred rather than human figures. Like the *Mérode*/Brussels *Annunciation*, this composition survives in a number of copies, all evidently issuing from David's workshop, suggesting that this was a popular stock image requested by many buyers.[18] They must have been drawn to the sight of the Virgin and Child looking and acting like ordinary human beings in an everyday setting, anticipating the development in later art of the domestic genre scene.

---

[15] L. Campbell, *National Gallery Catalogues: the Fifteenth-Century Netherlandish Schools* (London, 1998), pp. 92–9.

[16] M.W. Ainsworth (ed.), *Petrus Christus: Renaissance Master of Bruges* (New York, 1994), pp. 170–6.

[17] See *Spätmittelalter am Oberrhein. Vol. 1: Maler und Werkstätten 1450–1525* (Stuttgart, 2001), cat. 4, 6, 41, 42.

[18] M.W. Ainsworth, *Gerard David: Purity of Vision in an Age of Transition* (New York, 1998), pp. 295–308.

Figure 3.4 Circle of Robert Campin/Rogier van der Weyden, *Werl Altarpiece Wings***, 1438, Madrid, Prado Museum.**

Figure 3.5 Gerard David, *Virgin and Child with the Milk Soup*, *c*.1515, Brussels, Musées Royeaux des Beaux-Arts; photo copyright: IRPA-KIK, Brussels.

These images clearly accord with the expansion of late medieval devotional literature calling upon its readers to meditate on the humanity of Christ and the Virgin and identify emotionally with their human experiences. This type of religious spirituality originated among Benedictines in the late eleventh century, flourished among the new religious orders such as the Cistercians and Carthusians in the twelfth century, and was further developed by Franciscans in the thirteenth and fourteenth centuries, as exemplified by the *Meditationes vitae Christi* written by a Franciscan friar for a nun, which encouraged its readers/listeners to visualize the events of Christ's life in great detail as if they were direct witnesses ('Now then, here too watch closely, as if you were actually present, and take in mentally everything said and done').[19] Both the *Meditationes* and a similar work by the fourteenth-century Carthusian Ludolphus of Saxony, the *Vita Christi*, were widely read throughout the later middle ages in northern Europe. By the late fourteenth and fifteenth centuries, this type of affective piety had become popular in vernacular as well as Latin devotional literature, reaching its apogee in the *Devotio Moderna* movement that started in the northern Netherlands and appealed first and foremost to the laity rather than to religious orders.[20] In addition to the emphasis on Christ's life, such texts usually exhorted their readers to examine their consciences carefully and strive to make themselves worthy of God, often likening the soul to a dwelling place, an idea that has been compared with the interior depicted in the *Mérode Annunciation*.[21] By showing the Holy Family as visually equivalent to a contemporary family, these domestic Madonna images brought the biblical (and extra-biblical) narratives of Christ and the Virgin to life, making it easy for viewers mentally to recreate the details of their everyday existence. At the same time, they encouraged viewers to visualize how they might make their own lives fitting to God, by imitating the Virgin's pious reading or mothering.

Although there is little specific evidence to prove it, it is likely that these images were often used in conjunction with devotional texts and prayer books. Those who owned domestic Madonna panels were probably not immediate members of the *devotio moderna*, since the movement required its lay strand (the

---

[19] Taney *et al.* (eds), *Meditations on the Life of Christ*, p. 13.

[20] J. Marrow, *Passion Iconography in Northern European Art of the Late Middle Ages: a Study of the Transformation of Sacred Metaphor into Descriptive Narrative* (Courtrai, 1979), pp. 7–26; T.H. Bestul, *Texts of the Passion. Latin Devotional Literature and Medieval Society* (Philadelphia, 1996), pp. 35–68.

[21] R.L. Falkenburg, 'The Household of the Soul: Conformity in the *Mérode Triptych*', in M.W. Ainsworth (ed.), *Early Netherlandish Painting at the Crossroads: a Critical Look at Current Methodologies* (New York, 2001), pp. 2–6. For examples of *Devotio Moderna* writings in translation, see J. van Engen (ed.), *Devotio Moderna: Basic Writings* (New York, 1988).

Brothers and Sisters of the Common Life) to live communally and give up individual possessions.[22] But although only a small proportion of urban populations actually joined such communes, their influence was much more widespread through their writings.[23] As the late medieval laity were increasingly exhorted to focus on their inner spirituality and take responsibility for their own devotions, an increasing proportion of them acquired private devotional objects towards that purpose, including Books of Hours, which by the fifteenth century were widely owned by urban bourgeoisie as well as the nobility.[24] These prayer-books for the laity could be read while attending Mass, but the hours could also be said at home in between other activities, as is specifically advocated in the preface to an English Primer printed in Rouen in 1538.[25] Loosely based on the divine office as performed by canons and monks, the Hours of the Virgin at the heart of these books consisted of verses, psalms, and hymns grouped according to the canonical hours (Matins, Lauds, Prime and so on), though they tended to be shorter than the divine Hours proper, and they were supplemented by other elements such as a calendar, gospel lessons, and popular prayers. In contrast to expository texts like the *Legenda aurea* and the *Meditationes*, Books of Hours contained little narrative description: the poetic psalms that form the bulk of the Hours of the Virgin were viewed as thematic prefigurations of the New Testament and therefore operated by allusion rather than exposition.[26] Nevertheless, if a manuscript was prestigious enough to be figuratively decorated, these texts and the direct prayers to Mary and other saints were explicitly connected to biblical narratives through illustrations, such as the infancy cycle that usually accompanied the Hours of the Virgin.[27] The Annunciation normally appeared at Matins, the first and most widely read of the hours, and in Netherlandish Books of Hours (unlike French ones) the scene was most often represented as the domestic type.[28] This conjunction of text and image

---

[22] Ibid., pp. 12–25.

[23] N. Geirnaert, 'Bruges and the Northern Netherlands', in V. Vermeersch (ed.), *Bruges and Europe* (Antwerp, 1992), pp. 82–3.

[24] On Books of Hours generally, see L.M.J. Delaissé, 'The Importance of Books of Hours for the History of the Medieval Book', in U.E. McCracken, L.M.C. Randall and R.H. Randall, Jr (eds), *Gatherings in Honor of Dorothy E. Miner* (Baltimore, 1974), pp. 203–25; J.P. Harthan, *Books of Hours and their Owners* (London, 1977); R.S. Wieck (ed.), *Time Sanctified: the Book of Hours in Medieval Art and Life* (New York, 1988).

[25] R.S. Wieck, *Painted Prayers: the Book of Hours in Medieval and Renaissance Art* (New York, 1997), p. 22. See also Harthan, *Books of Hours and their Owners*, pp. 32–3; V. Reinburg, 'Prayer and the Book of Hours', in Wieck (ed.), *Time Sanctified*, pp. 39–44.

[26] See for example the description of the Matins texts in Wieck, *Painted Prayers*, pp. 52–4.

[27] Wieck (ed.), *Time Sanctified*, pp. 60–72.

[28] A few dozen Annunciation scenes from Books of Hours at the Koninklijke Bibliotheek (hereafter KB) and the Museum Meermanno-Westreenianum in The Hague can be viewed at

suggests that the owners of devotional panel paintings could likewise have contemplated them during private prayers, as the object of their thoughts and supplications. The images, in turn, mirror the act of devotion itself: the book that the Virgin reads in domestic Annunciation panels is sometimes explicitly shown by its decoration as a Book of Hours, and the manner of her devotions – reading in a private room with the book open on a prie-dieu – would have been immediately familiar to their viewers.[29]

In choosing to place the Virgin at home rather than in a church, domestic Madonna scenes identify her with daily home life rather than with ecclesiastical institutions, as if the living rooms of private homes were just as appropriate places as church interiors for the Holy Family to enter. It would be misleading, however, to view this development as an outright rejection of church spaces; it is more an evolution of a possible alternative.[30] In Books of Hours, domestic and sacred settings were by no means mutually exclusive: a single book might contain a range of images using both types of setting, and while the domestic scenes might reflect the experience of praying at home, a church-type Annunciation could equally resonate with the experience of reading a prayer-book during Mass. The paintings of Jan van Eyck, similarly, show a great deal of fluidity between ecclesiastic and domestic-looking spaces as settings for the Virgin. His *Madonna and Child with Canon van der Paele* (Figure 3.6) and the *Dresden Triptych* depict the Virgin and Child enthroned within a church at the place where we would expect to see an altar, but his *Lucca Madonna* in Frankfurt instead places the Virgin's canopied throne in an apparently domestic room, though with elements suggestive of a chapel.

While the Washington *Annunciation* is set in a church, the Annunciation on the exterior of the *Ghent Altarpiece* (Figure 3.7) is located in a more enigmatic interior, a large and apparently domestic room, though mostly empty. Between Mary and Gabriel are a niche with lavabo, bowl, and towel, and an unglazed

www.collecties.meermanno.nl. Of the fifteenth-century Annunciations shown in a specific setting, those in northern Netherlandish manuscripts are almost all of the domestic type; southern Netherlandish examples are mostly of the domestic type, though with a few of the church type or conflations between the domestic and church types (see for example KB, 76 G 21, ff. 28v–29); while the majority of French examples are either the church type or conflations, set in architectural spaces that look somewhat like private chapels.

[29] See Webb, pp. 27–47 above, for further discussion of private domestic devotions.
[30] Van Os, *Art of Devotion*, p. 87.

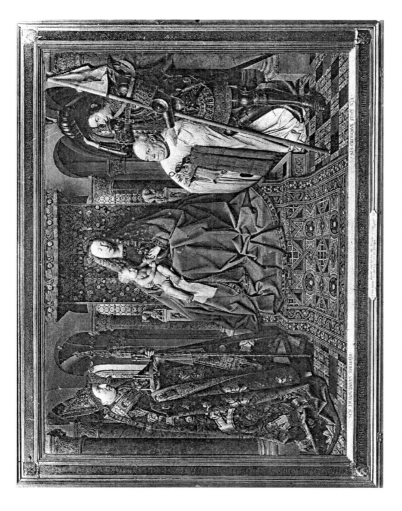

Figure 3.6 Jan van Eyck, *Madonna and Child with Canon van der Paele*, 1436, Bruges, Groeningemuseum; photo copyright: IRPA-KIK, Brussels.

Figure 3.7 Jan van Eyck, *Ghent Altarpiece* (exterior), 1432, Ghent, St Bavo Cathedral; photo copyright: IRPA-KIK, Brussels.

colonnaded window looking out onto a city landscape, apparently from the second storey. A smaller vaulted space that opens out behind the Virgin – by inference the space behind Gabriel is probably identical – looks more like an oratory, though nothing is actually in it, other than a glass water vessel on the window seat which possibly alludes to Mary's intact virginity.[31] The *Madonna and Child with Nicolas Rolin* in Paris depicts the Virgin and Child appearing to the kneeling donor in a much more richly-ornamented building with an open loggia but similarly difficult to identify conclusively as ecclesiastical or secular, being more like a palace or hall of justice than a church but with capitals carved with biblical scenes.[32] Compared with the Campin-circle images, Van Eyck's panels intertwine elements of the home with the church much more subtly, and his style of painting also retains a much more powerful sense of imbued sacrality; nevertheless, his works serve as a useful reminder that a growing interest in the domestic need not exclude the ecclesiastic, at least not for all viewers.

Even so, the increasing popularity of the domestic Madonna does raise significant questions about how people conceived of sacred space in this period. When praying at home in a secular room, did people perceive their actions as sanctifying the space around them, or was prayer simply becoming divorced from the need for a sacred context? This question applies to the images themselves as well as to the actions of their owners. Over the last few decades there has been much scholarly debate about how to interpret these works, particularly after Erwin Panofsky's influential *Early Netherlandish Painting* was published in 1953. Most writers agree with Panofsky's essential view that the rooms and objects portrayed in panels like the *Mérode Triptych* must be meant to convey theological meaning, though this symbolism has been interpreted in different ways.[33] In the *Mérode Triptych*, for example, the vase of lilies on the table, ubiquitous in scenes of the Annunciation, undoubtedly conveys the usual reference to the Virgin's purity, even while operating simultaneously as domestic decoration. The single candle whose flame has just been snuffed out, its smoke still rising, must have a specific symbolic intention as well, unless we are merely to think that Gabriel entered on a strong gust of wind; it is typically interpreted as signifying the light of Christ outshining all earthly illumination. Further symbolism has been read into virtually every other detail of the room including the lavabo and bowl (referring to liturgical

---

[31] Religious literature of the time often compared the conception of Christ to sunlight passing through glass, Panofsky, *Early Netherlandish Painting*, p. 144.

[32] For discussions and illustrations of all of these works by van Eyck, see C. Harbison, *Jan van Eyck: the Play of Realism* (London, 1991); C.J. Purtle, *The Marian Paintings of Jan van Eyck* (Princeton, 1982).

[33] See for example Panofsky, *Early Netherlandish Painting*, pp. 142–3, 164–5; Falkenburg, 'The Household of the Soul'; Thürlemann, *Robert Campin*, pp. 66–73.

hand-washing before the Mass),[34] the firescreen (shielding the Virgin from the fires of lust according to one view),[35] and the lions decorating the armrests of the bench (alluding to the Throne of Solomon).[36]

If such readings are accurate to contemporary perceptions, it would suggest that those who prayed at home might similarly have perceived the space and objects around them as carrying underlying spiritual significance, an attitude traditionally viewed as typical of the medieval mindset.[37] But symbolic interpretations of these panels have also been contested, either by interpreting the same objects differently[38] or by claiming that no such symbolism was ever intended.[39] The Brussels variation does not include many of the *Mérode* details such as the firescreen, back niche, or the smoke rising from the candle; on the other hand it adds a brush hanging on the wall in the back right corner, and above the fireplace hangs a hand-coloured print of St Christopher, which may act both as interior decoration (suggesting that this was one use to which inexpensive prints were put in this period) and as an allegory of the Virgin, since Christopher too was a bearer of Christ. But are all of these details necessarily symbolic, or could they simply indicate the sorts of objects typically found in contemporary homes? Only Gabriel's ecclesiastic vestments, a typical feature of angels in Netherlandish painting,[40] makes explicit reference to the church and its rituals. However far the detailed symbolisms construed by modern scholars were originally perceived in the fifteenth century, the artists and patrons did clearly make a conscious decision to show the Annunciation taking place inside an essentially secular space. Any symbolism contained or, to use Panofsky's term, 'disguised' in the domestic furnishings[41] must be read into them by a knowledgeable viewer; in other words, if this is still in essence a sacred space, it has been made to look first and foremost like a secular one instead.

---

[34] B. Lane, *The Altar and the Altarpiece: Sacramental Themes in Early Netherlandish Painting* (New York, 1984), pp. 42–3.

[35] C. Hahn, "'Joseph Will Perfect, Mary Enlighten and Jesus Save Thee": the Holy Family as Marriage Model in the *Mérode Triptych*', *Art Bulletin* 68 (1986), 60–61.

[36] Panofsky, *Early Netherlandish Painting*, p. 143.

[37] J. Huizinga, *The Autumn of the Middle Ages*, trans. R.J. Payton and U. Mammitzsch (Chicago, 1996), pp. 234–45.

[38] For instance Thürlemann, *Robert Campin*, p. 68, notes that the lions on the bench armrests are paired with dogs, interpreting these as symbolically 'male' and 'female' animals turned away from each other as a reference to the chaste relationship between Joseph and Mary.

[39] See Ainsworth and Christiansen (eds), *From van Eyck to Bruegel*, p. 90, and in the same volume J. Chapuis, 'Early Netherlandish Painting: Shifting Perspectives', pp. 11–12.

[40] M.B. MacNamee, *Vested Angels: Eucharistic Allusions in Early Netherlandish Paintings* (Leuven, 1998).

[41] Panofsky, *Early Netherlandish Painting*, pp. 140–44.

That this was a deliberate choice is further suggested by the fact that the great majority of fifteenth-century Netherlandish domestic Madonna paintings do not depict any specifically religious paraphernalia other than perhaps a prie-dieu, an object which, judging by its portrayal in visual representations, was used by individuals both in homes and in churches. There are a few exceptions where the setting does include more overtly sacred elements: in the *Annunciation* in Van der Weyden's *Columba Altarpiece*, the artist has added a small rose window with elaborate stained-glass tracery, reminiscent of chapel decoration, to the bedroom where the Virgin kneels saying her prayers. This was not a private devotional work but a large altarpiece probably commissioned for a private chapel in the church of St Columba, Cologne,[42] which may have something to do with the rose window's inclusion. Some Annunciation scenes appear to depict a domestic altar, for example in some manuscript illuminations[43] and in engravings by the Rhenish artist Master E.S. in the 1460s;[44] by the early sixteenth century representations of domestic altars had also become more common in Netherlandish panel paintings, as in an *Annunciation* by Joos van Cleve showing a small painted triptych in the background.[45] However, these are the exceptions that prove the rule: overtly religious features were rarely depicted at the time of the iconography's early development in the Netherlands, suggesting that the buyers of these works did not want or expect them to be included.

This brings us to an important question: who exactly did buy these images? By the second half of the fifteenth century, the domestic Madonna had become fairly common, readily available to be taken up by various audiences; a few decades earlier, it was a deliberate innovation. I think it likely that those who first commissioned or chose to purchase fully-developed domestic interiors tended to be those whose piety was better satisfied by pursuing private devotion at home than by attempting to appropriate actual ecclesiastical spaces for themselves. Of course these should not be taken as mutually exclusive aims, any more than portrayals of domestic and religious spaces were. Most of the developments in late medieval ecclesiastical art and architecture can be directly linked to the desire of individuals and groups, fuelled by concern over personal salvation, to patronize church spaces;

[42] D. de Vos, *Rogier van der Weyden: the Complete Works*, trans. T. Alkins (New York, 1999), p. 136 and cat. 21.

[43] For instance the Annunciation in a *c.*1450 south Netherlandish Book of Hours, KB, 76 G 22, f. 32 (www.collecties.meermanno.nl), though it is difficult to be sure whether the setting is meant to be a home chapel or a church one. In general, domestic altars appear more common in manuscript illuminations than in panels, particularly outside the Netherlands.

[44] See *Spätmittelalter am Oberrhein*, cat. 3, 49, 58. These scenes appear to have been partly inspired by earlier iconographies of Mary as a young virgin praying in the temple.

[45] Ainsworth and Christiansen (eds), *From van Eyck to Bruegel*, pp. 364–5.

hence the ever-increasing number of side chapels, altars, and donations of objects for their adornment, visible markers of individual and family patronage. But although a wide range of people sought to become active participants in and contributors to church spaces, not everyone had equal resources to do so. Ecclesiastic interiors could incorporate both what we might call collective sacred spaces – where a range of individuals, families, and groups worshipped and donated gifts – and more or less private ones, such as side chapels dominated by individual families. Most people could only participate in collective sacred spaces and had to be content with modest offerings that stood alongside those of their neighbours, or they contributed as part of a guild or confraternity. It was the nobility and the most wealthy of the urban patriciate or burgher classes who could establish 'private' ecclesiastic sacred spaces by founding entire religious institutions or chapels, and who could assume a dominant position in collective sacred spaces by donating especially prestigious objects or architectural features.

Such ambitions are easily traced, for example, among the ducal family. One of the most prominent cases is the Carthusian monastery at Champmol just outside Dijon, the capital city of Burgundy, founded by the first Valois Burgundian duke, Philip the Bold, not only as a religious institution but as a ducal memorial: the portal was decorated with life-size sculptures by Claus Sluter representing Philip and his Duchess Margaret of Flanders being presented to the Virgin and Child by their patron saints, and both Philip and his son John the Fearless were buried in the church, memorialized by artistically innovative tombs. Though it no longer survives, we know that the church also had a private oratory where the ducal family could watch the monks' services.[46] Somewhat paradoxically, the monastery attracted many visitors, particularly after Sluter's crucifixion sculpture in the centre of the cloisters, now known as the *Moses Well*, was granted papal indulgences in 1418.[47] Therefore, although nominally a sacred space dedicated to the monks' use, the monastery also served the interests of the dukes of Burgundy by giving them privileged access to the church and, more importantly (as the ducal family did not in reality visit the monastery that often), an arena for displaying their prestige to a large visiting public. In this case the ducal oratory was probably only occasionally put to use, but gaining private access to monastic sacred spaces was a long-established noble tactic. In the twelfth century, the counts' palace in Bruges had a

---

[46] On the Chartreuse de Champmol, see S.C.M. Lindquist, 'Women in the Charterhouse: the Liminality of Cloistered Spaces at the Chartreuse de Champmol in Dijon', in H. Hills (ed.), *Architecture and the Politics of Gender in Early Modern Europe* (Aldershot, 2003), pp. 177–92; K. Morand, *Claus Sluter: Artist at the Court of Burgundy* (London, 1991), pp. 58–132.

[47] Ibid., pp. 107–8.

private passage leading to their chapel in the collegiate church of St Donatian.[48] The English royal palaces at Greenwich, Richmond, and Bridewell were all deliberately built adjacent to, and with galleries leading into, friaries, so that the royal family could enter the church directly from the palace to observe services privately.[49] In the early sixteenth century Margaret of Austria, daughter of the emperor Maximilian I and regent of the Netherlands, had a similar direct passage connecting her palace in Mechelen to a parish church.[50] These private entrances provided an immediate link between the secular home and the sacred realm, allowing their inhabitants to pass freely between the two. In the process the boundaries between secular and sacred could become blurred, and this was particularly the case with domestic chapels, as Diana Webb discusses above in the case of both palaces and more modest households.[51] Palace chapels gave the household family a private place to worship, but they also typically foregrounded their social superiority by continuing a tradition going back at least as far as Charlemagne's palatinate chapel at Aachen, where the emperor's throne was placed on the upper level along the central axis, enabling him to look down onto the high altar while not being clearly seen himself.[52] As in other imperial and royal palaces, the Burgundian palace of Rihour in Lille follows a similar pattern, with the ducal oratory situated to the left of the chapel on a slightly higher level, a narrow squint and a larger closable window both providing visual access to the altar below.

A remarkable parallel example still survives in Bruges in the palace of the nobleman Louis de Gruuthuse, built immediately adjacent to the large parish Church of Our Lady (Onze Lieve Vrouwkerk). Instead of a private palace chapel, Gruuthuse acquired permission to build an extension from his house onto the choir ambulatory of the church. A door on the ground floor led directly into the ambulatory itself, while oratory windows above allowed Gruuthuse to look down onto the high altar (Figure 3.8), so that he and his family could watch what was

---

[48] M. Vale, 'An Anglo-Burgundian Nobleman and Art Patron: Louis de Bruges, Lord of la Gruthuyse and Earl of Winchester', in C. Barron (ed.), *England and the Low Countries in the Late Middle Ages* (New York, 1995), p. 122.

[49] B. Sloane, 'Tenements in London's Monasteries c.1450–1540', in D. Gaimster and R. Gilchrist (eds), *The Archaeology of Reformation, 1480–1580* (Leeds, 2003), pp. 293–6.

[50] D. Eichberger, 'A Noble Residence for a Female Regent: Margaret of Austria and the Construction of the "Court of Savoy" in Mechelen', in Hills (ed.), *Architecture and the Politics of Gender*, pp. 28–9.

[51] See above, pp. 36–42.

[52] C. Heitz, *L'Architecture religieuse carolingienne: les formes et leurs fonctions* (Paris, 1980), pp. 64–81.

normally closed off from the laity by the choir screen.[53] Perhaps initially constructed in wood, Gruuthuse was given permission by the church in 1472 to build the lower part of the oratory in stone, and the new construction was given an impressively ornamented façade on the inside of the church. Thus although the oratory effectively allowed Gruuthuse and his family to attend church while staying at home, this was less an act of private devotion than a means of projecting their presence within the community, singling them out even while allowing them to remain essentially unseen.

A similar inference can be drawn about a well-known miniature of the Burgundian duke Philip the Good attending Mass in a church. As the Mass takes place, Philip kneels before a devotional diptych – probably with the Virgin and Child on one side and his own portrait on the other – in a space to the right of the altar closed off by hangings.[54] Although the curtains are open enough to allow the duke to see what takes place on the altar, they clearly mark off his space as separate. Sometimes interpreted as depicting the contrast between private devotion and the liturgy of the Mass,[55] the image also emphasizes the public face of the nobility's 'private' devotion: as with Gruuthuse's oratory, Philip here can announce his presence within the church and his proximity to the altar, even while remaining closed off from others.

Would Gruuthuse or the Burgundian duke have been the type of patron who typically commissioned domestic Madonnas? Probably not; on the whole, they were likely more interested in viewing the saints as heavenly counterparts to the earthly nobility than as private individuals living quiet domestic lives. That is not to say that they never owned domestic Madonna images – a profusely illustrated Book of Hours made for Philip the Good, for instance, contains a mixture of church and domestic scenes, including several portraits of the duke himself

---

[53] M.P.J. Martens, *Lodewijk van Gruuthuse: Mecenas en Europees Diplomaat ca. 1427–1492* (Bruges, 1992), pp. 39–41; Vale, 'An Anglo-Burgundian Nobleman', p. 122.

[54] *Traité sur l'oraison dominicale*, Brussels, Bibliothèque royale Albert I, MS 9092, f. 9. See J. Chipps Smith, 'Portable Propaganda: Tapestries as Princely Metaphors at the Courts of Philip the Good and Charles the Bold', *Art Journal* 48 (1989), 34–5; M. Belozerskaya, *Rethinking the Renaissance: Burgundian Arts across Europe* (Cambridge, 2002), pp. 133–4.

[55] S. Ringbom, *Icon to Narrative: the Rise of the Dramatic Close-Up in Fifteenth-Century Devotional Painting* (Doornspijk, 1984), pp. 31–2.

Figure 3.8 Gruuthuse Palace, view from oratory into choir of Onze Lieve Vrouwkerk, Bruges. At the left is the high altar, at the right the tomb of Mary of Burgundy completed in 1502.

kneeling alternately in front of an altar and the Virgin and Child[56] – but such examples are rare. The domestic Madonna was, for the most part, better attuned to a different type of patron, those of urban burgher origins: administrators, financiers, merchants, upper craftsmen, those who were reasonably well-off and had access to urban art markets. It is difficult to judge the precise social status signified by the interiors depicted in these scenes, since the type of furniture used by the upper nobility in the fifteenth century did not differ from that used by well-off urban classes; differences in rank and wealth were displayed by the size of house, the quality of flooring and interior stone carving, and by displays of possessions like plate and wall hangings.[57] Van Eyck and Hans Memling often depicted the Virgin and Child on a canopied throne with expensive cloth hangings like the royal or ducal thrones shown in illuminated manuscripts, thus analogizing the Virgin to a secular ruler, but domestic Madonna panels generally omit this feature. Lacking displays of tapestries or plate but otherwise suggestive of a reasonably well-off owner, the domestic Madonna tends to be situated at the blurred boundary between noble and upper bourgeois living, like the interior shown in Jan van Eyck's *Arnolfini Double Portrait*, which was painted in Bruges for an Italian merchant.[58]

Of the images considered here so far, in those cases where we can identify the patron there are interesting parallels between the depicted spatial context and the owner's social background. Van Eyck's *Madonna with Canon van der Paele* (Figure 3.6), one of his largest surviving works, was commissioned by a canon of the highly prestigious collegiate church of St Donatian in Bruges.[59] It is not surprising therefore that this image chooses to situate the Virgin and Child not merely in a church, but specifically at the apse of a choir rather than in the nave. For Canon van der Paele, the Virgin was clearly identifiable with the institutional Church, placed in that part of a physical church to which he himself had privileged clerical access. Nicholas Rolin, on the other hand, the patron of Van Eyck's panel

---

[56] KB, 76 F 2 at www.collecties.meermanno.nl; A. de Breuck *et al.* (eds), *The Tavernier Book of Hours* (Brussels, 2002), pp. 24, 46–8.

[57] C. Reynolds, 'Reality and Image: Interpreting Three Paintings of the *Virgin and Child in an Interior* Associated with Campin', in Foister and Nash (eds), *Robert Campin*, pp. 187–9; J. Chipps Smith, 'The Practical Logistics of Art: Thoughts on the Commissioning, Displaying, and Storing of Art at the Burgundian Court', in L.S. Dixon (ed.), *In Detail: New Studies of Northern Renaissance Art in Honor of Walter S. Gibson* (Turnhout, 1998), pp.35–41.

[58] See Campbell, *Fifteenth-Century Netherlandish Schools*, pp. 174–211; M. Koster, 'The Arnolfini Double Portrait: a Simple Solution', *Apollo* 158, no. 499 (2003), 3–13.

[59] On St Donatian as an institution, see R. Strohm, *Music in Late Medieval Bruges* (Oxford, 1990), pp. 10–14, and on van der Paele, Harbison, *Jan van Eyck*, pp. 48–64.

in Paris, was a man of bourgeois origins in Burgundy who rose through the ranks to become the Burgundian chancellor, one of the most powerful and wealthiest men in the realm. The painting hung in a chapel that Rolin founded and richly endowed in Notre-Dame-du-Chastel in his home town of Autun; Rolin also commissioned another famous Netherlandish painting, Rogier van der Weyden's *Last Judgement Altarpiece*, for the chapel in the hospital that he and his wife founded in Beaune, not far from Autun.[60] He was thus a distinctive type of patron, a man of bourgeois origins who acquired through the Burgundian court enormous personal wealth and prestige, enough to found entire religious and charitable institutions. He is depicted in Van Eyck's painting as an overtly wealthy man, wearing an ostentatious brocaded robe and originally intended also to wear a large money-bag at his belt, though this detail was omitted in the painting stage. The panel was on the one hand intensely personal, a small panel (far smaller than Canon van der Paele's) depicting him experiencing a private vision of the Virgin and Child, but on the other hand it was meant to be seen by his native community as part of his highly visible acts of patronage there. These multivalent qualities correlate with the lavish but ambiguous palatial setting of the painting, which takes the Virgin out of an explicitly ecclesiastic setting and brings her instead into a prestigious space to which Rolin himself belongs.

Similarly spatially ambiguous, but much more an identifiably domestic interior, the *Ghent Altarpiece* (Figure 3.7) was commissioned by the wealthy financier Jodocus (or Joos) Vijd and his wife Elizabeth Borluut, both from leading families of Ghent. Vijd was active in the city's administration, holding for a time the position of First Alderman. The altarpiece was made for a chapel whose restoration the couple financed in the parish church of St John, now St Bavo cathedral, and it was dedicated on the same day that Vijd acted as godfather at the christening of Duke Philip the Good and Isabella of Portugal's short-lived second son Joos; Vijd had previously served in Philip's retinue in Zeeland and Holland for five months.[61] The patrons were thus of burgher origins and proud of their civic identity, commissioning a radically new type of altarpiece for their chapel in a large community church whose other chapels were similarly patronized by leading Ghent families like themselves. But they also held court connections of which they could be equally proud, and the final dedication of the altarpiece (which must have

[60] On van Eyck's panel and Rolin, see P. Lorentz, 'The *Virgin and Chancellor Rolin* and the Office of Matins', in Foister, Jones and Cool (eds), *Investigating Jan van Eyck*, pp. 49–57; Harbison, *Jan van Eyck*, pp. 48–64, 100–23; B. Maurice-Chabard (ed.), *La Splendeur des Rolin: un mécénat privé à la cour de Bourgogne* (Paris, 1999).
[61] A.L. Dierick, *The Ghent Altarpiece: van Eyck's Masterpiece Revisited* (Ghent, 1996), introduction (unpaginated).

been under construction for several years) was made to coincide with an extraordinary personal privilege offered by the ducal family. This couple at the top of the urban elite chose to have Van Eyck show the Annunciation in an apparently domestic interior, though one with hints of the sacred. Despite the sparse furnishings and the over-proportioned size of the holy figures (who are likely to smack their heads on the ceiling if they stand up straight), compared with the Campin-circle images like the *Mérode Annunciation* this one comes across as a more palatial setting of impressive size and grandeur, well matched to the social status of its patrons.

In contrast, the much smaller and more plainly domestic *Mérode Triptych* (Figure 3.2) displays in the back window a coat of arms identified as that of a family from Mechelen, whose name occurs in a number of variants including Ymbrecht, Engelbrecht, and Inghelbrechts. The individual who commissioned the triptych may have been the merchant Peter Engelbrecht, who was originally from Cologne and like his father and older brother acted for a time as alderman there.[62] It appears likely that he bought the central panel as an existing stock from the painter's workshop and then commissioned the two wings to be added, turning the work into a small triptych depicting the donors praying not only to the domestic Virgin but, unusually, to Joseph at work in his shop as well. The different tone of this painting from those of Jan van Eyck accords with the different type of patron who commissioned it, a family that was moderately well-off but without the higher pretensions of figures like Rolin or Vijd. However, when the Master of Catherine of Cleves adapted the composition for a Book of Hours owned by the aristocratic Catherine of Lochhorst, he copied the figures of Gabriel and the Virgin virtually identically – although giving the Virgin much richer clothing, her gown covered with embroidered or brocaded initials – but changed the setting, adding a private chapel in the background and placing the Virgin in front of a canopied chair rather than a bench.[63] There is no evidence of who originally owned the Brussels *Annunciation* or most of the other versions of the composition, since they lack donor figures, inscriptions, and identifiable coats of arms, which in itself points to the more modest status of these works compared with the other examples just considered. Nor do we know who purchased the multiple versions of Gerard David's *Virgin and Child with the Milk Soup* (Figure 3.5), but given that they were

---

[62] Thürlemann, *Robert Campin*, pp. 70–73; Ainsworth and Christiansen (eds), *From van Eyck to Bruegel*, p. 95, are somewhat sceptical of this theory, particularly Thürlemann's identification of the female donor (who was added slightly later) as Peter's second wife.
[63] Thürlemann, *Robert Campin*, pp. 206–7.

repeated from a pattern and largely executed by assistants, it is likely that they were relatively affordable and aimed at a mass market.[64]

In all of these cases, then, the spatial setting appears to have been correlated to the interests of their particular buyers, which supports the argument that the domestic Madonna, placed in a deliberately secular-looking interior, held greatest appeal for middle-class buyers who practised private devotions at home and thought of a secular setting as a highly suitable location for the Holy Family. But although most of the earliest domestic Madonna panels were probably bought by urban burghers, it is of course the case that merchants and officials were not the only people who consumed devotional literature: certain religious orders and lay women, including noble women, were especially receptive to affective piety, and women may have owned proportionally more Books of Hours than men.[65] It is unsurprising therefore that such donors also commissioned or bought domestic Madonna images, particularly later in the fifteenth century. An early case is the *Werl Altarpiece Wings* (Figure 3.4), where the Franciscan friar Heinrich Werl of Cologne kneels in an interior space (painted over what was originally depicted as a landscape), matched in the other wing by a scene of St Barbara looking much like the Virgin in a domestic sitting room.[66] Measuring a full metre in height, these panels must have been part of an altarpiece rather than a private devotional work, and as the central image has been lost we do not know the ultimate object of Werl's devotions. Towards the end of the century, on the other hand, we see that Christiaan de Hondt (Figure 3.1), abbot of the Cistercian monastery Ter Duinen near Bruges, kneels in adoration of the Madonna in a church, thus envisioning the churchly Virgin as appropriate for his own devotions. De Hondt himself, however, is not in the church when he has this experience, but in a bedroom that looks like part of an abbot's spacious and well-appointed house, with a small devotional diptych hanging above the bed. This interior appears to have been a stock pattern, reusable for different types of upper-class donor figures. It is unknown if it too was copied from Van Eyck, as only his original Virgin panel has survived, and another diptych copy of the *Madonna in a Church* by Jan Gossaert, now in the Galleria Doria in Rome, depicts its donor kneeling in a landscape instead;[67] but the Master of 1499 used the same interior again in a diptych made for Margaret of Austria, the

[64] Ainsworth, *Gerard David*, pp. 276–80, 308.

[65] S. Penketh, 'Women and Books of Hours', in L. Smith and J.H.M. Taylor (eds), *Women and the Book: Assessing the Visual Evidence* (London, 1997), pp. 270–71; M. Clanchy, 'Images of Ladies with Prayer Books: What Do They Signify?', in R.N. Swanson (ed.), *The Church and the Book* (SCH 38, Woodbridge, 2004), pp. 106–22.

[66] On the construction of the panels, see Carmen Garrido, 'The Campin Group Paintings in the Prado Museum', in Foister and Nash (eds), *Robert Campin*, pp. 56–61.

[67] Harbison, 'Miracles Happen', p. 162.

Netherlands' regent, depicting her in the right panel in the same position in the same room, paired with a different left wing showing an abstract architectural space with the enthroned Virgin and Child being crowned by two angels.[68] Both types of patrons, a Cistercian abbot and the female regent of the Netherlands, were apparently comfortable with being shown praying in an identical well-furnished private domestic room while visualizing the Virgin in a more glorified setting.

There are several other instances of noble women shown praying in domestic spaces, suggesting that while noble men may not have had a great deal of interest in the domestic Madonna, perhaps their wives and sisters did. A particularly intriguing example can be found in a manuscript owned by Margaret of York, third wife of the last Burgundian duke, Charles the Bold. Devotional works were heavily predominant in Margaret's library – more so than the ducal library, which had an unusually large collection of history volumes[69] – and at around the time of her marriage she commissioned from her private chaplain, Nicolas Finet, the *Dialogue de la duchesse à Jesus Christ*. This text, recounting an imagined personal dialogue between Margaret and Christ, tellingly opens with a miniature (Figure 3.9) that depicts this conversation literally taking place in the duchess's bedroom, in a composition reminiscent of the *Noli me tangere*, Christ's appearance to Mary Magdalene after his resurrection.[70] Clearly Margaret and the artist both expected that she would read this text alone in her room, not in an oratory or chapel, and that she would visualize the risen Christ coming to her where she was.

These images demonstrate that sacred experiences often took place in spaces that were distant from the church, places whose primary purpose was secular and only occasionally, temporarily, religious. What impact could such experiences have had on conceptions of what it was that made space sacred? One key difference between a church and a home as the setting for devotions was that the church was far more fixed as a sacred space. Of course churches could sometimes be used for purposes other than the liturgy, such as for business meetings, and the

---

[68] Ghent, Museum voor Schone Kunsten, Inv. 1973–A.

[69] Margaret's known library is listed in K.A. Barstow, 'Appendix: the Library of Margaret of York and Some Related Books', in T. Kren (ed.), *Margaret of York, Simon Marmion, and the Visions of Tondal* (Malibu, 1992), pp. 257–62. For a study of the manuscripts commissioned by the previous Duke Philip the Good, see W. Blockmans, 'Manuscript Acquisition by the Burgundian Court and the Market for Books in the Fifteenth-Century Netherlands', in M. North and D. Ormrod (eds), *Art Markets in Europe 1400–1800* (Aldershot, 1998), pp. 7–18.

[70] T. Kren and S. McKendrick, *Illuminating the Renaissance: the Triumph of Flemish Manuscript Painting in Europe* (London, 2003), pp. 215–16.

Figure 3.9 Follower of Dreux Jehan, *Margaret of York with the Risen Christ*, **from Nicolas Finet,** *Le Dialogue de la Duchesse à Jesus Christ*, **c.1468, London, BL Additional MS 7970, f. 1v. By permission of The British Library.**

particulars of their decoration changed frequently: precious objects like reliquaries and liturgical vessels were brought out at certain times and otherwise locked away, the wings of altarpieces were opened and closed according to the time of the week and liturgical calendar, church hangings and vestments changed according to the season. But throughout such changes, the essential purpose of the space, a permanent setting for sacred rituals, remained constant. Private chapels or oratories, or sections of rooms used on occasion for prayers, were likely to be much more variable. Even a palace chapel, whose architecture and altar would have remained consistently indicative of sacred purposes, might not retain an aura of active sacrality at all times: the highest nobility like the French royalty and Burgundian dukes not only moved frequently from palace to palace, but they took their furniture with them, leaving most palaces virtually empty when they were not resident.[71] Their chapels, then, must often have been silent and bare, awaiting the return of the court to come back to life.

But it was particularly more humble household spaces that would only occasionally, and temporarily, become 'sacred' by the introduction of devotional images and books. It is likely that such objects were often kept locked away until brought out for use. Some Annunciation scenes depict the Virgin kneeling in front of a cupboard built into the wall, partly open to reveal books, scrolls, vessels, or rosaries: clearly the Madonna keeps her religious paraphernalia shut in the cupboard until she brings them out for her devotions.[72] Books were portable objects, often transported in carrying bags (depicted in both the *Mérode* and Brussels Annunciations); similarly, although diptychs could sometimes be hung on a wall, as shown within the diptychs by the Master of 1499, they were also designed to be transportable, as must be the case with the diptych used by Philip the Good in his temporary oratory in the manuscript illumination discussed earlier. Most portrait and devotional diptychs, including Van Eyck's *Madonna in a Church*, were painted on the reverses, either with imitation marbling or with emblems or devices, implying that they were frequently closed and seen from the outside.[73] So while domestic Madonnas do occasionally include a devotional image

---

[71] Smith, 'Practical Logistics', p. 33; G. Blieck, 'Le Château royal de Lille sous le règne du duc de Bourgogne Philippe le Hardi (1384–1404)', in G. Blieck *et al.* (eds), *Le Château et la ville: conjonction, opposition, juxtaposition (XIe–XVIIIe siècle)* (Paris, 2002), pp. 123–4.

[72] For example the *Annunciation* by Dirk Bouts in the Calouste Gulbenkian collection in Lisbon, and one of the Annunciations in the Book of Hours of Philip the Good at The Hague, KB, 76 F 2, f. 116 (www.collecties.meermanno.nl).

[73] See A. Dülberg, *Privatporträts: Geschichte und Ikonologie einer Gattung im 15. und 16. Jahrhundert* (Berlin, 1990), pp. 107–53; H. Verougstraete and R. van Schoute, 'Frames and Supports of Some Eyckian Paintings', in Foister, Jones and Cool (eds), *Investigating Jan van Eyck*, pp. 110–11.

or two, usually in the background, such private devotional spaces must generally have looked like what they were, secular rooms primarily used for non-sacred purposes. It was not the space in and of itself that was sacred: it only became so by the prayers of the people inside it.

Chapter 4

Private Rooms in the Monastic Architecture of Habsburg Spain

Lisa A. Banner*

A feature of many monasteries, convents and hospitals founded in Spain during the sixteenth and seventeenth centuries is the incorporation of a private room for the house's patron.[1] These rooms provided an important and vital connection between the sacred space of the religious house and the religious devotions of the patron in supplying a place for prayerful observances. Often built with direct access to the altars and reliquary rooms in the religious house, such rooms thereby granted the patron privileged access to the most holy spaces within these foundations.[2] Probably the most well-known examples of these apartments were the private quarters built for Charles V at the monastery of Yuste in 1548 and Philip II's oratory which adjoined his bedroom, and overlooked the high altar, constructed at the Escorial.[3] These rooms provided a place of retreat from the world, especially during key periods of religious observance or mourning, thereby establishing a place of lay devotion within the sacred space of the religious house. The Habsburg kings were, however, merely continuing a long Spanish tradition, which was emulated on a more modest scale by their wealthier subjects. The provision of private accommodation within religious houses had been customary for royalty,

* I am grateful for the comments of Constancio del Alamo, Priscilla Muller, Peter Brown and Antonio Feros, who all read early drafts of this paper.
[1] F. Chueca Goitia, *Casas reales en monasterios y conventos españoles* (Bilbao, 1982), p.38, cites E.E. Viollet-le-Duc, *Dictionnaire raisonné de l'architecture française* (10 vols, Paris, 1875), I, pp. 264, 278, 305, who recognized this development in France and gave numerous examples of French kings staying in convents and monasteries.
[2] P. Brown, 'Enjoying the Saints in Late Antiquity', in S. Lamia and E. Valdez del Álamo (eds), *Decorations for the Holy Dead: Visual Embellishment on Tombs and Shrines of Saints* (Brussels, 2002), pp. 3–17.
[3] M. Ángel Zalama, 'Carlos V, Juste y los jerónimos. Sobre la construcción del Aposento del emperador', in *El arte en las cortes de Carlos V y Felipe II. Actas de las IX jornadas de arte del Consejo Superior de Investigaciones Científicas (CSIC)* (Madrid, 1999); C.Wilkinson Zerner, *Juan de Herrera, Architect to Philip II of Spain* (New Haven, 1993), p.108; Chueca Goitia, *Casas reales*, pp. 141 ff.

bishops and the highest nobility since the eighth century in Spain, with certain religious orders being particularly favoured by patrons, most notably the Dominicans, Augustinians and Franciscans from the thirteenth century onwards, and the Jeronimites from the fifteenth century.[4]

During the reign of Charles V, 'the reform of the laws and spiritual precepts' of the military orders,[5] in particular the *Regla*, the rule book for the Order of Santiago, led to a significant expansion in the construction of private rooms within monasteries. This development was due both to an increase in the numbers of nobles admitted to the military orders, and also to changes in the requirements for members of these orders. While these rooms had often in the past provided a place for private devotion, they became sacred spaces in which members of the nobility could fulfil their spiritual obligations for retreat and meditation, obligations that were tied to their observance of the written rules for spiritual behaviour. Usually built overlooking, or else behind, the altar, these private rooms allowed patrons a retreat from the conjugal bed during times of prescribed abstinence, as well as, in some cases, being a place for repentance. By providing ready access to the holiest parts of the church as well as accommodation for the elite members of society, these private rooms caused a further blurring of the boundaries between the sacred and the profane during the early modern period.

Private oratories or chapels within a domestic setting were a relatively common feature of the homes of the Spanish elite during the late middle ages, as elsewhere in Europe. The construction of windows opening onto the church or private passageways, connecting domestic accommodation with an adjacent church, was also found in northern Europe.[6] However, the requirement that, as part of a religious house's obligation to a founding patron and his family, private rooms should be built within the monastic precincts, close to the church, or with a connecting passage, or *pasadizo*, to the church, was more peculiar to Spain.[7] The incorporation of such *pasadizos* in monastic designs began in royal houses, but gradually spread to those of the aristocracy. The use of *pasadizos* to private chapels, linking palaces to churches, or to rooms in a church with access to or sight of the altar, provided entrance to a sacred space without allowing the lay person to be seen as they entered the church or monastery. An example of the use of such *pasadizos* is found at the monastery of Santa Creus, dating from *c*.1350. A series of

---

[4] Ibid., pp. 38–40; S. Brindle, 'Some Aspects of Religious Architecture in Castile, 1400–1550, with Special Reference to the Province of Burgos. A Study in Patronage' (3 vols, unpublished D.Phil. thesis, University of Oxford, 1991), p. 31.

[5] Francisco de los Cobos, *Regla de la orden de la cavallería de señor Santiago del espada* (Valladolid, 1527) [hereafter: *Regla* (1527)], f. iiii. See Joseph de Sigüenza, *Tercera parte de la historia de la orden de San Geronimo, doctor de la Iglesia* (Madrid, 1605), pp. 90–91.

[6] See above, pp. 27–79.

[7] Chueca Goitia, *Casas reales*, pp. 36–7.

pasadizos connected the palace to a private oratory located above the lateral chapels on the epistle side of the church, allowing private access to the holy space.[8] Another example might be the *pasadizo* connecting the palace of Doña Juana (1479–1555), mother of Charles V, to the adjacent church of San Antolín in Tordesillas where she attended Mass.[9] *Pasadizos* were usually enclosed and thus maintained the invisibility of their aristocratic or royal patrons as they walked to and from the sacred spaces. In some cases, such as the rooms of the Duke of Lerma (1553–1625) in San Pablo, the rooms also opened through a screen to a family pantheon or familial tomb established within the monastery, creating a link between living and deceased patrons.[10] However, the connection was not always intimate. In Medina de Rioseco (Valladolid), the Franciscan convent merely faced the palace of the Enríquez family, Almirantes of Castilla, whose family pantheon was in the main chapel.[11]

Pasadizos became architectural symbols of noble privilege in Spain and in particular for those nobles who had the protection of a military order, which granted them the right to build private rooms within churches of which they were patrons.[12] Such a *pasadizo* provided a transitional passage, from a secular palace into a sacred space. Starting work in 1599, Diego Sarmiento de Acuña, Conde de Gondomar, built a *pasadizo* from his palace, the Casa del Sol to the nearby Benedictine monastery of San Benito in Valladolid.[13] In the same city, the Duke of Lerma was building, by 29 August 1601, a *pasadizo* across the street from his palace to the corner of the religious house opposite.[14] Yet it was an architectural feature that at times provoked opposition for its ostentatious display. A thinly veiled attack upon the *pasadizo* built by several nobles in Valladolid was made in 1602 by Fernández de Medrano, in a book dedicated to Lerma that criticized a *pasadizo* constructed across the street from his palace in Florence by Cosimo de'

---

[8] Ibid., p. 79.

[9] M.Á. Zalama, 'Juana I de Castilla y el Monasterio de Santa Clara de Tordesillas', *Reales Sitios* 39 (2002), 14–27.

[10] Chueca Goitia, *Casas reales*, p. 114.

[11] About the military orders and funerary monuments, see M. Cortés Arrese (ed.), *El Espacio de la muerte y el arte de las Órdenes Militares* (Cuenca, 1999).

[12] Chueca Goitia, *Casas reales*, p. 74; García de Medrano, *La Regla y establecimiento de la cavallería de Santiago del espada. Con la historia del origen y principio della* (Valladolid, 1603) [hereafter: *Regla* (1603)], f. 15v. The 1603 *Regla* summarized rules that had been in effect previously, and added new ones. This rule was among those already granted.

[13] A description by Pinheiro da Veiga of the *pasadizo* erected for the baptism of Philip IV notes the grandeur of the structures, see J. Urrea, *La Plaza de San Pablo, Escenario de la Corte* (Valladolid, 2003), p. 31. Another contemporary *pasadizo* built by Cardinal Bernardo de Sandoval y Rojas in Toledo is described in Pedro de Herrera, *Descripcion de la Capilla...* (Toledo, 1617), f. 6v.

[14] L. Cabrera de Córdoba, *Relaciones de las Cosas Sucedidas en la Corte de España, 1599 hasta 1614* (Madrid, 1857), p. 110.

Medici.[15] The construction of *pasadizos* also often occurred in seignorial villages, where the isolation of a noble from curious eyes was of great importance, for instance in Medinaceli, where the Colegiata of Santa María de la Asunción, renovated in 1562, was connected to the ducal palace by a gallery.[16] This particular construct of privilege became a hallmark of building practice, especially in the religious *conjuntos* built during the reigns of Philip II and his son, Philip III, where some nobles connected their palaces to several adjacent monastic foundations with *pasadizos*.

The demands of patrons and their temporal world even intruded upon the enclosed sacred space of the convent in early modern Spain. The decoration of burial chapels with a family's noble arms, the frequent practice of widows' residence in convents without taking the veil, and the presence of secular apartments within convents together 'blurred the ideal of a boundary separating the sacred from the secular'.[17] However, the inclusion of private rooms for patrons within the walls of a monastery or convent, allowed nobles the ideal space to meet the sacred, and undertake contemplative prayer, spiritual reflection, and penance. While noble residence was, as we shall see, required at certain times in the liturgical year, it was not intended to be permanent.[18]

The importance of the private room in the life of a noble becomes readily apparent in the increase in monastic architecture built by nobles between 1520 and 1550, a trend which seems to have slowed under the reign of Philip II, and resumed again briefly under the reign of Philip III.[19] Two factors directly influenced this widespread monastic building programme and its character: Charles V increased the number of people admitted to the military Order of Santiago, and he made changes to the requirements for the members of this Order which, amongst other things, emphasized the need for private rooms. Although private apartments had been included in some monastic buildings for centuries, their purpose, clearly stated and outlined by Charles V, suddenly affected a wider group of people.[20]

Upon acceding to the throne of Spain, Charles V began a systematic revision of the military orders, primarily the Orders of Santiago, Alcántara and Calatrava,

---

[15] J. Fernández de Medrano, *Republica mista* (Madrid, 1602), p. 133.

[16] I am grateful to Steven Brindle for this reference.

[17] E. Lehfeldt, 'Spatial Discipline and its Limits: Nuns and the Built Environment in Early Modern Spain', in H. Hills (ed.), *Architecture and the Politics of Gender in Early Modern Europe* (Aldershot, 2003), pp. 140–41, 145.

[18] *Regla* (1527), f. x.

[19] Brindle, 'Some Aspects of Religious Architecture in Castile', II, p. 303.

[20] The importance of the Order for architectural patronage has yet to be fully examined. Its undeniable influence has been recognized in a brief but seminal essay by J.J. Martín González, 'Hacia una metodología para el estudio del arte de las órdenes militares en Castilla la Vieja y León', in F.J. Pizarro Gómez (ed.), *Actas del simposio, El arte y las Órdenes Militares* (Cáceres, 1985), pp. 159–63.

founded in the twelfth and thirteenth centuries.[21] The order of Santiago was considered the richest of the three main Orders and it was regarded as the most historically important. There was a dramatic rise in membership under Charles V with 45 members invested between 1521 and 1525, 107 in 1526–30, and 136 in 1531–35.[22] The background to this increase in membership was the Bull issued in 1523 by Pope Adrian IV, incorporating all the Orders into the Crown in perpetuity. This Bull set the stage for the reforms of the Order of Santiago, and its rulebook, published by Charles V in 1527. In the *Regla*, Charles V announced that he was going to 'correct and amend' the spiritual rules.[23] The *Regla*, initially presented as a 'spiritual rulebook' had social and legal implications in Habsburg Spain, and although the order of Santiago was the most prestigious, each order had similar rules, set out in a handbook for members.[24] The rules were 'what they [the members of the Order] are obliged to do and accomplish, and what they have to guard, and from what abstain'.[25] Thus, in the context of the 1527 reforms, the '*fuero de caballeros*' or oath of knighthood – obedience, poverty and conjugal chastity – was the same for the three main orders.[26]

The spiritual rule followed by the Order of Santiago, and therefore the basis of its rulebook, was the rule of Saint Augustine. As described in the 1527 edition, spiritual and temporal rules for members of the order were set out in two volumes. The spiritual rules in the first volume were said to be the most important and mandated the building and maintenance of churches and monasteries; they also included explicit directions to members of the order to observe periods of

---

[21] The Order of Santiago was formalized in 1170 when the first royal privilege for its existence was issued by Ferdinand I, king of Castile, León and Portugal. Antonio Ruiz de Morales y Molina, *La Regla y establecimiento de la órden de la cauallería de Santiago del Espada, con la hystoria del origen y principio della* (1565), ed. M.I. Viforcos Marinas and J. Paniagua Pérez (León, 1998) [hereafter: *Regla* (1565)], pp. 94–5.

[22] L.P. Wright, 'Military Orders in Sixteenth- and Seventeenth-Century Spanish Society: the Institutional Embodiment of a Historical Tradition', *P&P* 43 (1969), 55. These figures reflect only the early part of the reign of Charles V; the numbers varied and were at their lowest point in the five-year period 1551–55, when Philip II ascended the throne and tightened the membership. Under Philip III the numbers were consistently more than 100 in each five-year period until, at the accession of Philip IV, the numbers skyrocketed to 515 in the first five years of his reign.

[23] Wright, 'Military Orders', 35. See also *Regla* (1527), f. iii.

[24] E. Postigo Castellanos, 'Las Órdenes Militares de la monarquía Hispana. Modelos discursivos de los ss. XVI–XVIII', in I.R. Izquierdo Benito and F. Ruiz Gómez (eds), *Las Órdenes Militares en la península Ibérica* (2 vols, Cuenca, 2000), II, pp. 1585–636.

[25] *Regla* (1527), f. iii.

[26] E. Postigo Castellanos, *Honor y Privilegio en la Corona de Castilla: el Consejo de las Órdenes y los Caballeros de Hábito en el s. XVII* (Soria, 1988), p. 43. See also *Difiniciones de la Orden y Cavallería de Calatrava Conforme al Capítulo General Celebrado en Madrid, 1652* (Madrid, 1661). On the role and importance of the earliest printed version of the *Regla* (1503), see ibid., pp. 189–90, 219.

separation from the world in monasteries, emphasizing the retreat to sacred spaces, fasting and abstinence.[27]

The importance of Charles V's reform of the rulebook for the Order cannot be underestimated. It had a direct impact on architecture. The *Regla* articulated the spiritual rules and norms of behaviour for the group of nobles who were permitted membership of the order, and set up a system of vigilance, the *visitadores*, who monitored compliance. By outlining the spiritual rules and aligning these with the maintenance and building of churches and monasteries, Charles V and his Habsburg descendants thrust the protection and creation of sacred space into the hands of the nobles. By 1603, the *Regla* enjoined that a tenth of a noble's fortune should be given for repairs, ornamentation and maintenance of churches each year.[28] The *Regla* thus gave weight and purpose to the sacred spaces constructed in Spain. Those among the members of the orders of Calatrava, Alcántara, or Santiago who benefited most from the king's favour were able to build *conjuntos* (an architectural ensemble of buildings, usually arranged around a central plaza, and often connected by *pasadizos*), that most closely mirrored the requirements of the order as written in their rulebooks.

As a reward for loyalty, Charles V expanded the membership of the Order of Santiago, which had previously been limited to a very few nobles. The expansion in membership was thus reflected in a sudden increase in the building of churches, convents and monasteries. The appearance of private rooms in monastic architecture built by nobles thus seems to escalate from the time of Charles V's revisions to the rulebook in 1527.[29]

Patronage of religious foundations was not only expected and required of knights of the military orders like Santiago, it also documented a verifiable Old Christian pedigree. Family burial places within churches were frequently cited as 'proof of nobility', and nobility was the required pedigree for entry into the military orders.[30] Against the background of the spectacular increase in the numbers of Masses for the dead during the sixteenth century, the *Regla* of 1603, which expanded upon the initial requirements of 1527, required knights to pay for thirty Masses every year.[31] Each religious house was expected to pray for the souls of its founder, his descendents and family. For example, an agreement between the Duke of Lerma and the Dominicans of San Pablo arranged for Masses for the dead to be said and for payments to be made on St John's day, in June, and at

---

[27] Ibid., ff. viii verso, ix–x verso.
[28] *Regla* (1603), ff. 152 ff. The *Regla* also mandates repairs, ornaments and gifts of books.
[29] Ibid., ff. 15v, 152v.
[30] Chueca Goitia, *Casas reales*, p. 39.
[31] C.M. Eire, *From Madrid to Purgatory: the Art and Craft of Dying in Sixteenth-Century Spain* (Cambridge, 1995), pp. 178–9; *Regla* (1603), f. 46.

Christmas.[32] In a monastery with four or more friars, the family of a *caballero* (knight of noble status) was permitted to have a private chapel in which only those friars and the family were permitted to hear divine offices and receive ecclesiastical burial.[33] The provision in the *Regla* for the renovation of older churches may help to explain the constant restoration and redecoration of ancient churches in Spain apart from the obvious prestige gained from patronage of an ancient monastery, especially a royal foundation. Knights were first required to repair and endow their *encomiendas* (the property held in trust for the order, or an entailed estate), and the churches under their auspices, before beginning fresh projects.[34]

A few examples dating from 1520 to 1620 illustrate the diversity of these secular rooms created in monastic settings. In Úbeda, a *pasadizo* connected the palace of Francisco de los Cobos, secretary to Charles V and author of the 1527 *Regla*, to the church of San Salvador, where the contract of 1536 specified his burial chapel and also a private room would be built. When he was taken ill, he asked that the luxurious addition of marble pillars and other architectural details of the private room be removed and only kept in the sacristy and around the doors.[35] García de Padilla, son of Pedro López de Padilla, became *comendador* of Lopera and Malagón in the order of Calatrava, and later *comendador mayor* of that order, serving Charles V in the councils of State and Justice before he died in 1542.[36] He rebuilt and expanded part of the monastery of Fresdelval, including a domestic apartment in the southern end of the building, decorating it with the carved heraldry of the family and the order of Calatrava, following the ancient tradition of Castilian nobility.[37]

Although there was a decline in aristocratic building of monastic structures in the Burgos region after about 1550, during the reign of Philip II, the building effort revived again during the reign of Philip III. The king's favourite, the Duke of Lerma, was named *comendador mayor* of the Order of Santiago at the end of 1599, and immediately began renovating monasteries and churches. His efforts are a perfect example of the construction of private accommodation within a sacred setting for a secular prince, and were emulated by many of his contemporaries. In Valladolid, Lerma acquired the palace of the adviser to Charles V, Francisco de los

---

[32] Valladolid, Archivo de la Casa Ducal de Medinaceli [hereafter: Medinaceli], Leg. 71–24, ff. 7–16.

[33] *Regla* (1603), f. 15v.

[34] Ibid., f. 132.

[35] M. Gómez-Moreno, *Las Aguilas del Renacimiento Español: Bartolomé Ordóñez, Diego Siloé, Pedro Machuca, Alonso Berruguete* (Madrid, 1983), pp. 80–81, 186–93.

[36] Brindle, 'Some Aspects of Religious Architecture in Castile', I, p. 134. Other members of his family were members of the Order of Santiago, a not uncommon practice.

[37] Ibid., I, p. 141.

Cobos, and also the patronage of the adjacent Dominican monastery and church of San Pablo. After connecting the palace to the church with a *pasadizo*, he began to build a private tribune within San Pablo, overlooking the main chapel, screened from and overlooking the altar. His burial chapel was also in San Pablo, adjacent to the main chapel, and visible from the private rooms through a screen.[38] In his seignorial town of Lerma, the Duke built the Dominican convent of San Blas adjacent to his palace, and connected it to the palace with a *pasadizo*. The small *pasadizo*, now destroyed, initially connected to a series of three rooms that overlooked a private garden for the patron's use. On the original drawing for the convent, the private rooms and an adjacent, private walled garden are clearly labelled.[39]

Private rooms were not intended to mimic the austerity of monastic cells, but were specially designed places for secular patrons and nobles to spend time in retreat from the world. The rooms, and even the *pasadizos* leading there, were at times elaborately decorated with paintings and tapestries, usually religious or biblical in nature. Paintings could reflect the intensely personal and intimate focus of a prayerful patron.[40] For instance, a genre of painting specifically created for devotion was that of a saintly figure, often the Virgin or Christ crucified, ringed with roses. The roses symbolized the Passion, and at the same time the rosary. As one concentrated on the painting, one would also pray, focusing the eyes and following the circular ring of roses as if they were beads on a rosary. This created a meditation on the religious figure at the centre of the picture while praying. Paintings of this nature might have been found in oratories or private rooms in convents as well as in domestic settings for the lay elites.

Through inventories prepared for the *visitadores* of the Order of Santiago, we have a good record of the luxury of the decoration in the Duke of Lerma's private rooms. At Valladolid there were fine paintings, among them one of *Susanna and the Elders* in a gold and black frame, a reminder to resist worldly temptations.[41] In Lerma there were pictures by Titian, Bassano, and one ascribed to Tintoretto.[42] On

---

[38] J. Martí y Monsó, *Estudios histórico artísticos relativos principalmente a Valladolid* (Valladolid, 1898), p. 602, fn. 2. See also L. Cervera Vera, *El conjunto palacial de la villa de Lerma* (Lerma, 1996), p. 99, fn. 264.

[39] Madrid, Biblioteca Real, IX/M/242/2 (9), attributed to Francisco de Mora, c.1610. Some scholars date the drawing a few years later, and attribute its authorship to Juan Gómez de Mora or Fray Alberto de la Madre de Dios. See the discussion in *Las trazas de Juan de Herrera y sus seguidores* (Madrid, 2001), pp. 258–9.

[40] D. Freedberg, *The Power of Images: Studies in the History and Theory of Response* (Chicago, 1989). For similar paintings in the Low Countries in the fifteenth century, see above, pp. 43–46, 49–79.

[41] Medinaceli, 29 April 1609, Leg. 71–29.

[42] Medinaceli, *Entrego de San Blas de Lerma*, Leg. 74–13. See the discussion of these rooms and their decoration in S. Schroth, 'The Private Picture Collection of the Duke of

6 December 1617 Lerma recorded that he gave thirty-nine additional religious pictures to the convent, including twenty-four scenes of the miracles of Saint Charles Borromeo, along with portraits of himself, Borromeo, Saint Sebastian and Francisco de Borja; but he kept the most important paintings in his private room in the convent.[43]

Time spent apart from the demands of the secular world in monasteries was mandatory in the rulebooks of the military orders, and considered healthy, both spiritually and physically. This secular accommodation for the lay elites within the confines of monastic houses needs to be viewed in this context. The rooms served as places for retreat, meditation, and conjugal chastity, that is as places to renew spiritual commitment or serve penance. The literature of the early sixteenth century can be directly connected with spiritual practice in the private rooms. Nobles tried to emulate meditation and prayer as explored by mystics like Francisco de Osuna, who published the *Abecedario Espiritual (tercera parte)* in Toledo in 1527, and later Luis de Granada, who wrote the *Libro de Oracion y Meditación*, published in Salamanca in 1554.[44] Mystical works, like that by Osuna, created a religious movement called *recogidos*, urging the practice of recollection as a means to union with God.[45] This exercise, like the spiritual exercises of St Ignatius of Loyola, was a means of moving towards contemplative prayer. According to Osuna the three requirements for such contemplation were the right place, virtuous company, and the disposition of the will.[46] In a private room in a convent (the right place), isolated from the world and literally surrounded by monks or nuns (virtuous company), one could find the right atmosphere for such prayer. Aids to contemplation, like paintings, portable altarpieces and reliquaries, strengthened one's disposition for contemplation and recollection by providing a beautiful focal

Lerma' (unpublished Ph.D. thesis, New York University, 1990), pp. 83–4; L. Cervera Vera, *El Monasterio de San Blas en la Villa de Lerma* (Valencia, 1969), pp. 110 ff.

[43] Schroth, 'The Private Picture Collection of the Duke of Lerma', p. 84.

[44] Luis de Granada's many texts enjoyed several reprintings. Although studying later religious texts, see H. Dansey Smith, *Preaching in the Spanish Golden Age. A Study of Some Preachers of the Reign of Philip III* (Oxford, 1978); M. del Pilar Davila Fernández, *Los sermones y el arte* (Valladolid, 1980).

[45] Francisco de Osuna, *The Third Spiritual Alphabet*, trans. M.E. Giles (New York, 1981), p.xii. Hans Belting, James Marrow and David Freedberg have written extensively about the responses of a contemporary viewer to a work of art. See for instance D. Freedberg, 'A Source for Rubens's Modello of the Assumption and Coronation of the Virgin: a Case Study in the Response to Images', *The Burlington Magazine* 120 (1978), 436.

[46] Many of these ideas were developed in a seminar with Jonathan Brown at the Institute of Fine Arts, New York University, in 1994. I am especially grateful to Miguel Falomir Faus and Luisa Elena Alcalá, other participants in the seminar.

point.[47] At their death knights were required by the *Regla* to bequeath to these houses 'their books, and good and saintly writings that they owned, so that they remain, and are in the libraries of the said convents'.[48]

The construction of private accommodation within the confines of a religious building also reflected the importance for members of the Order of Santiago to have a place to withdraw to, at times, from the marriage bed. The *Regla* of 1527 followed the rule of St Augustine and stated that those who wanted to have wives could have them in conjugal chastity, and those who did not want wives should live chastely.[49] The brief description of this state was listed in the same passage as the exhortation not to have worldly goods except those allowed by the Master (after 1523, the king) or the *comendador mayor*, his deputy, and chief of all the castles in Castile. When a knight was nominated and preparing to take his vows as a member of the Order of Santiago, he would be asked to live celibately for one year, physically isolated in a monastery. After that trial, if he so chose, he was permitted to marry the woman who had previously been approved by the Master, or the king. The woman's background had to be similar to the knight's own.[50]

The Order's involvement in a knight's marriage did not stop here. In Chapter 13, folio 10, of the 1527 *Regla*, there is a description of how knights should behave with their wives, when they should abstain from sexual relations, and at what times they are obliged to reside in convents.[51] Charles V also set out to modify the harsh penalty for adultery, and printed a 'Moderation' amending the requirement in the rulebook. He confirmed the wording of the Infante Don Enrique, who had

---

[47] For example, St Teresa of Avila describes being transported to a place of religious ecstasy by contemplating a sculpture: *Libro de la Vida*, ed. Ottger Steggink (Madrid, 1986), pp. 167–8.

[48] *Regla* (1603), f. 66.

[49] *Regla* (1527), f. 12. The term 'conjugal chastity' derives directly from St Augustine's writings on marriage. For further discussion and the most current interpretations of the dating of these sermons, see D.G. Hunter, 'Augustine, Sermon 354A: its Place in His Thought on Marriage and Sexuality', *Augustinian Studies* 33 (2002), 39–60; P. Brown, *Augustine of Hippo* (Berkeley, 1967); P. Brown, *The Body and Society: Men, Women and Sexual Renunciation in Early Christianity* (New York, 1988), pp. 387 ff., 400 ff.

[50] The choice was subject to prior approval, as recorded by *Regla* (1603), f. 66a. Also see, *Copilación delos establescimientos spirituals dela orden de cavall'ia de señor Santiago* (Toledo, 1539) [hereafter: *Regla* (1539)], f. xix verso. There were papal dispensations for all these categories, a loophole that became more widely used after Charles V took over as Master of the Orders.

[51] *Regla* (1527), f. 10, ch. 13: 'Como se han de aver los freyles con sus mugeres y en que tiempos se deuen abstener de convenir con ellas. E como en ciertos tiempos los freyles y sus mugeres an de estar en los conuentos' [How the knights should comport themselves with their wives and in which times they should abstain from sexual relations with them. And how in certain times the knights and their wives have to be in the convents]. For the definition of *freyles* as a knight of one of the military orders, see *Diccionario de la lengua castellana* (3 vols, Madrid, 1729–39), III, p. 794.

originated the rule, except in the last case of fornication. If a married, engaged, or cleric knight was found in fornication or adultery, the new rules ordered that, the first time, he could serve a penance of one year, isolated in a monastery. If found offending a second time, the knight would serve a double sentence, two years. Penalties were meant to discourage, yet increased in severity for recidivism. If it was found 'that the second penance of two years did not punish him, we establish that for the third time, as for a man hardened and obstinate in his sinning, he will be returned to the monastery to serve perpetual penance, and will also be deprived of his *encomienda* or benefice, if he has one'.[52] As the rulebooks evolved, the rules became more clearly defined. In 1603, it was written categorically, that 'penances [must] be completed [by knights] in their own convents, ... and in no other'.[53]

The penalties for sexual promiscuity by those who were not married were gradually eased, first by Ferdinand the Catholic in 1513, and then further by Charles in 1527. After 1527, those caught in fornication were spared the loss of their *encomienda* if they served one year of penance in a monastery.[54] Keeping concubines had been categorically outlawed in both the secular courts and at the *Capitulo General* (general meeting) of the Order in 1403. Until 1527, the rule of the Infante Don Enrique had stood, that anyone found keeping a mistress should immediately lose his *priorazgo* or *encomienda*, or whatever office or benefice he held. If he were living in a convent, as a celibate knight, he would be required to serve penitence of one year; if married, and found in fornication, he would lose his *encomienda* and any offices, and serve a year-long penance. Caught in adultery, a knight was immediately subject to a year's penance and the loss of his *encomienda*.[55] The importance of secular accommodation within a monastery was thus increased by Charles V's innovations. Rather than lose their benefice, knights now chose to serve their penance in their own private rooms within the family monastery. The *Regla* thus instituted a form of social control, using these rooms within sacred spaces as retreats and places of punishment. The rules were maintained by a group of Visitors (*Visitadores*) loyal to the king, who periodically inspected, and reported any irregularities.[56]

---

[52] See *Regla* (1539), f. xx recto-verso.
[53] *Regla* (1603), f. 119: 'Que las penitencias se cumplan en los Cónventos propios. Ordenamos que los Freyles, que por alguna causa huuieren de ser penitenciados, cumplan sus peniténcias en los Conventos, y no en otro...'.
[54] *Regla* (1539), f. xx verso.
[55] Ibid. See also *Regla* (1565), pp. 347–8.
[56] Postigo Castellanos uses the phrase 'social control' in describing the importance of Confession for the Orders. Indeed, many aspects of membership in the Orders constituted social control for those who were members: *Honor y Privilegio en la Corona de Castilla*, p.262.

Charles V also introduced new regulations which sought to prohibit marital relations at times of great sanctity in the Church's calendar. During these festivals, members were expected to live in the family convent or monastery. Special devotion to certain saints and at particular festivals was obligatory, including those dedicated to the Trinity, the Virgin Mary, Saints Peter and Paul, and of course, Santiago. During the vigils before such feast days sexual relations were not permitted, and residence was required in a monastery.[57] The *Quaresmas*, or lenten periods, and the period from Christmas to Epiphany were to be similarly spent in monasteries; the end of such periods of abstinence and withdrawal from the world was marked by large, public celebrations mixing military and religious promenades. These celebrations became a hallmark of the Habsburg court in Spain. Married women were also required to stay in convents during these times, with their unmarried daughters, as well as single women and widows.[58] The explosion of 'twin' monasteries for the same orders, one for nuns and one for monks, allowed married couples to spend time apart yet close together within their own private rooms.[59]

Secular accommodation in these religious houses could also be used for other purposes as well, such as isolating and controlling the lives of widows of members of the Order. Some widows, whose husbands had died whilst they were away on business, and therefore while the wife was staying in the monastery, were expected to remain in the convent, unless they had the Master's permission to leave and live honestly.[60] Any widow who wished to remarry had first to obtain permission from the Master to ensure that her choice of husband was of a similar status and background. In order to be seen as indulgent, the king preferred that young widows should remarry, and have children so as 'not to give the devil an opportunity for evil'. If a young widow did not wish to remarry she should remain perpetually in the monastery. If she married without the blessing of the Master of the Order she would violate her vow of obedience, and was consequently required to live in the monastery for one year as penance.

Private rooms within monasteries were only one form of sacred space built and decorated by nobles who were members of the Order of Santiago, and the other

---

[57] *Regla* (1527), ff. ix–x. This was reiterated in subsequent editions of the *Regla*; for instance in the 1565 edition, transcribed by Antonio Ruiz de Morales, ff. 39v–40. See also *Regla* (1603), ff. 31b, 44b and 66a, about 'Castidad conjugal'. The new *Regla* also specified the duration of a year of penance and sexual isolation prior to making a profession (ff. 62, 67): 'cavallero que fuere a hazer profession que tiempo ha de estar en el convento' [The knight who is going to make profession; what amount of time he had to be in the convent].
[58] *Regla* (1527), f. x.
[59] C.A. Vañes, *Doña Ana de Austria: abadesa del Real Monasterio de las Huelgas. Sus primeros años de gobierno (1611–1614)* (Madrid, 1990), p. 24.
[60] *Regla* (1527), f. x.

military orders, but they were perhaps the most important manifestation of the interaction between the laity and sacred space. Domestic chapels, or small oratories built within their palaces also increasingly afforded nobles the opportunity to bring the sacred into their domestic spheres, where they and their families could privately hear divine offices.[61] The original plans by Francisco de Mora for the palace in Lerma indicate such a private chapel within the palace.[62] The Luján palace plans, though later, also include chapels within the palace.[63] Building such places for personal devotion within their palaces was a privilege of the *caballeros* of Santiago, allowing them to create a sacred space within their own homes.

The tradition of building private apartments within conventual buildings, whilst having well-established roots in earlier royal practice, was transformed in this period as a result of the demands of the *Regla* into a new opportunity for nobles to create sacred spaces of their own. Although the *Regla* did not dictate the specific form or placing of these rooms, it allowed them to be erected, and protected, as private spaces within otherwise enclosed religious buildings. As integral parts of the sacred spaces of churches and the monasteries attached to them, such private rooms expressed the relationship of a patron to the holy space they had created. As a consequence, the boundaries between the sacred and the secular were not clearly defined, but blurred by the presence of knights and their wives in these havens within monasteries.[64] While they were intended to be used for religious purposes, the private rooms instead often reflected the comforts of their own domestic situation rather than the austerities of a monastic cell. The intimacy of the relationship between patrons and the church thus allowed the secular luxuries of the noble's existence to be included in a monastic religious setting.

---

[61] *Regla* (1603), f. 15v.

[62] *Las trazas de Juan de Herrera*, pp. 223–4. The drawing for the palace has been dated *c*.1604–5, although there is much discussion about its dating and attribution.

[63] V. Tovar Martín, 'La Familia Luján y sus construcciones en el Madrid del siglo XVII', in E. Bermejo and A.E. Pérez Sánchez (eds), *Miscelánea de arte* (Madrid, 1982), pp. 124–9.

[64] Lehfeldt, 'Spatial Discipline and its Limits', p. 145.

Chapter 5

Forbidden Sacred Spaces
in Reformation England

Richard L. Williams

Although Eliade's seminal work might arouse certain post-structuralist suspicions of any analysis which seeks to elucidate underlying rules or universal norms, his notion of sacred space can be seen as both relevant and enlightening when applied to the specific context of Reformation England. This chapter will focus on the determination of the English Catholic hierarchy to maintain some semblance of continuity in the use of sacred space in Elizabethan England even though this left priests increasingly exposed and vulnerable to arrest. By contrasting these risks taken by priests and Catholic laity with the hostile response of the Protestant government, the chapter will seek to draw out continuities and discontinuities in concepts of sacred space, and examine how the issue became so crucial in Reformation England.

The notion of 'Catholic spaces' in early modern England has already begun to attract the attention of scholars. Lisa McClain has recently explored the creativity of English Catholics in claiming new forms of space to help foster a sense of community and identity. Even the adverse environment of a courtroom or a site of execution could be interpreted as Catholic space through a pious act of imagination in which symbolic meaning and significance could be projected onto the bleak surroundings.[1] The present study, however, will focus more specifically on 'sacred' space, following Eliade's notion of 'an irruption of the sacred that results in detaching a territory from the surrounding cosmic milieu and making it qualitatively different'.[2] What might be called 'hierarchies of sanctity' continued to condition responses of English Catholics to religious spaces and this was something the Catholic leadership and their missionary priests sought to promote and control. This chapter will examine the means by which Elizabethan priests articulated sacred spaces specifically for the celebration of Mass.

---

[1] L. McClain, 'Without Church, Cathedral, or Shrine: the Search for Religious Space among Catholics in England, 1559–1625', *SCJ* 33 (2002), 381–99.
[2] Eliade, *The Sacred and the Profane*, p. 26.

Prior to the Reformation, hierarchies in the sanctity of space had even operated within the churches themselves: the holiest part of the building was usually considered to be the high altar. The rood screen acted as a physical barrier to prevent all but the clergy from approaching this most sacred of consecrated ground.[3] However, the extent to which this sacred status might be compromised was a dilemma facing Catholics in England since the churches, monasteries and other consecrated sites had fallen into the hands of their Protestant enemies. These spaces had, after all, been lawfully consecrated under the authority of the Roman Catholic Church.

Issues such as these were debated at the English seminary colleges abroad. Records survive in various archives of cases of conscience discussed at the English College at Douai in 1578 and 1579 (by which time it had relocated to Rheims). This college and its teaching became the model for English seminaries founded soon after at Rome, Valladolid and Seville. These casuist texts typically follow a standard formula in which a question is posed, the issues are discussed and then the resolution is given. One case ruled that consecration of the ground on which a church stood remained potent even after the church itself had burnt to the ground or been otherwise destroyed. The site could not be converted into a private dwelling or put to any other profane use except under special dispensation granted by the Pope.[4]

Another case asked, 'Are Catholics bound at present in England to keep the churches in good repair?' The verdict explained that Catholics should not repair anything in the church associated with Protestant worship '(if there are any)'. However, repairs to the fabric of the church building were proper to undertake,

> ... because to do so tends to the welfare and benefit of the church itself, which, it is hoped will, God willing, in a short time, be restored to its former state when the faith is re-established in England, although unfortunately at the moment the churches are in the hands of the heretics. But if there were no reasonable hope of this, I think that Catholics would not still be bound to make these repairs, because when there is no hope that to do so will redound to the benefit of the Catholic Church, it seems to be done for the benefit of heretics and is therefore intrinsically evil.[5]

However, Elizabethan Catholics were increasingly urged by their clergy to keep away from the churches. Most seriously, church attendance as an outward display

---

[3] For an introduction to the pre-Reformation Church in England, see E. Duffy, *The Stripping of the Altars. Traditional Religion in England 1400–1580* (London, 1992).

[4] P.J. Holmes (ed.), *Elizabethan Casuistry* (Catholic Record Society Records Series lxvii, London, 1981), pp. 26–7.

[5] Ibid., p. 110.

of conformity by 'Church Papists' presented a threat to the unity of the faith which the English Catholic hierarchy was resolved to resist.[6]

Yet, a small number of fully consecrated spaces were still available for the celebration of Mass in late sixteenth-century England. These were private chapels dating from before the accession of Elizabeth I, which survived in the houses of the Catholic gentry and nobility. Private chapels had traditionally been created under licence by the local bishop, under whose jurisdiction they fell.[7] After attempts to enforce their reformation by the Protestant government of Edward VI, their traditional function as a site for the Mass had enjoyed a brief revival during the reign of Mary Tudor. For instance, a charter granted by Cardinal Pole, archbishop of Canterbury, survives which granted Henry, Lord Berkeley

> permission to use his chapel in his Manor of Callowden, co. Warwickshire, as his ancestors used the same before the schism, and to have there a portable altar, to say Mass, to celebrate the Holy Eucharist, to keep the sacred elements in a befitting box with fair linen cloth, with candle burning before it etc.[8]

By formally confirming the licence and consecrated status of private chapels the Marian Church reasserted its authority and proclaimed the importance attached to the legitimacy of consecration.

Naturally, for Catholic priests operating in Elizabethan England such chapels were especially prized. A house thirty miles from London belonging to Richard Bold, courtier and former member of the earl of Leicester's household, was described as 'most suited to our work' by the Jesuit, William Weston, 'because it possessed a chapel, set aside for the celebration of the Church offices'.[9]

In the grandest houses, private chapels and their furnishings could still be equally grand. For example, the leading Jesuit priest operating in Elizabethan England, Father John Gerard, described the private chapel at Lord Vaux's house at Harrowden as fitted with

> ... many fine vestments for the altar: two sets of each colour which the Church uses; one for ordinary use, the other for great feasts; some of these with figures of exquisite workmanship were embroidered with gold and pearls. Six massive silver candlesticks

[6] A. Walsham, *Church Papists: Catholicism, Conformity and Confessional Polemic in Early Modern England* (Woodbridge, 1993).

[7] R. Burn, *Ecclesiastical Law* (2 vols, London, 1797), I, pp. 296–8; J.H. Denton, *English Royal Free Chapels 1100–1300* (Manchester, 1970), p. 10; G.H. Cook, *Medieval Chantries and Chantry Chapels* (London, 1963), p. 54.

[8] I.H. Jeayes (ed.), *Descriptive Catalogue of the Charters and Muniments at Berkeley Castle* (1892), p. 215, Selected Charters no. 730.

[9] W. Weston, *William Weston: the Autobiography of an Elizabethan*, trans. P. Caraman (London, 1955), p. 71.

stood on the altar and two smaller ones at the side for the elevation. The cruets, the lavabo bowl, the bell and thurible were all of silverwork; the lamps hung from silver chains, and a silver crucifix stood on the altar. For the great feasts we had a golden crucifix a foot high.[10]

Thus in rare, privileged enclaves such as these it was evidently possible to follow the feast days of the liturgical calendar with many of the appropriate trappings associated with a great church.

There are even rare instances of new chapel buildings being constructed by rich Catholic families during the reign of Elizabeth. Ralph Sheldon built what was effectively a chantry chapel onto the north side of his parish church at Beoley in Worcestershire. Not only did the chapel house family tombs; an elaborate stone altar was erected which still survives. The doorway leading directly into the churchyard is a characteristic feature of such chapels,[11] but in this instance it might have served to gain the Catholic patrons direct access thereby avoiding the need to enter the main body of the Protestant church.

More commonly, new Catholic chapels were built within or connected to private houses. Father John Gerard recounts that Sir Everard Digby and his wife 'set up a small domestic church like the one in the house where I was staying. They built a chapel and sacristy and provided it with rich and very beautiful vestments'. According to Gerard they were not alone in this but established a trend: 'What this family did, others did too. Many Catholic gentlemen, when they visited this house and saw the arrangements there took it as a model. They founded congregations centred round their own homes, furnished their chapels, and designing accommodation suited to a priest's needs...'.[12]

Whether Sir Thomas Tresham's celebrated Triangular Lodge at Rushton falls into this category is far from clear. Its iconography and inscriptions would certainly have made an appropriate backdrop for the saying of Mass. Although there is no surviving documentary evidence that it was used as anything other than 'The Warryners Lodge', it is, perhaps, the exposed position of the building which counts most against its use for liturgical celebration.[13] A chapel in the large house nearby would have afforded a priest many avenues of escape and places to hide unlike the solitary lodge. The lodge might have served better as a place of private

---

[10] Ibid., p. 195.

[11] H. Colvin, *Architecture and the After-Life* (London, 1991), pp. 257–8. My thanks to Andrew Spicer for bringing this example to my attention.

[12] Ibid., pp. 168–9.

[13] G. Isham, *Rushton Triangular Lodge* (London, 1991); G. Isham, 'Sir Thomas Tresham and his Buildings', *Reports and Papers of the Northamptonshire Record Society* 65 (1964/5), 48–52.

contemplation and prayer for Sir Thomas, away from family and servants in the house.[14]

No doubts, however, attend the function of the elaborate chapel erected by Lady Magdalen, Viscountess Montague at Battle Abbey, her country house in Sussex. It was described by one of the three priests who officiated there in his panegyrical biography of Lady Montague:

> She built a chapel in her house (which in such a persecution was to be admired) and there placed a very fair altar stone, whereto she made an ascent with steps and enclosed it with rails, and, to have everything conformable, she built a choir for singers and set up a pulpit for the priests, which perhaps is not to be seen in all England besides. Here almost every week was a sermon made, and on solemn feasts the sacrifice of the Mass was celebrated with singing and musical instruments, and sometimes also with deacon and subdeacon. And such was the concourse and resort of Catholics, that sometimes there were 120 together, and 60 communicants at a time had the benefit of the Blessed Sacrament.[15]

Despite periodic raids, Lady Montague's chapel in Sussex continued to function; acquiring such notoriety that locals referred to the house as 'Little Rome'. However, in 1607, a year before she died, the Privy Council ordered that she remain 'free from molestation' on account of her age, her status as a noblewoman and 'by reason of her fidelity in the time of Queen Elizabeth was never in question'.[16]

Virtually everything about this story is exceptional and wholly unrepresentative of the experience of the majority of Catholics in England, most of whom might never have encountered a priest. The biography in which it is recounted, and indeed the autobiographies of the Jesuit priests William Weston and John Gerard, was clearly intended to fortify and inspire a new generation of novices and lay folk. That such texts are highly tendentious in no way serves to impugn their sincerity. Yet, their value for the present study is to demonstrate that the defiant use of traditional sacred space was celebrated and encouraged by senior English Catholic figures as an ideal to which others might aspire. The Mass was the lifeblood of Catholic survivalism in England, and although opportunities for its celebration remained scarce, the situation was expected to improve. After all, the mission to England was still thought to be in its early stages; as in the case of Sir Everard Digby's newly-built chapel, where one Catholic gentleman led, others would surely follow.

---

[14] For spaces selected for private devotion, see above pp. 27–93.

[15] A.C. Southern (ed.), *An Elizabethan Recusant House Comprising The Life of Lady Magdalen Viscountess Montague (1538–1608)* (London, 1954), p. 43.

[16] See the order of the Privy Council to the Attorney General dated 19 April 1607, printed in ibid., p. 54.

Unless formally consecrated or licensed, such new structures could not claim a status equivalent to pre-Reformation private chapels. This appears, however, not to have been a pressing issue at the time. Had it been so, the descriptions of new chapels by Gerard, Weston and others would surely have laid great stress on any acts of consecration or any reception of a licence. Similarly, no mention is made of the formal affiliation of new chapels in the casuist texts cited earlier, which sought to prepare a new generation of priests for the difficult conditions in England. There are most likely several reasons for this. Jesuit and seminary priests operating in Elizabethan England presumably had neither the authority nor jurisdiction to license or consecrate chapels. Alternatively, to send licences from competent senior clergy abroad would surely have proved an unnecessary and potentially fatal risk. Such a document would have constituted *prima facie* evidence of illegal activity against the owners of the site named, and simply to bring into the country any such instrument from the 'Sea of Rome' was treason.[17] Perhaps this was an issue that could wait until the Catholic Church regained its authority in England.

In the meantime, many of the 'chapels' described by Gerard and other priests would not, technically, have been chapels at all. Their official status would have been no different from any other room in a house where Mass might be celebrated. However, it became customary to refer to a room prepared for the Mass as a 'chapel', and such usage will be adopted in this chapter. The fact that it could be quite legitimate to celebrate the liturgy of the church on unconsecrated ground meant that licences and rites of consecration would not have been necessary for informal 'chapels'.

When unconsecrated locations were selected for the celebration of Mass a great deal of care was taken to confer what might only be a fleeting moment of sanctity upon the space. This emerges as an important issue in the training of novices at the English seminary colleges. The casuist texts referred to earlier posed the question, 'In what place may masse be sayde nowe in England?' The official response was

> On a portable altar, if the other things necessary for the Mass are present, in any place except at sea or on a river. But a prudent man will choose the most suitable place he can, and in the absence of a church will not even shrink from a bridal chamber if it is the most suitable place because it is not polluted since it is not a church.[18]

A portable altar or 'superaltar' would indeed allow a priest to say Mass almost anywhere including 'in a wood' in Glamorganshire, according to one government

---

[17] 1571 Act of Parliament entitled 'An Acte agaynste the bringing in and putting in Execution of Bulls and other Instruments from the Sea of Rome': *The Statutes of the Realm*, ed. A. Luders *et al.* (12 vols, London, 1810–28), IV, pp. 528–31.

[18] Holmes, 'Elizabethan Casuistry', p. 23.

report.[19] However, it was usually more practical to celebrate indoors. In their present state the churches were clearly excluded since they had been 'polluted' by Protestant occupancy. Although the casuist cases cited earlier had insisted that the consecration of a church was indelible, perhaps an act of reconciliation or confirmation was envisaged before these sites would have been deemed fit for the Catholic liturgy. The latter is suggested by the grant quoted above in which the Marian Church confirmed Lord Berkeley's right to celebrate Mass in his private chapel 'as his ancestors used the same'.[20]

A 'suitable' place for the Mass was not only free from Protestant 'pollution'; the same casuist text explained further that 'everyone must be careful, as far as time and place are concerned, that what he does is edifying and not offensive'.[21] Such considerations were put into practice when Father William Weston arrived at a house approximately nine miles from London. He described it as a 'large and suitable house in a remote place', continuing, 'In the morning I prepared to say Mass. A fine room had been chosen, well suited for it, and the time settled'.[22] Unfortunately, it is not made clear whether the room was judged to be 'fine' because it was spacious or because it was a well appointed room of high social status, such as the great chamber.

That a 'bridal chamber' could be a suitable setting for the Mass in certain circumstances, as mentioned in the extract above, is borne out by the activities of John Gerard. When it became apparent that a certain gentleman, probably Sir William Browne of Walcot, was dying, Gerard 'set up an altar in his bedroom (I had brought all I needed with me) and I said Mass at which he assisted...'.[23] Similarly, a Catholic gentlewoman's bedchamber was used as a site for the Mass following the death of her husband. Every night following her bereavement she had seen a flickering light enter her bedchamber and pass the bed-curtains. She was told that the light represented the soul of her husband pleading for intercessory prayers. Following old tradition, Mass was said for the deceased over a period of thirty days, but the lady 'had Mass said in that room [her bedchamber] for a long time'.[24]

However, in the absence of such special considerations, the choice of room appears to have been a highly flexible matter. In 1583, a spy in the Arundel family's London residence, Howard House, believed that Lady Arundel and Lady

---

[19] J.J. Scarisbrick, *The Reformation and the English People* (Oxford, 1988), p. 143.

[20] For Mary Tudor's own concerns about the consecration of the chair for her coronation, see below p. 104.

[21] Holmes, 'Elizabethan Casuistry', p. 15.

[22] *William Weston*, p. 23.

[23] John Gerard, *John Gerard: The Autobiography of an Elizabethan*, trans. P. Caraman (London, 1951), p. 183.

[24] Ibid., pp. 38–9.

Margaret heard Mass every morning in one particular room. According to the spy, 'The said chamber was first the erle of Arundels wardrop and after the lord william … did ly there himself'.[25] The status of the room was clearly not the reason for its selection in this instance. Privacy, discretion and, above all, security seem, more generally, to have been the obvious determining factors in finding an appropriate space. A room near the top of a house, even an attic room, was a particularly suitable place to establish a chapel since, in the event of a government raid, the time it took the pursuivants to find the room would allow priests to hide themselves and conceal any other incriminating evidence. However, a more satisfactory precaution was to establish the chapel in a building that had not fallen under suspicion. Gerard achieved this by jointly renting a large house in London under a name not known to the authorities in which he was able to 'set up a large and well-equipped chapel'.[26]

Establishing a chapel for the Catholic liturgy was always dangerous, yet away from London and the surrounding counties other parts of the country could be less hazardous. Lancashire, in particular, remained notorious throughout Elizabeth's reign as a place where popery had not lost its grip.[27] In a letter sent to Rome in 1600, the priest Richard Cowling related that, whilst lodging with a widowed Catholic gentlewoman in that county, so many of the faithful flocked to the house to receive the sacraments that 'it was quite impossible to accommodate them in the room that I used as a chapel, spacious as it was'. Large numbers would arrive on Sundays and ordinary feast days, whereas 'on the greater feasts we had to keep the doors shut and admit only a selection'.[28] One solution to this was for the priest to adopt a more peripatetic ministry, or else to celebrate Mass at a much larger venue. This is presumably why there are several instances in Lancashire of Masses being held in barns.[29]

In some instances, a room had evidently been set aside exclusively for use as a chapel, whereas in others it had been specially prepared for what might only have been an infrequent or unique event. Once William Weston agreed to say Mass in a private house, he mentions members of the household busily arranging an upstairs room.[30] John Gerard would say Mass 'in the morning wherever I happened to

---

[25] J.H. Pollen and W. MacMahon, 'The Venerable Philip Howard Earl of Arundel 1557–1595, English Martyrs II', *Catholic Record Society* 21 (1919), 45.

[26] *John Gerard*, p. 142.

[27] C. Haigh, *Reformation and Resistance in Tudor Lancashire* (Cambridge, 1975).

[28] Father Richard Cowling to Claude Aquaviva, 25 September 1600, quoted in P. Caraman (ed.), *The Other Face. Catholic Life under Elizabeth I* (London, 1961), p. 121.

[29] For example, see 'Quarter Sessions Roll 32 Eliz. (1590)', in J. Tait (ed.), *Lancashire Quarter Sessions Records, Volume I* (Chetham Society New Series lxxvii, Manchester, 1917), p. 12; C. Haigh, 'The Continuity of Catholicism in the English Reformation', in C.Haigh (ed.), *The English Reformation Revised* (Cambridge, 1987), p. 184.

[30] *William Weston*, p. 34.

lodge', suggesting a readiness to adapt and make use of whatever space was available.[31] When a room was returned to its former function it is not clear whether a special respect remained for the space in which the Mass had been celebrated. As noted above, English novices were taught not to 'shrink' from using 'a bridal chamber' as opposed simply to referring to a bed chamber, which suggests that profane uses, even the conjugal use of space, need not sully the dignity of the temporary chapel. In fact, the squalid and hostile space of a prison cell was frequently the rather unlikely setting for a temporary Catholic chapel. A combination of corruption and laxity enabled priests to celebrate Mass with all the requisite liturgical paraphernalia. It was even sometimes possible for Catholic lay people to come from outside to attend such services.[32]

The question remains, however, how bedrooms, former wardrobes, barns and even prison cells could have been considered appropriate or 'edifying' locations for the saying of Mass. In other words, how were such unpromising sites transformed into sacred spaces? The fundamental answer to this question is that the sacred rites conducted within them, especially the Mass, made the spaces sacred. Yet, this, in turn, was dependent on the sanctified objects that were essential to the legitimate celebration of Mass.

In spite of the oppressive conditions created by the Elizabethan state, the casuist texts formulated at Douai and Rheims made few concessions for the priests on the English mission in matters concerning consecration. They declared that a portable altar was a necessity. It was ruled acceptable to use an altar that did not contain relics and such altars could be recovered and reused as long as they were not 'so badly broken as to lose their shape'. However, it was crucial that the altar be consecrated or else the priest committed a mortal sin. 'All the vestments' were another requirement in conducting the Mass. If the priest knew his vestments were not consecrated another mortal sin was committed. A missal was required for the Mass, even if the priest was able to enact the ritual from memory. Key liturgical vessels were a practical requirement, including the chalice, which could however be made of tin. Yet all such vessels too needed consecration.[33]

These strictures added to the vulnerability of priests. Many of those arrested were captured dressed in the full vestments that unmistakably marked them out. Moreover, items connected with the Mass could be admissible as corroborative evidence that Mass had been celebrated in cases when suspects had not been caught in the act. For instance, at the trial of Francis Tregian and the priest

---

[31] *John Gerard*, p. 40.
[32] P. McGrath and J. Rowe, 'The Imprisonment of Catholics for Religion under Elizabeth I', *Recusant History* 20 (1991), 415–35; McClain, 'Without Church, Cathedral, or Shrine', 386–91.
[33] Holmes, 'Elizabethan Casuistry', pp. 15, 18–19.

Cuthbert Maine in 1577, the presiding judge told the jury that the discovery of liturgical paraphernalia at Tregian's house meant that 'it must needs follow that he hath said Mass'. 'You must remember', the judge remarked, 'that in causes where direct proofs cannot be had, there presumptions must be allowed'.[34] Possession of consecrated objects could lead to charges of high treason,[35] and so the insistence by the Catholic hierarchy on their continued use indicates how vital consecration was considered.

Consecrated objects embodied God's holiness and conveyed it into the terrestrial realm. Writing for an audience of Elizabethan Catholics, Thomas Hill remarked that the Roman Catholic Church required reverence to be shown to 'all holy things in regard of Him from whom proceedeth all holiness'.[36] It was this essential holiness which enabled consecrated objects to help transform mundane spaces into sacred spaces. Whether the power of consecration could be undermined by Protestant 'pollution' of individual objects was another matter of concern for many Catholics. Mary Tudor feared that the medieval coronation chair at Westminster Abbey might have had its sanctity corrupted by the earlier Protestant coronation ceremony of Edward VI. She therefore broke with established tradition at her own coronation by sitting in a new chair for her anointing, one which had been specially consecrated by Pope Julius III.[37]

In Elizabeth's reign as in Edward VI's, church goods had been sold off and adapted to secular functions, so that chalices were used as wine cups, sacred vessels became saltcellars, and pyxes given to children to play with as toys.[38] This was another subject of controversy addressed by the Elizabethan casuist texts which clearly sought to settle earlier confusion. They directed attention to vestments, copes and 'church cloths' that had been converted into cushions, bed hangings and curtains, and intriguingly 'stageplayers clothes'. The ruling declared authoritatively that 'The consecration of ecclesiastical vessels is indelible'. Vestments converted into secular furnishings could be returned to their former shape and then worn by a priest without the need for further intervention. When

---

[34] J. Morris (ed.), *The Troubles of our Catholic Forefathers, Related by Themselves* (3 vols, London, 1872–77), I, pp. 79–83.

[35] For a general introduction to the deteriorating position of Catholics in England see P..McGrath, *Papists and Puritans under Elizabeth I* (London, 1967), pp. 161–204.

[36] T. Hill, *A quatron of reasons of Catholike religion* ([English Secret Press], 1600), p. 129.

[37] C. Wilson, P. Tudor-Craig, J. Physic and R. Gem, *Westminster Abbey* (London, 1986), p.108.

[38] For these and many more examples, see the documents relating to the visitation of the diocese of Lincoln in 1565/66 in E. Peacock (ed.), *English Church Furniture: Ornaments and Decorations at the Period of the Reformation* (London, 1866), especially pp. 36, 53, 55. The remainder of the documents are printed in C.W. Foster, *Lincolnshire Notes and Queries* 14 (1917), 78–88, 109–16, 144–51, 166–73. See the discussion in Duffy, *The Stripping of the Altars*, pp. 572–3.

restoration proved impossible, then the objects were to be set to some other ritual use or alternatively burnt, but never used for any profane purpose.[39]

Nevertheless, many of these reclaimed liturgical objects were badly worn and, more seriously, there were simply not enough available. The problem intensified as increasing numbers of seminary and Jesuit priests arrived, each needing to be equipped to serve the religious needs of the Catholic laity in England. John Gerard had to bring his own specially designed equipment with him from abroad. However, in the course of his ministry Gerard noticed a marked improvement in the situation.[40]

One reason for this transformation was that some of Gerard's hosts had made the equipment themselves. Sir William Browne's dying wish was that the purple and red robes he had received on becoming a Knight of the Bath be 'turned to use at the altar'. Mrs Wiseman seems to have established something of a cottage industry for the production of vestments at Braddocks: 'She devoted all her time to prayer and needlework – she made vestments and other things for the altar and sent them to different people'.[41]

Altars, crosses, chalices and the like were not, however, so easily improvised. It was largely their importation into England from the Continent that made these liturgical objects more freely available. The scale of this smuggling operation was sufficient to provoke the intervention of Parliament and other Protestant authorities. Officials at the ports and borders were instructed to seek out what were called 'Certaine of the Popes Merchandize lately sent ouer into Englande'.[42] The latter was the title of a woodcut broadsheet print intended to help officials identify these subversive Catholic goods. The print (Figure 5.1) was issued with a book by Bernard Garter entitled *A new years gifte, dedicated to the popes holiness* (London, 1579), which offered further written description. The objects illustrated range from different versions of an Agnus Dei to rosary beads. A cross is included, but the first item in the list is a superaltar which, as Garter commented, would 'serve to say Masse on in any secret place'.[43]

[39] Holmes, 'Elizabethan Casuistry', p. 18.
[40] *John Gerard*, p. 40.
[41] Ibid., pp. 184, 52.
[42] R.L. Williams, 'Collecting and Religion in Late-Sixteenth-Century England', in E. Chaney (ed.), *The Evolution of English Collecting: Receptions of Italian Art in the Tudor and Stuart Periods* (London, 2003), pp. 180–86; R.L. Williams, 'Religious Pictures and Sculpture in Elizabethan England: Censure, Appreciation and Devotion' (unpublished Ph.D. thesis, Courtauld Institute of Art, 2003), pp. 52–66.
[43] B. Garter, *A New yeares gifte dedicated to the popes holiness and all Catholikes addicted to the Sea of Rome* (London, 1579), sig. hii[r].

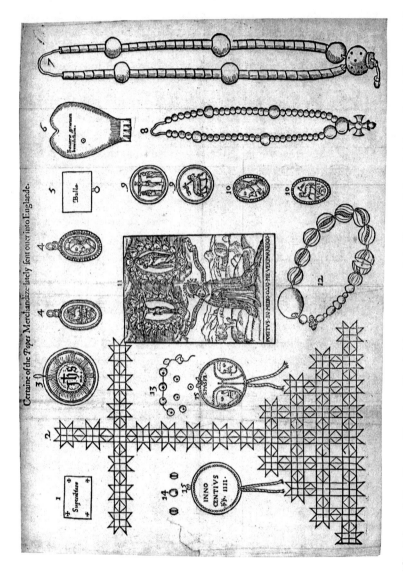

Figure 5.1 'Certaine of the Popes Merchandize lately sent ouer into Englande', print issued with Bernard Garter, *A New Years Gifte, dedicated to the Popes Holiness* (London, 1579). By permission of the British Library.

Although consecrated objects can be seen as crucial in the articulation of sacred space, other signifiers not officially prescribed for liturgical celebration could also play an important role in this process. Elaborate settings and decoration of the altar were not a necessity but nonetheless were highly valued. John Gerard boasted that a 'beautifully furnished altar with Mass vestments laid out beside it' greeted the eyes of government searchers upon entering the chapel of a Catholic house in 1599. So beautiful were the altar and its vestments that 'Even the heretics were amazed at them'.[44] Yet, such display was not merely a matter of pride, it played a part in evoking the reverence appropriate for worship. Conversely, a poor display could have a directly detrimental effect. Thus Gerard had serious misgivings after visiting a house at Lawshall because 'the altar furnishings were old and worn and anything but helpful to devotion'.[45]

Visual imagery was another means to draw attention to the centrality of the altar. Altarpieces were not prescribed for the celebration of Mass according to Catholic canon law.[46] Yet, their quasi-liturgical status was held in high esteem. Altarpieces and other images rescued from the churches were still to be found hidden in the houses of Elizabethan Catholics. At Sir Thomas Tresham's house in Hoxton in 1584 the authorities seized 'A new fashioned picture of Christ in a great table, and a tabernacle of sondrie painted images w[i]th leaves to fold serving as should seeme for a tabernacle or screene to stand upon the altar'.[47] No indication is given of the age of this altarpiece, but its picture of Christ was judged to be 'new fashioned' which indicates that religious imagery of this nature continued to be made illegally in Elizabethan England for those few Catholics with the means and opportunity to commission it. One of the few examples to survive was also produced for Tresham, at his country seat at Rushton in Northamptonshire. Dated 1577, the image is a large and brightly painted plaster relief of the Crucifixion, set high into an east wall of a room located at the rear of the house. It is possible that what survives originally formed part of a much larger display, acting as a reredos behind an altar table.[48]

Evidence of the production or importation of more modest imagery for Elizabethan Catholics comes from the inventories of objects seized by officials from the houses of suspected Catholic militants. Several of these inventories survive in the National Archives and these reveal the different media used. For example, among the items seized from Mistress Hampden's house in Buckinghamshire in 1583 were 'v picktures payntd upon past bords'. The firm

[44] *John Gerard*, p. 151.
[45] Ibid., p. 24.
[46] P. Hunfrey and M. Kemp (eds), *The Altarpiece in the Renaissance* (London, 1989), p. 11.
[47] NA, London, SP12/172/113.
[48] R.L. Williams, 'A Catholic Sculpture in Elizabethan England: Sir Thomas Tresham's Reredos at Rushton Hall', *Architectural History* 44 (2001), 221–7.

foundation of pasteboard made it ideal to hang from the wall or stand upon a table, either for private prayers or as an altarpiece. The same could be said of the 'ii pictures of nedlework sett into Frames of bordes' found in the 'Litel gallery' of Mistress Hampden's house.[49]

In the same lady's own bedchamber was 'a pickture made upon yewloe sarssarnet', and in the room assigned to Mr Fitton were 'ii pictures one upon yellowe sarcnet, thother upon parchment which are wrapped togeither in a paper'. Sarsanet was a kind of silk and thus a costly material.[50] The images might have been painted onto the fabric. For example, an image on satin confiscated from Tresham's Hoxton house in 1584 was said to be a painting: 'a painted crucifix upon orenge colored satten'.[51] The widespread distribution of these silk pictures is indicated by the large numbers intercepted by the constables of Lewes in 1584. Upon opening a fardel containing numerous Catholic books, rosary beads and relics, the constables noted 'Pictures in sylks: of the greater sorte, xix / Pictures in silke of the lesser sorte xxvii'.[52] Presumably, these objects were destined for distribution among the Catholic households in the area. It seems quite possible that the 'greater sorte' of silk pictures in particular were intended to adorn an altar, either as an overfront, a netherfront or even a reredos.

Religious pictures printed onto single sheets of paper were also in circulation. In 1584, 'xii prynted superstycyous pyctures' were found in a house in Holborn.[53] The 'xii sevrall pictures rolled togeither' discovered at Mistress Hampden's house might also have been prints on paper.[54] Bernard Garter fulminated against the illegal importation of 'Pictures of Saintes' into England and printed an example at the centre of his broadsheet. What appears to be a faithful reproduction of a Catholic single leaf print from the Netherlands depicts St Nicholas praying between Christ and the Virgin Mary.[55]

Pictures on fabric, painted onto pasteboards or printed onto paper were light and compact, thereby making them relatively easy to transport and to conceal. They could be smuggled into prison along with equipment necessary for the Mass. In fact, one of the clearest examples of the part such pictures could play in the articulation of sacred space occurred in a prison cell. Recalling his time of

[49] NA, SP12/167/113.

[50] S. Foister, 'Paintings and Other Works of Art in Sixteenth-Century English Inventories', *Burlington Magazine* 123 (1981), 275.

[51] NA, SP12/172/113.

[52] NA, SP12/156/15.

[53] NA, SP12/172/111.

[54] NA, SP12/167/113.

[55] See Williams, 'Religious Pictures and Sculpture in Elizabethan England', pp. 212–13 for a correction of T. Watt, *Cheap Print and Popular Piety, 1550–1640* (Cambridge, 1994), p.179.

incarceration, William Weston described a cell which had been turned into a chapel 'where the priests offered their daily Mass'. 'It was here', Weston wrote, 'that the table stood which served as an altar. On the wall behind it were attached a number of pictures of the saints, to form a reredos'.[56]

Although examples such as this illustrate the centrality of the altar in marking out a chapel area as sacred space, the surrounding room could also be adorned with religious symbolism. Evidence survives, although fragmentary, demonstrating that sometimes walls and ceilings were painted. An attic room at Harvington Hall in Worcestershire, thought to have been used as a recusant chapel, still bears what appear to be symbolic drops of blood and water painted in distemper on the walls. Croft-Murray makes the convincing suggestion that the blood shed by Christ and the water that issued from the wound in his side are being represented in a symbolic allusion to the Passion.[57] Another attic room at Quendon Hall in Essex retains the barely visible remnants of a scheme of saints and cherubs' heads painted onto the sloping roof.[58] Sir Thomas Tresham recorded how he and his fellow Catholics interned at Ely in 1597 painted the crucifix and other religious symbols onto cloth or directly onto the walls of their rooms.[59] These painted images were likely to have been intended as an aid to private devotion rather than to create a chapel for the Mass since, at least officially, their place of detention at the bishop's palace at Ely was reserved for Catholic lay gentlemen and their servants rather than priests. The episode, nevertheless, is instructive in that it indicates the value attached to wall paintings and painted cloths of religious themes by the Catholic gentry.

In addition to painted cloths or walls, in the privacy of their houses some of these Catholic gentlemen would surely have owned tapestries with which to fill the space of their chapel chambers. Even while in custody at Sheffield Castle, Mary Queen of Scots was able to borrow 'hangings of the Passion' for her rooms from her very captor, the Protestant earl of Shrewsbury.[60] In this case, the hangings were most likely to have acted as a stimulus to private devotion since it is difficult to imagine that Mary would have had the opportunity to hear Mass whilst under such close supervision. Yet it seems highly probable that wealthy Elizabethan Catholics

---

[56] *William Weston*, p. 166.

[57] E. Croft-Murray, *Decorative Painting in England 1537–1837* (2 vols, London, 1962), I, p.188.

[58] G.M. Benton, 'Wall Paintings at Quendon Hall', *Essex Archaeological Society* 18 (1928), 290–92.

[59] BL, Additional MS 39832, f. 5. Printed in Historical Manuscripts Commission, *Report of the Manuscripts in Various Collections III*, 55 (1904), p. 91.

[60] Lambeth Palace, Talbot Papers MS 3198, vol G, 150. In this 1582 inventory of the household goods and furniture at Sheffield Castle and Lodge, 'hangings of the Passion and of warres, peces viii' were listed 'In the Quenes chambers' in a subsection headed 'An Inventorye … Queen of Scotts and her People hath of my Lords'.

might have adorned their chapels with costly hangings in continuation of a tradition established long before the Reformation. Even Catholics of a less exalted status could have used the moveable images on fabrics and paper discussed above, not just to adorn the altar but to fill small rooms with colour and holy symbols.

The actions of the prisoners at Ely and of Mary Queen of Scots demonstrate that rooms in which the Mass might never be celebrated could also be embellished. Rooms set aside for prayer alone were usually described as oratories. Prior to the Reformation a distinction had been made between a private chapel, being a consecrated space licensed for the celebration of the official liturgy of the Church, and a private oratory, being a space generally ordained exclusively for prayer. Although an oratory officially required a licence from the bishop, this stipulation appears to have been generally overlooked.[61] Under the oppressive conditions of Elizabethan England, in the same way that virtually any space might serve as a temporary chapel, so informal oratories were established. Even within a cell of the Tower of London John Gerard found that an earlier inmate, the martyr Father Henry Walpole, had marked out the space of 'a little oratory' by chalking on the walls the orders of the angels and other devout inscriptions. After being moved to another cell Gerard secured permission to visit Walpole's cell with its oratory to say his prayers.[62] This suggests that great care was taken not only in the selection of a space for the celebration of Mass, but also for prayer and meditation.

Nevertheless, a room used as an oratory would have risen in status the moment the Mass, with its priest and consecrated objects, transformed it into a chapel. The use of imagery was thus a contributory factor, not an exclusive means by which the physical space of a chapel could be set strikingly apart from the profane world.

It should also be acknowledged, however, that the visual was not alone among the senses employed in the creation of sacred space. A room could also be filled with religious music, perhaps heightening the emotional response and the spiritual awareness of those present.[63] William Weston was not only impressed that Richard Bold owned a private chapel but because

> The gentleman was also a skilled musician, and had an organ and other musical instruments and choristers, male and female, members of his household. During those days it was just as if we were celebrating an uninterrupted octave of some great feast.[64]

---

[61] Burn, *Ecclesiastical Law*, I, pp. 296–8; Denton, *English Royal Free Chapels*, p.10; Cook, *Medieval Chantries and Chantry Chapels*, p. 54.
[62] *John Gerard*, pp. 104–5.
[63] A question asked by John Goodall at the Exeter conference stimulated consideration of the role of music in this chapter, for which the present author is most indebted.
[64] *William Weston*, p. 71.

This entire Latin tradition of ecclesiastical music had been rendered obsolete, in fact illegal, in the Church of England. In the days of the 'old religion' this repertoire had helped mark the important feasts and holy days of the liturgical calendar.[65] Indeed, it was hearing this music that helped transport Weston back to a memory of happier times. Similarly, when arriving at the same chapel, Father Robert Southwell hoped to 'have sung Mass with all the solemnity accompanied by choice instrumental and vocal music, on the feast of St Mary Magdalen'.[66]

Weston remembered that William Byrd, 'the very famous English musician and organist', was present at this sung Mass. As a Gentleman of the Chapel Royal, Byrd was afforded a degree of protection in spite of his Catholic faith. His settings of the Roman Catholic liturgy, such as his Masses for four and for five voices, were secretly printed and distributed in England. This at least kept alive the English tradition of ecclesiastical music, and was encouraged by key Jesuits operating in England. Henry Garnet was one such priest. He was a life-long friend of Byrd, and the two shared their passion for music.[67] In a letter dated 1601, Garnet commented, 'Notwithstanding all our troubles we sing Mass'.[68] Byrd's music had the power and weight to fill a space on the scale of the chapel built by Viscountess Montague with its 'choir for singers' and musical instruments.[69] Yet it was equally suited to the intimate setting of a small room or cell where it could have added immeasurably to the numinous atmosphere of the sacred space.

This sense of a numinous atmosphere was constructed within the realm of personal experience. To some extent it was yet another act of pious imagination; a projection of private significance onto the perception of the senses. The elements examined above, such as the consecrated objects, the vestments worn by the priest, the sacred ritual, the music and the adornment of the space with imagery all combined to heighten sensation. That stimulation of the senses by these means evoked an atmosphere of the sacred was recognized by James Pilkington, bishop of Durham. Writing in 1562, the bishop's attack on the 'pope's church' amounts to an analysis of the Catholic conception of sacred space:

> The pope's church hath all things pleasant in it to delight the people withal: as for their eyes, their god hangs in a rope, images gilded, painted, carved most finely, copes, chalices, crosses of gold and silver, banners, etc. with relics and altars; for their ears,

---

[65] For an introduction to music in sixteenth-century England, see J. Milsom, 'Music', in B.Ford (ed.), *Renaissance and Reformation. The Cambridge Guide to the Arts in Britain* (9 vols, Cambridge, 1989), III, pp. 168–205.

[66] *William Weston*, p. 77 fn. 10.

[67] Ibid., pp. 71, 77 fn. 11.

[68] Stonyhurst MS Grene, P 553, Henry Garnet to Thomas Strange, 30 June 1601, printed in Caraman, *The Other Face*, pp. 211–12.

[69] A.C. Southern (ed.), *An Elizabethan Recusant House Comprising The Life of Lady Magdalen Viscountess Montague (1538–1608)* (London, 1954), p. 43.

singing, ringing, and organs piping; for the nose, frankincense sweet; to wash away sins (as they say) holy water of their own hallowing and making; priests of infinite sort, Masses, trentals, diriges, and pardons, etc.[70]

Although such stimuli appealed to the individual consciousness, a sense of the sacred seems to have been more acute when experienced collectively. This would not merely have come from the excitement of group identity observable today in the audience at a live concert. Elizabethan Catholics were in a position to experience the high emotions and close sense of identity often associated with clandestine groups who perceive themselves to be persecuted minorities.

However, the stimulus afforded by the display of liturgical trappings and non-liturgical dressings was not in itself sufficient to create a sacred space. According to Eliade's conception, 'Every sacred space implies a hierophany', defined as 'the act of manifestation of the sacred'.[71] A Catholic chapel was a truly sacred space because those within it experienced a manifestation of the divine. During Mass the miracle of transubstantiation occurred in which the 'real presence' of Christ was manifested. This was the hierophany common to all Catholic chapels. It was stressed to the next generation of English Catholics in Laurence Vaux's catechism that the altar was 'the place of Christes residence'.[72] Even more explicitly, in a story reminiscent of the *Golden Legend*, William Weston claimed that a child attending Mass enquired after 'That wonderful little baby', following a vision in which the Mass wafer visibly transformed into the body of Christ.[73]

The presence of the divine might even be confirmed through further miraculous intervention. William Weston believed that another hierophany, or what Eliade more properly calls a *sign*, had blessed his creation of a sacred space within the Clink jail.[74] When the ceiling of a fellow Catholic's cell caved in, 'the part of the room where priests offered their daily Mass was completely untouched'. This was the cell mentioned earlier in which pictures had been attached to the wall to form a reredos but, to the amazement of those present, 'None of the pictures nor any part of the altar was so much as soiled by the falling dust and rubbish'. Weston and the other inmates were in no doubt over the interpretation of this event, commenting, 'And this, we all remarked, was something more than happy chance'.[75] Not only

---

[70] *Exposition upon the Prophet Abdias, 1563*, in *The Works of James Pilkington D.D.* ed. J.Scholefield (3 vols, PS xxxv, Cambridge, 1842), III, p. 256.

[71] Eliade, *The Sacred and the Profane*, pp. 26, 11.

[72] L. Vaux, *A catechisme, or a Christian doctrine, necessarie for chyldren and the ignorant people* (Rouen, 1583), sig. lvi^v. Printed first in 1568, this book was published in eight further editions.

[73] *William Weston*, p. 36.

[74] Eliade, *The Sacred and the Profane*, p. 27.

[75] *William Weston*, p. 166.

had their faith in the True Religion been vindicated, so had their creation and articulation of sacred space.

This divine vindication of Catholic sacred space was in stark contrast to what Catholics perceived to be God's wrath at the sacrilegious attack on English churches at the hands of the Protestants. The latter was experienced by Francis Woodhouse of Norfolk who, after years of resistance, succumbed to pressure to go to church. 'Immediately I entered the church', he confessed, '... my bowels began to torture me'. With his stomach raging like a fire, Woodhouse rushed to the nearest tavern where he managed to down eight pints of beer, but still his inflammation was not quenched.[76] The story served, perhaps primarily, as a warning against the perils of adopting the ways of the Church Papist. Yet, it also suggested that God's spirit was no longer present in the churches of England.

In the eyes of English Catholics the Protestant government's calculated attack on the very notion of sacred space had left the churches desecrated. According to the Catholic polemicist, Thomas Hill, the effects of this upon the common people had been catastrophic: 'they enter into their churches with no greater reverence than they enter into taverns; they bow or make reverence to nothing therein, for that they have made all sacred things away ...'. The destruction of images and wall paintings, although not consecrated, still had a detrimental effect. Hill scorned the Protestants for their bare, sterile churches and spartan services, observing that 'they have leaft their churches as fit to mooue people to pietie and deuotion, as theyr barnes are, when all the corne and hay is out of them, and nothing left to be seene besides the roofes, walles and silles'. The consequences of this were devastating, since such an environment 'giveth the people occasion to be undeuout, irreligious and unreuerent for that they see nothing worthy of reuerence'.[77]

Such concerns make more understandable the motivations of the Catholic leadership in insisting that its priests employ fully consecrated equipment, and encouraging them to use imagery and other non-essentials in the articulation of sacred space despite the increased risks of detection this undoubtedly involved. However, the issue of sacred space in Elizabethan England had become much more than a matter of theological controversy. Intermixed with matters of faith were matters of power relations. This was not only from the perspective of the English government, for which the establishing of a forum for Roman Catholic worship was treated as an act of political defiance. The position of the English Catholic hierarchy can be examined in the same terms. Its insistence that priests must wear full vestments and the encouragement to use crosses, images and the like was a call for defiance amongst English Catholics against the government of Elizabeth I. This command to be uncompromising was very much in tune with the message Robert

[76] Ibid., p. 148.
[77] Hill, *A quatron of reasons of Catholike religion*, pp. 66–7, 85–6, 120.

Persons emphasized in his many books, that Catholics should stand defiant rather than compromise with the heretics as the so called 'Church Papists' had done. As Alexandra Walsham has shown, the problem of the outwardly conforming Catholic was of growing concern to the Catholic leadership.[78] From the Catholic perspective, the threat was to the absolute authority of the Pope and his Church.

In conclusion, many devout Catholics in Elizabethan England might well have considered their desire to create sacred spaces for ritual enactment to be nothing more than a continuation of Church tradition and a simple act of faith. However, the combined actions of the English government and of the Catholic hierarchy had transformed such reverence towards sacred space into a provocative act of political defiance.

[78] Walsham, *Church Papists*.

Chapter 6

Designing for Protestant Worship:
the Private Chapels of the Cecil Family

†Annabel Ricketts
with Claire Gapper and Caroline Knight*

The members of the Cecil family whose chapels are discussed in this paper built their houses in the eighty years following the Reformation begun during the reign of Henry VIII. The period saw continuing religious upheavals as the Church of England gradually emerged with the English monarch as its Supreme Governor. Changes in liturgy and the manner in which churches were used were matched by the ways in which patrons and their architects approached the design of the domestic chapel.

Before the Reformation private chapels were common and might be consecrated, thus permitting the celebration of the sacraments, though it was also possible for Mass to be celebrated in such unconsecrated places by episcopal licence.[1] After the Reformation, consecration appears to have ceased, for there are no records of private chapels being consecrated during the Elizabethan period. Bishop Pilkington's view that 'honest places for Christian services had no need for hallowing' best captures the feeling for simplicity that characterizes the period.[2] More practically, no approved Protestant service of

* This paper was edited by Claire Gapper and Caroline Knight using notes prepared by the late Annabel Ricketts and her 'The Evolution of the Protestant Country House Chapel, c.1500–c.1700' (unpublished Ph.D. thesis, University of London, 2003). The editors have revised and expanded this material and provided footnotes for the full text. They would like to thank Margaret Aston, Pauline Croft and Andrew Spicer for reading and commenting on drafts of this paper and for providing invaluable advice and support. We are also grateful to Robin Harcourt-Williams, for making available to us the resources of the Hatfield House archive.
[1] For medieval domestic chapels in general, see E.L. Cutts, *Parish Priests and their People in the Middle Ages in England* (London, 1898), pp. 408–37. See also, pp. 27–47 above.
[2] *The Works of James Pilkington*, ed. J. Scholefield (3 vols, PS xxxv, Cambridge, 1842), p. 129.

consecration existed. In the early years of the seventeenth century, the creation of a Protestant consecration service was in its infancy with patrons, in conjunction with their bishops, playing an important role in creating services.[3]

Protestant private chapels are surprising in both their originality and variety. In contrast to parish churches where, in most cases, space designed for Catholic worship was adapted to Protestant use, noblemen and gentry could devise spaces in their houses that allowed them to worship as they wished, free from the traditions that had governed the layout of the Catholic Church.

In the absence of any direction from central authority, patrons were at first uncertain as to what constituted a Protestant domestic chapel. Subsequent experiments included the development of the 'assembly chapel', as patrons were at liberty to reinterpret the spaces they required for Protestant worship, whether they were regarded as 'sacred spaces' or not. By the end of Elizabeth's reign there is evidence of a revival of interest in the form of the traditional pre-Reformation chapel, culminating in the building of new chapels such as that at Hatfield House. As a family, the Cecils played a significant role in all these developments.

The purpose of this article is to convey something of the range and inventiveness of these chapels in the late sixteenth and early seventeenth centuries. This will be accomplished by analysing what is known of the architectural form and interior space of the household chapels of three Protestant members of the Cecil family, who were all building or adapting important houses between 1560 and 1612. These are: William Cecil, created Lord Burghley in 1571, who served as Lord Treasurer to Queen Elizabeth until his death in 1598; and his two sons, the elder son Thomas, who was born in 1542 and created earl of Exeter by James I in 1605, and his half-brother Robert, who was twenty-one years younger, served as Principal Secretary of State to King James, and was ennobled at the same time as Thomas, becoming earl of Salisbury. It will be shown that the three men had very different attitudes to chapel building, resulting from their own differing responses to Protestantism, but none of the chapel types discussed was unique to the Cecil family.

Before the Reformation most good-sized country houses had a private chapel: aristocratic families had the right to one, while gentry families had to apply to the church authorities. Sometimes chapels were attached to the house;

---

[3] Ricketts, 'Protestant Country House Chapel', p. 19; Wickham Legg, *English Orders*. Also see below, pp. 207–30.

sometimes they were free-standing. In either case, the chapel was architecturally distinguished, a clearly visible and instantly identifiable part of the building, often placed across a range and only rivalled in visual importance by the great hall. But perhaps the most important characteristic of the early Tudor chapel was the way in which all aspects of its design were centred on the altar. From the exterior, the east end was usually marked by an apse or a large east window; the interior space was divided into two clearly defined areas, often of different dimensions, and the division could be emphasized by a change in the pitch or structure of the ceiling. A screen was often used to divide the two spaces. Just as the architecture and fittings worked together to create a separate, and emphasized, east end space, so too was the decoration carefully controlled to build up to a climax in the chancel and, in particular, the area immediately round the altar.[4]

Most chapels were for the use of the family and household only, but if the parish church was some distance away, the chapel might be used by the local community as well.[5] Pre-Reformation chapels can be seen today at country houses such as The Vyne, Hampshire, Haddon Hall, Derbyshire, and Cotehele, Cornwall.[6] Following the Reformation, these were simply converted for Protestant use, and Snape Castle in North Yorkshire exemplifies this process. Here, George Nevill, a younger son of the earl of Westmorland, and later Lord Latimer, had built himself a large courtyard house *c*.1426–50, with a splendid private chapel, which was probably free-standing.[7] The house built by Nevill is now in ruins, but the chapel, attached to the later south range, has survived and is now used as the parish church.[8] This chapel provides a Catholic benchmark against which to judge the later Protestant chapels. Although much altered internally, it gives an idea of an aristocratic pre-Reformation chapel in that it would have formed an important and clearly identifiable part of the domestic complex. Thomas Cecil's wife, Dorothy Nevill, inherited the castle in 1577 and a major reconstruction, which will be discussed below, was carried out in the 1580s.

---

[4] Ricketts, 'Protestant Country House Chapel', pp. 247–8.

[5] Ibid., p. 27. Ricketts discusses the 'grey area' between a private chapel, and one also used as a chapel of ease.

[6] Ibid., p. 37. Both Haddon and Cotehele originally had chapels that were free-standing buildings, but which were incorporated into the house in the sixteenth-century expansions.

[7] G. Worsley, 'Snape Castle, Yorkshire', *Country Life* (6 March 1986), 570–75.

[8] The village of Snape has no church, but is part of the parish of Well; the Nevills were buried in Well church. It is possible that the chapel at Snape also served as a chapel of ease for the villagers.

William Cecil (1520–98) was the most powerful figure in England throughout the reign of Elizabeth I. He had established a reputation as an outstanding administrator during the Protectorate of the Protestant Duke of Somerset, and had kept a low profile during the reign of Queen Mary. His father and grandfather had built up substantial estates in Northamptonshire, Lincolnshire and Rutland, which he inherited along with the house at Burghley at his father's death in 1553. He transformed this house from the late 1550s until 1587. With the birth of a second son, Robert, he bought the estate of Theobalds in Hertfordshire in 1564, and built himself a substantial house there, which was to be Robert's inheritance. His career meant that he was mainly in London, and he inherited his father's house in Canon Row, close to Westminster Abbey and Whitehall Palace. He later acquired an existing house on the north side of the Strand, which he enlarged considerably, creating a magnificent courtyard house.[9] None of William's three most important houses, Burghley House, Lincolnshire, Cecil House, London, and Theobalds, Hertfordshire, appears to have had a chapel with an identifiable architectural character. Indeed, Theobalds was the only house of the three known for certain to have had a chapel.

At Burghley it appears that the speedy building of a chapel was not a high priority for William. The building records for 1553–65 indicate that a chapel was intended at the high end of the hall, and this was to have included a 'high' window following the pre-Reformation tradition.[10] However, during the second building phase of 1573–87 the position formerly allocated to the chapel was given over to the splendid new south-eastern great stair. It was when William's mother, Jane, moved back to Burghley from Stamford in 1573 and complained of the lack of a chaplain that another chapel may have been hurriedly constructed in the north-east corner of the house, from rooms that had previously been part of the apartment of Mildred, William's second wife. It appears likely that William's eldest son, Thomas, who lived mainly at Burghley after his marriage in 1564, had adopted a more 'low-church', that is, less ceremonial, regime and the temporary lack of a chapel may not have been

---

[9] For the plan and a discussion of the house, see P. Henderson and J. Husselby, 'Location, Location, Location! Cecil House in the Strand', *Architectural History* 45 (2002), 159–93.

[10] J. Husselby, 'The Architecture at Burghley House: the Patronage of William Cecil, 1553–1598' (3 vols, unpublished Ph.D. thesis, University of Warwick, 1996), III, Appendix B, p. 415, contains William Cecil's memorandum of 1558 to masons, referring to 'a high window for ye chappell', suggesting that it still had not been built. We are grateful to Jill Husselby for her help in interpreting the evidence for the siting of the chapel at Burghley House.

important.[11] Thus, in one of the most splendid of Elizabethan prodigy houses, the early intention for a prestigious chapel gave way to more secular concerns, and the provision of a magnificent processional route through the state apartments took priority.[12]

The omission of a chapel was not unusual in the Elizabethan period, and is reflected in a number of contemporary household regulations which refer to the 'chapel or chamber used for prayers'. What was important was to have a place where the household could assemble to pray, even if it was in the great hall or great chamber.[13] As an example, Protector Somerset, builder of Somerset House in the Strand and fiercely Protestant, does not seem to have had a chapel, and John Knox records that Somerset went to the great hall to hear a sermon.[14] A specifically differentiated 'sacred space' was not considered necessary, and because of this, a chapel was no longer essential.

Cecil House in the Strand was substantially extended by William in the 1560s, and may well provide another example of the use of domestic space for worship. The recently discovered plan does not include an identifiable chapel but, since only one floor is shown, this is not conclusive evidence. However, by this date the majority of chapels were on the ground floor, since they had specific access requirements for the various members of the family and household, and hardly ever contained a fireplace, so they are often easy to identify. In this case, Norden's manuscript description of the house suggests an alternative arrangement, for he describes 'the oratory placed in the angle of the great chamber'. Since an oratory is usually thought of as a small room set apart for prayer, this inclusion of an oratory within the principal chamber of state is surprising. However, John Florio's *Dictionary* published in 1598 provides a possible explanation as his entry for 'oratory' reads: 'a place dedicated only to prayers. Also a pulpit'.[15] Hence it seems likely that at Cecil House assemblies were held in the great chamber with the chaplain addressing the household

[11] The terms 'high-church' and 'low-church', although anachronistic, are used for convenience since they have commonly understood, but not too specific, religious and social connotations.

[12] Ricketts, 'Protestant Country House Chapel', pp. 31–2.

[13] Ibid., pp. 30–31.

[14] *The Works of John Knox*, ed. D. Laing (6 vols, Bannatyne Club cxii, Edinburgh, 1846–64), III, p. 176, quoted in N. Pevsner, 'Old Somerset House', *Architectural Review* (September 1954), 163.

[15] John Florio, *A Worlde of Wordes or most copious and exact Dictionarie in Italian & English* (London, 1598), p. 247.

from the 'oratory'.[16] Although no other examples of an oratory/pulpit have been discovered, there is evidence that a number of large houses both in London and the country did not have chapels but instead used the great chamber, and sometimes the great hall, for religious assemblies.[17]

At Theobalds, William was building a house that was also a quasi-palace, providing accommodation for the Queen and her courtiers, as well as for his own household. According to Summerson, the chapel was on the ground floor, rising through two storeys, but there is no evidence as to the appearance of its windows.[18] The chapel was sited adjacent to the lodgings used by the Queen and it may have been included primarily with her visits in mind. The famous description of Theobalds by Baron Waldstein in 1600 gave a great deal of attention to the rooms of state and the gardens and yet made no mention of the chapel.[19] In this the baron is not unusual for no account of the house mentions the chapel and it is therefore difficult to avoid the conclusion that, devoid of decoration, the chapel was simply not interesting enough to mention.[20] It appears therefore that William, like a number of his Protestant contemporaries, rejected the imposing pre-Reformation chapel of the type seen at Snape and, in two of his major houses, favoured an assembly held in a secular room.

The next generation was more radical, and Thomas (1542–1623) showed himself at Wimbledon to be in the vanguard of Protestant chapel design. He seems to have belonged to that mainstream, Calvinist-conformist group which was predominant in the Elizabethan Church. He was Cecil's only child by his first wife, and was not entrusted by his father with any responsible posts in government, although he does seem to have spent much time at Burghley, which he was destined to inherit, supervising his father's rebuilding work.

---

[16] According to Sir Michael Hickes (demonstrated by A.G.R. Smith to be the author of the *Anonymous Life* and resident in Cecil House), the members of Cecil's household were expected to attend twice-daily prayers in the chapel. See A.G.R. Smith (ed.), *The 'Anonymous Life' of William Cecil, Lord Burghley* (Lampeter, 1990), pp. 90, 114–15. It may be that the word 'chapel' was used for the space where the prayers took place, although this may have been a room used for prayers, rather than one specifically built as a chapel. We are grateful to Pauline Croft for this reference and for the suggestion that the oratory may have been part of the pre-Reformation fabric of the original house of the parson of St Martin-in-the-Fields that had survived the subsequent rebuildings.

[17] Ricketts, 'Protestant Country House Chapel', p. 30. Two Yorkshire examples cited are Hackness Hall, where prayers were held in the great chamber rather than the chapel and Ledston Hall, where the chapel was converted into a parlour in 1588.

[18] J. Summerson, 'The Building of Theobalds 1564–1585', *Archaeologia* 97 (1959), 107–26. Plate XXXIII shows the position of the chapel on the plan.

[19] *The Diary of Baron Waldstein*, ed. G.W. Groos (London, 1981), pp. 81–7.

[20] Ricketts, 'Protestant Country House Chapel', p. 194. See above Nuechterlein, pp. 76–8.

When in London, he may have used his father's house, but in the 1570s he began to amass a suburban estate in Wimbledon, about eight miles south-west of central London, and about 1585 began to build a substantial and innovative house there, with elaborate terraced gardens and a large park. This was a U-plan house, with a single-storey hall with the great chamber above; one wing contained the state apartments and long gallery, the other the service and family rooms. There were two staircases, identical on the plan, giving access to these upper rooms.[21]

Here, in about 1588, Thomas created one of the first of the new assembly chapels that began to appear in private houses in the 1580s. These were chapels designed to create a practical space for specifically Protestant household worship and they represent a complete break with traditional conventions. To understand them it is necessary to be aware of two key changes to household worship instituted by Protestants. First (as the *Northumberland Household Book* describes), in pre-Reformation houses it was usual to hold four or five services a day, some of which were designed for members of the household unable to attend at other times because of their duties.[22] In other words, the everyday life of the house did not come to a halt when a service was held, and because the normal business of the house continued, the idea of a sacred, and often consecrated, space set apart in a secluded area for worship was important. This contrasted with the Protestant custom of holding two services a day, which everyone, without exception, was required to attend. Thus all normal duties were suspended when the household was at prayer. Secondly, the provision of a specifically sacred space was not central to

---

[21] There are no surviving building accounts or early inventories to tell us more about this house and its chapel at this date. The house was sold by Thomas Cecil's granddaughters in 1639 and was demolished *c.*1717. The house is discussed by Caroline Knight, 'The Cecils at Wimbledon', in P. Croft (ed.), *Patronage, Culture & Power: the Early Cecils 1558–1612* (London, 2002), pp. 47–66.

[22] *The Regulations and Establishment of the Household of Henry Algernon Percy, the Fifth Earl of Northumberland at his Castles of Wressle and Leckonfield in Yorkshire Begun Anno Domini MDXII* (London, 1905), pp. 311–13, 354–63.

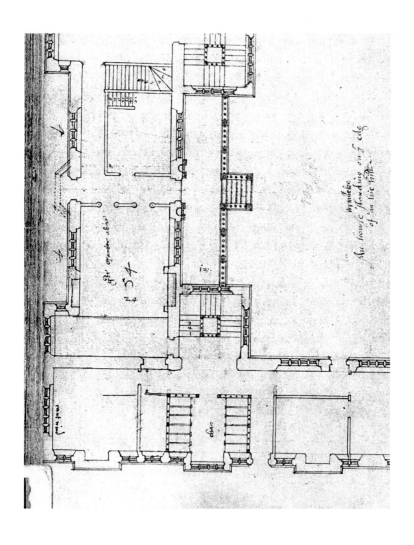

Figure 6.1 Detail from the Plan of the Ground Floor of Wimbledon House by John Thorpe. T 113. By Courtesy of the Trustees of Sir John Soane's Museum.

Protestant ideas about worship (indeed, was specifically challenged by some) and no approved service of consecration existed during Elizabeth's reign.

Taken together, these two facts meant that there was no need for a space set apart for worship, and the pre-Reformation chapel was therefore no longer a practical way of serving the spiritual needs of a modern Protestant household. The assembly chapel was devised as an alternative, based on the idea that, although the chapel would need to hold the entire household, its space did not need to be clearly defined and, in particular, ordinary domestic spaces could be co-opted. The importance and originality of this development cannot be overstated. At a time when parish churches were adapting space designed for Catholic worship, private chapels were responding to the specific needs of Protestant worship by creating an entirely new chapel type.[23]

Wimbledon is a very clear example of this new approach. Thorpe's plan shows that there is a core chapel area fitted with pews. The window relates both to the main axis and to the arrangement of seating, producing an integrated space.[24] But this central space is contained only by open-work screens, rather than walls, and is surrounded by a series of peripheral chapel spaces which also have a domestic function. Most obvious is the way the west screen, with its wide central opening, allows the chapel space to flow almost uninterrupted into the area of the great stair. A room to the south of the core space has its northern wall replaced with a screen, and to the north a passageway leading from the garden door to the great stair is also only separated from the chapel by an open screen. These are not sacred spaces, but they can be co-opted for religious assemblies only because no one would be using them while a service was taking place. This is a highly rational and practical solution. The Protestant assembly chapel had no need of sacred space, since consecration was not an issue, and the idea of shared space therefore caused no problem. The core chapel area was available for private prayer, but the dual-function areas surrounding it meant that the space needed for the chapel proper could be far smaller than would be possible if it had to house the entire household.

At the same time that Thomas was building Wimbledon, he was also carrying out a major reconstruction of Snape Castle. As it now stands, the bulk of the house is Elizabethan, dwarfing Nevill's chapel and testifying to the ambitious scale of Thomas's work. It may seem ironic that although Thomas was an enthusiastic seeker-out of recusants, even writing from the north to his half-brother Robert in

[23] Ricketts, 'Protestant Country House Chapel', p. 81.
[24] Ibid., p. 49.

Figure 6.2 Exterior of Snape Castle, North Yorkshire, from the South East; photo copyright: Caroline Knight.

London that 'Since my coming I have filled a little study with copes and Massbooks',[25] he continued to use a building that had been a Catholic chapel, but this was paralleled in English parishes during this period, where everything of a Catholic nature was stripped from the interior, leaving the shell intact for Protestant worship. (We must presume that he or the Nevills had adapted the interior for Protestant worship.)

To this day, in its fenestration the exterior retains the pre-Reformation character that made it so different from the chapel at Wimbledon, which had no architectural features to distinguish it from other parts of the house. Possibly Thomas never intended to spend much time in Yorkshire – his position as President of the Council of the North was much later – and therefore he could live with a chapel which in its outward form did not entirely match his religious ideas. But a more likely explanation is that Thomas, ever conscious of his *arriviste* position in society, wished to create a house that spoke of ancient lineage, even if it was that of his wife's family rather than his own. The chapel of the Nevills, one of the most ancient and powerful families of the north, would go far towards creating exactly the right atmosphere of tradition and antiquity. As such, the decision to keep the medieval chapel and to build the battlemented south range could well be seen as a statement of Thomas's worldly aspirations rather than of his spiritual concerns.

Thomas's half-brother, Robert (1563–1612), was involved in many building projects in the early seventeenth century: Salisbury House and the New Exchange in the Strand, Cranborne Manor, Dorset, and Hatfield House, Hertfordshire. But one of the least known is his involvement with a house in Chelsea, though whether he considered living there, or was looking on it as a speculation, is unclear.

The Great House, Chelsea, later known as Beaufort House, had been built by Sir Thomas More in the 1520s. It was a long brick house set back from the Thames, with large gardens on all four sides. By the late sixteenth century it belonged to the Dacre family and the widowed Lady Dacre bequeathed it to William Cecil, with a remainder to Robert. She died in 1595, and William appears to have passed the house on to Robert in 1597. Its interest lies in the six plans connected with it that survive in the Hatfield archives, and in particular, in the wide range of chapel types that are depicted. One plan, a survey of the ground floor, shows an assembly type chapel to the east of the stairwell.[26] This was there

---

[25] Cited in R. Milward, *Tudor Wimbledon* (London, 1972), p. 99.
[26] Hatfield House, Cecil MSS, CPM II.7.

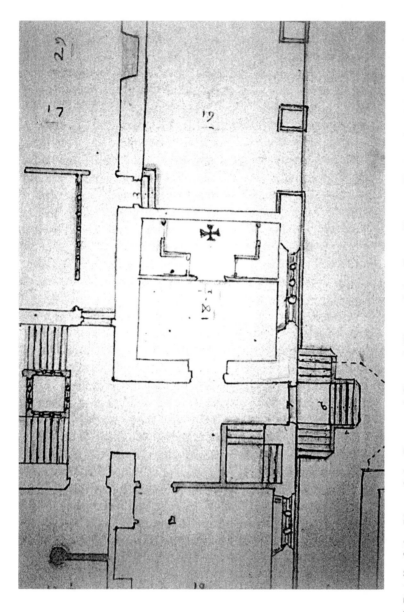

Figure 6.3 Detail of the Plan of the Proposed Ground Floor of the Great House, Chelsea by John Symonds, c.1595. Hatfield House, Cecil MSS, CPM II.10; copyright: the Marquess of Salisbury.

when the Dacres owned the house; the other five plans (dated *c.*1595) reflect Cecil's ideas for enlarging and improving the house. All these other plans place the chapel elsewhere in the house.[27]

Two plans by John Symonds show ideas for a stacked chapel, that is, a ground-floor chapel with a room of the same size above it, in the east range.[28] This is positioned well away from the service rooms in the west range, but is close to the high end of the hall, on the main circulation route leading to what is probably a parlour and to the famous terrace walk. This appears to be a Protestant adaptation of a standard pre-Reformation form.[29] A Catholic chapel would be expected to focus on the altar, so the upper spaces would be in the western half of the chapel giving a view of the east end. Here, in contrast, the upper space is the same size as the lower chapel and has a simple railed opening immediately over the centre of the east end. This would not provide a satisfactory view of the communion table below and its purpose was almost certainly to allow those in the upper room to hear the service. In a sense this is a Protestant adaptation of the Catholic squint – as it were an 'aural squint'.

The other three surviving designs for Chelsea show alterations that would have enlarged the house in various ways, but it is the extraordinary variations in chapel design that are of interest here. All by William Spicer, they suggest variations that would appeal more to a high-church patron. One ground-floor plan exists, showing a traditional chapel that followed a standard pre-Reformation layout.[30] It is set apart from the main circulation routes, and the large ante-chapel, which can be entered either from the house or the forecourt, is divided from the main body of the chapel by a screen. Some members of the household might have stood in this ante-chapel during prayers.

Two first-floor plans for upper chapels or closets in this same position survive and the differences between them are instructive. The first shows a traditional

[27] These plans are illustrated in *Survey of London* (45 vols, London, 1900–), IV, *Parish of Chelsea, Part II*, pp. 18–27.

[28] Hatfield House, Cecil MSS, CPM II.9 (ground floor) and CPM II.10 (first floor).

[29] The ground-floor arrangement of this chapel space seems most unusual. Its walls are extremely thick, with none of the transparency one might expect in an assembly chapel. There is only one point of access to a relatively small space, and there seems to be no obvious explanation for the arrangement of partitions around the communion table. It is not at all clear how this space was supposed to function.

[30] Hatfield House, Cecil MSS, CPM II.16. This plan is endorsed, 'Mr Spicers platt w^{th}out a gallery/Allowed', but there is nothing to suggest that it was ever built.

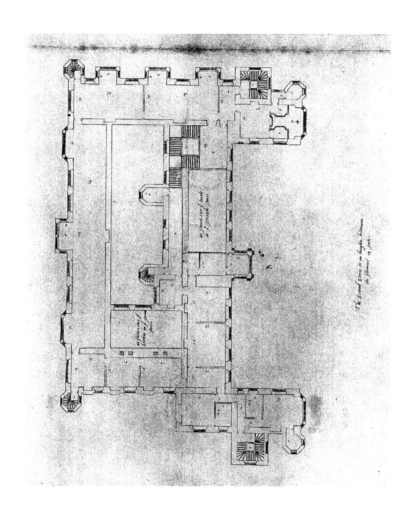

Figure 6.4 Plan of the Proposed First Floor of the Great House, Chelsea, by William Spicer, c.1595. Hatfield House, Cecil MSS, CPM II.6; copyright: the Marquess of Salisbury.

arrangement of two bay openings directly facing the (liturgical) east end, which is reminiscent of the arrangement of the Holyday closets in Henry VIII's chapel at Hampton Court.[31]

The second version proposed a grander upper chapel, with a central bay with an opening which gives a good view of the communion table.[32] This is flanked by two doors, both giving access to closets with windows facing each other rather than the east end. It is significant that although there would be no problem about hearing the chaplain, the two closets would barely have had a view of the communion table. While the first option is uncomplicatedly high-church, with its emphasis on the 'altar',[33] the second design appears to provide two types of space, for while the main part of the upper chapel focuses on the 'altar', the two closets beyond it appear to offer space with a very restricted view.

No similar post-Reformation chapels are known and the purpose of these spaces remains unclear. However, the use of traditional ideas in the positioning and design of some of these chapels point to a high-church patron, and it is significant that the design is unlikely to be later than 1597. Could this be evidence of a relatively early move towards high-church ideas and also of a sharp difference between Robert's and Thomas's ideas about chapel design? Pauline Croft has shown that, as he grew older, Robert's views became more high-church, and it is a tempting interpretation, although it can remain only a possibility.[34] The house was sold to Henry Clinton, earl of Lincoln, in 1599, who is unlikely to have carried out any of Cecil's schemes.[35]

Robert was only briefly the owner of the Great House, and it appears that he never lived there, but evidence survives for the chapels in two other houses of his. In 1599 he bought Worcester House in the Strand, on the desirable south side of the street, with its gardens going down to the Thames. He immediately rebuilt it as Salisbury House with Simon Basil, the Surveyor of the King's Works, as his architect. Was it this purchase which persuaded him to sell the Great House in Chelsea?

---

[31] Hatfield House, Cecil MSS, CPM II.15. See also P.E. McCullough, *Sermons at Court. Politics and Religion in Elizabethan and Jacobean Preaching* (Cambridge, 1998), pp. 11–49.

[32] Hatfield House, Cecil MSS, CPM II.6.

[33] In his will, Robert Cecil uses the words 'holy table' for the altar; it was only in the 1620s and 1630s that the word 'altar' came back into use. We are grateful to Pauline Croft for pointing out this distinction.

[34] P. Croft, 'The Religion of Robert Cecil', *Historical Journal* 34 (1991), 773–96.

[35] Since the plans are still in the Hatfield archives it is improbable that they were used by Clinton. The John Thorpe plan, T63 and T64 in the Sloane Museum, probably records Clinton's alterations to the house, showing a chapel in the middle of the east range. The house was demolished in 1739–40 by Sir Hans Sloane.

Although the house no longer survives, inventories show that there was a well-furnished chapel. In the upper chapel or closet, the crimson hangings were embroidered with 'pillars and my Lordes armes', and there were matching window cloths and crimson damask coverings for the furniture. No hangings were listed for the lower chapel. According to an inventory of 1640 the pulpit was sited in the upper chapel, but this was most unusual.[36] Usually the upper chapel or gallery was for members of the family and their guests.

In addition, there was also a 'room over the Chapel where my Lord goeth to prayers', perhaps an oratory with a view into the chapel below.[37] Salisbury House also provides evidence for the existence of another subsidiary room-type associated with the chapel. Inventories list a 'praier house', a room containing only curtains and curtain rods. This would appear to be a further room set aside for religious purposes, in the continuing development of subsidiary spaces suitable for a Protestant patron.[38] Perhaps similar functions were intended for the otherwise unexplained rooms adjacent to the chapel on some of the plans of the Great House, Chelsea; for example, the octagonal space adjacent to the chapel on CPM II.6 (see Figure 6.4), or the long, thin room alongside the chapel on CPM II.15.

Fortunately the final example, Hatfield, survives, and provides fascinating evidence of Robert's views on the design of chapels. His father's house at Theobalds had always been intended as Robert's inheritance, but was so favoured by James I that in 1607 Robert offered it to the King, and was given lands at Hatfield in exchange. The old royal palace there was largely demolished, and a new house built nearby on a hilltop site, from 1609 to 1612. The design was at least partly Robert's, with the assistance of Robert Lyminge as master-carpenter and on-site supervisor.[39]

At Hatfield there is no doubt that the chapel was created for a high-church patron, and although it is its decoration that most obviously confirms this, in its plan it marks a return to the pre-Reformation ideas that were first suggested in the Chelsea designs. The chapel is sited across the west range, interrupting the sequence of state apartments in that range. Externally, the chapel breaks the symmetry of the original main entrance front. The east end projects slightly

[36] Ricketts, 'Protestant Country House Chapel', pp. 167, 217.
[37] Cited by L. Stone, 'The Building of Hatfield House', *Archaeological Journal* 112 (1965), 122.
[38] Ricketts, 'Protestant Country House Chapel', p. 89; Hatfield House, Cecil MSS, Box C/8.
[39] For details of the design and building of Hatfield, see C. Gapper, J. Newman and A. Ricketts, 'Hatfield: a House for a Lord Treasurer', in Croft (ed.), *Patronage, Culture & Power*, pp. 67–98. The Appendix to this chapter contains a detailed reconstruction of the interiors of the chapel and its antechamber and Colour Plate IX illustrates the east end of the chapel.

forward from the main façade of the west range, a feature which is not repeated on the east range, and the chapel is easily identifiable by its imposing east window which, spanning two storeys, is the largest window on the façade. The fact that this is a cross-range chapel facilitates the emphasis on the east window, and this is further enhanced by the use of a different fenestration pattern. Instead of variations on the rectangular mullion and transom type, the lights of the chapel window are arched, and this distinctive form is repeated on the west window of the lower chapel. However, the west window which lights the upper chapel reverts to the standard domestic form, perhaps because the area which it lit was likely to have been separated from the main body of the chapel, forming an independent passageway linking the Queen's withdrawing chamber to her bedchamber. What Hatfield demonstrates is that differentiated windows were carefully controlled, and that only windows directly connected with the chapel, and perhaps intended to contain painted glass, were given this treatment.[40]

The great east window still contains painted glass with scenes from the Old Testament; accounts show that it was designed and made by two foreign craftsmen, Louis Dauphin and Martin van Bentheim, and one Englishman, Richard Butler. Although parts have been damaged, enough survives to give an idea of its quality and richness of colour. The west window, now filled with plain glass, was also supplied with painted glass by the same group of craftsmen. Although glass was considered the least dangerous medium from the point of view of idolatrous imagery, Hatfield's window avoided the issue by reviving the medieval typological approach, where Old Testament scenes (or ante-types) are linked to New Testament types by means of inscriptions.[41]

[40] Ricketts, 'Protestant Country House Chapel', p. 107.

[41] Ibid., pp. 207–8. Today the order in which the scenes are arranged is puzzling, but since the glass has been removed from the window at least once, this may be due to a later re-arrangement.

Figure 6.5 Interior of the Chapel at Hatfield House, Hertfordshire, looking North East. Photo copyright: the Marquess of Salisbury.

Internally, a large upper chapel with long side galleries looked down onto a communion table which was raised on a platform approached by two steps.[42] This upper chapel or closet, unusually, had a fireplace, and was richly decorated with textiles, some being embroidered pictures of prophets and patriarchs, framed and hung on the walls.

The side walls of the lower chapel were given an architectural treatment with *trompe l'oeil* Ionic pilasters which were painted in blue and gilded. Numerous other entries in the building accounts refer to the paintwork (usually blue) and gilding in the chapel, and perhaps the best surviving example of this type of small-scale repetitive decoration is the frieze which runs round the chapel at two levels. Largely executed in blue and gold, its design incorporates winged cherub heads, flaming urns (which can often be used to symbolize piety), and bibles/books, perhaps pointing to the importance of the word, and thus conveying a simple Protestant message.[43]

There was also a great deal of painted decoration, including a painting on the ceiling (and probably also on the ante-chapel ceiling beneath the upper chapel). The subject(s) are not recorded and the main ceiling, whitewashed in 1644, was finally destroyed by fire in the nineteenth century. Two of the most important survivals are the six prophets painted on the reveals of the east window, and the plaster roundels set into the upper galleries which depict Christ and various apostles and saints. At least four roundels must have been added to the series when the upper chapel was shortened in the late eighteenth century, thereby extending the side galleries. Thus it is not certain that the image of Christ (the third of four images set below the west gallery) was part of the original scheme, although the reference in the accounts to Rowland Bucket painting 'Christ and the apostles' must make it likely.

The surviving fixed decoration shows a mix of Old Testament and New Testament figures which became (with minor variations) one of the standard features of seventeenth-century schemes. If this had been the total extent of the decoration at Hatfield, it would have appeared as a carefully thought-out attempt to revive biblical imagery (in both glass and paint) which managed to avoid direct reference to the most contentious subjects. However, the scheme also includes a series of six paintings of scenes from the Life of Christ which are documented as being in the chapel in 1611. The brightly coloured canvases are large, of various sizes, and by at least two hands. There was no attempt to produce a rational scheme since, despite the fact they were all framed in the same way, the pictures were of different heights and lengths, and must have

---

[42] Ibid., p. 163. This was clearly an afterthought, carried out with some difficulty in 1611, when the chapel was nearing completion.
[43] Ibid., pp. 216–17.

formed an irregular, but almost continuous, band of very strident colour round the main body of the chapel. In addition, on 9 March 1611/12, Bucket the painter was paid £23 for 'paintinge 2 picktures upon cloth ... for the Chappell at Hatfield and done by my lords appointment'. These were the Annunciation and the Angels appearing to the Shepherds, both of which are still at Hatfield.

What is puzzling about all these pictures is that they appear to upset an otherwise carefully considered scheme. The absence of any scenes from Christ's life after the Agony in the Garden perhaps reflects a desire to avoid contentious subjects, but it is surprising that, only a year or so after the installation of the typological window, apparently designed to refer obliquely to 'difficult' New Testament scenes through the use of texts, such vivid and obvious depictions of subjects such as the Annunciation were used in, and indeed specifically commissioned for, the chapel. It is also the case that the scenes from the Life of Christ do not relate to the texts in the east window, since some of the scenes illustrate the New Testament texts, whilst others do not. Although it is possible that the scheme may appear more confused than it actually was because elements are now missing, this can only be a partial reason. A more convincing explanation is likely to be that it is simply mistaken to assume that schemes would be co-ordinated across different media. There is no evidence that this was done in pre-Reformation examples and no evidence has come to light of any early seventeenth-century decorative schemes that demonstrate sustained cross-media co-ordination. Indeed, Hatfield is increasingly being recognized as revolutionary in the way that some room schemes co-ordinated the colour of the woodwork with the colour of the textiles. Although it is certainly the case that in the chapel the glass and the painted wall decoration work well together, one should not expect to find a fully co-ordinated cross-media scheme at this date. However, it does appear that there was a change of plan during the creation of the scheme, perhaps caused by a new and more relaxed attitude to the use of certain images.[44]

The upper chapel at Hatfield was decorated with black hangings, hung in orange baize cases, which were embroidered with the prophets and patriarchs in coloured satins. A similar hanging, of David, was placed over the fireplace. This matches the evidence from other inventories, often showing that the upper chapel at this period had particularly rich hangings, whilst in the lower chapel panelling or plainer textiles were used. The rich effect of the upper chapel was further enhanced by the way in which the furniture was upholstered to match the hangings. At Hatfield, black cloth was embroidered with 'gold and orange tawnie'. This emphasis on the west end of the chapel is one of the few areas of

---

[44] Ibid., pp. 211–12.

continuity with the Elizabethan period, but it is only in the seventeenth century that textiles were used both to emphasize the communion table and the pulpit in the chapel proper, and to balance this concentration of colour at the west end. At Hatfield (at least from 1621), a red curtain hung behind the communion table, and the table itself was covered with a black velvet cloth embroidered with vine leaves. The pulpit and reading desk had similar black cloths embroidered with silver and gold thread.

As at Salisbury House, the inventories list a subsidiary room that seems to have had some religious function. The ante-chamber to the chapel, which could be arranged as a bedchamber if the state rooms beyond were in use, did not otherwise contain a bed. Joiners' work for this room in 1610 included 'plain seeling sipher and square with seat round about' and this suggests that the room, adjacent to the chapel on its south side, could have served as an assembly room to be used for prayers and readings.[45]

Again a Cecil was in the vanguard of chapel design, but what was created at Hatfield was very different from Thomas's assembly chapel at Wimbledon. Robert's was a chapel designed to be consecrated (as it was in 1610–11), and therefore used for communion, and everything about it marks a return to ideas that had last been seen in the early sixteenth century. Because of its sacred nature, an assembly design was clearly inappropriate, and Robert's scheme at Hatfield demonstrates how a high-church Protestant chapel could adopt pre-Reformation ideas to signal the arrival of a new type of Protestant space: one which emphasized the significance of the Passion and the celebration of the sacraments as well as preaching and prayer. Like Snape, the Hatfield chapel could be clearly identified, both externally and internally, as a sacred space, and it is one of the first chapels of the seventeenth century to return to pre-Reformation ideas about chapel design.

The chapels of the three Cecil patrons clearly demonstrate the way in which domestic chapel design evolved during a period of about sixty years, reflecting the evolution taking place in the Church of England itself. During a period which witnessed the church in a state of flux as the Elizabethan settlement was worked out, patrons were at liberty to experiment with the form of the Protestant chapel in their own houses, and the attitude to the domestic chapel depended very largely on the individual viewpoint of the patron. At Burghley, William Cecil saw the provision of a grand state apartment as a higher priority than a chapel. At Wimbledon, where he was building from scratch, his first son Thomas adopted that practical Protestant model, the assembly chapel, although at Snape he retained at least the shell of the earlier Catholic chapel. Finally (and

---

[45] Ibid., p. 89.

possibly after some experimentation in connection with Great House, Chelsea), Robert created an ostentatiously high-church space where the whole family of the Church – the prophets, patriarchs and disciples – gathered round the focal point of the communion table, to celebrate Christ's sacrifice with the members of the Cecil family and household.

PART 2

Chapter 7

A Northern Jerusalem:
Transforming the Spatial Geography
of the Convent of Wienhausen

June L. Mecham

'O special soul, when you shall determine to walk in the footsteps of Christ … take care to follow in his footsteps in spirit and body to visit devotedly *the actual locations* where the spiritual suffering occurred'.[1] So began a fifteenth-century nun's journey through the monastic complex of the Cistercian community at Wienhausen in Lower Saxony.[2] The observance of the Stations of the Cross, recorded in two late fifteenth-century manuscripts produced within the convent, reveals how this community of Cistercian nuns combined spiritual imagination and imitative action to transcend time, space, and geography to unite with the divine. Increasingly restricted both spatially and ideologically, the fifteenth-century nuns of Wienhausen used the Stations of the Cross to define the holy and their relationship to it, both in terms of an individual, mystical union with Christ, as well as a communal, sororal membership among the ranks of the earthly and heavenly Jerusalem. Manipulating communal space and artwork to recreate the *via crucis* within their convent, the nuns of Wienhausen transformed a chilly, northern cloister into the historical Jerusalem of Christ's Passion, thereby asserting both the sacral nature of their monastery and their status as privileged inhabitants of this space.

Because the Stations of the Cross united various spiritual trends, this devotion provides unique insight into the pious practices and spiritual concerns of Europeans on the eve of the Protestant Reformation. The Stations combined the traditional mnemonic practices of monastic *meditatio* with emphasis on a human Christ and his suffering, yet the observance demanded the visual and physical expression of piety through action and movement. Additionally, the Stations of the

---

[1] Wienhausen, Klosterarchiv (hereafter KlA), MS 86, f. 1 [emphasis added].
[2] The convent was founded *c*.1228 by Duchess Agnes of Landsberg.

Cross engaged medieval ideas about the creation and use of sacred space, art, and architecture.[3]

While devotion to the Stations of the Cross shared these latter features with the liturgical rituals of the church, they emerged in particularly sharp relief in the confined spaces of female monastic enclosure.[4] With its focus on the human frailty and suffering of Christ, the Stations of the Cross emphasized spiritual trends that had particular resonance for religious women.[5] At the same time, fifteenth-century reforming concerns about the restriction of sacred space, and female claustration in particular, gave the Stations heightened significance for religious women. For the nuns of Wienhausen, performing the Stations of the Cross evoked a series of dichotomies. It promised an unmediated, personal experience of the divine, re-lived through Jesus' suffering. However, the accessibility of such a mystical union was achieved through the regulation, restriction, and re-negotiation of the sacred space of the monastery. In a similar manner, the practice elevated a visual experience through the use of religious artwork and demonstrable expressions of piety and compassion. Yet, it was through such visual acts of piety that the nuns hoped to achieve the invisible: unity with Christ and a place within the heavenly Jerusalem. The nuns' observance of the Stations of the Cross thus magnified the issues and concerns of this devotional practice, demonstrating how piety and space interacted within a restricted framework.

Negotiating Space: Access and Enclosure

Throughout the Middle Ages, the architectural control of space played an important role in dividing the sacred from the profane and directing an individual's thoughts toward the eschatological. Nowhere was this more evident than within the confines of the monastic enclosure. Historians of medieval monasticism have placed great emphasis on the restrictive and negative aspects of claustration,

---

[3] Numerous German cities established civic Stations of the Cross in the later fifteenth century. In such urban settings, the demarcation of sacred space through the creation of religious art and architectural features played a particularly important role. E. Kramer, *Kreuzweg und Kalvarienberg: Historische und Baugeschichtliche Untersuchung* (Kehl, 1957), pp. 15–20, 99–129.

[4] See Bossuyt, pp. 187–206 below.

[5] C. Walker Bynum, '"… And Woman His Humanity": Female Imagery in the Religious Writing of the Later Middle Ages', in her *Fragmentation and Redemption: Essays on Gender and the Human Body in Medieval Religion* (New York, 1992), pp. 171–5; C.Walker Bynum, *Holy Feast and Holy Fast: the Religious Significance of Food to Medieval Women* (Berkeley, 1987).

particularly with regard to female communities.[6] However, claustration did not function merely to discipline; it also reinforced the unique and sacral nature of the convent. Stricter enclosure emphasized the interior cloister as a liminal space where the earthly and the heavenly might combine and coexist. Indeed, monks and nuns manipulated the spatial geography of their monasteries to suit their spiritual needs.[7]

The restriction of access to certain locations played an important role in establishing sacred space. Within a monastic setting, systems of outer courts, open to the secular community, and inner cloister courts, accessible only to the religious inhabitants of the house, controlled the level of contact between people of different social or religious status as well as members of the opposite sex.[8] Such architectural features delineated spatial boundaries and outlined a hierarchy of space. Restrictive levels of access combined with structural elements to consolidate the sacred in certain locations: a chapel within an inner cloister, an altar behind a rood screen. Those sites with the most restricted access often signified the most sacred locations, where only a select few might approach union with the divine.

Issues of spatial segregation had particular importance for religious women. Not only were women purposefully distanced from certain sacred locations, such as altars or particular shrines and monasteries,[9] but even consecrated religious women faced greater enclosure from physical as well as ideological barriers.[10] Caesarius of Arles' rule for nuns, written in the sixth century, already prescribed strict claustration for female communities.[11] In the twelfth century the resurgence

---

[6] Gilchrist, *Gender*; C.A. Bruzelius, 'Hearing is Believing: Clarissan Architecture, *ca*.1213–1340', *Gesta* 31 (1992), 83–91; L.N. Simmons, 'The Abbey Church at Fontevraud in the Later Twelfth Century: Anxiety, Authority and Architecture in the Female Spiritual Life', *Gesta* 31 (1992), 99–107; J.F. Hamburger, 'Art, Enclosure and the *Cura Monialium*: Prolegomena in the Guise of a Postscript', *Gesta* 31 (1992), 108–26; J. Tibbetts Schulenburg, 'Strict Active Enclosure and its Effects on the Female Monastic Experience (*c*.500–1100)', in J.A. Nichols and L. Thomas Shank (eds), *Medieval Religious Women I: Distant Echoes* (Kalamazoo, 1984), pp. 51–79.

[7] M. Cassidy Welch, *Monastic Spaces and their Meanings: Thirteenth-Century English Cistercian Monasteries* (Turnhout, 2001).

[8] Welch, *Monastic Spaces and their Meanings*; Gilchrist, *Gender*; B.H. Rosenwein, *Negotiating Space: Power, Restraint, and Privileges of Immunity in Early Medieval Europe* (Ithaca, NY, 1999).

[9] J.Tibbetts Schulenburg, 'Pilgrimage Centers: the Construction of Gendered Spaces and Miracles: Policies of Access and Exclusion, *c*.500–1200', paper presented at the *Defining the Holy* conference.

[10] Gilchrist, *Gender*, pp. 165–6; Bruzelius, 'Hearing is Believing'; Simmons, 'The Abbey Church at Fontevraud'.

[11] Césaire d'Arles, *Oeuvres Monastiques*, ed. A. de Vogüé and J. Courreau (Sources chrétiennes 345, Paris, 1988), p. 206.

of double monasteries re-invigorated concerns about space, discipline, and gender segregation. Indeed, the elaborate regulations and architectural measures taken to prevent any contact between the monks and nuns at Fontevrault bespeak a profound 'proximity anxiety' on the part of the ecclesiastical hierarchy.[12]

The definitive statement regarding such segregation came in 1298 with Pope Boniface VIII's promulgation of the decretal *Periculoso*, which established strict active enclosure for religious women. In the wake of this decree, walls, locked doors, and windows with bars and grates increasingly separated religious women, not only from the external, secular world, but also from the religious advisers who provided them with spiritual care: their priests and confessors. Whether the nuns of Wienhausen felt the effects of *Periculoso* in the years following its publication and reception remains unclear.[13] References to efforts to regulate female monastic enclosure in Lower Saxony did not appear prominently until the mid-fifteenth century, when they emerged as part of the reforming programme led by Johannes Busch.

Medieval visitors regularly included female enclosure as part of their standard repertoire of emendations, and Busch's reforms turned rhetoric into reality in several female houses through architectural changes.[14] However, Busch did not suggest the need for greater claustration at Wienhausen. Indeed, an image of the convent on the north wall of the nuns' choir, painted *c.* 1330, indicates that a wall with a gate and gatehouses had surrounded the monastery since the early fourteenth century (Figure 7.1).

Nevertheless, like many other female monastic communities throughout Europe, the nuns of Wienhausen shared their church with the local parish.[15] In northern Germany, the problem of maintaining proper female enclosure while sharing a church was often resolved by the construction of an upper-level nuns'

---

[12] Simmons, 'The Abbey Church at Fontrevaud'.

[13] The extent to which *Periculoso* was received and enforced varied greatly across Europe. E. Makowski, *Canon Law and Cloistered Women: Periculoso and its Commentators, 1298–1545* (Washington, 1997).

[14] At the neighbouring Benedictine convent of Ebstorf in Lower Saxony, higher walls and a grille in the entrance hall provided material reminders of Busch's visit. C. Borchling, 'Litterarisches und geistiges Leben in Kloster Ebstorf am Ausgange des Mittelalters', *Zeitschrift des Historischen Vereins für Niedersachsen* 56 (1905), 392–3.

[15] M. Oliva, *The Convent and the Community in Late Medieval England: Female Monasteries in the Diocese of Norwich, 1350–1540* (Woodbridge, 1998); J. Hamburger, 'Art, Enclosure, and the Pastoral Care of Nuns', in J. Hamburger (ed.), *The Visual and the Visionary: Art and Female Spirituality in Late Medieval Germany* (New York, 1998), pp.44–57.

Figure 7.1 Nuns' Choir, Wienhausen: Image of the Convent of Wienhausen guarded by Seraphim, First Bay from the East on the North Wall; copyright: Lüneburger Klosterarchive.

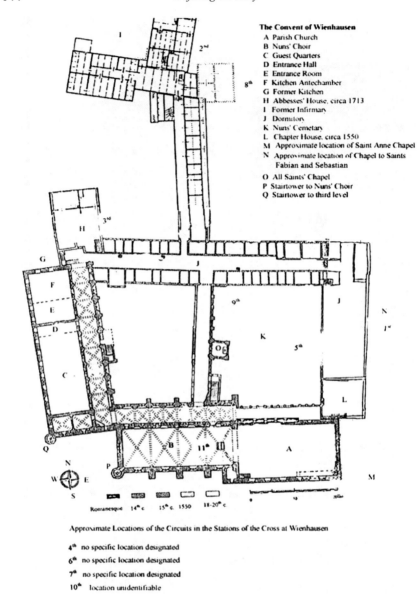

The Convent of Wienhausen

A Parish Church
B Nuns' Choir
C Guest Quarters
D Entrance Hall
E Entrance Room
F Kitchen Antechamber
G Former Kitchen
H Abbesses' House, circa 1713
I Former Infirmary
J Dormitory
K Nuns' Cemetary
L Chapter House, circa 1550
M Approximate location of Saint Anne Chapel
N Approximate location of Chapel to Saints
   Fabian and Sebastian
O All Saints' Chapel
P Stairtower to Nuns' Choir
Q Stairtower to third level

Approximate Locations of the Circuits in the Stations of the Cross at Wienhausen

4th no specific location designated
6th no specific location designated
7th no specific location designated
10th location unidentifiable

Figure 7.2 Plan of the Convent of Wienhausen with the approximate locations of the Stations of Cross indicated; J. Mecham after Coester.

choir.[16] The community of Wienhausen adopted this measure. Yet even within a segregated nuns' choir, religious women faced the problem of sharing this space with the priests and clerics responsible for performing the Mass. The community at Wienhausen resolved this dilemma by erecting two polygonal staircase towers next to the west wing and the nuns' choir, which provided access to storage areas and the second-storey nuns' choir (Figure 7.2).[17] This allowed the priests responsible for holding the Mass and the farm workers responsible for provisioning the nuns to perform their tasks without entering the inner cloister.

Even with such regulations and architectural divisions, the boundaries between the enclosed nuns and the external world always remained to a certain degree permeable. The nuns of Wienhausen and their local parishioners shared access to other sacred spaces besides the church, primarily the chapel dedicated to Saints Fabian and Sebastian and the chapel of Saint Anne. Indeed, when Abbots Herman and Bertram from the communities of Saints Michael and Godehard in Hildesheim visited the convent in 1483, they expressed considerable concern over the nuns' contact with secular society. Citing *Periculoso*, they ordered that enclosure be strictly observed at Wienhausen.[18]

The visitors wished to restrict both physical access to the monastic complex, regulating entrance and egress from the community, as well as visual access to the nuns and the interior cloister. Several statements reflected the visitors' concern that the nuns neither see the external world nor be seen by it. The abbots decreed that the nuns guard against opening the window for the 'incautious sight' of men and women, and to this end they suggested that the nuns have not only a double iron grating to separate them and a window with wooden slats but also a drape between the two. The visitors insisted further that the nuns not open the doors to their choir on account of the 'delight of [its] ornaments' nor permit any secular persons to enter the choir in order to view its crosses. If certain images or crosses were necessary for a procession or any other church rite, they should be gathered at the

---

[16] Hamburger, 'Art, Enclosure, and the Pastoral Care of Nuns', pp. 50–57; E. Coester, *Die einschiffigen Cistercienserinnenkirchen West- und Süddeutschlands von 1200 bis 1350* (Mainz, 1984), pp. 1–4, 12, 89; E. Coester, 'Die Cistercienserinnenkirchen des 12. bis 14. Jahrhunderts', in A. Schneider (ed.), *Die Cistercienser: Geschichte, Geist, Kunst* (Cologne, 1986), pp. 358–65; H.F.H. Zomer, 'The So-Called Women's Gallery in the Medieval Church: an Import from Byzantium', in A. Davids (ed.), *The Empress Theophano: Byzantium and the West* (Cambridge, 1995), pp. 290–306.

[17] The west wing and nuns' choir at Wienhausen were built between 1308 and 1335. Coester, *Die einschiffigen Cistercienserinnenkirchen West- und Süddeutschlands*, p. 392.

[18] Wienhausen, KlA, Urkunde (hereafter Urk.) 554 (7 July 1483).

altar in the lower church.[19] Apparently, the nuns had shown off their choir and its decorations to the view of local parishioners and other secular visitors.

The visitors also increased the level of division between the monastic community and the local parish through the creation of new architectural structures. Along with the barriers they advised for the window, the abbots ordered the construction of a new, extended wall that would enclose the area around the kitchen.[20] The Wienhausen chronicle further mentioned the erection of a wall between the infirmary and dormitory as well as the renovation of a wall surrounding the courtyard and chapel to Saints Fabian and Sebastian, both of which occurred during the abbacy of Wienhausen's post-reform abbess, Susanna Potstock (1470–1501) (see Figure 7.2).[21]

In addition to the construction and extension of walls, the visitors ordered the nuns to fill the entrance door to the chapel of Saints Fabian and Sebastian with stone and fill in its windows up to the level of the nuns' cloister.[22] The visitors thus eliminated both the parishioners' physical and visual access to this chapel, restricting it for the nuns' use alone. Under Abbess Potstock, the Saint Anne chapel was likewise relocated within the cloister and its previous location restored to secular use.[23] Since parishioners probably had had access to this chapel as well, its relocation within the cloister emphasized the increasing division between the nuns and the parish with its concomitant restriction of sacred locations.[24]

The fifteenth-century decrees regarding locked doors, double bolts, walls, grating, and curtains created a more elaborate system of entrance and egress, a multiplication of levels of permeability that hindered both visual and physical access to the convent and separated the nuns more forcefully from the local parish. Such separation and isolation reinforced the sacral nature of the convent, particularly those interior parts of the complex that became more restricted, such as the nuns' choir and chapels. Such restrictions affirmed the interior cloister as a liminal space where the miraculous might become manifest to a select few through ritual and devotion. One such ritual that transcended the divide between the mundane and the sublime was the Stations of the Cross, and it was within the context of this fifteenth-century movement towards greater enclosure that the nuns of Wienhausen began to observe this devotion.

---

[19] Ibid.

[20] Ibid.

[21] H. Appuhn, *Chronik und Totenbuch des Klosters Wienhausen* (Celle, 1986), pp. 28–9.

[22] Wienhausen, KlA, Urk. 554 (7 July 1483).

[23] Appuhn, *Chronik und Totenbuch*, p. 28.

[24] Wienhausen, KlA, Urk. 470 (13 March 1448); Wienhausen, KlA, Urk. 452 (13 December 1433); Appuhn, *Chronik und Totenbuch*, pp. 28, 37–9, 41, XIV.

Walking in the Footsteps of Christ: the Stations of the Cross at Wienhausen

Two manuscripts, dating from the late fifteenth or early sixteenth centuries and catalogued in the Wienhausen convent archive as *Handschriften* 85 and 86, recorded the nuns' observance of the Stations of the Cross. Internal references to the chapel of Saints Fabian and Sebastian, to 'our cemetery' and 'our sepulchre', together with the lack of a professional hand, indicate that the nuns produced these works specifically for use within their convent. The sepulchre mentioned in these texts presumably referred to the one commissioned by Abbess Katharina von Hoya and consecrated in 1448, thereby establishing this date as a *terminus post quem* for the manuscripts' production.

As early examples of the Stations of the Cross, the Wienhausen manuscripts provide little information about the specifics of the nuns' observances. Neither work indicated a particular season, day, or time for performing the Stations, nor did either specify whether such spiritual pilgrimages were undertaken individually or communally. Both manuscripts followed a similar path through the monastic complex, accompanied by a set number of *Paternosters* and indulgences, but each work varied in the associations attached to certain locations. Such variations suggest that the nuns of Wienhausen personalized their observances and very likely performed the ritual individually. Of the two works, MS 85 included the most detailed meditations and prayers, but MS 86 exists in a better state of preservation.

Each manuscript directed its reader on a spiritual journey that involved the imaginative recreation of the *via crucis* and the *loca sancta* of Jerusalem within the convent of Wienhausen. The practice demanded both mental or interior devotion through pious meditation on the events and scenes of the Passion as well as exterior action: movement from one location to another, contemplation of religious artwork, and physical expressions of pious compunction. Performance of the Stations thus dictated that a nun use the material space of the monastic complex, defined and regulated through architectural structures, to construct the imagined spaces of the earthly and heavenly Jerusalem, which were created through a combination of memory, movement, and religious art.[25]

---

[25] I follow Lefebvre in defining space in both material and imaginary terms. I follow de Certeau in emphasizing the mutable nature of space, particularly in terms of the construction of sacred space through movement. H. Lefebvre, *The Production of Space*, trans. D. Nicholson-Smith (Oxford, 1991), pp. 229–91; M. de Certeau, *The Practice of Everyday Life*, trans. S. Rendall (Berkeley, 1984), pp. 97–117; Welch, *Monastic Spaces and their Meanings*, pp. 3–5.

This transformation began in the nuns' choir, located on the upper level of the south wing (Figure 7.2). Here the nun imagined the residence of Pilate, 'where Christ, in the presence of all the people, was unjustly condemned to be yoked to the cross and punished with death'.[26] As the nun descended the steps from the nuns' choir to the ground level, she contemplated 'in [her] mind's eye the house of Pilate, where the impious imposed the cross on Christ and the 28 steps which he was forced to go up and down pitiably with the cross, [and how] while doing [this] he brutally fell down on the steps'.[27] Although the manuscripts differed in the manner of devotion an individual should assume, each directed the nun to mimic Christ's actions by humbling herself as Jesus had been humbled. Thus both directed the nun to either genuflect or walk with bare knees on the steps.[28] This devotional practice may have recalled the *scala sancta* in the Lateran, a series of 28 steps reputedly brought to Rome by Saint Helen from Pilate's palace, which devotees climbed upon their knees.

In both manuscripts, the first circuit began when the nun walked through the door to the cemetery where the chapel of Saints Fabian and Sebastian stood. Continuing to recreate the *loca sancta* of the Passion within the monastic complex, a nun recalled 'that place where Saint Helen ordered two marble stones to be erected, formerly placed over the steps before the residence of Pilate, where Christ, burdened by all the people, was dressed in a purple robe'.[29] Here the text emphasized the recollection of such realistic details as were commonly found in accounts of the 'Secret Passion', in which Christ was dragged by his hair and beard, taunted by youths throwing mud and stones, and ridiculed with indecent songs and shouts.[30] Such details helped a nun to achieve closeness to Christ by experiencing the cathartic emotions of humiliation and suffering.

This second circuit, in which the nun circumnavigated the infirmary, introduced the sympathetic figure of the Virgin as a model for the nun's observance. Wienhausen MS 86 narrated how Mary suffered under the burden of the cross just as Christ did, using mirror imagery to describe the bond between mother and son:

---

[26] Wienhausen, KlA, MS 86, f. 1.

[27] Ibid., f. 1v.

[28] Wienhausen, KlA, MS 85, f. 2v; Wienhausen, KlA, MS 86, f. 2.

[29] Wienhausen, KlA, MS 86, f. 2v.

[30] Ibid., f. 4; Wienhausen, KlA, MS 85, f. 4v. Accounts of the Secret Passion, which gained popularity in the fourteenth and fifteenth centuries throughout the Netherlands and Germany, described sensational, non-Gospel episodes extracted from prophetic statements found in the Old Testament. J.H. Marrow, *Passion Iconography in Northern European Art of the Late Middle Ages and Early Renaissance: a Study of the Transformation of Sacred Metaphor into Descriptive Narrative* (Kortrijk, 1979), pp. 9–25.

Seeing and hearing all this your most just mother cried out and herself fell to the ground when she had seen you weakened through your most bitter Passion. And with compassion [for] your mother herself, weakened by all the blows to [your] body, [you fell] to the ground, still burdened and wearied with the cross.[31]

Identifying with Mary thus became itself a form of identifying and uniting with Christ. Following the same path within the confines of her monastic enclosure, a nun might imagine herself in the role of the Virgin, suffering mentally and physically with Jesus as he progressed from Jerusalem to Calvary. Indeed, the story of Mary walking the *via crucis* in memory of Christ's Passion gained popularity in the later Middle Ages.[32]

Performing the Stations of the Cross asserted the nuns' symbolic status as intimates of Christ by building on the gendered imagery of a sympathetic bond between Mary and Jesus – a bond premised on their common humanity and Mary's intimate care of Jesus' physical body. In this regard, the nuns reflected the affective spirituality of female saints and mystics, who often drew upon the associations between Christ, Christ's humanity, and Mary.[33] The location of this second circuit emphasized the associations between woman, physicality, human suffering, compassion, and female care. The infirmary, a site of Christian compassion towards the diseased and dying, where the nuns cared for their fellow sisters, provided an appropriate context for meditating on Mary and her unique empathy with Jesus' suffering in the Passion.

In the third circuit, a nun proceeded to the *lavatorium*. Here, according to MS 86, she attended 'in spirit that place where Christ, exhausted and weary, fell and lay prostrate on the ground beneath the weight of the cross'.[34] In contrast, MS 85 associated the *lavatorium* with the account of the Veronica.[35] The fourth circuit allowed the nun to choose the location of her meditations; each text merely noted that the Station occurred in 'no particular place'. Thus each nun was free to

---

[31] Wienhausen, KlA, MS 86, f. 4.

[32] Towards the end of the fifteenth century woodcuts of the Stations of the Cross sometimes depicted Mary's sympathetic suffering by portraying her heart being pierced by a sword in every scene. N. Eckmann, *Kleine Geschichte des Kreuzweges: Die Motive und ihre künstlerische Darstellung* (Regensburg, 1968); R. Zittlau, *Heiliggrabkapelle und Kreuzweg: Eine Bauaufgabe in Nürnberg um 1500* (Nuremberg, 1992), p. 80. See also A. Storme, *The Way of the Cross: a Historical Sketch*, trans. K. Dunlop (Jerusalem, 1984), p. 61; H.Thurston, *The Stations of the Cross: an Account of their History and Devotional Purpose* (New York, 1906), p. 3.

[33] For example, Elisabeth of Schönau, *Liber Visionum tercius*, transcribed by G. Jaron Lewis, 'Christus als Frau: Eine Vision Elisabeths von Schönau', *Jahrbuch für Internationale Germanistik* 15 (1983), 74–6.

[34] Wienhausen, KlA, MS 86, f. 4v.

[35] Wienhausen, KlA, MS 85, f. 6.

combine her meditations with locations within the convent that held particular significance to her.[36]

In the fifth circuit, the nun approached the 'sepulchre of the Lord', presumably the sepulchre donated by Abbess Katharina von Hoya in the mid-fifteenth century, which held the community's effigy of Christ. Here MS 86 focused the nun's meditation on the Veronica.[37] By associating the tale of the Veronica with the sepulchre, the author of this manuscript united two scenes of the Passion in which women played an important role. In contrast, MS 85 directed the nun to contemplate how Christ was thrown repeatedly to the ground beneath his cross when she reached the fifth circuit and the sepulchre.[38] The author of this text thus linked the sepulchre with Christ's suffering.

In the sixth and seventh circuits a nun could again choose more personalized sites for her contemplation; the manuscripts merely directed their readers to 'implore divine thanks as may seem appropriate' as well as pray for the deceased.[39] Returning again to the infirmary in the eighth circuit, each manuscript directed that the nun should ponder Christ's journey through the city of Jerusalem and up to Mount Calvary.[40] The ninth circuit ceased to make direct connections between locations within the convent and places in Jerusalem, yet it reaffirmed the association between the infirmary and Christ's suffering. MS 86 instructed the nun to walk to the end of the infirmary and contemplate 'with a devoted mind the first horrible fall of Christ with the cross'. She then approached the steps to the nuns' cemetery, where she pondered the second fall of Christ under the burden of the cross.[41]

In the tenth circuit, while the nun progressed 'before the home on the right side', MS 86 directed her to 'imagine with the eyes of the heart the third most bitter fall of Christ with the cross'.[42] The meditation thus shifted from the contemplation of specific *loca sancta* in Jerusalem to a more abstract consideration of Christ's suffering. Nevertheless, physical location continued to play an

---

[36] Wienhausen, KlA, MS 86, f. 5: 'quarto circuitu qui nulli loco specialiter est deputatus...'; cf. Wienhausen, KlA, MS 85, f. 7.

[37] Wienhausen, KlA, MS 86, f. 5v. The account of Veronica, which did not enter descriptions of the Stations of the Cross until the mid-fifteenth century, provides another indication of the Wienhausen manuscripts' date. Storme, *The Way of the Cross*, pp. 95–7.

[38] Wienhausen, KlA, MS 85, f. 7.

[39] Wienhausen, KlA, MS 86, f. 6r–v; Wienhausen, KlA, MS 85, f. 7v.

[40] Wienhausen, KlA, MS 86, f. 6v; Wienhausen, KlA, MS 85, f. 8.

[41] Wienhausen, KlA, MS 86, ff. 7v–8. This devotion to the falls of Christ also developed in the fifteenth century. M.-J. Picard, 'Croix (chemin de)', in *DSp* II, col. 2602. MS 85 combined the ninth circuit with a meditation on Christ's suffering on Mount Calvary and Christ's 'great misfortune' under the cross: Wienhausen, KlA, MS 85, f. 9.

[42] Wienhausen, KlA, MS 86, f. 8.

important role in enhancing the devotional impact of the exercise. A nun's recollection of Christ falling beneath the weight of the cross when she reached the infirmary and cemetery associated Christ's suffering and weakness with visual reminders of mankind's own bitter suffering (in illness) and weakness (in death).

Concluding the nun's observance of the Stations, the eleventh circuit reasserted the direct association between locations within the convent and the city of Jerusalem. As the nun climbed the steps up to the choir once again and approached its permanent altar, the manuscripts directed her to

> Ascend spiritually Mount Calvary to [the place] where Christ suffered much, yoked to the cross, and bore [it] with great weariness and bitterness – to where he mounted fifty steps with the cross, and then fell down, [and] was forced to climb again – [to the place] where he was finally crucified and died for the salvation of the whole world.[43]

The high altar, the place where the convent's most prized relic of a drop of Christ's blood may have been displayed, thus became Mount Calvary and the physical location of Christ's crucifixion.[44] The observance of the Stations and meditation on the Passion therefore concluded, appropriately enough, in this most sacred location. Having returned to the choir and re-enacted the story of Christ's journey from Pilate's palace to the crucifixion on Mount Calvary, the nun had completed her spiritual *via crucis*.

The texts clearly demonstrate that the nuns' devotions focused on three locations in particular: the nuns' choir, the cemetery, and the infirmary. The emphasis on the nuns' choir may be attributed to the presence of the altar and the community's relic of Christ's blood, as well as the lavish artistic decoration of its walls and vault. Moreover, the choir was where the nuns of Wienhausen heard Mass and performed the liturgical hours; it represented the devotional heart of the community.

The emphasis placed on the cemetery and infirmary likewise reflected the symbolic associations attached to these sites. Both locations evoked Jesus' common bond with humanity through bodily suffering and death – fundamental features of the recollection of the Passion in the Stations of the Cross. Likewise, each symbolized Christ's promises of healing, salvation, resurrection, and eternal life. In fact, cemeteries and hospitals often served as sites for devotion to the Stations of the Cross in urban settings. In the city of Nuremberg, the Stations of the Cross sponsored by Martin Ketzel and created by Adam Krafft between 1490–93

---

[43] Ibid., ff. 8v–9; Wienhausen, KlA, MS 85, ff. 10–10v.

[44] H. Appuhn, 'Der Auferstandene und das heilige Blut zu Wienhausen: über Kult und Kunst im späten Mittelalter', *Niederdeutsches Beiträge zur Kunstgeschichte* 1 (1961), 98; Hamburger, 'Art, Enclosure, and the Pastoral Care of Nuns', p. 97.

culminated in the cemetery of Saint John. This site was located between three hospitals: the leprosarium of Saint John, the Holy Cross hospital for syphilitics, and the hospital of Saint Sebastian, which ministered to victims of the plague.[45] The nuns' emphasis on the infirmary and cemetery thus reflected a general recognition of such sites as sacred and liminal spaces. However, the symbolic associations between woman and corporality would have imbued cemeteries and hospitals with additional meaning for religious women.

The nuns' devotions also illustrate that a hierarchy of sacred space existed within the confines of the monastic complex. Locations associated with the mundane, such as the dormitory, kitchen, or refectory, did not form a part of the nuns' observance of the Stations, unless a nun chose to visit these places when the manuscripts did not prescribe a specific site. In general, however, the nuns' observance of the Stations emphasized the delineation of the sacred from the profane even within the restricted and holy space of the monastery.

Theological Imagination, Memory and Space: Constructing a Northern Jerusalem

By performing the Stations of the Cross, a nun entered the space of theological imagination and transformed the monastic complex into the city of Jerusalem. Instead of the choir, she saw the residence of Pilate; she climbed the 28 steps to his house. In place of the convent cemetery, with its chapel dedicated to Saints Fabian and Sebastian, she envisioned the marble stones erected by Saint Helen.[46] Instead of the infirmary and *lavatorium*, a nun saw the locations where first Mary and then Christ lay prostrate on the ground. She stood before Christ's sepulchre and recalled his humiliation; she ascended Mount Calvary with him.

The fifteenth-century nuns of Wienhausen thus defined the space of the convent by devotional memory and theological imagination as well as material objects. This ability to reconstruct the sacred locations and events of the Passion built upon the skills the nuns learned and practised in their daily meditations. Meditative

---

[45] Zittlau, *Heiliggrabkapelle und Kreuzweg*, pp. 139–40. Similar associations between cemeteries and Stations of the Cross existed in the cities of Fulda and Bamberg. Kramer, *Kreuzweg und Kalvarienberg*, pp. 16, 100.

[46] This may have referred to the churches established by Saint Helen in Bethlehem near the Grotto of the Nativity and on the Mount of the Ascension near Jerusalem. The association between objects of the Passion from Jerusalem and Saint Helen also appeared when the nun mentally climbed the steps of Pilate's palace, supposedly preserved in the *scala sancta* of the Lateran and brought to Rome by Saint Helen. 'Helena II (Kaiserin)', in E. Dassmann *et al.* (eds), *Reallexikon für Antike und Christentum* (Stuttgart, 1987), no. 107, p. 366.

exercises sought to transcend the limits of time, space, and personality to allow an individual to become mystically present at important events in Jesus' life and thereby unite with him.[47] Medieval beliefs about time, particularly the concept of *duratio*, or God's time, further provided the fluidity that allowed a pious believer to experience the miraculous past in the present.[48] Indeed, this conceptual framework functioned more broadly in the liturgical rituals of the medieval church. In particular, processions of the paschal season allowed the laity to experience Christ's Passion re-enacted in the present as well as identify their own community or town with the heavenly Jerusalem.[49] Coupled with the spatial restrictions of their enclosure, the nuns' recreation of the *via crucis* and re-enactment of the events of the Passion elevated the liminal nature of the monastic enclosure, creating spaces within the convent that were fluid, active, and saturated with meaning.[50]

Observing the Stations of the Cross further transformed the space of the cloister into a performance space.[51] In fact, the Stations may have provided an alternative to the performance of Passion plays in places where this had been forbidden.[52] The Stations collapsed the boundaries of time, space, and gender, allowing a nun to become Christ as s/he walked to Calvary and as s/he recalled the events of each location. A nun literally walked 'in the footsteps of Christ', visiting devoutly 'the actual locations where the spiritual suffering occurred'.[53]

Performance of the Stations united action and contemplation, even artistic 'props', with the goal of demonstrating the individual piety of the performer to both a divine and monastic audience. The practice functioned as a living drama: a 'performance of body, imagination, and heart'.[54] Like medieval theatre, which collapsed space and time by constructing the biblical past in the material present, the nuns who performed the Stations of the Cross symbolically recreated Jerusalem and Christ's Passion within the confines of the monastery at Wienhausen.[55]

---

[47] Even the monastic hours were associated with the Passion. Eckmann, *Kleine Geschichte des Kreuzweges*, p. 10; Welch, *Monastic Spaces and their Meanings*, p. 41.

[48] *Duratio* described the extra-temporal time of creation and judgement that allowed for the history of Christian salvation to replay itself in the present moment. D. Dox, 'Theatrical Space, Mutable Space, and the Space of the Imagination: Three Readings of the Croxton Play of the Sacrament', in B.A. Hanawalt and M. Kobialka (eds), *Medieval Practices of Space* (Minneapolis, 2000), pp. 187–8; A.D. Breck, 'John Wyclyf on Time', in W.Yourgrau and A.D. Breck (eds), *Cosmology, History, and Theology* (New York, 1977), p. 217.

[49] See below pp. 191, 194–5, 200–201.

[50] Dox, 'Theatrical Space, Mutable Space', p. 182.

[51] Ibid., pp. 187–8.

[52] Zittlau, *Heiliggrabkapelle und Kreuzweg*, p. 140.

[53] Wienhausen, KlA, MS 86, f. 1.

[54] Picard, 'Croix (chemin de)', col. 2602.

[55] Dox, 'Theatrical Space, Mutable Space', p. 176.

Material objects and artwork reinforced this identification of the inner cloister with both the historical and the heavenly Jerusalem.

Several of the community's most important artworks connected the convent of Wienhausen with the historical and heavenly Jerusalem. The wooden effigy of Christ, or *Grabchristus*, created in the late thirteenth century and used by the nuns in the *depositio* and *elevatio* rites of the Easter liturgy, reinforced the association between the community and the historical Jerusalem of Christ's burial.[56] The wooden sarcophagus, commissioned by Abbess Katharina von Hoya and consecrated in 1448, made this association between Wienhausen and the historical Jerusalem even more explicit. Although the exact placement of the effigy and sarcophagus within the convent remains unclear, both artworks would have transformed their location into the symbolic *locum sanctum* of Jesus' burial. A wooden statue of Christ carrying the cross, also donated by Abbess Katharina von Hoya in the later fifteenth century, likewise helped to transform the convent into the Jerusalem of Christ's Passion.[57] In this case, an almost life-size Christ literally walked the *via crucis* within the convent walls.

Other artwork within Wienhausen associated the historical Jerusalem of Christ's Passion with the heavenly Jerusalem of Christ's resurrection. Thirteenth-century murals on the ceiling of the chapel of All Saints depicted the heavenly Jerusalem with Christ enthroned and surrounded by nine angelic choirs, while paintings on the walls portrayed scenes from the Passion (Figure 7.3a).[58] In a similar fashion, the iconography of the nuns' choir, painted between 1330 and 1335, united the two Jerusalems.

The paintings in the fourteenth-century nuns' choir portrayed Christian history as a unified narrative along the lines of texts such as the *Speculum humanae salvationis*.[59] The south wall depicted the creation of the world, ending with the fall from grace on the western wall, while the north wall portrayed scenes from the Old Testament believed to prophesy Christ's life and death. Painted medallions on the vaults of the ceiling illustrated the life of Christ, beginning with the Annunciation

---

[56] The *depositio* rite symbolized the burial of Christ on Black Friday, while the *elevatio* portrayed Christ's resurrection on Easter Sunday. Hamburger, 'Art, Enclosure and the Pastoral Care of Nuns', p. 83.

[57] Appuhn, *Chronik*, p. 15.

[58] K. Maier, *Kloster Wienhausen* (Celle, 1972), p. 39.

[59] The convent's large embroidery of the *Speculum humanae salvationis* or 'Heilsspiegelteppich' also depicted scenes from the New Testament followed by scenes from the Old Testament. The use of this iconography in two different media suggests that the nuns were familiar with this theological view of the Bible as offering a unified, prophetic narrative. P. Wilhelm, *Kloster Wienhausen: Die Bildteppiche* (Celle, 1979), pp. 34–5; T. Kohwagner-Nikolai, 'Zur Funktion des Heilsspiegelteppichs in Kloster Wienhausen', *Die Diözese Hildesheim in Vergangenheit und Gegenwart* 69 (2001), 105–37.

in the west and culminating with Christ enthroned in the heavenly Jerusalem in the east above the altar.

Conveying the impression of the nuns' choir as a cityscape, a crenellated wall with towers divided the Old Testament images from the swirling vine motifs that led to the vaults of the ceiling. This architectural motif multiplied in a dizzying array of towers, windows, walls, and arches surrounding the figures in the heavenly Jerusalem (Figure 7.3b). Such iconography gave visual form to medieval associations of the church, and specifically the church vault, with the heavenly Jerusalem.[60] Notably, the nuns' choir, where this connection between Wienhausen and the heavenly Jerusalem appeared so prominently, was one of the locations that the visitors of 1483 sought to make most restricted, and thereby emphasized as the most sacred.

Just as the paintings in the chapel of All Saints and nuns' choir visually created a heavenly Jerusalem within the convent of Wienhausen, so too did the community assert its place within this celestial city. Included within the heavenly choirs surrounding the enthroned Christ were the convent's founders, Duke Henry of Saxony and Duchess Agnes of Landsberg, accompanied by the abbesses and provosts of Wienhausen (Figure 7.4a). The monastic complex itself was also placed in close association with the heavenly Jerusalem in the images of the nuns' choir. Painted on the northern wall, almost directly below the image of the founders and abbesses in the heavenly Jerusalem, stood the complex of Wienhausen guarded by two seraphim (see Figure 7.1).

An illuminated miniature of Christ enthroned in the heavenly Jerusalem in the Wienhausen responsorial, created by the nuns around 1480, similarly included the convent and its abbesses within the scene (Figure 7.4b). In the image, crowned female figures surround an enthroned Christ. On each side stand two figures with crosiers, probably representing Wienhausen's abbesses. The angel on the right-hand side of Christ also holds a church, perhaps intended to represent Wienhausen. In this miniature, the nuns of Wienhausen once again placed their community, and even the monastic structure itself, within the heavenly Jerusalem. Such images made it clear that both the inhabitants of Wienhausen and the monastic complex had a place within the celestial city. The heavenly Jerusalem was in Wienhausen and Wienhausen in the heavenly Jerusalem; the two were united both symbolically and visually.

---

[60] B. Kühnel, *From the Earthly to the Heavenly Jerusalem: Representations of the Holy City in Christian Art of the First Millennium* (Rome, 1987), p. 87; M. Parsons Lillich, 'Constructing Utopia', in M. Parsons Lillich (ed.), *Studies in Cistercian Art and Architecture* (2 vols, Kalamazoo, 1982), I, xi–xiv; see below p. 191.

Figure 7.3 (a) Wienhausen, All Saints' Chapel, detail of Christ Enthroned in the Heavenly Jerusalem, late thirteenth century; copyright: Lüneburger Klosterarchive; (b) Wienhausen, Nuns' Choir, detail of the Heavenly Jerusalem, *c.*1330; copyright: Lüneburger Klosterarchive.

Figure 7.4 (a) Wienhausen, Nuns' Choir, detail of the Heavenly Jerusalem depicting the founders of the convent, Duke Henry of Saxony and Duchess Agnes of Landsberg, surrounded by the abbesses and provosts of the convent; copyright: Lüneburger Klosterarchive; (b) Wienhausen, Convent Archive, MS 29, p. 21, *c*.1480; copyright: Lüneburger Klosterarchive.

The nuns of Wienhausen were not unusual in equating their convent with the heavenly Jerusalem. Indeed, Bernard of Clairvaux expressed similar sentiments in the twelfth century when he described the monk as a 'citizen of Jerusalem' and his own monastery of Clairvaux as a 'heavenly Jerusalem on earth'.[61] Nor was the recreation of the *via crucis* in a physical progression through the monastic complex unique to the nuns of Wienhausen. In the fourteenth century, the Dominican mystic Henry Suso (d. 1365) followed devotions similar to the Stations of the Cross. Suso progressed through his monastery each night, re-enacting the episodes of the Passion from the Last Supper to the Crucifixion as he moved from the chapter room to the chapel and through the cloister.[62] The combination of prayers, psalms, and physical prostration at each site demonstrated Suso's individual piety to his community, and specifically to the author of his *Vita*. The practice also facilitated a close, personal relationship between Suso and Christ, just as it did for the nuns of Wienhausen. By mentally transforming certain locations within the monastery into the sites of the Passion, Suso achieved a 'Christ-like feeling of sympathy' and was able to nail 'himself to the cross with his Lord'. Indeed, it became so real that he felt as if he were 'walking at Christ's side'.[63] Suso's union with Christ likewise involved a sympathetic connection with the Virgin Mary. His *Vita* noted another 'mournful way of the cross' that Suso made wherein he envisioned himself accompanying the Virgin Mary from the grave to her home.[64]

Many religious women in the later Middle Ages enacted the Passion through physical movement and pious performance or made spiritual pilgrimages similar to Suso's. Elisabeth of Spalbeek (d. 1306) and Catherine de' Ricci (d. 1590) were both notable for their physical re-enactments of Jesus' suffering.[65] Indeed, a close connection existed between the development of the Stations of the Cross and female devotional practices. According to her *Vita*, Eustochium of Messina (d. 1491) fashioned in her chamber representations of the holy places in Jerusalem, especially those associated with the Passion. To these sites, the devout Eustochium came daily 'as if present at the real places' and 'contemplated tearfully the

---

[61] Bernard of Clairvaux, *S. Bernardi abbatis primi Claræ-Vallensis opera omnia: sex tomis in quadruplici volumine comprehensa*, PL 183, col. 1045, and PL 182, col. 169.

[62] Henry Suso, *The Life of Blessed Henry Suso by Himself*, trans. T.F. Knox (London, 1913), pp. 41–3; Picard, 'Croix (chemin de)', col. 2603; Storme, *The Way of the Cross*, p. 108.

[63] Suso, *The Life of Blessed Henry Suso*, pp. 41–3.

[64] Ibid., p. 44.

[65] Raffaele Cai, 'Catherine de' Ricci', *DSp* II, cols 326–7; S. Rodgers and J.E. Ziegler, 'Elisabeth of Spalbeek's Trance Dance of Faith: a Performance Theory Interpretation from Anthropological and Art Historical Perspectives', in M.A. Suydam and J.E. Ziegler (eds), *Performance and Transformation: New Approaches to Late Medieval Spirituality* (New York, 1999), pp. 299–356.

gentleness of her spouse – each deed and act in succession'.[66] Like Suso and the nuns of Wienhausen, the depth of her meditations allowed her to feel the crucifixion. Saint Rita of Cascia (1382–1457) also progressed around her cell, stopping at certain points that marked the important stages of her mental journey.[67] The lives of Saints Columba of Rieti (d. 1501) and Osanne of Mantua (d. 1505) mentioned similar practices, as did the chronicle of the Cistercian convent of Lorvão near Coimbra dating from 1300 to 1550, which recorded that one of its lay-sisters made such a spiritual pilgrimage around the convent.[68]

Finally, at the turn of the sixteenth century the nuns of Saint Katherine's convent in Augsburg acquired six panel paintings for their chapter hall. The nuns used these images to make a spiritual pilgrimage to the churches in Rome, which in turn represented important locations in Jerusalem and functioned in place of making an actual pilgrimage to the Holy Land.[69] The nuns of Saint Katherine's thus followed the way of the cross through a spiritual pilgrimage that was twice removed from the Holy Land. However, like the nuns of Wienhausen, their devotions associated the sacred spaces of Jerusalem and Rome with the interior space and artwork of their convent, thereby reflecting the layered symbolic associations that allowed medieval Christians to re-enact scenes of the Passion and define the holy in a variety of locations and ways.

While the fifteenth-century nuns of Wienhausen were thus not unique in adopting the Stations of the Cross as a devotional ritual, the surviving textual and visual materials from Wienhausen do reveal how religious women created and manipulated sacred space to suit their spiritual interests and needs. The nuns of Wienhausen combined theological imagination, meditation, imitative action, and pious performance to achieve a personal and emotional identification with the suffering of both Mary and Jesus. By following the way of the cross within the confines of her monastery, a nun could cast herself in the role of the Virgin Mary and thereby unite with Christ. This sympathetic union, premised on a gendered identification with Mary and relationship with Christ, and facilitated by the realistic details drawn from narratives of the Secret Passion, enabled a nun to

---

[66] L. Wadding, *Annales Minorum seu Trium Ordinum, a S. Francisco institutorum* (32 vols, Florence, 1931–3), XIV, p. 580; Picard, 'Croix (chemin de)', col. 2603; Thurston, *The Stations of the Cross*, pp. 12–13.

[67] Storme, *The Way of the Cross*, p. 109.

[68] Picard, 'Croix (chemin de)', col. 2603; Wadding, *Annales Minorum seu Trium Ordinum*, XV; Thurston, *The Stations of the Cross*, pp. 16–19, 93–5.

[69] Eckmann, *Kleine Geschichte des Kreuzweges*, p. 10; Kramer, *Kreuzweg und Kalvarienberg*, p. 16; P.F. Cuneo, 'The Basilica Cycle of Saint Katherine's Convent: Art and Female Community in Early Renaissance Augsburg', *Women's Art Journal* 19 (1998), 21–5.

internalize Christ's Passion as a personal memory and associate it with significant locations within her own convent. The nuns of Wienhausen thus relived Jesus' humiliation and suffering by walking in his footsteps through their own 'northern' Jerusalem.

For the nuns of Wienhausen, the space of the convent – at once restrictive, distancing, and enclosed – created a space that was sacral, liminal, and mutable. The spatial geography of the convent of Wienhausen, with its enclosure and artistic decoration, fostered both a mode of thinking (the space of the imagination) as well as the means of recreating (the space of performance) that allowed the religious women of this community to transform their monastic complex into the earthly and heavenly Jerusalem. Manipulating medieval concepts about time, space, gender, and religious art, each nun fashioned her own spatial and spiritual narrative as she performed the Stations of the Cross. In such a way, the nuns of Wienhausen negotiated the restricted space of their enclosure and defined their privileged relationship with the holy, both as individuals and as a community.

Chapter 8

Using Material Culture to Define Holy Space: the Bromholm Project

Tim Pestell

Medieval monasteries have long enjoyed the image of enclaves 'in places unfrequented and remote'.[1] Yet the need for religious institutions to be self-sufficient and economically viable enforced a dialogue with the secular 'outside' world. Recognition of this paradox has led scholars to take various approaches to understanding the uneasy relationship between the contemplative, spiritual life and the less godly world without. Indeed, in much recent work archaeologists and historians have looked away from the cloister, stressing instead the economic aspect of monasteries and the way in which many institutions, in particular Cistercian houses, were big businesses concentrating economic functions in substantial precincts.[2] Perhaps nowhere was the tension with the laity more acute

[1] P. Matarasso (ed.), *The Cistercian World: Monastic Writings of the Twelfth Century* (Harmondsworth, 1993), p. 7. The phrase, from §15 of the *Exordium Parvum* of Stephen Harding, written *c.*1120, has been particularly applied to the Cistercians, although in following St Benedict's Rule it stands for monastic ideals more generally. For reassessments of the isolated nature of monastic houses, see N.J. Menuge, 'The Foundation Myth: Yorkshire Monasteries and the Landscape Agenda', *Landscapes* 1 (2000), 22–37; T. Pestell, *Landscapes of Monastic Foundation* (Woodbridge, 2004). I should like to thank Sarah Hamilton and Andrew Spicer for inviting me to contribute to this volume and for their patience as unforeseen circumstances led to a delay in the final submission of this chapter. My principal debt is to Phil Emery, with whom I have co-directed work at Bromholm since 1997; the results outlined here are as much his work as mine, and I am grateful for his comments on an earlier draft of this paper. The Bromholm Project has been carried out by a dedicated team who have stuck to their task over six years in both fair and (often) foul Norfolk weather: Wendy Brinded, Andy Carter, Tom Dunn, Tim English, Geoff Featherstone, Mick Nudd, Barrie Sharrock, the late Allan Taylor, and his son Peter. We also owe a great debt to the landowners, the late Mr Edward Deane and Mr Jonathan Deane, who have supported our work and donated all the finds made to Norwich Castle Museum (accession numbers 2001.224 and 2003.184).
[2] Glyn Coppack has observed that approximately two-thirds of British Cistercian abbeys have precincts averaging at 60 acres (24ha) compared to the average precinct size of 30

than in those monasteries that were destinations of pilgrimage. Such institutions not only encouraged the veneration of their relics, which brought them prestige and wealth, but also necessitated the negotiation of sacred space between members of a religious community and its visitors. This paper attempts to examine how a secular presence was accommodated in one particular religious house, Bromholm Priory, using the evidence of material culture rather than the idealized views of monastic authors.

Hitherto, studies of spatial dynamics have tended to focus upon or be structured by architectural layout. For instance, access analysis is frequently applied to the arrangement of buildings to develop a picture of ingress or visitor flow.[3] However, such methodologies rely upon the maintained structural integrity of the buildings being examined, within which fixtures and fittings like fencing or gates could play a fundamentally important role in the regulation of movement between sacred and profane spaces. For the vast majority of monasteries such an approach is simply not possible. Even if excavations can reveal a legible ground plan, potentially important details may be missing, like the decorative vaulting corbels and bosses explored by Roberta Gilchrist at Lacock Abbey to signal areas of male and female space.[4] The sample of monasteries with sufficient remains to permit detailed analysis is consequently reduced and investigation then limited to those buildings with suitable extant structures remaining rather than those that might pose interesting questions.

Such architecturally-derived interpretative models, focused upon the structure of the claustral church, have generally been to the detriment of the wider monastic precinct. While the last twenty years has seen new work helping to redress the balance, this has usually been motivated by a desire to explore economic and industrial processes undertaken in those precincts.[5] Integration of both concerns is clearly required to reconstruct the wider spatial relationships between those

---

acres (12ha) for Benedictine or Augustinian monasteries. G. Coppack, *The White Monks: the Cistercians in Britain, 1128–1540* (Stroud, 1998), p. 105.

[3] Recent examples include analyses of Canterbury cathedral. See B. Nilson, 'The Medieval Experience at the Shrine', in J. Stopford (ed.), *Pilgrimage Explored* (York, 1999), pp. 95–122; T. Tatton-Brown, 'Canterbury and the Architecture of Pilgrimage Shrine in England', in C. Morris and P. Roberts (eds), *Pilgrimage: the English Experience from Becket to Bunyan* (Cambridge, 2002), pp. 90–107. For a recent example of access analysis, see A. Richardson, 'Gender and Space in English Royal Palaces *c.*1160–*c.*1547: a Study in Access Analysis and Imagery', *Medieval Archaeology* 47 (2003), 131–65.

[4] Gilchrist, *Gender*, pp. 159–60.

[5] The most impressive recent overview is J. Bond, *Monastic Landscapes* (Stroud, 2004). For a good example of the more specific investigation of an industrial aspect to a monastery, see G. Coppack, 'The Excavation of an Outer Court Building, perhaps the Woolhouse, at Fountains Abbey, North Yorkshire', *Medieval Archaeology* 30 (1986), 46–87.

spiritual and economic dimensions to religious houses that were all contained within one ostensibly 'sacred' space, the monastic precinct. Thus, while gatehouses created both a symbolic and physical restriction upon ingress into a monastery, the reality of intramural life was more complex.[6] Within the precinct, the weighting, exploitation and meaning of this sacred space was varied and could be structured by far more than those buildings or walls that created what we might term 'hard' spaces. Potentially equally important was the 'soft' space in a monastery, that is, those areas not necessarily enclosed by buildings or fenced off but which, through their sheer size, emptiness or proximity to other features, might have led them to be used or regarded in particular ways.

In the case of those sites subject to pilgrimage, the significant yet mobile human component passing through them also needs to be considered. In particular, to what extent might such pilgrims have influenced the physical layout of the wider monastery beyond the presence of (say) a guest house? If evidence such as earthworks or architecture no longer survives, or survives in insufficient detail, how might tangible evidence for the interaction and definition of these sacred and profane spaces be given a voice? A tentative first step is being made by a research project examining Bromholm Priory in the parish of Bacton in north-east Norfolk. Here, a small, unremarkable priory acquired a relic of the True Cross and came to generate a pilgrim trade of national repute.

Bromholm Priory's Foundation

Bromholm was founded in 1113 by William de Glanville as a cell of the Cluniac priory of Castle Acre.[7] Autonomy was achieved in 1195, shortly before the relic of the True Cross first became actively promoted by Bromholm.[8] Like many contemporary monasteries, the house was probably intended by its founders to articulate essentially secular ideologies through the creation of spatial divisions

---

[6] P. Fergusson, '*Porta Patens Esto*: Notes on Early Cistercian Gatehouses in the North of England', in E. Fernie and P. Crossley (eds), *Medieval Architecture and its Intellectual Content: Studies in Honour of Peter Kidson* (London, 1990), pp. 47–59.

[7] W. Dugdale, *Monasticon Anglicanum*, ed. J. Caley, H. Ellis and B. Bandinel (8 vols, London, 1817–30), V, p. 59. The foundation charter occurs on the first, near-illegible, folio of the house cartulary, Cambridge, University Library MS Mm.2.20.

[8] Bromholm's independence from Castle Acre was formalized by a bull of Pope Celestine III in 1195, although disputes continued into the thirteenth century, with Acre claiming the right to appoint Bromholm's priors. The matter was finally concluded by Pope Gregory IX in 1229: Dugdale, *Monasticon Anglicanum*, V, pp. 61–5 and nos iii and v; W. Page (ed.), *VCH: Norfolk* (2 vols, London, 1906), II, pp. 359–60.

within the landscape. The priory was sited on a small gravel holm or knoll immediately north of a now-extinct river in a belt of low-lying coastal land quite probably prone to flooding.[9] A further watercourse appears once to have flowed further to the east of the holm, with a second extinct river slightly further east again, approximately following the parish boundaries of Bacton and Ridlington (Figure 8.1). Thus positioned, Bromholm could be argued to constitute a 'typical' monastic location, cut off within the landscape. This relatively small site caught between two river valleys may therefore have been attempting to mediate the idea of poor religious, removed or set apart from society, their island of sacred space standing out physically and mentally, as an enclave within the surrounding secular landscape. Certainly, this theme appears to have been particularly popular among monastic foundations in twelfth-century East Anglia.[10]

In fact, it is far from certain that the priory was ever particularly isolated from contemporary secular settlement. Bacton appears to have been a polyfocal parish with a number of berewicks including Keswick which, with its church, lay immediately to the east of the priory precinct. These must have been near-contemporary with Bromholm's foundation as the land of Stanard the Priest and his church at Keswick were confirmed to the priory by Bartholomew de Glanville, son of the founder.[11] Bromholm was therefore probably established within a well-populated landscape and designed to dominate the local area rather than hide away in isolation.

While the priory remains prominent in the surrounding landscape today, the effect must have been magnified for a twelfth-century audience looking at a complete building, probably gleaming in a white external render, from which came the regular sound of bells signalling the call to prayers. As a spatial marker, Bromholm must have projected a less than subtle message of social control to the local lay population, and the Glanville family's favoured position in the natural order of society.

Bromholm's rise from a provincial, familial monastery to a national venue for pilgrimage was only secured by the priory's acquisition of a fragment of the True

---

[9] Domesday Book shows a reduction in most of Bacton's valuations between 1066 and 1086, unlike most other vills in north-east Norfolk. P. Brown (ed.), *Domesday Book Norfolk* (2 vols, Chichester, 1984), ff. 155b–156a. The situation was clear by the fourteenth century, Berdewelle church being appropriated in 1385 to support the priory after their lands had been 'wasted by the inundations of the sea': *The Calendar of Patent Rolls Preserved in the Public Record Office*, eds H.C. Maxwell Lyte *et al.* (London, 1891–), 1381–5, p. 579.

[10] See further my *Landscapes of Monastic Foundation*, pp. 201–8.

[11] The confirmation charter of Bartholomew de Glanville occurs in both the Bromholm cartulary and at fol. 62 in the Castle Acre cartulary (BL, Harley MS 2110, in the course of publication by Professor C. Harper-Bill). It is published in W. Dugdale, *Monasticon Anglicanum*, V, p. 63.

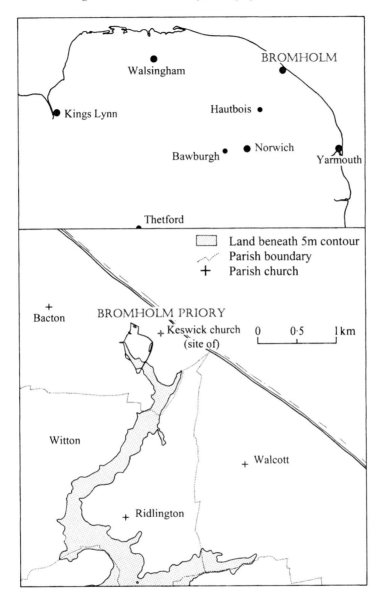

Figure 8.1 (a)   Site Location showing Principal Settlements and Nearby Shrines; (b)   Bromholm Priory in its Local Setting.

Cross. The relic was reputedly acquired from an English priest who fled the sack of Constantinople in 1204.[12] Pilgrimage is first recorded in 1223 and in its early years the monastery was a fashionable venue, being patronized among others by Henry III and by Edward II.[13] Evidence for popular pilgrimage is witnessed by a papal indult of 1401, allowing priests appointed by the community to hear 'the confessions of, and grant absolution to ... the multitude who resort from afar to the church on account of a certain notable piece of the true wood of the cross'.[14] The shrine remained popular with pilgrims until the Dissolution, gaining a place in the national consciousness with mentions in the *Canterbury Tales* and in Langland's *Vision of Piers Ploughman*.[15]

Pilgrimage, while welcome for the prestige and increased revenues that it brought,[16] introduced issues of controlling visitor flow and spatial regulation. How might this have been approached by the community at Bromholm? Conventional access analysis is limited because relatively few of the monastic buildings that survive as ruins on the site are in a complete enough form to reconstruct accurately points of entry or control. In many respects Bromholm appears to have had an entirely typical claustral layout, placed to the south of the priory church, set within a precinct entered through two gatehouses, one to the north, the other to the west. The surviving architectural remains include much of the priory east range including the chapter house, and the north transept of the church.[17]

---

[12] The story of Bromholm's acquisition of the relic is recounted by Ralph of Coggeshall and is discussed, and the text printed, by F. Wormald, 'The Rood of Bromholm', *Journal of the Warburg Institute* 1 (1937), 31–45.

[13] For these illustrious visitors and some of their gifts see ibid., 36–40.

[14] Indult of 19 August 1401: *CEPR*, V, p. 432.

[15] For the Miller's wife of Chaucer's *The Reeve's Tale* ('Helpe, holy croys of Bromholme!'), see *The Complete Works of Geoffrey Chaucer Edited From Numerous Manuscripts*, ed. W.W. Skeat (6 vols, Oxford, 1894), IV, p. 124 [l. 4286 (366)]. For Avarice's repentant, 'And bidde the rode of Bromholme, bryng me oute of dette', see *The Vision of William Concerning Piers Plowman*, ed. W.W. Skeat (2 vols, Oxford, 1886), I, p. 148 (Text B, Passus V, l. 231).

[16] Bromholm was particularly geared towards two celebrations, having been granted a market on Holy Cross Day (14 September) and the two following days, by Henry III in 1229. The grant also gave the monks a regular Monday market: *The Calendar of Close Rolls Preserved in the Public Record Office*, ed. H.C. Maxwell Lyte *et al.* (London, 1896–), 1227–31, p. 153. The other principal festival is likely to have been Passion Sunday (two weeks before Easter Sunday), a day particularly associated with the cross: Wormald, 'Rood of Bromholm', 37.

[17] The transitional Norman/Early English north transept apparently dates to much the same time, as the priory was fostering pilgrimage and asserting its independence from Castle Acre. One suspects that all three events were connected. The construction of the north transept, in an obviously expensive and up-to-date architectural style, suggests a wealthy and self-confident community that might indeed look for independence from the mother

To some extent this provides a means of determining which spaces within the monastic precinct might have been regarded as more sacred than others, focusing in particular on the High Altar and relic of the True Cross within the conventual church. Unfortunately, the only ground plan of the priory church is a reconstruction made in 1854 that relies for its more interesting details upon a survey made in 1822 by 'the late Mr Spurdens' of 'the foundations visible ... which are not now to be seen'.[18] As a result specific analysis of those areas of the priory church used daily by the laity and monks appears impossible.

That there could be contestation of these holy spaces is provided in a rare historical snapshot from the priory. When Sir John Paston was buried at Bromholm on 29 May 1466, there was a lavish funeral involving over seventy servants, copious quantities of food and drink and many guests. Some of the workmen were clearly put up within the priory as the Prior 'toke to bord diverse persons laboryng abought the enterment' and charged the Pastons for it. The Pastons incurred other incidentals including twenty pence 'for viii peces of peuter lost of the Priors' while the huge quantities of wax burned as part of the obsequies led to another twenty pence being paid 'to the glaser for takyn owte of ii. panys of the windows of the schyrche for to late owte the reke of the torches at the deryge, and sowderyng new of the same'.[19] One can easily imagine the impact upon the priory for a few breathless days while the Pastons descended upon the monastery to which they were by now patrons. But this was a brief event in the life of the house – what might the more typical situation have been?

Given Bromholm's prominence as a venue for pilgrimage our lack of architectural or other documentary evidence is unfortunate and retards our understanding of the impact of pilgrimage upon the layout of a modestly-sized monastery. An alternative approach that has been adopted in trying to identify those areas that were of a sacred or profane nature has been to use the presence and distribution of different types of material culture recovered through fieldwalking and metal-detection. Although the large-scale evidence for buildings has been almost entirely removed, those smaller, portable items used in everyday life that were most easily dropped or disposed of are less easy to expunge. Might they provide a dataset able to explore the individual circumstances and dynamics of space prevailing at Bromholm?

house. The promotion of a cult was an obvious method of further helping the priory to raise its profile and income.

[18] H. Harrod, *Gleanings Among the Castles and Convents of Norfolk* (Norwich, 1857), opposite p. 220.

[19] *The Paston Letters*, ed. J. Gairdner (6 vols, London, 1904), IV, pp. 227–9.

Clearly, investigation of the wider precinct using such finds can only be conducted at a level less precise than the familiar spatial architectural models. The results, however, are no less interesting. They rely first upon an understanding of reconstructing arrangements in the wider precinct area; and second, of the types of material culture remaining and the caveats associated with their study.

Using Material Culture

Bromholm Priory is now all under arable land with the exception of the farm buildings and farm house at its centre, a regime in operation since at least the mid-nineteenth century. No earthworks remain to aid the process of reconstructing the priory precinct layout, although some early cartographic sources and aerial photographs are available.[20] Archaeological techniques like geophysics would undoubtedly do much to enhance our understanding, but have yet to be undertaken in any systematic way.[21] The result of these sources is a somewhat superficial composite plan of the Bromholm Priory precinct in which there is only a basic understanding of the divisions of monastic space (Figure 8.2). This can, however, be amplified by other survey techniques.

Fieldwalking, the collection of archaeological material exposed on the surface of ploughed fields, was undertaken in a detailed survey by dividing those precinct areas under arable into 25×25m gridboxes. Quantification of the fieldwalked finds has demonstrated the structured spatial distribution of pottery within the priory precinct, indicating both the preferential exploitation of space in certain parts of the monastery and, in some measure, its change over time. For instance, the precinct's western gatehouse has good evidence for occupation between the twelfth and fourteenth centuries, given the spread of 'Local Medieval Unglazed' (LMU) sherds clustering around it (Figure 8.3a). By contrast, in the later medieval period, represented by 'Late Medieval/Transitional' (LMT) wares, no pottery whatever was discarded here (Figure 8.3b).

---

[20] The cartographic sources are limited. The 1886 Ordnance Survey 25" map (Norfolk, sheet xx.16, surveyed 1885) shows the farm layout to be fundamentally that of today, except for a larger barn complex to the south-east of the priory. The 1845 Tithe Apportionment map (Norfolk Record Office DN/TA 873) again shows nothing of note. The apportionment (Norfolk Record Office MF755, pp. 23–5) even makes it clear that most of the monastic precinct was already under full arable cultivation.
[21] Trial resistivity survey by Dr Peter Carnell between December 1998 and February 1999 suggested that the remains of the church walling may be minimal, probably as a result of almost complete robbing. However, more geophysics is needed and trial work using a ground-penetrating radar by Mr Malcolm Weale has begun.

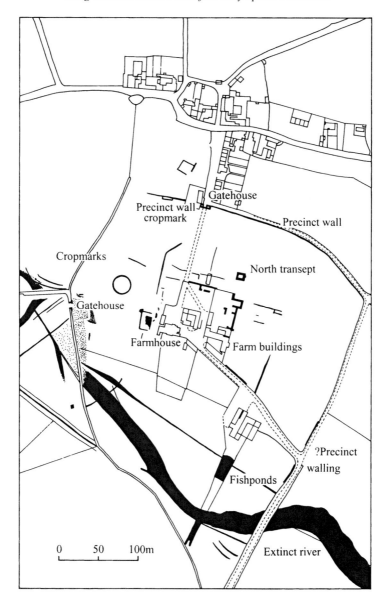

Figure 8.2 Bromholm Priory Precinct as Reconstructed from Maps, Aerial Photographs and Building Surveys.

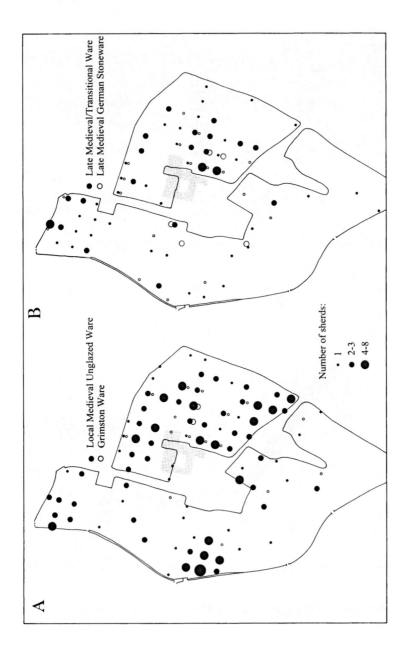

Figure 8.3 Results of the Fieldwalking Survey: (a) The Distribution of Local Medieval Unglazed Ware Sherds (c.12th–14th cent.); (b) Late Medieval/Transitional Ware and Contemporary German Stoneware Sherds(c.14th–15th cent.).

However, does this represent secular or religious use of the site? In this case, the pottery seems to indicate lay space within the monastery. The pottery vessel forms recovered are predominantly of cooking jars, suggesting the preparation of food, a task normally undertaken by priory servants. More important, the gatehouses were important symbolic structures regulating traffic into and out of the precinct, but normally staffed by lay servants. The pottery also helps to show the fluidity of space, whether 'holy' or not, over time. Even if the western gatehouse was still standing in the later medieval period, the lack of pottery around it suggests that it had simply gone out of use. If so, was ingress to the precinct now controlled using only the other, large, northern gatehouse? Perhaps the main frustration with the fieldwalking is the relative bluntness of the data, since it principally samples ceramic materials, notably pottery, which can have a broad date range of production and a restricted function.

Metal detection, by contrast, is effectively a non-destructive archaeological technique in deep ploughsoil.[22] It has the capacity to yield a far larger range and number of objects than fieldwalking, since it also locates items beneath the surface, and provides many metal finds that are far more closely datable than pottery.[23] The challenge is to determine the extent to which the deposition of those finds recovered are representative of use patterns from the life of the priory. Similarly, to what extent might artefacts, and thus spaces, be capable of definition as 'holy' or 'secular'?

The metal-detecting at Bromholm has reused the site grid established for the fieldwalking but subdivided into 12·5×12·5m boxes, to provide even higher resolution to the mapping of finds. Eighteen acres (7.3ha) of the site have now been metal-detected completely, three times, with each gridbox scanned across its entire surface area. Quantification of the finds is difficult as analysis is continuing, but in excess of 8000 have been recovered. The vast majority of this material is undatable lead scrap probably relating to the use and repair of lead roofing on the monastic buildings. However, over 600 objects have been allocated specific

---

[22] Bromholm's ploughsoil has probably been extended in recent years by the deep working depth of modern agricultural machinery. A straw-poll of the detectorists working at Bromholm suggests 80 per cent of all finds have been made in the top 4" (100mm) of ploughsoil. The recovery depth of artefacts is thus often limited (contrary to the claims of detector manufacturers) and shows how repeated detection of the same area is necessary to recover finds after ploughing has turned over the topsoil.

[23] Metal-detecting has generated considerable debate in archaeological circles, see T. Gregory and A.J.G. Rogerson, 'Metal-Detecting in Archaeological Excavation', *Antiquity* 58 (1984), 179–84; C. Dobinson and S. Denison, *Metal-Detecting and Archaeology in England* (London, 1995); M. Lewis, 'The Portable Antiquities (Voluntary Recording) Scheme: its Impact in Kent and the Future for London', *London Archaeologist* 9 (2002), 330–37.

'smallfind' numbers because they have a recognizable function or are easily dated. When classified, dated and plotted these finds have the potential to say something about the way the space within Bromholm Priory's precinct was used and subjected to the loss or deposition of objects. The remainder of this paper will examine some of the more easily identifiable categories of find and their possible implications for the definition of sacred space.

Some of the Finds Considered

The most obvious analogue to the fieldwalked pottery from Bromholm are fragments of cast copper-alloy cooking vessels, principally a phenomenon of the fourteenth century and later.[24] While difficult to date any more accurately these metal vessels are broadly contemporary with Late Medieval/Transitional pottery. The distributions of fieldwalked pottery and metal-detected vessels is of interest. To date, 30 fragments of copper-alloy vessel walling or rim, and 14 legs have been recovered. They appear in two spreads, one a small cluster within the western field of the site, the other in a more diffuse distribution to the east (Figure 8.4a). The Late Medieval/Transitional pottery (Figure 8.3b) by contrast, is almost totally absent from the western field. Where it does appear to the east, the pottery and metal vessel fragments do not share concentrations – instead they appear to be mutually exclusive, suggesting either subtly different uses or users.

If the pottery associated with the western gatehouse was a consequence of occupation by lay priory servants, might the pottery to the east have had a similarly profane origin? There is nothing relating this pottery to specific priory functions as seen, for instance, at Kirkstall Abbey in West Yorkshire, which had a concentration of dripping pan sherds near the monastic kitchens.[25] Two suggestions may be offered. First, the cluster of metal vessels in the west perhaps suggests another, previously unsuspected, kitchen area within the monastic precinct, for guests, corrodians or pilgrims. Whatever the case, this was clearly not a 'holy' area of the precinct, but one associated with provisioning its guests or residents. Second, if the differences between metal and pot vessel fragment distributions do indeed relate to different users, might the former have originally been brought into

---

[24] The Bromholm fragments are all here described as 'vessels', although a range of types are probably represented, for instance basins, ewers, cauldrons and skillets. The evidence from London suggests that tripod ewers or cauldrons and long-handled skillets were the most common forms: G. Egan, *The Medieval Household: Daily Living c.1150–c.1450* (Medieval Finds From Excavations in London 6, London, 1998), p. 161.

[25] S. Moorhouse and S. Wrathmell, *Kirkstall Abbey I: the 1950–64 Excavations: a Reassessment* (Yorkshire Archaeology 1, York, 1987), p. 107, Fig. 63.

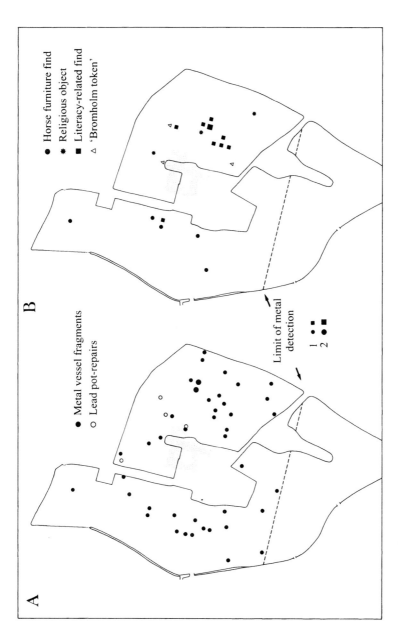

Figure 8.4 Distribution of Metal Finds: (a) Metal Vessel Fragments and the Lead Repair Plugs Used on Broken Ceramic Pots; (b) Various Specific Find-Types.

the precinct by travellers requiring vessels more robust than earthenware pots for food preparation? Indeed, do they indicate areas of *consumption* as well as preparation, and (given the lack of surviving evidence for buildings here) are they associated with a seasonal pilgrim trade?

Less subtle, although from a far smaller sample, is the distribution of horse furniture like harness pendants. These small bronze ornaments were generally attached to the breast-band or *peytrel* of a horse with a *floruit*, as carriers of armorial designs, in the thirteenth and fourteenth centuries.[26] Three pendants, the suspension-hanger of a fourth and the star-rowel from a spur have been found at Bromholm and all derive from the field to the west of the priory buildings (Figure 8.4b). The relative scarcity of medieval finds from this part of the site appears consistent with a more open, outer, precinct area available for stables or even paddocks. That the community itself used this area is suggested by the discovery of one pendant bearing the Cross of Bromholm. Such pendants were a common feature of secular society, mediating social position through vivid visual displays into which churchmen were inevitably drawn. While the prior of Bromholm is unlikely to have needed the twenty-six horses used by Abbot Samson of Bury St Edmunds ('thirteen horses are sufficient for some other abbots, but not for me'),[27] he would almost certainly have had his horses furnished with tack reflecting the status of his monastery. The objects provide evidence for a use of the priory space that would otherwise have only ephemeral remains such as paddock fences and perhaps stables. They also emphasize that this is most likely to be a working part of the priory, frequented principally by laymen and thus a scene of secular activities.

If the area west of the priory church is more easily explicable as 'outer' precinct, those parts surrounding, or close to, the claustral complex would be expected to have been considered holier. Access to these spaces should also have been more difficult as the monastic community would have wanted to restrict visitors to these areas.

Objects of a religious nature would be most likely to occur in the area of the priory church and this seems to be borne out by the presence of a thirteenth-century Limoges-style champlevé enamelled and gilt plaque probably once attached to a processional cross arm, and a small cast copper-alloy bottle probably used for storing holy oil.[28] However, not only are these the only specifically liturgical items

---

[26] See in particular S.J. Ashley, *Medieval Armorial Horse Furniture in Norfolk* (East Anglian Archaeology 101, Norwich, 2002), pp. 27–32.

[27] *Jocelin of Brakelond Chronicle of the Abbey of Bury St Edmunds*, ed. D. Greenway and J. Sayers (Oxford, 1989), pp. 24, 49.

[28] An increasing number of enamelled plaques are known, both from existing museum collections and metal-detector finds. For recent finds see Museums, Libraries and Archives Council, *Portable Antiquities Scheme Annual Report 2003/04* (London, 2004), pp. 42, 62.

to have been identified from Bromholm so far; neither is within the projected area of the priory church (Figure 8.4b). Indeed, the oil bottle was found close to the south-east corner of the precinct eastern field. The two finds are clearly not enough to define areas as being of 'holy' use, but a collection of material that perhaps suggests this better relates to literate practice (Figure 8.4b).

Books are most commonly associated with religious ownership in the medieval world, both for devotional practices and liturgical use. The far higher proportion of books owned by religious personnel compared to the laity is amply shown in Norman Tanner's study of wills and inventories made in medieval Norwich 1370–1549. Only 65 (3.8 per cent) of 1,705 lay people's wills and inventories mention books, compared to 104 mentions (or 33.2 per cent) in the corresponding sample of 313 for the clergy.[29] Similarly, large numbers of book clasps have recently been recovered from excavations at the Norwich Carmelite friary.[30] The decorative bosses and clasps once attached to book covers that have been recovered from Bromholm are most likely to indicate ecclesiastical use, and more sacred areas of the monastic precinct. This impression is emphasized by the tight distribution of the objects, which cluster within a 25m radius to the east of the cloister east range.[31] Also associated with the use of documents is a lead seal matrix, the silver openwork knop of a matrix and the cut half of a lead papal bulla of Clement VI (1342–52).[32] Might these demonstrate an area of the priory precinct related to the use or perhaps possession of books by members of the community? Or to the disposal of rubbish collected within the claustral areas? An analogue might be the discovery of six papal bullae in a drain at the archiepiscopal manor of Otford in Kent.[33] While such items could represent a single dumping event from a Dissolution-period clearance of the priory buildings, there are no specific

---

The holy oil bottles are less well known, but the discovery of an example inscribed 'olevm chrism' (chrism oil) from East Clandon, Surrey, confirms the identification: D. Williams, 'East Clandon', *Medieval Archaeology* 48 (2004), 244–5.

[29] Calculated from the figures in N.P. Tanner, *The Church in Late Medieval Norwich 1370–1532* (Studies and Texts 6, Pontifical Institute of Medieval Studies, Toronto, 1984), App. 6. Although the proportions changed over time, the range of book mentions for the laity was between 1.8–5.5 per cent, while the clergy ranged between 16.6–38.4 per cent.

[30] Peter Rilings, personal communication.

[31] The only exception is a copper-alloy mount with a central glass 'stone', probably a book boss, found in the western field.

[32] For the silver matrix knop see Department for Culture, Media and Sport, *Treasure Annual Report 2002* (London, 2004), p. 82. The occurrence of papal bullae that have been deliberately cut in half is a phenomenon becoming increasingly recognized.

[33] One was of Lucius III (1181–5), the other five of Urban III (1185–7), supporting the impression they were dumped in a single event as part of a tidying exercise: R.D. Clarke, 'Researches and Discoveries: Otford', *Archaeologia Cantiana* 87 (1972), 225.

concentrations of other material types in this area to support more general clearances at this date.

It is true that there is indirect evidence for the production of 'literate' objects for pilgrims to Bromholm. Lambeth Palace Library now holds a fourteenth-century Book of Hours containing a vellum leaf on which is a picture of the Holy Rood of Bromholm within a heart shape, accompanied by a short hymn to the cross.[34] The leaf would appear to have been a type of 'devotional card' sold to visiting pilgrims as keepsakes.[35] Likewise, a fifteenth-century prayer roll sold by Sotheby's in 1963 carried depictions of, and prayers to, the Holy Rood of Bromholm.[36] If pilgrims were able to buy such devotional materials at the shrine, it is a short step to suppose that they may also have carried, used, and lost, books or pieces of them. However, the tight distribution of these 'literate' finds seems far easier to reconcile with a 'religious' use of this part of the site, or at least the dumping of material derived from sacred areas occupied by the literate ecclesiastics close by. The fact that the claustral range is within 50m of the spread provides a ready source for such artefacts but again emphasizes the more visibly 'holy' aspect to this part of the site and the loss or deposition of material culture more associated with the religious way of life.

One of the defining features of Bromholm's existence was pilgrimage. Might it therefore be possible to examine those areas of the priory precinct accessible to pilgrims? An obvious find-type to attempt this correlation would appear to be pilgrim badges, those mass-produced trinkets collected by visitors to shrines as proof of their pilgrimage. In fact, remarkably, not one single pilgrim badge or ampulla has been found to date during the metal-detector survey, although a number celebrating Bromholm are known to exist and have been found as far afield as Holland.[37] This absence has been something of a surprise (and disappointment!), and suggests that if such trinkets had been sold at Bromholm, they were so highly treasured at the shrine itself that few appear to have been dropped. One possible devotional object found is a small cast rectangular lead sheet, 73×25mm, depicting a woman in the swaying posture common in early fourteenth-century art. With no attachment points or obvious function, this may have been some form of *ex voto* offering. Perhaps significantly, this was found

---

[34] Lambeth Palace Library, MS 545, f. 186.

[35] Wormald, 'The Rood of Bromholm', 32–4.

[36] The manuscript was sold to Dawsons of Pall Mall in their sale of 9 December 1963, lot 120. D.J. Hall, *English Medieval Pilgrimage* (London, 1967), p. 208.

[37] For a range of designs depicting the Holy Rood, see B. Spencer, *Pilgrim Souvenirs and Secular Badges* (London, 1998), pp. 160–65. For the Dutch find, from Middelburg, see A.M. Koldeweij, 'Medieval Pilgrim Badges Found in the Netherlands', *Pre-printed Papers, Medieval Europe 1992:7, Art and Symbolism* (York, 1992), pp. 41–2.

immediately outside the priory church north transept, an area certainly associated with holy space, but it does little to inform us about the wider division of precinct into areas of sacred or profane use.

Three more lead-alloy objects clearly related to Bromholm are equally difficult to define. These small cast discs, essentially identical, depict the Holy Rood on one side, and a face, apparently Christ wearing the Crown of Thorns, on the other.[38] All three have been found in the eastern field, but widely spread out (Figure 8.4b). It is unclear whether they formed some kind of token for use in the precinct, or were simply keepsakes, but they have no liturgical function and must therefore relate to secular rather than monastic use. In turn, this implies both a lay presence in the inner precinct space immediately adjacent to the priory church, and thus that this area of the priory need not have been purely 'sacred' after all. This observation is considerably amplified by the discovery of large numbers of dress accessories.

Dress formed one of the most readily-identifiable means for religious personnel to distinguish themselves from 'seculars' in the medieval world, the subscription to a common identity being the antithesis of individual statements made through fashion. It should therefore be expected that everyday dress accessories from the precinct would relate to their use, and loss, by a lay audience. This is not to say that religious personnel never wore 'secular' accoutrements. A 1440 visitation of Kirby Bellars Priory, Leicestershire, heard that some canons 'do wear clasps in their boots' and purses of embroidery and silk 'that hang down from their belts to their knees'. Similarly, in 1531 John Longland, bishop of Lincoln, ordained in his visitation of Elstow nunnery, Bedfordshire, that no sister should wear 'ther apparels upon ther hedes under suche lay fashion as they have now of late'.[39] Crucially though, it was the 'unholy' nature of such fashion statements that led to them being recorded in our documentary sources and to steps being taken to stop this practice.

If the eastern field represents an inner precinct with associations of 'deeper' sacred space, to which access was more tightly restricted, it might be supposed that within it there would have been fewer losses of items like dress fittings. A caveat to this is the presence of priory servants who would have access to these areas but whose dress code would have been more relaxed than that of the monks. Some restrictions on the servants were, presumably, in force, as the Bromholm cellarer's

---

[38] Both the plate and token are illustrated in T. Pestell, 'New Surveys at Bromholm Priory', *Church Archaeology* 3 (2000), p. 53.

[39] A.H. Thompson (ed.), *Visitations of Religious Houses in the Diocese of Lincoln, 1420–1449* (3 vols, Canterbury and York Society, London, 1915–27), II, p. 166. For Elstow, see E. Power, *Medieval English Nunneries c.1275 to 1535* (Cambridge, 1922), p. 304.

roll of 1415/16 makes it clear that many wore liveries provided by the house.[40] A mechanism therefore exists for dress accessories to have been lost by members of the wider priory community within the precinct. However, the fact that numbers of pilgrims are known to have visited the site, that such outsiders had no dress restrictions, and that some losses of dress fittings could be expected from them, means it is also reasonable to anticipate that metal dress accessories should reflect the presence of these pilgrims. In turn this begs questions about the degree of 'sacredness' associated with those areas yielding such finds.

Dress-fittings so far recovered include buckles, buckle plates, belt stiffeners, strap-ends, lace-tags and purse frames, and range in quality from scrappy thin sheets of copper-alloy to an ornate cast bronze Romanesque belt buckle. Several items of jewellery including annular brooches and a gold ring have also been found. Of the 58 pieces identified within the precinct area, only 15 come from the western field, the remainder forming a spread to the north and east of the priory church (Figure 8.5a). This pattern seems most readily interpreted as including the losses of a visiting population, rather than solely from monks and their servants, who (all things being equal) could have lost such accoutrements throughout the precinct.

The dress fittings therefore suggest that this eastern part of the precinct was not a 'sacred' area *per se*, but one that saw a secular presence. But how significant was this? Could it have been seasonal, limited to short periods of influx in the same way that the Paston funeral led to brief disruption? Or was it an ongoing area of lay involvement? Two final classes of artefact, lead weights and silver coins, bear on this question. Their importance derives from their likely use in mercantile activity, more specifically markets, held within the priory precinct. This has obvious implications for understanding which parts of the precinct were held sacred and those that saw regular profane ingress and activity.

---

[40] *The Cellarer's Account for Bromholm Priory, Norfolk 1415–16*, ed. L.J. Redstone (Norfolk Record Society 17, Norwich, 1944), p. 50, §33.

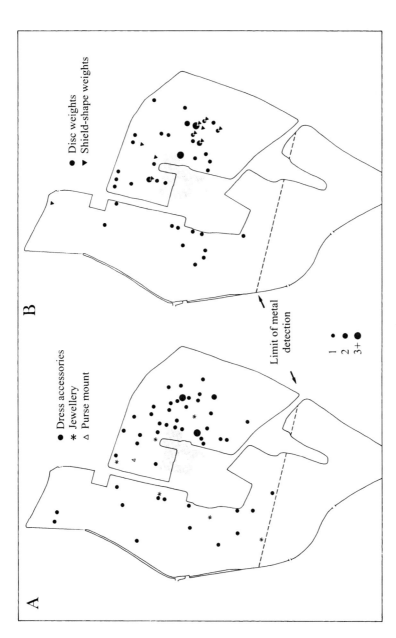

Figure 8.5 Distribution of Metal Finds: (a) Dress Accessories and Allied Objects; (b) Lead and Copper-Alloy Weights.

'My House Shall Be a House of Prayer': Markets in the Monastic Precinct[41]

The indication that traders conducted business at the heart of the priory is of some interest given the Church's various pronouncements about markets. Many churchyards became informal market places on Sundays when people gathered to worship, and many churches were granted market rights of supervision.[42] However, attempts to prevent Sunday trading had been ongoing since the tenth century with law-codes issued by, among others, King Æthelstan. The process was pressed home increasingly from the thirteenth century, for example, the 1285 Statute of Winchester prohibiting the holding of fairs and markets in churchyards for the 'Honour of the Church'.[43] Despite such injunctions, Whitby Abbey changed its market from Sunday to Saturday only in 1445.[44] That monastic churchyards were used for other purposes too is made clear in Jocelin of Brakelond's *Chronicle of Bury St Edmunds*. He describes how contests and competitions between the abbey servants and townspeople were held there on Boxing Day 1197, only for a bloody punch-up to erupt. Abbot Samson thereafter banned the cemetery as a venue for 'assemblies and shows'.[45]

These illustrations are somewhat at variance to a more traditional picture of monastic market-places being situated outside the precinct, often directly in front of the gatehouse, as at Peterborough or Bury St Edmunds.[46] It seems possible that the evidence from Bromholm is in fact more representative of the commercial arrangements at many smaller or medium-sized monasteries, and it is simply the lack of structured archaeological surveys, particularly using metal-detectors, that disguises this. For instance, metal-detecting at Newark Priory, Surrey, by John and Paul Buckingham in the 1980s yielded 89 medieval coins, suggesting that a sustained level of commercial transactions were taking place on the site.[47] The very temporary nature of markets and fairs, which leave few archaeological features, may have left most other such sites completely unrecognized, and excavation, even

---

[41] Lk. 19:45: 'And he entered the temple and began to drive out those who sold, saying to them "It is written 'my house shall be a house of prayer'; but you have made it a den of robbers"'.

[42] R. Morris, *Churches in the Landscape* (London, 1989), pp. 212–13.

[43] Ibid., p. 212. For Æthelstan's law-code of 926–*c.*930 issued at Grately (II Æthelstan 24.1), see D. Whitelock (ed.), *English Historical Documents c.500–1042* (London, 1979), p. 421.

[44] Bond, *Monastic Landscapes*, p. 269.

[45] *Jocelin of Brakelond*, ed. Greenway and Sayers, pp. 82–3.

[46] Bond, *Monastic Landscapes*, pp. 271–4. The importance of markets for monastic income is made by J. Burton, *Monastic and Religious Orders in Britain, 1000–1300* (Cambridge, 1994), p. 245.

[47] For details of the coins I am grateful to Dr Martin Allen of the Fitzwilliam Museum, Cambridge.

if on a suitably large scale, would be unlikely to recover the quantities of weights and coinage needed to make the case.

Lead weights are notoriously difficult objects to define as they could be used for a variety of purposes. While many were used for commerce, acting as specific weight units, they also acted as sinkers for fishing nets and as plumb-bobs in construction, uses which did not demand metrologically significant masses.[48] Those weights that can most clearly be accorded an economic function, such as shield-shaped weights, or discs suitable for stacking, cluster together at Bromholm to the north and south-east of the priory church. Equally important, exclusion of those few weights that are more obviously akin to net-sinkers, or which are unusually irregular, leaves an overall distribution that has a rationale within the precinct and which accords with some of the other patterns already examined (Figure 8.5b). The most important overlap in distribution relates to the coinage recovered from Bromholm which suggests that these lead weights indeed relate to mercantile or commercial use.

To date, some 165 coins of all dates have been recovered from Bromholm, in addition to 15 jettons or tokens of thirteenth- to early seventeenth-century date. Although still small in statistical terms, the 76 English and Continental coins from Bromholm, dating to between 1100 and 1603 compare favourably to the 109 catalogued from all the large-scale excavations in York undertaken 1971–81.[49] Analysis by Dr Martin Allen of the Fitzwilliam Museum, Cambridge, has enabled the numismatic assemblage to be dated very accurately, enabling a clearer chronological understanding of spatial use within the monastic precinct.

In particular, the coins form coherent patterns when plotted using their minting dates (Figures 8.6a and b).[50] Those dating from the twelfth and thirteenth centuries

---

[48] The metrology of weights is a thorny matter as many different standards and units have been used over time, often concurrently. As a branch of numismatics, the literature is voluminous. An important starting point is R.E. Zupko, *British Weights and Measures. A History from Antiquity to the Seventeenth Century* (London, 1977), while summaries and presentations of important archaeological assemblages are M. Biddle, 'Weights and Measures', in M. Biddle (ed.), *Artefacts From Medieval Winchester II: Object and Economy in Medieval Winchester* (Winchester Studies 7, Oxford, 1990), pp. 908–23; G. Egan, 'Weighing Apparatus', in G. Egan (ed.), *The Medieval Household: Daily Living c.1150– c.1450* (Medieval Finds from Excavations in London 6, London, 1998), pp. 307–22. The range of sizes and shapes that lead weights could take is amply illustrated in N. Biggs and P.Withers, *Lead Weights in the David Rogers Collection* (Llanfyllin, 2000).

[49] E.J.E. Pirie, *Post-Roman Coins from York Excavations, 1971–81* (The Archaeology of York 18:1, York, 1986), pp. 58–67.

[50] Of course, mint-dates need not necessarily relate to loss-dates, and the sterling coinage of the fourteenth century (for instance) was long-lived. However, it is remarkable how coherent the patterns are when analysed in this way.

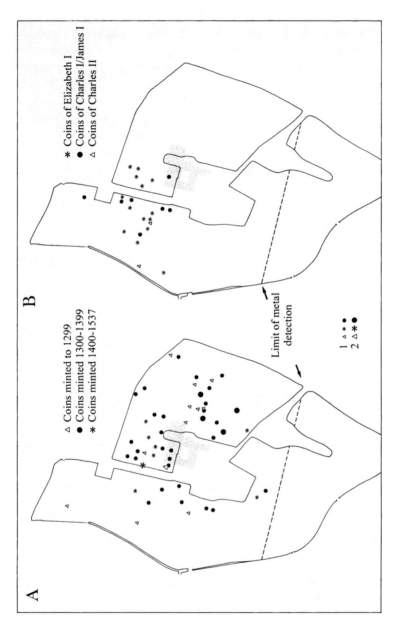

Figure 8.6 Distributions of Coinage: (a) Hammered Silver Coins from the Lifetime of the Priory; (b) Hammered Silver and Copper-Alloy Coins of Tudor and Early Stuart Date.

A

△ Coins minted to 1299
● Coins minted 1300–1399
✳ Coins minted 1400–1537

B

✳ Coins of Elizabeth I
● Coins of Charles I/James I
△ Coins of Charles II

Limit of metal detection

1 △ ✳ ●
2 △ ✳ ●

are distributed within and to the north of the priory church (three coins), while twice as many (six coins) extend in an eastwards line east of the chapter house.[51] The fourteenth century, during which half of the medieval coinage recovered from Bromholm was struck, is in three spreads, one to the north of the priory church, another in a spread to the east of the claustral range, and a third in a thin scatter in the western field (again coinciding with a few lead weights). Finally, those coins struck from the start of the fifteenth century until the Dissolution are wholly concentrated to the north of the priory church. A few odd outliers only help to demonstrate the rule.

The fact that there appear to be three distinct concentrations containing fourteenth-century coins is perhaps due to the long-lived nature of such sterling issues, although further analysis may allow some narrowing down of the periods that these zones were in use. Regardless, the underlying point is clear: the coins show that space within the religious precinct was organized for profane activities, meaning coin use, and loss, was most likely to occur in specific areas. Essentially, people were guided into distinct zones within the precinct before they might be in a position to lose their cash.

Perhaps more interesting is to speculate upon how the coins and weights may help us to understand the modification or changing use of space within the monastic precinct over time, and whether the nature of such spaces might have been considered 'holy' or not. As a preliminary, it is important to consider whether the finds do indeed represent mercantile activity beyond the monetized nature of a community managing its estates. The latter is certainly possible, but the coincidence of coinage and weights seems far more plausibly interpreted as representing the exchange and sale of goods at a retail level, rather than the administration of bulk produce from the monastic demesne. The Bromholm coins are also broadly similar in the proportion of issues to other assemblages of single coin finds noted by Christopher Dyer, representing coins formerly 'circulating in the countryside, many [of which] came from the purses of peasants', rather than to the coin-loss patterns argued by Stuart Rigold to represent the monetization of monastic estates.[52] These similarities only emphasize the probably 'secular' nature of the Bromholm coin assemblage.[53]

---

[51] A tenth coin, a penny of Edward I (*c.*1283–6), is an outlier and was actually found outside the area of the medieval priory.

[52] C. Dyer, 'Peasants and Coins: the Uses of Money in the Middle Ages', *British Numismatic Journal* 67 (1998), 36.

[53] S. Rigold, 'Small Change in the Light of Medieval Site Finds', in N.J. Mayhew (ed.), *Edwardian Monetary Affairs (1279–1344): a Symposium held in Oxford, August 1976* (BAR, British Series 36, Oxford, 1977), pp. 60–68, 70–72.

This being the case, the two most likely sources for such coin losses surely relate to the influx of pilgrims to Bromholm on particularly auspicious days, perhaps two or three times a year, and to the priory's weekly market, regularly used by local traders and consumers. Either market or fair may have resulted in the loss of other medieval detritus like belt buckles and strap-ends, many of which may, in any case, have been sold there. The presence of thirteenth-century coins predominantly to the east of the claustral range may suggest this was where the weekly market and annual fair were held. The fourteenth-century coins, with spreads to the south-west, north and east of the claustral complex appear to signal a period of change, the site of the market being shifted away from the east as, by the fifteenth century, coinage is only found to the north. This in turn suggests that the community wished to regulate visitor flow within its precinct more closely, shifting the disturbance of the public away from those 'deeper' spaces near to the private areas of the cloister. This might well coincide with the development of the pilgrim trade through the fourteenth century, with an increasing influx of visitors.

A possible alternative is that the limited early coinage to the north of the church indicates the weekly market site, close to the gatehouse providing access to the priory. Those areas to the east of the claustral buildings might then represent a temporary overflow area, perhaps for the annual fair in September around Holy Cross day. In this scenario, space that was predominantly 'holy' in being restricted from lay access was used only briefly, providing a temporary nuisance to the priory community. By the fifteenth century, however, this space was no longer being exploited; either a reduction in the size of pilgrim crowds, or a desire finally to shut off an area, saw the shift to the north of the priory church. Lay ingress into this 'deep' monastic space had finally been curtailed.

That the coins and weights relate to a market or fair at Bromholm is, finally, proven by post-Dissolution examples showing a continued commercial use of the site long after the monastery's internal economy had ceased to exist. A number of Elizabethan and later coins have been recovered from Bromholm that, when plotted, show a concentration to the north of priory church and to the west of the trackway running up to the northern gatehouse (Figure 8.6b). This spread, drifting slightly to the north-west compared to the medieval coinage, continued into the early seventeenth century with a halfgroat and four royal farthing tokens of Charles I being recovered. The mercantile interpretation to these finds is reinforced by the discovery of a two-ounce 'Norwich Series' lead trade weight, clearly datable to this phase of the site's use by the royal cipher of Charles I.[54]

---

[54] For identical examples see Biggs and Withers, *Lead Weights*, pp. 63–4, nos 250–51.

Thereafter, the distribution of coins within the monastic precinct becomes far less focused. No coins of the Commonwealth, and only two Charles II farthings have been found. The reduction in numbers of later coins, despite the rise of coinage in circulation, and their increasingly widespread and random findspots, indicates these coins were stray losses, unstructured by the functional use of space seen in the lifetime of the priory. Given that the site was by now a farm, many must surely have been lost by labourers working the land.

Was the traditional market site at Bromholm ended by religious fervour evinced by men such as William Dowsing in the mid-seventeenth century, or due to simple economic decline?[55] It is impossible to be sure, but the fact that one of the two fairs was still in existence in Bacton parish as late as 1842 hints at the former.[56] It is something of an irony that the removal of a market site from within the sacred space of a Cluniac monastery, urged for so long under the Roman Church, should only have occurred a century after that institution's closure by a new religious philosophy.

Conclusion

Bromholm has provided an interesting opportunity to examine questions of space on a religious site, and to question how we may define particular areas as 'holy' or 'profane'. The expanding body of theoretical work that has chosen to investigate issues of space, and in which the writings of contemporary monastic authors is often cited in support, provides a counterpoint to the analysis of material culture. Because objects found in the ground are the consequence of actions rather than aspirations, the correct reading of this archaeological record has much to say about the realities of life or ideas actually being put into practice.

The presence of holy space has long been recognized in monastic studies, and techniques like access analysis have highlighted cases where hierarchies of space might exist, with 'deeper' areas more restricted in access usually equating to zones considered more sacred or private. Typically these depend upon the identification and definition of 'hard' architectural spaces, with specific barriers and points of access. For the spreads of material across the ill-defined 'soft' space of

---

[55] Dowsing was even concerned at St Benet's church, Cambridge, being called 'Benet Temple': *The Journal of William Dowsing: Iconoclasm in East Anglia During the English Civil War*, ed. T. Cooper (Woodbridge, 2001), pp. 167–8.
[56] C. Green, *The History, Antiquities and Geology of Bacton, in Norfolk* (Norwich, 1842), p.8. Green described one being held on the first Monday in August and constituting nothing more than a 'pleasure market', the other, on 30 November 30, being obsolete.

Bromholm's arable fields, the situation is more complex. Yet certain types of material culture show that, underlying their findspots, structured spaces once existed, ordered in ways that reflected their functional or sacred natures. The metal-detector project has, for instance, shown items of a religious nature to be found, unsurprisingly, closest to the holy space of the priory church.

However, the Bromholm Project has also illustrated the ultimate contradiction of a holy space like a monastic precinct. That secular people entered such a space is obvious; less appreciated perhaps is the sheer pervasiveness of their material culture throughout its area, not least as most archaeological studies of monasteries have focused upon architectural elements and fittings like floor tiles, sculpture and window glass. Indeed, few items of the material culture recovered from Bromholm can be specifically related to the needs or use of the monastic community alone. Yet as those small items of material culture show, the very visible display of holy space through buildings was, in reality, often compromised by extensive lay access to the wider precinct in which they lay.

Bromholm helps to illustrate the difficulties many medieval monks must have faced in separating the profane aspects to their life from the cloister. Their writings, so powerful in structuring our notions of sacred space, may not be 'wrong', but they surely emphasize the idealized view many wanted to convey to others – and indeed the world they themselves would have wished to inhabit.

Chapter 9

The Liturgical Use of Space
in Thirteenth-Century Flanders

Stijn Bossuyt

Introduction

The processional culture of towns in the Low Countries in the late medieval and early modern periods is well known to historians.[1] The different roles played by space within the liturgies which supported such a culture has not, however, been the subject of detailed study. This chapter seeks to rectify this *lacuna* through a study of the liturgical evidence from two medieval Flemish collegiate churches: the *Liber ordinarii* from the church of Notre Dame in Saint-Omer (*c*.1264–96), and that from the church of Saint Peter in Lille (*c*.1280–83). For the concept of sacred space is first and foremost embodied in the liturgy; the Church's rites make the sacred relationship between man and God visible to all Christians through the use

---

[1] Studies very often pay attention to the many 'civic rituals' in the town of the Low Countries. For example, N. Mosselmans, 'Les Villes face au prince: l'importance réelle de la cérémonie d'entrée solennelle sous le règne de Philippe le Bon', in J.-M. Duvosquel and A. Dierkens (eds), *Villes et campagnes au Moyen Age. Mélanges Georges Despy* (Liège, 1991), pp. 533–48; D. Nicholas, 'In the Pit of the Burgundian Theatre State. Urban Traditions and Princely Ambitions in Ghent, 1360–1420', in B.A. Hanawalt and Kathryn Reyerson (eds), *City and Spectacle in Medieval Europe* (Minneapolis, 1994), pp. 271–95; P.Arnade, *Realms of Ritual. Burgundian Ceremony and Civil Life in Late Medieval Ghent* (Ithaca, NY, 1996); A.D. Brown, 'Civic Ritual: Bruges and the Count of Flanders in the Later Middle Ages', *English Historical Review* 112 (1997), 277–99; W. Hüsken, 'Civic Patronage of Early Fifteenth-Century Religious Drama in the Low Countries', in A.F.Johnston and W. Hüsken (eds), *Civic Ritual and Drama* (Amsterdam, 1997), pp. 107–23; J. Huesmann, 'La Procédure et le cérémonial de l'hospitalité à la cour de Philippe le Bon, duc de Bourgogne', *Revue du Nord* 84 (2002), 295–317.

of space and symbols, as well as words.[2] Drawing upon the rites of these two churches, this chapter explores how this sacred relationship was expressed in the liturgical use of space during the later medieval period.

Because of the nature of the *ordinaria*, this study focuses on the rituals which recur annually.[3] Analysis of these rites reveals, as we shall see, four different categories for the liturgical use of space; these distinctions become clear through a description of the rituals involved, and the ways by which they should be interpreted. With regard to the liturgy, it should be kept in mind that rituals – though they may sometimes seem to be constant – are in fact subject to change and altered interpretation.[4] Nonetheless, although the sources derive from two Flemish towns at the end of the thirteenth century, they can contribute to our broader understanding of the liturgical use of sacred space. In particular the processions included in the liturgy express the physical and spatial experience of the liturgy in a very special way.[5]

God's invisibility means that the liturgy can only represent His acts in a symbolic way. Space plays an important role in such symbolism, but through the

---

[2] Furthermore, liturgy may also be an expression of interhuman relationships, more particularly, of a certain kind of social prestige. T.A. Boogaart, for example, studies participation in the procession of the Holy Blood in Bruges as evidence for social cohesion: 'Our Saviour's Blood: Procession and Community in Late Medieval Bruges', in K. Ashley and W. Hüsken (eds), *Moving Subjects: Processional Performance in the Middle Ages and the Renaissance* (Amsterdam, 2001), pp. 69–116. Although this is the main subject of my Ph.D. research, it cannot be denied that the primary function of liturgy was to express the relationship between man and God.

[3] *Libri ordinarii* originated in the eleventh century, and thrived from the end of the twelfth century onwards. They are the result of the increasing literalization of medieval liturgy. Mostly, they offer a dull description of the rituals performed and the incipits of chants and lectures. Non-recurrent or rare rituals are not described in *ordinaria*, but in *pontificals* or *ceremonials*. A.-G. Martimont, *Les «Ordines», les ordinaries et les cérémoniaux* (Turnhout, 1991), pp. 62–7, 89–90; F. Kohlschein, 'Der mittelalterliche *Liber ordinarius* in seiner Bedeutung für Liturgie und Kirchenbau', in F. Kohlschein and P. Wünsche (eds), *Heiliger Raum. Architektur, Kunst und Liturgie im mittelalterlichen Kathedralen und Stiftskirchen* (Munster, 1998), pp. 1–5.

[4] J.L. Nelson, 'Ritual and Reality in the Early Medieval *Ordines*', in J.L. Nelson (ed.), *Politics and Ritual in Early Medieval Europe* (London, 1986), pp. 329–39; G. Koziol, *Begging Pardon and Favor. Ritual and Political Order in Early Medieval France* (Ithaca, NY, 1992), pp. 292–3.

[5] J. Bärsch, 'Raum und Bewegung im mittelalterlichen Gottesdienst. Anmerkungen zur Prozessionsliturgie in der Essener Stiftskirche nach dem Zeugnis des Liber ordinarius vom ende des 14. Jahrhunderts', in Kohlschein and Wünsche (eds), *Heiliger Raum*, pp. 163–9.

study of both *Libri ordinarii* it becomes clear that the use of space is not a one-dimensional phenomenon; depending on the liturgical service involved, and on the way things were done, there were four alternative ways in which space could be regarded. At times the distinctions between these four definitions of sacred space were very subtle and often two or more perceptions of the sacred were included within one liturgical act.

The Restoration and Confirmation of Sacred Space

The first and perhaps most important role ascribed to space within the medieval liturgy was the restoration and reconfirmation of the hallowed nature of a pre-existent sacred space. This is the primary function of most rituals and liturgical acts. Such acts exclusively take place within a sacred space in the strict sense of the word: a church or chapel. Acts performed within such a context derive their sanctity from their environment. The reverse is also true: by performing a sacred act, the hallowed nature of the space in which it takes place is confirmed.

The first category of rituals which restore sacred space are those rituals which return the sacred space to the Sacred. These are cleansing rituals. Their function resembles that of baptism, since the baptismal water is used to wash away all human sins. The most common example of this sort of ritual is, of course, the blessing of the church-goers by sprinkling holy water (*asperges*) on them. Here, the surrounding space is symbolically cleansed of impurities. Purification can, in some cases, be interpreted in a still more literal way than is the case when some drops of water are merely being sprinkled. Take, for instance, the rituals on Maundy Thursday. Both in Saint-Omer and Lille – as, indeed, in many other churches – the altars were stripped and washed with a mixture of holy water and wine.[6] In Lille, spices were even added to this mixture;[7] they represented either the bitter herbs which are eaten during the Jewish meal of Pesach (Seder),[8] or the wine

---

[6] L. Deschamps de Pas, 'Les Cérémonies religieuses dans la collégiale de Saint-Omer au XIIIe siècle. Examen d'un rituel manuscrit de cette église', *Mémoires de la Société Academique des Antiquaires de la Morinie* 20 (1886–87), 165.

[7] *Documents liturgiques et nécrologiques de l'église collégiale de Saint-Pierre de Lille*, ed. E. Hautcoeur (Lille, 1895) [hereafter: *Documents*], p. 45.

[8] Ex. 1:8; H. Haag, 'Passah', in M. Buhlberger, J. Hofer and K. Rahner (eds), *Lexikon für Theologie und Kirche* (14 vols, Freiburg, 1957–63), VIII, pp. 133–7; M. Joseph, 'Seder', in

with bitter herbs in it which was offered to Christ on the cross.[9] Guillielmus Durandus, the thirteenth-century bishop of Mende and author of one of the most important medieval liturgical treatises, described this washing of the altars in his *Rationale divinorum officiorum* (c.1286). To him, the altar symbolized the true body of Christ. The mixture of holy water and wine referred to the stab wound in the side of Christ from which blood and water oozed.[10] In the preparations for the *triduum* of Easter, the purification of the altar indicated that the sacred nature of the entire space was being restored: it became part of the most sacred body of Christ. That this was the aim of this ritual becomes even clearer in the Lille ordinary, which even describes the order in which each of the altars was washed. From this text we learn that the altars were washed according to the importance of the saints to whom they were dedicated. First came the altars in the main body of the church: the collegiate high altar of Saint Peter, the parochial altar of the Virgin Mary, the altar of Saint Mary Magdalene, the altars of Saints Dionysius, Piatus and Quentin, and Saints John and John the Baptist. Afterwards came those in the crypt dedicated to Saints Peter, Stephen, Lawrence and Nicholas respectively.[11] These cleansing rituals reveal much about not only contemporary perceptions of sacred space, but also of the hierarchy of sanctity in general and the relative importance of individual cults within a particular church.

The second and most common category of rituals which confirm the sacred nature of a space are those involving the burning of candles or incense. Indeed, on all important and less important feasts, candles and incense were burned on one or more altars. Candles and incense were also frequently placed in front of the statue of the Virgin Mary and on the tomb of Saint Omer, even on feast days which were in no way connected to either saint, namely the great feast days of Epiphany, Easter, Ascension and Whitsun.[12] At the end of the Lille *ordinarium*, there is an exhaustive enumeration of the number of candles which had to be placed on and around the main altar, depending on the rank of the feast within the Church calendar. On certain specific ecclesiastical feasts, additional candles were placed on the side altars. For instance on all feasts connected to Our Lady, as well as on

---

Isaac Landman (ed.), *The Universal Jewish Encyclopedia* (11 vols, New York, 1969), IX, pp. 453–6.

[9] Mk. 15:23.

[10] Guillelmus Durandus, *Rationale divinorum officiorum*, ed. A. Davril and T.M. Thibodeau (CCCM 140, 140A and 140B, 3 vols, Turnhout, 1998), VI.lxxvi.5, II, pp. 367–8.

[11] *Documents*, pp. 45–6.

[12] Deschamps de Pas, 'Les Cérémonies', 151, 176, 184.

Christmas, Epiphany, Easter, Ascension, Whitsun, All Saints' Day and the feast of the church's consecration, two candles were burned on the main altar, and two on the altar of Our Lady. Also on the feasts of Saint Eubertus and of Saints Peter and Paul, extra candles were lit, in front of the entrance to the choir and of the main altar.[13] In Saint-Omer, incense was burned outside the choir only on feast days of the rank *magnum duplex*; at all other times, this was done within the choir. On these feast days, incense was also burned on the altar of Our Lady and on the tomb of Saint Omer. As a symbol of the prayer which rises up to God, the incense thus filled the sacred space with the scent of divine sanctity. The same is true for the burning candles (of course, we are here discussing the candles which were used in a liturgical context, not the devotional candles provided by individuals as part of their private prayers). The divine light filled the entire space. But the incense and the light were limited to the space in which they were burned or lit, and in this way, they helped to define the sacred space in which the ritual took place, and differentiate it from the secular space outside.[14] In the medieval liturgy, the church building was traditionally seen as a representation of the heavenly Jerusalem.[15] Everything in it served to represent eschatological expectations. Even though the End of Time had not yet arrived, Jerusalem was made present in the building and in the liturgy which took place within.[16] In the case of Saint-Omer and Lille, such symbolic representations can only be found in the *ordinarii*; no clear reference to Jerusalem can be found in the actual architectural setting of the respective church buildings. Indeed, there had apparently been no attempts to visualize the heavenly Jerusalem by architectural means.[17]

---

[13] *Documents*, pp. 102–3.

[14] Koziol, *Begging Pardon*, p. 297.

[15] Bärsch, 'Raum und Bewegung', p. 184; E. Parker, 'Architecture as Liturgical Setting', in J. Hefferman and E.A. Matter (eds), *The Liturgy of the Medieval Church* (Kalamazoo, 2001), pp. 273–326.

[16] One might also study the use of space within the architectural concept as an expression of the Jerusalem of the End of Time; however, this would take us too far from the main theme of this chapter.

[17] This is, however, not an unfamiliar theme in medieval architecture, for instance through the copying of buildings from the town of Jerusalem or by building an imitation grave within the church complex. See R. Ousterhout, 'The Church of S. Stefano: a "Jerusalem" in Bologna', *Gesta* 20 (1981), 311–21; C. Morris, 'Bringing the Holy Sepulchre to the West: S. Stefano, Bologna, from the Fifth to the Twentieth Century', in R.N. Swanson (ed.), *The Church Retrospective* (SCH 33, Woodbridge, 1997), pp. 31–59. This architectural interest in the Holy Land fits within a broader devotion in which relics, liturgy and architecture

We can thus conclude that one of the aims of the liturgy was to restore and confirm the hallowed nature of sacred space. Indeed, the religious person – in this case, medieval man – starts from the assumption that the world is not a homogeneous place. Certain places are sacred, that is more closely connected to the centre of the cosmos. Consecration rituals are thus essential for confirming or reconfirming this sacrality. The importance of such rituals is mainly to be found in their demarcation of the sacral and the profane orders. These aspects of reality exist side by side. It should be borne in mind, however, that the sacral order is not present as such: human intervention is required for the transition from one order to the other. It is precisely this transition which is brought about by consecration rituals, and which is also reconfirmed, as we have seen, in the liturgy on a regular basis. A thirteenth-century canonistic saying confirms this: 'Locus non sanctificat hominem, sed homo locum'.[18] Indeed, no sanctifying power radiates from a sacred space in itself; it is man who lends a place its sacred character, that is, its orientation towards the divine. Because of this, it is important that the sacred nature of such spaces is reaffirmed on a regular basis through the liturgy so that the site does not lose its special nature. These rituals, which symbolically reconfirm and visualize the sacrality of the space, are the most common in the liturgy. In them, the use of space is often not immediately striking. Nevertheless, such rites confirm sacral space as a place where a connection is forged between the earthly space, and all who are in it, and the transcendent reality.

The Sacralization of Profane Space

The second distinction which can be made comes with those rituals which sacralize profane space; through the performance of the ritual, a certain degree of sanctity is conferred upon 'everyday', 'normal' secular reality. In order to achieve this goal, it is essential that these rituals or liturgical acts are performed outside a space that is

---

interact, as is demonstrated by C. Morris, 'Memorials of the Holy Places and Blessings from the East: Devotion to Jerusalem before the Crusades', in R.N. Swanson (ed.), *The Holy Land, Holy Lands, and Christian History* (SCH 36, Woodbridge, 2000), pp. 90–109.

[18] 'Not the place sanctifies man, but man sanctifies the place'. A. Angenendt, *Geschichte der Religiosität im Mittelalter* (Darmstadt, 1997), p. 208; E.H. Kantorowicz, *The King's Two Bodies. A Study in Mediaeval Political Theology* (Princeton, 1997), p. 204, n. 35. He refers to Henricus de Segusia, card. Hostiensis (c.1200–1271), *Summa aurea* (Lyons, 1537), X. 1, 8, n. 3, col. 155.

already considered to be sacred – such as, for instance, a church or chapel. Notwithstanding this limitation, rituals of this type have to be performed within a strictly liturgical context. The Palm Sunday processions probably provide the best examples of this sanctifying of profane space. The ordinary of Saint-Omer offers three possibilities as to the route the procession should take, depending on the weather. In normal circumstances, when the weather was fine,[19] the chapter and the parishioners went to the church of the Holy Cross, situated outside the town walls. There, the Gospel was sung, the palm leaves were blessed and distributed, and a sermon was delivered. From thence, the covered cross and the Gospels were brought to the town in procession. The town gates remained closed until the actual arrival of the procession. The chant 'Gloria, laus' was sung en route to the town and on reaching the gates the famous chant 'Ingrediente Domino, in sanctam civitatem' was performed, the gates were then opened and the procession entered the town. From the gate, it proceeded to the church of Our Lady. There was a short pause in front of the house of the dean of the chapter, where the chant 'Collegerunt pontifices' was sung. There also, the cross was divested of its coverings and venerated by those present who knelt down in front of it and kissed it. Finally, the procession entered the church of Notre Dame, where Mass was celebrated. When the weather was bad, a similar scenario was followed, but the procession remained within the city walls, and set out from the church of Saint Denis before going on to Notre Dame. The actual rituals remained the same but because of the shorter distance the procession had to travel, fewer anthems were sung. The entry into the town was symbolically staged at the gate of the college of Notre Dame. When the weather was really terrible, the procession was confined to the collegiate buildings of Notre Dame beginning in the cloister; in such an event, the door between the ambulatory and the church symbolized the town gate. In this chapter, we will take only the good-weather scenario into account, as this best reflects the intentions of the participants in the ritual.

In Lille there were two options depending on the weather. Usually, the chapter and the faithful went in procession to the church of the SS. Apostles, outside the town walls, which was later renamed the church of Saint Andrew. There, palm leaves were blessed and distributed, the Gospel was sung and the excommunication of heretics, profanators and witches – prescribed by the synodal statutes – was promulgated. While the same chants as at Saint-Omer were being sung, the

---

[19] 'Si pulcrum tempus fuerit': Deschamps de Pas, 'Les Cérémonies', 157.

participants processed to the town. During the singing of 'Ingrediente', the town gates opened, the procession entered and proceeded to the church. The alternative scenario – in the case of bad weather[20] – had the procession take place within the church itself, in which case the main door to the choir symbolized the town gate.[21]

There are clearly two different aspects to the uses of space made by these processions. First, the biblical entry of Christ into the town of Jerusalem was physically re-enacted. We will discuss this aspect later. A second aspect of the use of space which stands out here is the fact that the faithful identified their own town with the heavenly Jerusalem. Just as Christ had entered Jerusalem on Palm Sunday,[22] so Christ, now symbolized by the cross and the Gospels, entered their town in procession and accompanied by singing. Indeed, in the Middle Ages, every church functioned as an earthly gate to the heavenly Jerusalem.[23] Since there is always a temporal dimension present in liturgy, this procession also symbolized that Christ was travelling with the participants to the heavenly End of Time. In this ritual, past, present and future converged. That same coincidence of the profane and the sacred is also visible where space is concerned. The earthly town is identified with God's sacred town. This analogy was certainly strengthened by the same chant which accompanied the entry through the town gate: 'Ingrediente Domino, in sanctam civitate'.[24] In the liturgy, the traditional views of the Christian community as a '*civitas christiana*' were confirmed. Apart from this, there is the (equally important) fact that the spectators almost certainly would have related the text to their own situation, both aligning the '*civitas christiana*' with their own town, and also by viewing the '*civitas christiana*' as their own community. The combination of the location, the chants which were sung and the acts performed symbolically enclosed the profane towns of Saint-Omer and Lille within the sacred. In a way, they were – if only for the duration of the ritual – lifted on to a higher level; they were raised up to the heavenly Jerusalem. The German examples, the *Liber ordinarius* of the abbey of Essen and the *Liber ordinarius* of the Dom of Munster, which were studied by Jürgen Bärsch and Benedikt Kranemann respectively, offer a slightly different view. There, the liturgy almost

---

[20] 'Si vero tempus pluviosum fuerit et processio egredi non poterit': *Documents*, p. 42.

[21] Ibid., pp. 41–2.

[22] Lk. 19:28–40.

[23] P. Leupen, 'Pelgrims naar Jeruzalem', in H. de Dijn and W. van Herck (eds), *Heilige plaatsen. Jeruzalem, Lourdes en shopping malls* (Kapellen, 2002), pp. 15–27; Angenendt, *Geschichte*, pp. 436–7.

[24] 'When the Lord entered the holy city': Deschamps de Pas, 'Les Cérémonies', 158.

exclusively took place within the church building.[25] Nonetheless, similar conclusions also applied to the northern French towns where not only did the church building symbolize the heavenly Jerusalem, but during the large processions, the setting of which was the entire town, the town itself represented Jerusalem.[26]

Benedictions with holy water were a common part of all the processions in Saint-Omer and Lille. Through it, the secular town was symbolically cleansed and assimilated within sacred space. For instance, on each of the three Rogation Days in Saint-Omer and in Lille a procession went to a church just outside the town walls.[27] In this way, on each successive day, the towns' communities were enlarged to include a different area outside the walls. At the rear of each of these processions, the relics of Saint Omer were carried along.[28] The three churches visited during the processions were in different sectors of the town, so that by the end of the third day the entire town had been sanctified through these rituals with holy water and relics. In fact, these rituals had the same effect as the rites performed by the monks of Lobbes in 1060, when they journeyed through the country with some relics. By drawing a circle around the relics, a sacred space was created, distinguishing and separating good from evil.[29] In the same way, the processions to the three churches outside the walls created a protective circle around the town of Saint-Omer. A similar sanctifying function is found in the evidence of the Rogation Days' processions from Montpellier.[30] Of course, not all

[25] Bärsch, 'Raum und Bewegung', pp. 184–5; B. Kraneman, 'Beobachtungen zum Verhältnis von Liturgie und Raum in der mittelalterlichen Kathedralsliturgie des Münsteraner Domes', in Kohlschein and Wünsche (eds), *Heiliger Raum*, p. 132.

[26] Similar dynamics are described elsewhere in this volume; see below pp. 153, 155.

[27] In Saint-Omer, the Rogation Days' processions went to different churches just outside the town walls. On the first day, the procession went to the church of the Holy Cross, on the second day to the church of Saint Michael, and finally to the church of Saint Magdalen: Deschamps de Pas, 'Les Cérémonies', 182–3. In Lille, there was also a procession on each of the three Rogation Days: on the first day to the hospital of La Maladrerie, on the second to the church of Saint Andrew, and on the third day to the church of Notre Dame de Salle. Ascension itself was also lent lustre by a solemn procession: *Documents*, p. 60.

[28] Deschamps de Pas, 'Les Cérémonies', 182–3.

[29] Koziol, *Begging Pardon*, pp. 296–7. See also G. Koziol, 'Monks, Feuds and the Making of Peace in Eleventh-Century Flanders', in T. Head and R. Landes (eds), *The Peace of God. Social Violence and Religious Response in France around the Year 1000* (London, 1992), pp. 239–58.

[30] N. Coulet, 'Processions, espace urbain, communauté civique', in M.H. Vicaire (ed.), *Liturgie et musique (IXᵉ–XIVᵉ siècles)* (Toulouse, 1982), pp. 385–6.

of the numerous processions in the town had this kind of hallowing function; other aspects and functions of the liturgical use of space also have to be taken into account, such as their social function. The position and role of the participants in the procession can indicate their relative social status and reveal much about the relations and dynamics between those of different rank within the town. Unfortunately, due to the absence of any detail in the two *Libri ordinarii* about the role and position of the laity in these processions it is impossible to study the social aspects of these particular processions. Lay people are almost absent from these ceremonies. Their participation is merely mentioned in passing, but no important function is ascribed to them.[31]

The Pastoral Function

Liturgy can therefore be used both to sacralize profane space and to reconfirm and restore sacred space within the church. However, the last two functions of the liturgical use of space are not concerned to define 'sacred space', but rather approach space from a more practical angle. The evidence of the *Libri ordinarii* suggests that space was also used within the liturgy to reinforce its pastoral message. Space was one, practical element of religious communication with the faithful. At the same time, interpreting why space was used within the liturgy in a certain way is often difficult: is a particular custom inspired by symbolism or more practical considerations? In most cases, it was often probably a bit of both. In both of the written sources we are discussing, the pastoral function is only rarely to be found.

One exception to the silence of the *Libri ordinarii* on this point is the striking example of the celebration of Ash Wednesday in Saint-Omer.[32] Everyone present was either given an ash cross on their forehead, or some ash was sprinkled over

---

[31] In order to conduct such a study we would also need descriptive, narrative and administrative sources such as are available for the later Middle Ages. See A. Löther, *Prozessionen in spätmittelalterlichen Städten. Politische Partizipation, obrigkeitliche Inszenierung, städtische Einheit* (Cologne, 1999); M. James, 'Ritual, Drama and Social Body in the Late Medieval English Town', *P&P* 98 (1983), 3–29; M. Boone, 'Les Gantois et la grande procession de Tournai: aspects d'une sociabilité urbaine au bas moyen âge', in J. Dumoulin and J. Pycke (eds), *La Grande Procession de Tournai (1090–1992). Une réalité religieuse, urbaine, diocésaine, sociale, économique et artistique* (Tournai, 1992), pp. 51–8.
[32] Deschamps de Pas, 'Les Cérémonies', 154–5.

their heads. This was done according to social status: first the canons and the most worthy and the oldest, then the other clerics. All this took place in the choir of the church. Afterwards, the 'major canonicus ecclesie cum aliquo clericorum' went to the altar of Saint John, and distributed the ash to the lay people.[33] In the church of Notre Dame at Saint-Omer, there is only one altar dedicated to Saint John, that of Saint John the Baptist.[34] In the Gospel, this patron saint incited the people to repent with these words: 'Repent ye: for the kingdom of heaven is at hand'.[35] The ritual, that is the distribution of the consecrated ashes, and the location where it took place were both conducive to the promulgation of the message.

The message at the beginning of Lent is clear: through the ritual, the faithful are exhorted to repent. The forty-day period of Lent in preparation of Easter, the most important feast of the Christian year, was the time *par excellence* to contemplate one's sins and to repent. A Christian needed a pure heart to face the Lord at Easter. The Ash Wednesday ceremony heralded the beginning of this period of contrition and summoned the faithful to repent. This ritual is, however, only a dim reflection of the public expulsion of penitents on Ash Wednesday and their joyful re-entry on Maundy Thursday, as described in some of the Northern French pontificals for more heinous sinners.[36] Mary Mansfield's study of these pontificals ascribed the disappearance of these rituals of public penance in the late thirteenth century to a complex process of changing theological views on sin and penance, liturgical uses and social practices. Over the course of the mid-twelfth to the early fourteenth centuries these Ash Wednesday rites were replaced by a universal confession and absolution of all the faithful.[37]

---

[33] 'The most important canon of the church, with some clerics': ibid., 154.

[34] M. Gil and L. Nys, *Saint-Omer Gothique: les arts figuratifs à Saint-Omer à la fin du Moyen Age 1250–1550: peinture, vitrail, sculpture, arts du livre* (Valenciennes, 2004), pp. 230–31.

[35] Mt. 3:2.

[36] There existed a great variety of rituals of public penance. In general, Christians who had committed major sins were ritually expelled from the Church. This also meant that they were deprived of all sacraments. After a suitable period of time, these sins were forgiven, absolution was given granted and the sinners were once more joyfully received into the fold: M.C. Mansfield, *The Humiliation of Sinners* (London, 1995), pp. 92–129.

[37] Ibid., pp. 241–4. Another remnant of ritual penance is found in the morning liturgy of Maundy Thursday, in which the priest scourges the choir stalls with a hammer ('sacerdos percutit stallum eum malleo': Deschamps de Pas, 'Les Cérémonies', 163), at approximately the moment when – in earlier times – the expelled persons were once more taken in. The chastisement with the hammer could be interpreted as a symbol of penitence and absolution.

During that same Ash Wednesday celebration, apart from the need to repent, the need for humility was also emphasized. After the faithful had received the ashes on their heads, the priest called on them to be humble, and he did so by his pose as well as by his words. He held out his arms over the congregation and said: 'Inclinantes se Domine majestati'.[38] The combination of the priest's posture and instructions, and the precise moment in the course of the celebration – just after the distribution of the ashes – strengthened each other's call for humility and conversion. That same ideal of humility was represented in the washing of the feet. Humility was emphasized both in the first washing of the feet in the early hours of Maundy Thursday, during which the feet of some poor people were washed,[39] and in the washing of the feet of the chapter members during evening service. The ritual of Saint-Omer even explicitly mentions with regard to that evening service that the 'digniores seu seniores' should perform the actual washing.[40] The prescriptions in the Lille ordinary are more vague.[41] In both these examples the pose and the actual act are more important than the use of space in communicating the pastoral message, and showing to both the clerics and the laity how very real Christ's humility had been. Space sometimes, but not always, played a part in such pastoral rituals.[42]

Re-Enactment of the Biblical Past

Finally, space was also used within the liturgy to dramatically re-enact the biblical past. Clearly, this aspect is closely linked to the functions we have already discussed, where the rituals were predominantly concerned to represent Christ and His sanctity symbolically; other rituals, as we shall see, were concerned to represent Christ through performance.[43] A place is transformed through ritual into sacred space; for instance, during the Palm Sunday procession, a crucifix was

---

[38] 'Inclinantes se, Domine, maiestati tuae, propitiatus intende'[Look graciously, O Lord, upon us who bow down before Thy majesty]: Deschamps de Pas, 'Les Cérémonies', 154–5.
[39] Ibid., 163; *Documents*, p. 44.
[40] 'The most worthy and the oldest': Deschamps de Pas, 'Les Cérémonies', 166.
[41] *Documents*, p. 46.
[42] It would be worth exploring the spatial element within pastoral rituals in more detail – e.g., the use of doors and space in public penance – but that evidence is found mainly in other sources such as ceremonials and pontificals.
[43] Bärsch, 'Raum und Bewegung', p. 172.

carried along representing the Christ. But the re-enactment of the past was often of a far more evocative nature.[44] It was the dramatic fulfilment of the need to make the past occur once more, without using the liturgy to make the space holy. Whilst a play is visually far more explicit, it merely intends to offer a reconstruction of the biblical past: its message is not performative. On the contrary, the liturgy, as we have already seen, was concerned to put across a symbolic message. In this way, the biblical events could be explained to the faithful who had no knowledge of Latin. Such liturgical acts can only sometimes be characterized as being performative because through the performance of this *in casu* ritual act, not only reality, but also the performers and the public transcended the space and time in which the act took place. Those rites which served only to evoke biblical time, on the other hand, have no such effect. Indeed, this type of performance imitates its textual source as closely as possible, without aspiring to transform reality into another order, it merely aims to represent faithfully what is recorded as happening in the Bible. Apart from the more extensive examples found in the Holy Week liturgy, the Whitsun rites also offer a small example of such attempts to evoke the Biblical past. In both churches, while 'Veni Sancte Spiritus' was being sung, the descent of the Holy Spirit was physically represented: in Saint-Omer, a dove was released, while in Lille the release of the dove was accompanied by the lighting of a ball of fire and the strewing of petals. Because of these rather literal representations of the biblical story of Whitsun, the use of space in these rituals can not be interpreted as performative.

In this rather early period of liturgical history, the dramatic re-enactment of the Gospels was mostly restricted to Holy Week. Christ's washing of the disciples' feet at the Last Supper was staged as a kind of play: the chapter of Saint-Omer perhaps presented the most faithful rendering of this event.[45] The Last Supper was also staged in Saint-Omer, and much more expressively than was the case in Lille; in the latter town, the spectacle seems to have had a rather more formal character. The two priests – one on the side of the provost, one on the side of the dean – were assisted by acolytes, who took care of the actual washing of the feet.[46] In Saint-Omer, these events seem to have been represented in a more realistic fashion. The canons, the other clergy of the church of Notre Dame and even some citizens were

---

[44] Kraneman, 'Beobachtungen', p. 132.
[45] Deschamps de Pas, 'Les Cérémonies', 166.
[46] *Documents*, p. 46.

seated at a long table,[47] and there, the events of the Last Supper were re-enacted; historical elements, such as the washing of the feet and the words of institution, were mixed with liturgical acts, such as the singing of psalms and hymns, and the reading of the Gospels.[48] In this church, a similar form of expression was also used on Good Friday. During Lent, a cloth was hung in front of the main altar, separating the choir from the nave.[49] On Good Friday, at the ninth hour, it was pulled down and removed from the choir, giving shape to the words of Scripture: 'And Jesus cried with a loud voice, and gave up the ghost. And the veil of the temple was rent in twain from the top to the bottom' (Mk. 15:37–38).[50]

A few days afterwards, the most important feast of the Catholic liturgical year took place: Easter. On this feast also, the Bible's account was re-enacted through the well-known *visitatio sepulchri* (the visitation of the tomb). Although the ceremonies in both towns were similar, the ritual of Saint-Omer provides a more detailed description of this re-enactment. The complete staging of the consecutive biblical events took several days. On Good Friday, after the veneration of the cross, the crucifix was placed beside the tomb of Saint Omer,[51] to symbolize the funeral of Christ.[52] During the night office of Holy Saturday, three or four boys, dressed as soldiers, stood guard at the tomb. They pretended to sleep, while the chapter went in procession towards the tomb. The cross was lifted, and borne to the altar of Saint John.[53] This symbolized the Resurrection. Finally, the last scene was staged during Matins. After the singing of the Gospel, a boy, dressed in a white dalmatic, went with three *ampullae* 'in modum mulierum' (in the fashion of the women) to the tomb. There, he found two boys dressed as angels, and asked them where Jesus was. The angels pointed to the empty grave and told the boy that Jesus was

---

[47] Deschamps de Pas, 'Les Cérémonies', 165: 'et conveniunt omnes in ecclesiam tam canonici quam alii clerici et burgenses aliqui de majoribus, [...] quo prevento sedent ad mensas paratas'.

[48] Ibid., 165–6.

[49] Ibid., 155–6. This was only removed for important feast days or funerals.

[50] On the Saint-Omer ceremony, see ibid., 168: 'velum quod ante altare pendebat celitus ad terram prosternatur et extra chorus deportetur'. In this ritual, the particular nature of such *Libri ordinarii* can clearly be seen; this passage is only found in the text of Saint-Omer. Guillemus Durandus, in his *Rationale divinorum officiorum*, does not mention it either.

[51] The tomb of Saint Omer in the collegiate church served as the tomb of Christ: Deschamps de Pas, 'Les Cérémonies', 177–8. The precise location of the *visitatio sepulcri* was not recorded for Lille.

[52] Ibid., 171.

[53] Ibid., 176.

resurrected. After this, the choir started to sing.[54] This entire dramatic performance aimed to do little more than to visualize the events described in the Bible. It had a rather limited liturgical function because the church was not altered into a transcendent place through the play, it remained merely a suitable venue for the dramatization of the liturgy.[55] Here, the church building and the town did indeed represent Jerusalem, but not in the same way as was the case for the two first functions, which were described above. Jerusalem was not depicted as the heavenly Jerusalem, but rather as a historical background against which a past reality took place. In this sense, reality was not lifted to a higher level. The play did not so much add to the sacralization of time and space, but rather helped the faithful to understand the biblical stories. Durandus, however, regarded the liturgy as being self-explanatory and without the need for further visualization. His *Rationale divinorum officiorum* does not even mention the *visitatio sepulchri*.

This play was afterwards taken outside the church to be performed. Apparently, this type of Easter play was not yet sufficiently embedded in the liturgy to have become absolutely necessary to the religious ceremonies. However, such performances became the cradle of Western drama.[56] This last function clearly shows that, although liturgy occasionally made use of the consecrated space of the church, it was not always concerned with sacralizing that space. From time to time, space was used within the liturgy to remind the participants of biblical or historical events.

Conclusion

Four important aspects to the liturgical use of space can thus be distinguished. First, liturgy confirmed and reasserted the sanctity of sacred space. This is liturgy's most self-evident function, and most rituals which took place within a church belonged to this type. A second aspect can mainly be noticed in processions. Here, the use of profane, or secular space resulted in its sanctification. Thirdly, the use of space sometimes had a pastoral function. In this case it served to strengthen the message of a particular rite for the audience. Lastly, space was used within a

---

[54] Ibid., 177.
[55] Kraneman, 'Beobachtungen', p. 132.
[56] 'Drama, 1. Mittelalter', in *Lexikon des Mittelalters* (10 vols, Stuttgart, 1977–99), III, cols 1353–5.

liturgical context to re-enact the past. Here, the use of space was not strictly a part of the liturgy but rather of a dramatic performance in which a biblical scene was staged. Space and spatial elements, such as for instance a tomb, were part of the existing physical context, without having a sanctifying function.

Obviously, these four aspects cannot always be neatly distinguished from each other. In some ceremonies, they are present side by side, and one ritual might encompass different functions of the liturgical use of space simultaneously. Two examples of the use of liturgical space might help to clarify the polysemic nature of many rituals.[57] Such an overlap of functions can, for instance, be found in rituals involving the tomb of Saint Omer. On the one hand, candles were lit and incense burned on it on several feast days. In this way, the sanctity of the final resting place of this saint was reconfirmed – the function which we mentioned at the beginning. On the other hand, the tomb was also used as a background for the re-enactment of the *visitatio sepulchri*. Here, the last function, the re-enactment of the past, clearly comes to the foreground. In other words a particular sacred space may have two completely different functions within a specific church liturgy.

Another example is the ceremonial procession of Palm Sunday. In it, we find the four aspects of the liturgical use of space coming together almost simultaneously in one ritual. The confirmation of sacred space is present at the beginning of the ceremony, when the incense is blessed and burnt inside the church outside the walls, and, after the procession, when entering the churches of Notre Dame and Saint Peter in the city. When the procession moved through the towns of Saint-Omer and Lille respectively, profane space was hallowed and lifted on to a sacral plain. Even the apparently opposing anamnetic and mimetic aspects of the liturgy were simultaneously present. On the one hand, Christ was symbolically carried along in the Gospel book and the crucifix, through which He was anamnetically made present. On the other hand, the mimesis was present in the procession of Saint-Omer, which was a sufficiently faithful imitation of the evangelical procession to the town. These diverse aspects were encompassed in one liturgical act. In the liturgical description, there are no caesuras to indicate that these different dimensions were separated. The profane and the secular space co-existed. The first three functions in particular thus offer an insight into the way medieval man interpreted space. Through the symbolic use of space in a liturgical context, it is clearly shown how secular and sacred space were inextricably bound

---

[57] Koziol, *Begging Pardon*, p. 308.

up with each other. Processions clearly show that through the liturgical use of space, one could cross from one type of space to another.

It is clear that in medieval liturgy different aspects worked together to give liturgy its hallowing and dramatic character: acting, words, time and space interacted. In a broader European context, the liturgy of Saint-Omer and Lille can be considered to be illustrative of medieval liturgy at the end of the thirteenth century. It is a commonplace of scholarship on medieval liturgy that there is a close correlation between word and rite.[58] However, less attention has been paid to the fact that not all liturgical acts can be interpreted as sanctifying acts. This is probably due to the fact that medieval liturgical authors, such as Guillielmus Durandus, Rupertus Tuitiensis or Johannis Beleth, discuss almost exclusively these sanctifying aspects of liturgy in their treatises.[59] The analysis of the actual liturgical practices found in the *Libri ordinarii* of the kind studied in this article or, for instance, in Franz Kolschein and Peter Wunsche's collection teach us something different.[60] A single liturgical practice should not only be described as far as its hallowing or religious aspects are concerned, but its secular aspects should also be taken into account. The use of liturgical space was not always perceived as being sacred. In the context of medieval liturgy, on occasion, sacred and secular space could and did meet.

---

[58] Bärsch, 'Raum und Bewegung', p. 184.

[59] Durandus, *Rationale divinorum officiorum*; Rupertus Tuitiensis, *Liber de divinis officiis*, ed. H. Haacke (CCCM 7, Turnhout, 1967); Johannis Beleth, *Summa de ecclesiastices officiis*, ed. H. Douteil (CCCM 41, Turnhout, 1976).

[60] Kohlschein and Wünsche, *Heiliger Raum*.

Appendix: A Short Analysis of the Sources

The Saint-Omer Ordinary (*Ordinarium*)

The first manuscript studied was the *Liber ordinarius* of the chapter of Notre Dame, Saint-Omer. It can now be found in the Bibliothèque d'Agglomération Saint-Omer (BASO), no. 909. The manuscript is no longer intact: parts are missing and it was seriously damaged by damp. It measures 200 x 276 mm. At present, it consists of 81 folios, but there are several gaps. Folios 1–9, 16–20 and 23–25 are missing.[61] The manuscript was foliated in ink with Arabic numerals. In between folios 58/59, 61/62, and 64/65, there is each time an unfoliated folio; the text, however, is not interrupted in these places. The codex comprises 11 quires: 1 III (15) + 1 I (22) + 5 IV (63) + 1 I (64bis) + 1 IV (72) + 1 III^{-2} (76) + 1 IV (84) + 1 I^{-1} (85).[62] The manuscript has a regular page layout in two columns (140 x 75 mm). Only a few pages remained blank: ff. 64rb (1/1), $64bis^{ra–b}$ (1/1), $64bis^{va–b}$ (1/1), 75rb (1/2), $75^{va–b}$ (1/1), 76ra (1/2), 76rb (1/1), $76^{va–b}$ (1/1), 85vb (1/4). It is bound without flyleaves. The cover consists of the original leather over wooden boards. There are remnants of copper fittings and clasps. It is a plain manuscript, completely undecorated. It is written in black ink, and the first letters of each new section are rubricated in red or blue. The script is a small, but neat *littera gothica textualis*. As in almost all liturgical manuscripts, this one also is divided into a *temporalium* (ff. 10ra–$64bis^{vb}$), with descriptions of the liturgy for Sundays and for Holy Week, and a *sanctorale* (ff. 65ra–85vb), discussing the liturgy of the saints' days. On the basis of the *sanctorale* the manuscript can be dated between 1264 – when the feast of Corpus Christi was first introduced[63] –and 1297, the year in which Saint Louis,

---

[61] There is one loose, unnumbered folio which probably belongs somewhere between the first and the ninth folio. On the recto side, it contains a fragment from the office for SS. Remigius and Hilarius (13 January), on its verso side, a part of a calendar with the feast-days and an indication of their rank from the feast of SS. Filitis and Piscis (14 January) to Cathedra Petri (22 February).

[62] In its undamaged, original form, the codex probably consisted of 13 quires: 2 IV (16) + 1 V^{-1} (25) + 5 IV (63) + 1 I (64bis) + 1 IV (72) + 1 III^{-2} (76) + 1 IV (84) + 1 I^{-1} (85).

[63] M. Rubin, *Corpus Christi: the Eucharist in Late Medieval Culture* (Cambridge, 1991), p. 177; E. Strubbe and L. Voet, *De chronologie van de Middeleeuwen en de Moderne tijden in de Nederlanden* (Brussels, 1960), p. 525.

King of France, was canonized.[64] It is a very rich source, containing elaborate descriptions of the rituals that had to be performed, enumerating the *incipits* of the songs and saying how many had to be sung, and enumerating also the incipits of the lectures which should be read.

The Lille Ordinary

The second manuscript studied here is kept in the Bibliothèque Municipale (BM) of Lille, where it is no. 564.[65] It measures 317 x 221 mm. The manuscript contains 117 folios, numbered A–L and 1–105, divided into 22 quires: 1 VI^{-4} (H), 6 IV (XLVIII), 1 I (L), 12 IV (95), 1 IV^{-3} (100), 1 III^{-1} (105). Lille MS no. 564 has a careful layout which varies according to the position of the pages within the codex. The beginning and the ordinary are written in two columns (220 x 60–5 mm). Ff. A^r–B^r contain 32 lines, ff. I–L 30 lines. The calendar (ff. B^v–H^r) consists of a single column (240 x 16 mm), containing 33 to 34 lines. The obituary and the first part of the enumeration of rents (ff. 1^r–101^v) are also written in a single column, and contain 30 lines. The manuscript was ruled in hard point. The fifteenth-century addition (ff. 102^r–105^v) has an irregular page layout without ruling in a single column. Blank pages are: ff. A^{vb} (1/4), B^{ra} (1/2), B^{rb} (1/1), H^v (1/2), XXXI^{ra} (3/4), XXXI^{rb} (1/1), XLVII^{ra} (3/4), XLVII^{rb} (1/1), L^{rb} (2 lines), L^v (1/1). Catchwords: ff. VIII^v, XVI^v, XXIV^v, XXXII^v, XL^v, XLVIII^v, 7^v, 15^v, 23^v, 31^v, 39^v, 47^v, 55^v, 63^v, 71^v, 79^v, 87^v, 95^v, 100^v.[66] The manuscript is bound with a flyleaf, in a modern binding. An old numbering on the spine reads A4 5 and 32 323. It is written in black ink. Throughout the text, there is extensive rubrication: the first letters of each new section, as well as the *incipits* in their entirety are indicated in red and blue. The first letter of the beginning of each important feast-day is decorated with often beautifully wrought lombards. The writing can be described as a *gothica textualis formata*. Most of the additions, however, are written in a fifteenth-century *gothica cursiva*. The manuscript contains a calendar (ff. B^v–H^r), an Easter table (f.

---

[64] J. Richard, 'Ludwig, 15. L. IX., d. Hl., Kg. v. Frankreich', in *Lexikon des Mittelalters*, V, cols 2184–6.

[65] Previous number and number in the inventory: 38.

[66] This last catchword, however, refers to a lost folio.

H^v), an ordinary (ff. I^r–L^r) and an obituary (ff. 1–95^v) with an annexe (ff. 95^v–105^v) of the rents given to finance certain anniversaries.

It is possible to give a rather precise date for this codex. The obituary mentions the Countess Margaret of Constantinople as having died on 10 February.[67] This event took place in 1280. Beatrice of Courtrai, her daughter-in-law, who died on 16 November 1282, is mentioned in the ordinary,[68] and the obituary tells us that a Mass of the Holy Spirit was said for the benefit of her soul.[69] Later entries in the obituary mention her anniversary.[70] The most recent *obiit* of the original redaction dates from 28 June 1283.[71] As a result, we may conclude that the text was written between 1280 and 1283. It begins with a short prologue which describes what the reader can expect to find: 'Hic est Liber ordinarius ecclesie Beati Petri in quo continentur ejusdem ecclesie consuetudines, ad usum et ordinem divini officii pertinentes'.[72] The actual ordinary contains the usual humility topos, in which the scribe apologizes for his shortcomings. Once more, the same order is followed. In a first part, the *temporalium* is discussed, including Sundays and the Holy Week.[73] The second part, the *sanctorale*, describes the saints' days.[74] The latter part starts with the feast of Saint Saturnine (29 November) and ends with the feast of Saint Maxime (27 November). A third and shorter part discusses some of the lesser ceremonies. These mainly concern the liturgy with regard to death, and the lighting of candles in the church.[75] As is also the case for the Saint-Omer ritual, the Lille ordinary does not contain the actual texts themselves of the Masses and offices, but rather a short enumeration of the number of lectures, the *incipits* of the prayers and lectures, and an indication of the liturgical actions which had to be performed.

---

[67] *Documents*, p. 136.

[68] Ibid., p. 4.

[69] Ibid., p. 228.

[70] Ibid., p. 195.

[71] It concerns canon Gilles Maillart. He wrote his testament on 27 June 1283, and died the day after. E. Hautcoeur, *Cartulaire de l'église collégiale de Saint-Pierre de Lille* (2 vols, Lille, 1894), II, p. 500.

[72] 'This is the *Liber ordinarius* of the church of Saint Peter, in which are described the customs of that same church with regard to the uses and the order of the divine office': *Documents*, p. 17.

[73] Ibid., pp. 17–72.

[74] Ibid., pp. 73–98.

[75] Ibid., pp. 99–103.

Chapter 10

'God Will Have a House': Defining Sacred Space and Rites of Consecration in Early Seventeenth-Century England

Andrew Spicer

In 1641 the minister David Crawley published a pamphlet criticizing the liturgical changes and writings of the previous decade. His tract *Superstitio Superstes or Reliques of Superstition newly Revived* was concerned that 'there hath beene of late, amongst our selves a Controversie revived, concerning the Holinesse of Places' and 'whether the Church be more holy than other places, or one part of the Church more holy than another'.[1] This question, he argued, was 'the foundation of the succeeding Controversies' faced by the Caroline Church, and in the second part of his tract he focused on the particularly emotive issue of the positioning of altars, behind rails, at the east end of churches.[2] Crawley was responding to a series of divines and religious writers who during the 1630s argued that places of worship were sacred spaces. They defined churches as the house of God, regarding the building as being the actual dwelling place of God and suffused with his holiness. His divine presence meant that these buildings should be entered with reverence as the congregation came before their God to communicate with Him through prayer and the Sacraments. As late as 1642, Alexander Rosse argued that

> Christs voyce is more heard and his graces more seene in the Word and Sacraments within our Churches then anywhere else. Where should the King be more seene and heard then in his owne house? It is his house by inhabitation, for though all our houses

---

[1] D.C. [Daniel Crawley], *Superstitio Superstes or Reliques of Superstition newly Revived. Manifested in a Discourse concerning the Holinesse of Churches* (London, 1641), p. 1.
[2] See K. Fincham, 'The Restoration of Altars in the 1630s', *Historical Journal* 44 (2001), 919–40.

be his because the earth is the Lords, and all that therein is, yet this house is more specially his ... here he dwels more particularly.[3]

A church was therefore set apart from the world and more holy than the rest of God's divine creation. This identification of a church as a sacred place was reflected by another author who observed that once the church was 'dedicated or consecrated to the Lord, the propertie therof becomes so His as it is no longer Ours'.[4]

Peter Lake has broadly termed this early seventeenth-century understanding of the divine presence in the world, and the appropriate ritual response to it, as the 'Laudian style'. The belief in the holiness of the church building resulted, he argued, in 'an intense concern with the material fabric of the church and a heightened sense of the value of ecclesiastical ornament and decoration'.[5] A widespread programme of church rebuilding and refurbishment during this period evoked this 'Laudian style', ensuring that the decoration and appearance of the building reflected the 'beauty of holiness' and that the ceremonial and rituals of worship were fitting for God's presence chamber. The sacred character of the churches was further emphasized by policies banishing secular or profane activities from the buildings and surrounding churchyards.[6] Although such opinions reached their apogee during the Personal Rule of Charles I, Lake acknowledged that this perception of the sacred was shared by other ecclesiastics earlier in the seventeenth century and was not confined solely to those associated with the religious policies of William Laud.[7]

This evocation of the Laudian style and its perception of sacred space coincided with the gradual development of a rite of consecration during the early seventeenth century. Through the ritual of consecration, buildings, churchyards, altars or liturgical vessels were separated from the profane secular sphere and were dedicated to sacred purposes. Consecration therefore defined churches as sacred spaces, but it was a contentious issue in early seventeenth-century England. At his trial in 1644 William Laud was charged with having 'traitorously endeavoured to

---

[3] Alexander Rosse, *God's House or the House of Prayer, vindicated from prophanenesse* (London, 1642), p. 7. Rosse's comments reflected what Mircea Eliade later called 'the new religious conception' in defining sacred in contrast to profane space: Eliade, *The Sacred and the Profane*, pp. 58–9.

[4] John Swan, *Profanomastix or a Briefe and Necessarie Direction concerning the respects which wee owe to God and his house* (London, 1639), p. 57.

[5] P. Lake, 'The Laudian Style: Order, Uniformity and the Pursuit of the Beauty of Holiness in the 1630s', in K. Fincham (ed.), *The Early Stuart Church, 1603–1642* (Basingstoke, 1993), p. 165.

[6] See above pp. 13, 17.

[7] Lake, 'The Laudian Style', pp. 162–3.

alter and subvert God's true religion by law established in this realm, and instead thereof to set up Popish superstitions and idolatry' and for having 'urged and enjoined divers Popish and superstitious ceremonies'. In particular evidence was presented that he had introduced 'Innovations in consecrating churches and chappels after the Popish manner'.[8] While Laud's actions at the churches of St Katherine Cree and St Giles-in-the-Fields in 1631 are relatively well known, these are often seen as being indicative of the Archbishop's ceremonialism rather than being placed in the wider context of a rising number of services of consecration from the late sixteenth century onwards, as well as the gradual development of a liturgy of consecration.[9] The intention of this essay is not to focus on the liturgies of consecration themselves but to examine the development of the practice and its importance for defining sacred space in post-Reformation England.

The medieval rite of consecration had been abandoned at the Reformation as the leading continental Reformers rejected the notion that one place could possess a greater sanctity than another. Preaching at the inauguration of the new chapel in the castle of Hartenfels, Torgau, in October 1544, Martin Luther argued that:

> ... this house shall be built and appointed according to this freedom for those who dwell here in this castle and court or any others who desire to come in. Not that we are making a special church of it, as if it were better than other houses where the Word of God is preached. If the occasion should arise that the people did not want to or could not assemble, one could just as well preach outside by the fountain [in the courtyard] or somewhere else.[10]

Similar sentiments were expressed slightly earlier by Jean Calvin in the first edition of his *Institutes of the Christian Religion*.[11] In general terms, the Reformers considered the ritual of consecration as 'adiaphora', a matter which they regarded with indifference. Luther dismissed the rite because it lacked scriptural authority and noted that although the Pope aped 'Moses's example in consecrating churches and vessels, there is no reason for it all, except that it was instituted out of stupid imitation, not on the basis of the sure Word of God'.[12] Similarly Heinrich Bullinger

---

[8] *The Works of the Most Reverend Father in God, William Laud D.D*, ed. W. Scott and J.Bliss (7 vols, Oxford, 1853), III, p. 407, IV, pp. 197, 246–51; William Prynne, *Canterburies doome, or, The first part of a compleat history of the commitment, charge, tryall, condemnation, execution of William Laud, late Arch-bishop of Canterbury* (London, 1646), pp. 114–28.

[9] This was documented in Wickham Legg, *English Orders*.

[10] J. Pelikan *et al*. (eds), *Luther's Works* (54 vols, St Louis, 1955–76), LI, p. 337.

[11] Jean Calvin, *Institutes of the Christian Religion: 1536 edition*, trans. F.L. Battles (Grand Rapids, 1986), p. 73. See below, p.221.

[12] Pelikan *et al*. (eds), *Luther's Works*, XII, p. 360.

rejected the Catholic ritual, arguing that a church could not be hallowed or consecrated 'with the rehearsing of certain words, or making of signs and characters, or with oil, or purging fire'.[13] English divines also voiced their opposition to the practice. James Pilkington, for example, argued that it was 'popish' to believe that a certain place was 'more holy than the rest which they [the bishops] have hallowed ... with washing it with their conjured water, crossings, censings, processions etc.'.[14] The royal articles of 1547 reflected a widespread perception that the rite was 'superstitious and lucrative', and denounced those who took 'excessive sums of money for consecrating'.[15]

In spite of this unequivocal rejection of the concept of sacred space and its associated rituals at the Reformation, during the early seventeenth century the rite of consecration was unofficially and gradually revived. An estimated ninety-five churches or chapels were built or partly rebuilt between 1604 and 1642, although it may be necessary to revise this figure upwards in the light of recent research.[16] While chapels that underwent extensive repair and rebuilding traditionally did not require a further act of consecration, new churches and structures which had been completely rebuilt did need to be consecrated. As can be seen from the appendix to this essay, twenty-four parish churches and chapels of ease were consecrated over these forty years. Furthermore religious building was not confined to the parochial churches and chapels; there was also an expansion in the construction of private and institutional chapels. During the same period there were thirteen chapels associated with university colleges, schools or other institutions consecrated, as well as twenty-five private chapels and nine graveyards.[17] Although the number of consecrations gradually increased and reached a peak during the 1630s, it is

---

[13] Heinrich Bullinger, *The Decades of Heinrich Bullinger*, ed. T. Harding (PS, Cambridge, 1849–52), IV, p. 499.

[14] *The Works of James Pilkington*, ed. J. Scholefield (PS xxxv, London, 1842), p. 64.

[15] *Visitation Articles and Injunctions of the Period of the Reformation*, ed. W.H. Frere and W.M. Kennedy (3 vols, Alcuin Club Collections XV, London, 1910), II, p. 104.

[16] J.M. Schnorrenberg, 'Early Anglican Architecture, 1558–1662. Its Theological Implications and its Relation to the Continental Background' (unpublished Ph.D. thesis, Princeton University, 1964), p. 249. He states that 'at least one hundred and thirty-three churches are known to have been newly built or completely rebuilt on an old site between 1603 and 1662, and nearly four hundred were enlarged or remodelled in some architecturally significant way' (p. 52). Research on London suggests that for the capital at least this figure might need to be revised upwards, see J.F. Merritt, 'Puritans, Laudians, and the Phenomenon of Church-Building in Jacobean London', *Historical Journal* 41 (1998), 935–60.

[17] See Appendix. This list is principally derived from Wickham Legg, *English Orders*, pp. 318–23, but recent research has revealed further examples.

interesting to note that the total of thirty consecrations was only slightly higher than in the preceding decades.

The growing importance of the act of consecration was reflected in the writings of a number of early seventeenth-century divines, particularly during the 1630s. Consecration was the means by which a church, God's house, was dedicated to the Lord and his service. Walter Balcanquall argued that 'the consecration or setting apart persons or things to God both by God himselfe and men is very ancient'. Balcanquall was one of several writers who traced the history of the rite from the dedication of the Tabernacle and Solomon's Temple, as well as the later temples recorded in Scripture, through Jewish ceremonial law and its rites of dedication, to the practice of the Early Church. In particular he referred back to a church built in Jerusalem by Constantine – the Church of the Holy Sepulchre – whose consecration in 335AD had been recorded by Eusebius.[18] The precedents of the Early Church and the Church Fathers were also examined by John Pocklington, who concluded that they and 'diverse others in all ages, that have approved, and with great devotion and piety practised the Dedication of Churches'.[19] One of the fullest discussions on the subject, running to over two hundred pages, was *De Templis, A Treatise of Temples: Wherein is Discovered the Ancient Manner of Building, Consecrating and Adorning of Churches*, published in 1638. The author, R.T., argued that the definition of a temple was 'an edifice consecrated to God' and that 'when wee say, it is consecrated to God, we not only distinguish it from all profane buildings, but also teach the end, for which it was built'.[20] R.T. examined the Roman rite of consecration so 'that we Christians may learne even from the vaine superstition of the heathen, with what reverence places dedicated to the true God are to be used' as well as the Jewish ceremonies recorded in Scripture. He then went on to discuss the history and liturgy of the Christian rite which he argued 'has been used ever since the Apostles time'.[21]

The historical and scriptural precedents for consecration were also taken up by Fulke Roberts in his *Gods Holy House and Service* where he devoted three chapters to the subject. He similarly discussed the consecration and dedication of places of worship in the Early Church, arguing that these holy or sacred houses were 'set a part from common use; they are assigned to God's Worship, they are

---

[18] Walter Balcanquall, *Honour of Christian Churches and the Necessitie of Frequenting Divine Service and Publicke Prayers in Them* (London, 1633), pp. 17–19.

[19] John Pocklington, *Altare christianum: or The Dead Vicar's Plea. Wherein the Vicar of Gr. Being Dead, Yet Speaketh, and Pleadeth Out of Antiquity, Against Him That Hath Broken Downe His Altar* (London, 1637), p. 37.

[20] R.T., *De Templis, A Treatise of Temples: Wherein is Discovered the Ancient Manner of Building, Consecrating and Adorning of Churches* (London, 1638), pp. 33, 36.

[21] Ibid., pp. 73–97.

consecrated with speciall rites, and given up into Gods possession'.[22] Roberts also rejected the argument that consecration was merely a continuation of Jewish rituals, asserting that it was a moral issue (rather than a ritualistic or Levitical repetition of the Jewish ceremonial) that 'the Church is specially sanctified to our use, or to call it a consecrated or holy place, when it is a creature of God set apart for the worship of God for the benefit of the soule, and for the furtherance of the whole man, to everlasting Salvation'.[23] Although some authors had referred to aspects of the ritual – Balcanquall had drawn parallels between the dedication of the Temple and the consecration of churches – Roberts's tract explained the significance of the ceremony in defining the church as a sacred place and argued that churches were 'first made holy, by speciall dedication and consecration'.[24] There were three elements by which a church moved from being a secular place to a sacred one:

> 1. The Alienation is when the ground whereon a Church is built, together with the Church or building it selfe, and so much ground about it as is intended for the Churchyard, being all yet but common ground and buildings; such as the owner may retaine in his owne hands and convert to what use he will, either publicke or private, is surrendered into the hands of the Bishop, to the end that it may be made holy unto God whereby the right which the owner had therein, is quite determined; and the common use whereto it might have beene put, is for ever prevented and put by....

> 2. The Assignation is the investing of Almighty God in the right and possession of that ground and building. For when the owner hath surrendered it into the hands of the Bishop, and given livery and seizing thereof to the Bishop, so as now the Bishop is thereof fully possessed; yet is the Bishop herein but God's Atturny, so seized and possessed of this ground and building to God's use; to the which he does by speciall ceremony and solemnity assigne it. Whereupon it becommeth now the house and ground of God, and God himselfe is thereof specially possessed....

> 3. Solemnitie, did also, ever accompany this worke....[25]

Roberts's definition of a consecrated church as 'specifically possessed' by God therefore mirrored the Laudian perception of the divine presence in the world but also emphasized the role of the bishop in defining sacred space.[26]

---

[22] Fulke Roberts, *Gods Holy House and Service According to the Primitive and Most Christian Form thereof* (London, 1639), p. 25.
[23] Ibid., p. 13.
[24] Ibid., p. 9.
[25] Ibid., pp. 9–11.
[26] See below, p. 216.

While these tracts of the 1630s could be portrayed as reflecting a particularly partial and 'Laudian' attitude towards sacred space, they in fact reflected a more widespread desire to distinguish between the sacred and the profane amongst the second generation of Reformers. In Germany, rituals of consecration had begun to reappear amongst the Lutherans during the sixteenth century and were well-established by 1700; elsewhere there is even evidence of Calvinist consecrations.[27] A similar trend can be seen in England where four consecrations had taken place during Elizabeth's reign, principally during the 1590s, but as can be seen from the appendix the practice gradually increased during the early seventeenth century.[28] Sentiments similar to those of the Laudian divines had also been expressed before the 1630s. Sir Henry Spelman, for example, in a tract principally concerned with the appropriation of tithes (which was later cited by Roberts), published in 1613, expressed the view that

> Churches being erected and endowed they and their livings, were (as I say) dedicated unto God. First, by the solemne vowe and oblation of the Founders then by the solemne acte of the Bishop, who to seperate these things from the secular and prophane imploiments, not onely ratified the vowe and oblation of the Patron and founders but consecrated also the Church it selfe using therein great devotion, many blessings, praiers, works of charity, and some Ceremony, for sanctifying the same to divine uses. Therefore also, have the ancient Councels added many fearfull curses against all such as should either violate it or the rights thereof.[29]

Several early seventeenth-century divines, although from a very different ideological standpoint, similarly recognized the importance of separating a church from the secular world. John Donne welcomed the opportunity to publish the sermon which he had preached at the consecration of Lincoln's Inn Chapel in 1623 as 'the whole body and frame of the Sermon is opposed against one pestilent calumny of theirs [the Catholics], that wee have cast off all distinction of places'.[30] The following year, John Prideaux, Regius Professor of Divinity and Vice-Chancellor of the University of Oxford, preached at the consecration of the new

[27] R.W. Scribner, 'The Impact of the Reformation on Daily Life', in *Mensch und Objekt im Mittelalter und in der Frühen Neuzeit Lieben – Alltag – Kultur* (Vienna, 1990), pp. 327–8; A. Spicer, '"What Kinde of House a Kirk is": Conventicles, Consecrations and the Concept of Sacred Space in Post-Reformation Scotland', in Coster and Spicer (eds), *Sacred Space*, pp. 99–102. See below, pp.231–50.

[28] Wickham Legg, *English Orders*, pp. xviii–xix; see below, pp. 228–30.

[29] Henry Spelman, *De non temerandis ecclesiis. A tracte of the rights and respect due vnto churches* (London, 1613), pp. 28–9.

[30] John Donne, *Encaenia. The Feast of Dedication Celebrated at Lincolnes Inne in a Sermon Therevpon Ascension day, 1623* (London, 1623), p. A2.

chapel at Exeter College. Taking as his text Luke 19: 46, 'My house is the house of prayer', the preacher asked his congregation to witness how God reserves to himself a House, which is set apart as the house of prayer:

> God will have a house; this House must appeare to be his peculiar; this peculiar must not be made common, as an Ild-hall for playes or pleadings; or a shop for merchandice; or a cloister for idle-walkers; or a gallery for pleasure; or a banqueting-house for riot; much lesse a brothel for wantonnesse or a cage for idolatrous superstition: but reserved as a sacred Congregation-house where the penitent and submissive supplicants may learne their duty by Preaching; assure their good proceedings by Sacraments, obtaine their graces by Prayer. Though Heaven be God's throne, the Earth his footstoole, his Essence infinitely above all, through all, in all and beyond all; yet his delight is such to be among the children of men, that it liketh him to have a place of assembling them together for his publick worship, where he vouchsafed to be in the midst of them. And this must be, not a mountain, a cave, a grove or obscure hovel; but (as my Text hath it) a convenient house.[31]

Prideaux argued that consecration was the means by which the church was set apart from common or profane use.[32] Similarly John Brinsley preaching at the consecration of the church at Flixton, Suffolk, in 1631 noted that the church was sanctified and set apart: 'This house being denoted and destinated to unto the publique worship and service of God'.[33]

That the consecration of churches was not solely a 'Laudian' concern was reflected in the willingness of Calvinist episcopalians to officiate at these services. John King, bishop of London, consecrated a chapel at Oxhey and St Mary Mounthaw Church in London in 1612 and Sir Julius Caesar's Chapel in the Strand two years later.[34] Archbishop George Abbott himself officiated in 1623 at the consecration of St James' Church, Duke Place, London and where he did

> wholy devolve and dedicate this place this day for ever unto thee (utterly separating it henceforth from all prophane and domesticall uses or affayres) and are bold to consecrate it to thy service onely hearing they worde celebrating thy sacraments and offering up the sacrifices both of prayer and thanksgiving.

Although on approaching the altar he reflected the more Reformed sentiments praying: 'we may present unto thee our soules and bodies as holy temples of thy

---

[31] John Prideaux, *A Sermon Preached on the Fifth October 1624 at the Consecration of St Iames Chappel in Exeter Colledge* (Oxford, 1625), pp. A2–A2v.

[32] Ibid., p. A2.

[33] John Brinsley, *The Glorie of the Latter Temple Greater then of the Former* (London, 1631), p. 22.

[34] Wickham Legg, *English Orders*, pp. 318–19.

spirit, within this little temple'.[35] Julia Merritt has contrasted Abbott's consecration
with the ceremony performed by Laud at the neighbouring Church of St Katherine
Cree eight years later, but it nonetheless still represented a ritual defining of the
church as a sacred place.[36] The separation of sacred space by non-Laudian bishops
continued into the 1630s. Joseph Hall consecrated a chapel and a burial ground in
Exeter, the latter being commemorated with a large plaque bearing his coat of
arms.[37]

While early seventeenth-century divines recognized the importance of setting
apart a place of worship, their understanding of the means by which this was
achieved differed markedly. The Church lacked an official form of consecration
but two liturgies developed which provided the basis for many of the rites
employed during the period. The first was used by Bishop William Barlow at
Langley Chapel, Kent, in 1607, while the more influential liturgy was devised by
Bishop Lancelot Andrewes for the consecration of a chapel at Peartree near
Southampton in 1620. In practice, there was considerable variation in these
services – Andrewes's liturgy was not even published until 1659 – and in some
cases completely different rites were employed. This ritualistic confusion only
serves to obscure further the range of opinions about what actually defined a place
of worship as holy.

Echoing the marks of a True Church identified by the Reformers, some
churchmen recognized the building as being consecrated by the Word of God and
the proper administration of the sacraments rather than through episcopal rites.
Jeremiah Dyke at the consecration of a chapel at Epping in 1622 argued:

> Heere then is our direction, wee have here built a place, an house for the Lord. Now if
> we get not God into it what are we the neare for all the cost? Let our next care be to get
> God, and keepe God in it. How may that bee done? Let us get and keepe his *Name*
> *recorded* here. And if we have his Name here, his Ordinance of the Word, and Prayer,
> then hee himselfe is here, and wee shall have him here. This is the principall
> Consecration of all, without which other Consecrations are to little purpose.... The main

---

[35] Oxford, Bodleian Library, Rawlinson MS D818, ff. 31, 32; Merritt, 'Puritans, Laudians,
and the Phenomenon of Church-Building', 951. The previous year Abbott had consecrated a
private chapel at Bramhill House in Hampshire in 1621. H. Arthur Doubleday (ed.), *VCH:*
Hampshire and the Isle of Wight (6 vols, Westminster, 1900), IV, p. 41.

[36] Merritt, 'Puritans, Laudians, and the Phenomenon of Church-Building', 951, 958.

[37] I am grateful to John Allan of the Exeter Archaeology Unit for drawing my attention to
the plaque. The original is now housed in St Nicholas's Priory, Exeter, but an eroded
replacement can be found in St Bartholomew Street.

substantials therfore requirable in a Consecration, are the Word and Prayer, which have the promise of God's presence.[38]

John Donne meanwhile preached that as the faithful were temples of the Holy Spirit

These walls are holy because the saints of God meet here within these walls to glorifie him. But yet these places are not onely consecrated & sanctified by your coming, but to bee sanctified also your comming that so, as the Congregation sanctifies the place, the place may sanctifie the Congregation too. They must accompany one another; holy persons and holy places.[39]

Walter Balcanquall in 1633 similarly recognized that

Churches ought to be consecrated by prayer; for Salomon his dedication is conceived in the very forme of a prayer; next, Churches are to be consecrated by reading of the Word; for at the dedication of the Temple the law was ever read: Thirdly Churches are to be dedicated with the celebration of the Sacrament of our Saviour, his most precious body and bloud, as in all the three dedications of the Temple ever sacrifice was offered.

There was however a subtle difference, in that for Balcanquall these were elements in the ritual of consecration for which there was Biblical precedent, rather than effecting the consecration of themselves. Consecration itself remained an episcopal act as 'the rites of consecration are left to the Church and her bishops'.[40] Such principles were further asserted six years later by Fulke Roberts, who emphasized the special role of the bishop. The bishop acted as the intermediary between the founder and the divine; he was the agent of God and through his actions a church became holy. This reflected a heightened sense of the sacramental powers and authority of the episcopacy in the Caroline Church.[41] Perhaps the clearest expression of the power of the bishop in defining and setting apart places of worship comes from William Laud himself. At his trial he acknowledged that 'I did pronounce the place holy ... and that was in the solemn act itself of consecration', referring to his actions at St Katherine Cree and St Giles-in-the-Fields in 1631.[42]

---

[38] Jeremy Dyke, *A Sermon Dedicatory preached at the Consecration of the Chappell of Epping in Essex October, 28. 1622* (London, 1623), p. 17.

[39] Donne, *Encaenia*, pp. 2–3. See George Abbott's comments above, and also see below, p. 303.

[40] Balcanquall, *Honour of Christian Churches*, p. 19.

[41] J. Davies, *The Caroline Captivity of the Church: Charles I and the Remoulding of Anglicanism, 1625–1641* (Oxford, 1992), p. 54.

[42] *Laud's Works*, IV, p. 248.

The growing number of consecrations during the early seventeenth century reflected the increasing episcopal concern to regulate and define places of worship. For although there were diverse opinions about how a church came to be set apart, the rite of consecration remained an episcopal act just as it had been in the pre-Reformation Church. Nonetheless, this represented a redefinition and reassertion of the sacred during the second generation of the Reformation rather than the mere continuance of earlier medieval practices. This power to define what was and was not a place of worship was exploited, especially in the 1630s, as a means of regulating religious affairs and asserting episcopal authority.

Particularly noticeable during this period were the number of private chapels that were consecrated, which exceeded the number of parish churches and chapels of ease. Before the Reformation private chapels had to be licensed by the bishop and were certainly a concern for the ecclesiastical authorities because they stood outside the existing parochial system.[43] In the radically changed religious landscape of post-Reformation England, the parish church served as the principal or only place of worship for a community. The authorities attempted to ensure religious conformity through requiring regular attendance at the parish church. Fears of residual conservatism, or alternatively radical conventicles, meant that absentees were regarded with suspicion and were punished. The Henrician statutes had permitted 'certen honorable persons as well spirituall as temporall shall have Chaplayns ... to serve theyme in theire honourable houses', but had specifically limited the privilege to the upper echelons of society.[44] This privilege had gradually been eroded and private chapels had become increasingly a cause for concern, and with some justification, as in some cases they provided a venue for Catholic worship or a haven for radical dissenters.[45] In an attempt to curb radical and subversive preaching, Charles I ordered in 1629 'That the bishoppes suffer none under noble men, and men qualified by the lawe to have any private chapplaine in his house'.[46]

These royal instructions served to reinforce the efforts which were already being made by the episcopate to regulate non-parochial worship. During the early seventeenth century, episcopal visitations went beyond questioning whether worship was taking place outside the parish church, and began to enquire

---

[43] See above, pp. 37–40.

[44] *The Statutes of the Realm*, ed. A. Luders *et al.* (12 vols, London, 1810–28), III, p. 457.

[45] Frere and Kennedy (eds), *Visitation Articles*, III, p. 211; W.P.M. Kennedy (ed.), *Elizabethan Episcopal Administration. An Essay in Sociology and Politics* (3 vols, Alcuin Club 27, London, 1924), II, pp. 122–3, III, pp. 321–2. See above, pp. 97–8.

[46] *Laud's Works*, V, p. 308; Davies, *The Caroline Captivity*, p. 161; K. Fincham (ed.), *Visitation Articles and Injunctions of the Early Stuart Church* (2 vols, Woodbridge, 1994–98), I, pp. 88, 116, II, pp. 27, 38, 40, 41, 69, 141–2, 160.

specifically whether the sacraments were being administered in a place that had not been consecrated or was legally sanctioned. As early as 1607 Bishop William Chaderton enquired in his visitation of the diocese of Lincoln: 'Whether doe adie [*sic*] chaplens, in your parish preach or administer the sacrament in anie chappell not consecrated, or in anie house having no chappell allowed by law...'.[47] It was a question which was repeated by his successors in 1618 and 1622 but was also taken up and included by Richard Neile in his injunctions for the visitation of the diocese of Durham in 1624 and then in his provincial visitations of the archdiocese of York in 1633 and 1636.[48] Matthew Wren in his visitation of the diocese of Norwich in 1636 asked: 'have you in your parish any dwelling-house with a chappell therein; or in which any roome is ordinarily used for preaching, or saying the divine service, and administring their holy sacraments'.[49] He expanded further on this article for his visitation of the diocese of Ely in 1638–39:

> Is there any other kind of chappell or chappells within the precincts of your parish? To whom do they belong? When were they erected? And when consecrated? Have you in your parish any house or houses, whereof any roome is ordinarily used for preaching, or saying the divine service, and administring the holy communion? How long hath it beene so? And by what authority or licence?[50]

William Juxon in 1640 similarly enquired for the London diocese:

> Doth your minister, except it be in times and cases of necessity, preach or administer the holy communion in any private house in which there is no chappell dedicated and allowed by the ecclesiastical laws of this kingdome? Doth any chaplaine living within your parish, preach or administer the communion in any other place then in the chappell of the said houses? Doth the lords and masters of such chaplaines, or houses, at other times resort to their owne parish churches, and there receive the holy communion, at least once a yeare? And doe any under noble men, and men qualified by law keepe any private chaplaine in their house or houses?[51]

During the 1630s, some bishops attempted to limit and control the establishment of new places of non-parochial worship through restricting the consecration of private chapels.[52] Archbishop Neile refused Sir Henry Slingsby's request to consecrate a chapel for 'having as he saith express command not to

---

[47] Ibid., I, p. 75.
[48] Ibid., I, pp. 80, 82, 85, 86, 88.
[49] Ibid., II, p. 148.
[50] Ibid., II, p. 151.
[51] Ibid., II, p. 230.
[52] Davies, *The Caroline Captivity*, pp. 162–3.

consecrate any, least it may be occasion of conventicles, & so I think it may be abus'd'.[53] The Bishop of St Davids referred a request to consecrate a private chapel, made by Sir Rice Rudd of Aberglasney to Archbishop Laud in 1636. As Rudd was only a baronet, his status did not qualify him to maintain a chaplain and on such grounds it was perhaps inappropriate for the chapel to be consecrated. Laud proposed that the chapel should be consecrated, with the local minister being licensed as its chaplain, but on condition that 'he use this chapel but at times of some necessity, not making himself or his family strangers to the mother-church; and that there may be a clause expressed in the license for recalling thereof, upon any abuse committed'.[54] In another case, Laud granted permission in 1638 for the widowed Lady Dorothy Selby to worship in her chapel at Ightham Mote, which had been consecrated several years earlier, rather than attend the parish church, on account of her age and infirmity.[55] Even where a private chapel had been consecrated, there could also be other issues which caused concern for the Laudian bishops. In 1639, Matthew Wren consulted Laud about the private chapel belonging to Sir John Cutts at Childerly, which had been consecrated by Martin Heaton, bishop of Ely, between 1600 and 1609. Wren raised questions about whether the rite of consecration, which consisted of the bishop 'saying a service there himself, and having a sermon', was valid. The family, although not of noble status, maintained a 'chaplain', worshipped solely in their chapel, and did not frequent the parish church. This was probably the basis for this enquiry.[56]

While some of these chapels were free-standing buildings, others were constituted within the main structure of the house. In some households, oratories or even particular rooms provided space in a domestic setting for pious reflection, contemplation and prayer.[57] The ecclesiastical authorities were, however, more concerned with ensuring that there was an appropriate setting for preaching, divine service and the administration of the sacraments. In the domestic environment there was a particular need to separate the sacred from the profane. This sentiment provided a metatext in the visitation articles concerning private chapels, but the need 'to distinguish places sequestred for religious exercises from private houses

---

[53] *The Diary of Sir Henry Slingsby*, ed. D. Parsons (London, 1836), p. 19. In 1634, Neile expressed surprise and concern at the proximity of Leeds parish church and the new chapel of St John, hoping that they would not become focal points for differing religious opinions. BL, Additional MS 4274, f. 255.

[54] *Laud's Works*, V, p. 344.

[55] Kent Archives Service, Maidstone, U947 Q1/2; Wickham Legg, *English Orders*, p. 322. I am grateful to Bernadette Gillow and Joy Debney from Ightham Mote for their assistance.

[56] *Laud's Works*, V, pp. 364–5.

[57] See above, pp. 27–79, 115–36; also J.P. Walsh, 'Holy Time and Sacred Space in Puritan New England', *American Quarterly* 32 (1980), 89.

for the more convenient use of Christian assemblyes' was more clearly seen in the rites of consecration.[58] Bishop Barlow's liturgy for the consecration of the earl of Salisbury's chapel at Hatfield House in 1610–11 did

> devote and dedicate thys Place, this day, for ever unto thee; and (utterly separating it henceforth, from all prophane and domesticall uses and affaires) are bould to Consecrate it to thy Service only, for hearing thy word, celebrating thy Sacramentes and offring up the Sacrifices both of Prayer and Thanksgeeving.[59]

It was not only the validity of private chapels as places of worship that concerned the ecclesiastical authorities. Edward VI had granted letters patent in 1550 allowing 'the ministers of the Church of the Germans and of other foreigners an uncorrupt interpretation of the most Holy Gospel and administration of the sacraments, according to the word of God and apostolic observance'.[60] Although these churches had been reconstituted under the superintendence of the diocesan bishop and other communities had been established during Elizabeth's reign, these congregations were an anomaly which stood outside the parochial system. The exiles did not attend the parish churches but were granted redundant chapels and churches to serve as their temple, buildings which would have been consecrated in the centuries before the Reformation.[61] Here they worshipped according to their own liturgy rather than the Book of Common Prayer. Laud regarded these churches as 'great nurseries of inconformity' and attacked what he regarded as their great 'irreverence at their communion, sate altogether as if it were in a Tavern or Ale-house'.[62] He therefore challenged the privileges of these communities and required the children of exiles, who had themselves been born in England, to leave the foreign congregations for the local parish church.[63] While the assault on these foreign churches focused principally on encouraging religious uniformity, in some cases the fundamentally different attitudes held by these communities towards sacred space provided a further source of irritation for some bishops.

---

[58] Wickham Legg, *English Orders*, p. 133.

[59] Ibid., pp. 2, 21. On the chapel itself, see above, pp. 130–36.

[60] A. Pettegree, *Foreign Protestant Communities in Sixteenth-Century London* (Oxford, 1986), pp. 24–5, 31–2; J. Lindeboom, *Austin Friars. History of the Dutch Reformed Church in London, 1550–1950* (The Hague, 1950), p. 201.

[61] See A. Spicer, '"A Place of Refuge and Sanctuary of a Holy Temple": Exile Communities and the Stranger Churches', in N. Goose and L. Luu (eds), *Immigrants in Tudor and Early Stuart England* (Brighton, 2005), pp. 91–109.

[62] Jean Bulteel, *A Relation of the Troubles of the Three Forraign Churches in Kent* (London, 1645), p. 9; *Laud's Works*, V, p. 323.

[63] For an overview of this conflict, see K. Sharpe, *The Personal Rule of Charles I* (New Haven, 1992), pp. 349–51.

During the early seventeenth century new communities of foreign artisans were established for whom the provision of a suitable place of worship was also an important concern. Sir Cornelius Vermuyden, who had engaged Dutch artisans in the drainage of the Isle of Axholme/Hatfield Chase, was permitted by the crown in December 1628, 'to erecte or build one of more chappell or chappelles for the exercise of religion or devine service to be vsed or reade in the English or Dutch language'. Several local landowners were granted permission in 1636 'to erect and build one or more chapel or chapels ... in the premises most convenient, and at their own expense, to maintain in the same ministers sufficient to celebrate divine service there'.[64] In spite of these grants, the community had to rely on makeshift accommodation for its services.

Archbishop Neile of York wrote disparagingly about the congregation in a letter to William Laud in June 1636: 'A barn of Sir Phillibert Vernatty is the place which they use for their church, whether the whole company have resort on Sondaies, where they baptize in a dishe after their owne manner, and administer the sacrament after their homely fashion of sitting'.[65] The willingness to resort to a barn for worship reflected the places used by their co-religionists on the continent in the early years of the Reformed movement, but also a fundamentally different attitude towards sacred space. In the first edition of the *Institutes of the Christian Religion* Jean Calvin stated that places of worship did not

> by any secret sanctity of their own make prayers more holy, or cause them to be heard by God. But they [temples] are intended to receive the congregation of believers more conveniently when they gather to pray, to hear the preaching of the Word of God, and at the same time to partake of the sacraments....[66]

The belief of the foreign congregations that where they worshipped was not defined as sacred was understood by Archbishop Abbott. In 1622 he granted the Dutch tapestry weavers at Mortlake permission for a minister 'to celebrate divine sevice, preache the Worde of God, and administer the holy sacraments (if neede

---

[64] H.G.B. Le Moine and W.J.C. Moens, 'Huguenots in the Isle of Axholme', *Proceedings of the Huguenot Society* 2 (1887–8), 278–9; G.H. Overend, 'The First Thirty Years of the Foreign Settlements in Axholme, 1626–56', *Proceedings of the Huguenot Society* 2 (1887–8), 292–3.

[65] NA, SP16/327/47.

[66] Calvin, *Institutes of the Christian Religion: 1536 Edition*, p. 73. The wording is slightly different in the later editions of the *Institutes*. J. Calvin, *Institutes of the Christian Religion*, ed. J.T. McNeill (2 vols, Philadelphia, 1960), II, p. 893. For a discussion of Calvinist attitudes towards sacred space, see C. Grosse, 'Places of Sanctification: the Liturgical Sacrality of Genevan Reformed Churches, 1535–1566', and Spicer, '"What Kinde of House a Kirk is"', in Coster and Spicer (eds), *Sacred Space*, pp. 60–103.

shall require) either in the parish church of Mortlack if it may be done conveniently, or in the house of Sir Francis Crane knight or any other convenient place there'.[67] By the 1630s, when the Laudian episcopate was in the ascendancy, the failure to recognize a place as sacred was unacceptable. This was reflected in the stinging attack made by Richard Corbet, bishop of Norwich, who was trying to eject the Walloon congregation from his episcopal chapel. He condemned the congregation in the following manner:

> Your discipline, I know cares not much for a consecrated place, & any other roome in Norwiche that hath but breadth and length may serve your turne as well as a chappell. Wherefore I say unto, without a miracle, *Lazare prodi foras!* Depart, and hire some other place for your irregular meetings.[68]

The defining of sacred space by the bishops through the rite of consecration provided the pretext for the dispute between the community settled at Sandtoft and Dr John Farmery, the Chancellor of the diocese of Lincoln – who administered the see on behalf of Archbishop Laud during the confinement of Bishop Williams – over their place of worship. Following the failure of the local patrons to provide them with a building, the community decided in November 1637 to construct their own temple.[69] Their minister, Pierre Bontemps, left the following year and Farmery appointed Estienne Cursol as his replacement. Farmery reported to Archbishop Neile that Cursol 'having our Booke of Comon Prayer in French, doth officiate amongst them very conformably in all things ... administer the sacraments to them in some one of our consecrated churches, Belton or Epworth, and not in the new built wooden house where Bontemps officiated in his time'.[70] Although the settlers did not recognize the need to worship in a consecrated place, Farmery seems to have been determined to ensure that the congregation gathered in the parish churches and used the Book of Common Prayer rather than assembling in their own temple. Although the exact details are unclear, it seems that in spite of their Reformed beliefs, Farmery insisted that the Sandtoft temple was consecrated before it could be used for worship while at the same time he made this difficult for the congregation to achieve. It was alleged that Farmery attempted to raise £300

---

[67] J.H. Hessels, *Ecclesiae Londino-Batavae Archivum* (3 vols, London, 1887–97), III, p. 1296.

[68] NA, SP16/400/45. On the dispute over the episcopal chapel, see Spicer, '"A Place of Refuge"', pp. 101–2.

[69] Spicer, '"A Place of Refuge"', pp. 102–3; Hessels, *Ecclesiae Londino-Batavae Archivum*, III, pp. 1759–60; *Seventh Report of the Royal Commission on Historical Manuscripts: Report and Appendix* (London, 1879), pp. 136, 145.

[70] Overend, 'The First Thirty Years', 304.

from the congregation for the 'obteyninge the graunt for this said Chappell and immunityes' and 'alsoe for procuringe their said Chappell when it is builded to be consecrated'.[71] The settlers petitioned the House of Lords concerning this exploitation which

> procured them no immunities at all, more then they had in their Letters Patents, and left them to procure at their owne charges, their poore church to bee consecrated, which by that meanes remaynes still unconsecrated to this day. The poore strangers & refugees being harrowed in the meane tyme in the said Farmeryes Court Ecclesiasticall for not being present every Lords Day in the churches of Croole, Belton, Epport & Hoxalme pretended to bee their supposed parishes, where they understand nothing preached or officiated.[72]

While his actions were condemned by the House of Lords, by requiring the consecration of the Sandtoft temple in defiance of Reformed tradition Farmery asserted the episcopal rite in defining how places were set apart for worship.

While the bishops, particularly during the 1630s, were exercised by the problems raised by the use of places of worship which stood outside the normal parochial system, they were also concerned to ensure that the status of parish churches, as the focal point of regular worship, was unambiguous. As has been noted, twenty-four newly built churches and chapels of ease were consecrated during the early seventeenth century.[73] The bishops exercised this right to authorize places of worship with some care. The correspondence between Archbishop Neile and the Leeds merchant John Harrison, concerning the consecration of St John's church in 1634, is revealing in this respect. The archbishop wrote he had '... indeavoured to shew my willingness to further and accomplish the worke of your good intentions by consecrating and establishing to Gods Holy service the chapple which with very great charge you have built'. Nonetheless, Neile was reluctant to come to Leeds to perform the rite until he had been assured that the matter of patronage and the finances for the maintenance of the minister had been settled.[74]

It was not only new churches that concerned the bishops but also churches in use, which for various reasons had not been properly defined as sacred space. The church at South Malling, a peculiar of the archbishop of Canterbury, provides a particularly interesting example of an unconsecrated church which was being used for worship. The original church was in a ruinous condition and so had been

[71] House of Lords Record Office, London, Annexe to the Petition of James de Con, John le Houg and Gilley Rey, 10 December 1640.
[72] House of Lords Records Office, Petition of James de Con, John le Houg and Gilley Rey, 10 December 1640.
[73] See Appendix.
[74] BL, Additional MS 4274, ff. 253–5.

demolished in the mid-sixteenth century; a new church was built on the site between 1626 and 1628 and John Evelyn 'lay'd one of the first stone at the building of that church'. On the building's completion, the congregation petitioned Archbishop Abbott that 'they may hear divine service and celebrate the sacraments without trouble for new consecration'. When it became known to Abbott that the site had been desecrated in the past through being 'polluted by beasts and other animals', he imposed an interdict on the church (6 May 1631), forbidding the minister, churchwardens and parishioners from entering the building until it had been lawfully and legitimately consecrated. This did not however take place for almost a year, being carried out by Bishop Field of Oxford on 24 May 1632.[75]

It was the consecration of the two churches by Laud in 1630–31, that provoked the most opposition over this issue. Much of the controversy focused on the ceremonial employed by Laud, but one witness claimed that 'they were not new churches' thereby implying that they did not need to be consecrated.[76] St Katherine Cree Church had undergone major refurbishment/rebuilding, which began after several years of discussion and fund-raising in 1628, while St Giles-in-the-Fields had been part of the Jacobean wave of church building, being rebuilt between 1623–25.[77] Worship had resumed in both of these churches after the work had been completed without the bishop of London, George Monteigne, requiring the buildings be consecrated. On his succession to the bishopric, Laud suspended 'divine services, sermons and sacraments' for a period of two or three weeks at the two churches, 'so as the church doors were shut up even on the Lord's Dayes, and the Parishioners forced to repair to other churches, onely because the church had not been re-consecrated after its reparation'.[78] Laud argued that the consecration

---

[75] *The Diary of John Evelyn*, ed. E.S. de Beer (6 vols, Oxford, 1955), II, p. 8; E.H.W. Dunkin, 'Contributions towards the Ecclesiastical History of the Deanery of South Malling', *Sussex Archaeological Collections* 26 (1875), 82–3; J.R. Daniel-Tyssen, 'Survey of the Church of the College of Malling, near Lewes', *Sussex Archaeological Collections* 21 (1869), 178–86; Wickham Legg, *English Orders*, pp. xlviii, 321.

[76] *Laud's Works*, IV, p. 249.

[77] *The Survey of London ... begunne first by the paines and industry of John Stow* (London, 1633), pp. 149, 894–5; Merritt, 'Puritans, Laudians and the Phenomenon of Church-Building', 935–60; P. Lake, *The Boxmaker's Revenge. 'Orthodoxy', 'Heterodoxy' and the Politics of the Parish in Early Stuart London* (Manchester, 2001), pp. 298–308; J. Newman, 'Laudian Literature and the Interpretation of Caroline Churches in London', in D. Howarth (ed.), *Art and Patronage in the Caroline Courts* (Cambridge, 1993), pp. 175–80.

[78] William Prynne, *A Quench-Coale or A Briefe Disquisition and Inquirie in What Place of the Church or Chancell the Lords-Table Ought to be Situated, Especially When the Sacrament is Administered* (London, 1637), p. 219; Prynne, *Canterburies Doome*, pp. 113, 119–20.

was necessary because it was 'notoriously known, they were both new-built from the ground and St Giles not wholly upon the old foundations'.[79]

Concern about unconsecrated churches being used for worship continued when Laud moved to Canterbury. Papers found in Laud's study after his arrest reveal 'his Visitor or Vicar Generall interdicted the Chappell of Buckston and of Downe in Derbyshire (though long used) for want of consecration'.[80] The chapel at Buxton dated from 1625 and so presumably had been in use for ten years before the metropolitan visitation.[81] Interestingly the four surviving sets of injunctions for this visitation do not include any reference to questions relating to the consecration of a church, as earlier injunctions had done in relation to private chapels.[82]

The use of chapels which had not been consecrated was an issue in the dispute between the Archbishop and the University of Cambridge. Although not as potentially subversive as private domestic chapels, the bishops had similarly sought to ensure that institutional chapels were also ritually set apart for worship. In 1617 the minister Sampson Price had preached at the consecration of the chapel of Shrewsbury School by the bishop of Lichfield and Coventry, a chapel which had been completed in 1613 'yet was never consecrated till now'.[83] The chapel built by Sir John Lenthall in the Kings Bench prison 'after it been built & used as a Chappell above a yeares space ... it must needs be consecrated or else threatened to be sequestered and interdicted'.[84]

In 1635 Laud had announced his intention to visit the Universities of Oxford and Cambridge as metropolitan. Although the Universities protested against Laud's claim to have this right, the King found in his favour in June 1636. Laud's intention was to examine the religious practices of the universities and to ensure conformity, as these two institutions served as seminaries for most of the English clergy. The need for religious reform was seen to be most pressing at Cambridge and in September 1636 Laud received a dossier of evidence from John Cosin of the

---

[79] *Laud's Works*, IV, p. 249.

[80] Prynne, *Canterburies Doome*, p. 126.

[81] N. Pevsner, *The Buildings of England: Derbyshire* (London, 1986), p. 113.

[82] Fincham, *Visitation Articles*, II, pp. 106–9. In addition, Prynne refers to 'Articles to be inquired at the visitation of the Arch-deacon of Buckingham, Anno 1625', which he also found in Laud's study. These include the question 'Whether any Chaplains did Preach or administer the Sacrament in any Chappell not consecrated?', Prynne, *Canterburies Doome*, p. 126.

[83] Sampson Price, *The Beauty of Holiness or the Consecration of a House of Prayer* (London, 1618), 'The Epistle Dedicatorie'.

[84] The chapel seems to have come to the attention of Laud and Matthew Wren, but as it fell within the diocese of Winchester it was consecrated by Bishop Curle in 1636. Prynne, *A Quench-Coale*, pp. 220–21.

'common disorders in the universitie'.[85] Amongst these abuses, Cosin reported that 'now in Cambridge three chappells were never consecrated Corpus Christi Coll. Emmanuel Coll. and Sidney Coll. Whereof Sidney Coll. is said to have been an old stable And Emmanuel Coll. Chappell Mr Chatterton saith that he hath consecrated by fayth and a good conscience'.[86] The pre-Reformation chapel at Corpus Christi College had initially adjoined and opened onto the parish church of St Benedict, but work began in 1579 on a separate chapel under the patronage of Sir Nicholas Bacon.[87] Emmanuel and Sidney Sussex Colleges were both post-Reformation foundations established with an evangelical agenda. Cosin's dossier included a copy of 'the publicke disorders' identified at Emmanuel College in 1603. Foremost amongst these it was noted that 'whereas all the Chappells in ye University are built with the Chancell Eastward, accordinge to ye uniform order of all Christendome. The Chancell in ye Colledge standeth north, and their kitchen eastwarde'. The chapel at Sidney Sussex was similarly aligned on a north-south axis being formed out of the ruins of the Grey Friars refectory which had occupied the site.[88] Thomas Fuller who had been a fellow of Sidney Sussex since 1629 responded to criticism about the orientation of the chapel at Emmanuel and observed that at Sidney Sussex 'the continued series of Divine duties (Praying, Preaching, administring the Sacrament) publickly practised for more than thirty yeares (without the check or controul of those in Authority) in a Place set apart to that purpose, doth sufficiently consecrate the same'.[89] Political events prevented Laud from undertaking his visitation of the university but in 1639 he reported to the king 'the divers particulars of moment and very fit for redress' uncovered by Matthew Wren's visitation of the town and University of Cambridge. Laud drew attention to the fact that 'Emanuel, Sidney and Corpus Christi colleges have certain

---

[85] K. Fincham, 'Oxford and the Early Stuart Polity', in N. Tyacke (ed.), *The History of the University of Oxford. Volume IV: Seventeenth-Century Oxford* (Oxford, 1997), pp. 203–4.

[86] BL, Additional MS 32093, ff. 153, 176, 177.

[87] R. Willis, *The Architectural History of the University of Cambridge* (3 vols, Cambridge, 1886), I, pp. 271–95.

[88] BL, Additional MS 32093, f. 177; Willis, *Architectural History of the University of Cambridge*, II, pp. 700–701, 738–9; C.W. Scott-Giles, *Sidney Sussex College. A Short History* (Cambridge, 1951), pp. 22–3.

[89] Thomas Fuller, *The History of the University of Cambridge since the Conquest* (London, 1655), p. 155. These observations themselves led to a brief skirmish in print between Fuller and the apologist for the Laudian regime, Peter Heylyn. See Peter Heylyn, *Examen historicum, or, A discovery and examination of the mistakes, falsities and defects in some modern histories occasioned by the partiality and inadvertencies of their severall authours* (London, 1659); Thomas Fuller, *The appeal of iniured innocence, unto the religious learned and ingenuous reader in a controversie betwixt the animadvertor, Dr. Peter Heylyn, and the author, Thomas Fuller* (London, 1659).

rooms built within the memory of man which they use for chapels to all holy uses, yet were never consecrated'.[90] The king's marginal annotations recorded that this 'ill example' should not continue, but Corpus Christi College Chapel remained unconsecrated until 1662 and a newly built chapel was consecrated at Emmanuel in 1677.[91]

The dispute over the proposed visitation to the University of Cambridge reflected some of the key issues about attitudes towards the defining of places of worship through consecration. The use of the rite of consecration clearly fitted the Laudian perception of a church as a holy place, as through the actions of a bishop a church moved from the secular to the sacred realm. The role of the bishops in the ritual, as the agents of God, enhanced their sacramental status and their authority within the Church as the rite was employed to establish a building as a place of worship. It was certainly a power that was exercised during the 1630s as a means through which to challenge religious nonconformity, whether it was in the universities, private chapels or the exile communities. Nonetheless while the consecration of churches neatly fitted the Laudian understanding of the sacred and episcopal authority, it was not a rite that was exclusive to them. Men from very different ideological standpoints, such as Archbishop Abbott, similarly recognized the need to separate places of worship from the secular realm. The writings from the 1620s and the growing number of consecrations from the late sixteenth century onwards reflected a more widespread concern to designate chapels, churches and churchyards through consecration. The focus on Archbishop Laud's consecration of St Katherine Cree has meant that the rite has been seen to be indicative of the religious policies of his regime and has diverted attention away from the growing practice of consecration amongst the second generation of the Reformation.

---

[90] *Laud's Works*, V, p. 366.
[91] The consecration at Corpus Christi was conducted by Matthew Wren, while his nephew was the architect at Emmanuel. Willis, *Architectural History of the University of Cambridge*, I, p. 295, II, pp. 703–8; Wickham Legg, *English Orders*, pp. 268–79, 323, 324.

Consecrations between 1600 and 1649

Most of these consecrations are recorded in Wickham Legg, *English Orders*, pp. 318–23. Additions to this list, or further information, are marked with an asterisk.

Sources: Cheshire and Chester Archives, DDB/I/L; Dorset Record Office, PE/MCR/RE1/2; Gloucester Record Office, GDR 142a, pp. 32–3; London Metropolitan Archives, E/MW/C/62; Oxford Record Office, Dioc/5/B/23/1; Jeremy Dyke, *A Sermon Dedicatory preached at the Consecration of the Chapell of Epping in Essex. October 28, 1622* (London, 1623); Samuel Price, *The Beauty of Holiness or the Consecration of a House of Prayer* (London, 1618); Robert Aylett, *The Brides Ornaments viz. Fiue Meditations, morall and diuine. 1. Knowledge, 2. Zeale, 3. Temperance, 4. Bountie, 5. Ioy* (London, 1625), pp. 117–18; William Prynne, *A Quench-Coale or A briefe Disquisition and Inquirie in what place of the Church or Chancell the Lords-Table ought to be situated, especially when the Sacrament is administered* (London, 1637), pp. 220–21; John Hackett, *Scrina Reserata: a Memorial of John Williams D.D.* (London, 1693), II, p. 61; H. Arthur Doubleday (ed.), *VCH: Hampshire and the Isle of Wight* (6 vols, Westminster, 1900), IV, p. 41, V, p. 290; L.F. Salzman *et al.* (ed.), *VCH: Oxford* (13 vols, Oxford, 1907–2004), III, p. 128; *Survey of London* (45 vols, London, 1900–), XXXVI, *Parish of St Paul Covent Garden*, p. 103.

*c.*1600–9	Childerly, Cambridgeshire[92]	Private Chapel
*1606, 14 Sept.	Melcombe Regis, Dorset	Parish Church
1607, 26 July	Langley, Beckenham, Kent	Private Chapel
1610, 15 Apr.	St Olave, Silver Street, London	Parish Church
2 Aug.	St Bride's Churchyard, London	Churchyard
1 Nov.	Fulmer, Buckinghamshire	Parish Church
1610–11	Hatfield House, Hertfordshire	Private Chapel
1612, 2 June	St Sepulchre's, London	Churchyard
9 July	St Olave, Silver Street, London	Churchyard
14 Sept.	Oxhey, Watford, Hertfordshire	Private Chapel
1612?	St Mary Mount-haw, Fish Street, London	Parish Church
1614, 8 May	Cecil Chapel, Strand, London	Private Chapel
1615, 18 Apr.	St Botolph's Without Aldgate, London	Churchyard
1615, 24 May	Edmonton, Middlesex	Private Chapel

---

[92] Consecrated by Martin Heaton, bishop of Ely, 1600–1609.

1616, 1 Sept.	Dulwich College, Surrey	Institutional Chapel
15 Sept.	Clay Hall, Barking, Essex	Private Chapel
*	Charlton House, London	Private Chapel
1617, 24 Febr.	East Greenwich Hospital, London	Institutional Chapel
4 June	St Botolph's Outside Bishopsgate, London	Churchyard
17 July	Wapping, London	Chapel & Churchyard
* 10 Sept.	Shrewsbury School, Shropshire	Institutional Chapel
1620	Jesus Chapel, Peartree, Hampshire	Chapel
	Willoughby House, Barbican, London	Private Chapel
*1621	Bramhill House, Eversley, Hampshire	Private Chapel
13 May	Serjeants' Inn Chapel, London	Institutional Chapel
28 May	Jesus College, Oxford	Institutional Chapel
*c.1621–37	Willington, Bedfordshire[93]	Private Chapel
*1622, 28 Oct.	Epping, Essex	Chapel
1623, 2 Jan.	St James, Duke Place, Aldgate, London	Chapel & Churchyard
22 May	Lincoln's Inn Chapel, London	Institutional Chapel
1624, 18 July	Wyke Champflour, Somerset	Chapel
5 Aug.	St Margaret's, Lynn Regis, Norfolk	Churchyard
5 Oct.	Exeter College, Oxford	Institutional Chapel
1625, 28 Aug.	Abergwili, Carmarthenshire	Private Chapel
*c.1625	Eston Lodge, Essex	Private Chapel
*1626, 11 Mar.	Yarmouth, Isle of Wight	Parish Church
24 Aug.	St Bartholomew's Hospital, Chichester	Institutional Chapel
1627, 25 Dec.	Ludham, Norfolk	Private Chapel
1629, 4 Jan.	Blickling Hall, Norfolk	Private Chapel
6 Jan.	Santon, Norfolk	Parish Church
* 31 May	Prinknash Park, Gloucestershire	Private Chapel
1631, 16 Jan.	St Katherine Cree, London	Parish Church
23 Jan.	St Giles-in-the-Fields, London	Parish Church
5 Feb.	Flitcham/Flixton, Norfolk	Parish Church
7 June	Hammersmith, London	Chapel & Churchyard
11 Sept.	Teddington, Middlesex	Private Chapel
15 Sept.	Lincoln College, Oxford	Institutional Chapel
1632, 24 May	South Malling, Sussex	Parish Church

[93] Consecrated by John Williams, bishop of Lincoln from 1621; the consecration presumably dates from before his imprisonment in 1637.

26 May	Roehampton, London	Private Chapel
17 July	Stanmore, Middlesex	Parish Church
23 Sept.	Risley, Derbyshire	Chapel
14 Oct.	Mersham Hatch, Kent	Private Chapel
*c.*1632–41	Moor Monkton, Yorkshire[94]	Private Chapel
1633, 17 Mar.	Peterhouse, Cambridge	Institutional Chapel
13 Oct.	Ightham Mote, Kent	Private Chapel
*	Boughton Chapel, Eccleshall, Staffordshire	Private Chapel
1634	Middleton, Kirby Lonsdale, Cumbria	Chapel
*	St John's Leeds, Yorkshire	Chapel
1635, 22 Mar.	Abbey Dore, Herefordshire	Parish Church
9 Aug.	Crewe, Cheshire	Private Chapel
19 Sept.	Hospital of St John the Baptist, Canterbury	Burial Ground
*c.*1636	Lambeth, London	Churchyard
*	Hunslet, Leeds	Chapel
*	King's Bench Prison, London	Institutional Chapel
1637	Sissinghurst, Cranbrook, Kent	Private Chapel
1637, 24 Aug.	St Bartholomew's, Exeter	Churchyard
*1638	Cuddesdon Palace, Oxford	Private Chapel
* 27 Sept.	Covent Garden, London	Parish Church
1639, 3 Sept.	Chiddingston, Kent	Parish Church
21 Sept.	Hospital/Chapel of St John, Exeter	Institutional Chapel
*1642, June/July	Oriel College, Oxford	Institutional Chapel

---

[94] Consecration was refused by Richard Neile, archbishop of York, 1632–40, but the chapel was consecrated by Thomas Morton, bishop of Durham, 1632–41.

Chapter 11

'Pure and White': Reformed Space for Worship in Early Seventeenth-Century Hungary

Graeme Murdock

Reformed religious ideas identified the need for a strict division to be maintained between the world of material objects and the realm of the divine. Most significantly, the physical elements used in the sacraments of baptism and holy communion were thought only to signify how God's spiritual presence was made known to the faithful. God was not believed to be really located in the water, bread and wine of the sacraments. Neither was any spark of the divine thought to be made manifest in pictures, images, or in wooden or stone objects. These ideas were sometimes received with enthusiasm by ordinary sixteenth-century Christians, who responded by destroying traditional religious objects. Crowds ridiculed the host of the Catholic Mass as a 'god of paste', smashed idolatrous images and statues depicting God, Mary and the saints, and destroyed crosses and relics which had previously been venerated and adored. Some communities across the Continent certainly responded both positively and quickly to Reformed preaching in outbursts of popular iconoclastic anger. However, this should not be allowed to obscure the time which clergy often needed to foster understanding and acceptance of Reformed patterns of belief and styles of worship among many congregations. The experience of many ministers indeed suggests that years of preaching, teaching and disciplinary action were required to ensure popular acceptance of Reformed ideas.[1]

[1] Many thanks to Maria Crăciun and Andrew Spicer for their comments and suggestions on this article. L.P. Wandel, *Voracious Idols and Violent Hands. Iconoclasm in Reformation Zurich, Strasbourg, and Basel* (Cambridge, 1995); C.M.N. Eire, *War Against the Idols. The Reformation of Worship from Erasmus to Calvin* (Cambridge, 1986); P.M. Crew, *Calvinist Preaching and Iconoclasm in the Netherlands, 1544–69* (Cambridge, 1978); N.Z. Davis, 'The Rites of Violence: Religious Riot in Sixteenth-Century France', *P&P* 59 (1973), 51–91; D. McRoberts, 'Material Destruction Caused by the Scottish Reformation', in D. McRoberts (ed.), *Essays on the Scottish Reformation, 1513–1625* (Glasgow, 1962), pp. 415–62; S. Michalski, *The Reformation and the Visual Arts. The Protestant Image Question in Western and Eastern*

This article will consider the development and reception of Reformed attitudes towards church buildings, which had contained many sacred objects and had been thought of as sacred spaces. It will assess how Reformed notions about the true worship of God affected ideas about sacred space and the appearance and uses of church buildings. It will focus on the churches of the Hungarian Reformed community, in the first place setting out the resolutions about the appropriate decoration and use of church buildings agreed at synods held during the mid-sixteenth century. It will then assess the implementation of these reforms in Hungary over time, and consider how far the appearance of Reformed churches had been altered by the early seventeenth century. Drawing on examples from the settled Reformed communities in the north-eastern Hungarian county of Zemplén, it will be argued that parish churches had been remodelled according to Reformed beliefs. In particular, the appearance of a new church constructed in the village of Bekecs in Zemplén will be considered from records of the services of consecration held there on New Year's Day in 1625. This example will be used to illustrate the role of clergy, noble patrons and ordinary parishioners in shaping Reformed space in early seventeenth-century Hungary.

Synodal Regulations and Parish Visitations

The official doctrines and approved patterns of worship adopted by the Reformed church in Hungary were established at synods held during the middle decades of the sixteenth century. Among the resolutions agreed at various meetings of clergy were instructions about the acceptable forms of material culture in Reformed religious life. These included regulations which laid down the clothing which ministers were required to wear during services, the appropriate appearance of church buildings, and the permitted forms of decoration within churches. The reforms which were advanced by these synods challenged traditional patterns of religious expression, as well as attitudes towards the nature of space within and around church buildings, and ideas about the relationship between the divine and the physical world. Buildings which had been used for Catholic rituals had to be altered to be made acceptable for Reformed worship which was dominated by listening to, saying and singing words in the vernacular. Objects inside churches which had been thought to connect believers with God or to assist the worship of God were deemed idols and causes of superstition. Altars, screens, organs, pictures, crosses, statues, candles and decorated windows were ordered to be removed from the sight of congregations. The 1554 Óvár synod for

Europe (London, 1993); M. Aston, *England's Iconoclasts* (Oxford, 1988); J. Phillips, *The Reformation of Images: Destruction of Art in England, 1535–1660* (Berkeley, 1973).

example demanded that local civil authorities take responsibility for the destruction of all idolatrous images inside churches.[2]

During the middle decades of the sixteenth century, support for Reformed ideas spread in many towns and across the countryside, particularly in the eastern counties of Hungary and in Transylvania. The synod held at Debrecen in 1567 was the most significant attempt to establish clearly the beliefs, structure and identity of the Reformed church within Hungarian and Transylvanian society. Representatives at the Debrecen synod came from seventeen church districts across the region. The synod endorsed Heinrich Bullinger's *Second Helvetic Confession* and approved the *Confessio catholica*, which had been compiled by Gergely Szegedi and Péter Méliusz Juhász in 1562. This synod demanded that all representations of God be removed from church buildings, and ordered people not to pray to any images in churches. Instead, 'the churches of the faithful, whether they are built of wood or stone, must throughout lack any luxury or superstition'. Thus, all idols, 'scandalous pictures', and anything associated with false worship and 'pagan ceremonies' were to be removed from sight.[3] The reform of church buildings across the region proceeded in the wake of Reformed preaching and the regulations issued by clergy synods. In towns where there was a contest between supporters of different religions there is evidence of outbreaks of popular Reformed iconoclasm. However, the removal of objects which were seen as likely causes of idolatry from churches mostly proceeded as a result of the orders of town councils and nobles. Evidence of some variation in the speed of change in different parishes can perhaps be inferred from the repeated insistence of later synods on the need for action to alter the appearance of churches. The clergy of Szatmár (Satu Mare) county, for example, felt the need to demand again at the 1570 Csenger synod that the 'Papist filth' of altars and images must be removed from all churches immediately.[4]

The church articles agreed by the 1567 Debrecen synod also set out detailed regulations on the approved fabric and functions of Reformed church buildings. These articles declared that the Bible did not support the foolish idea that preaching was limited to only one place within a community. The faithful were thus instructed to find an alternative place to worship in rather than enter a 'brothel of the Papal Antichrist' where Catholic teaching continued. Reformed congregations were, however, permitted to occupy churches which had previously been used by Catholics so long as all the pictures, the musical instruments employed in the 'Antichrist's dancing Mass', and any other 'marks of and opportunities for idolatry' were discarded. The articles

---

[2] *A szatmármegyében tartott négy első protestáns zsinat végzései*, ed. Á. Kiss (Budapest, 1877), p. 29.
[3] *A xvi. században tartott magyar református zsinatok végzései*, ed. Á. Kiss (Budapest, 1881), pp. 188, 189, 196–7, 200. All translations are my own.
[4] Ibid., p. 671.

justified this use of cleansed Catholic churches by noting that at least the stone walls and church bells had not been infected by Catholic prayers. The articles also cited the example of Old Testament kings who had cleared the temple at Jerusalem of idols and then used the building for the true worship of God once more.[5] After a church had been cleared of all idols, Reformed congregations were instructed to show respect for their place of worship and to keep it clean. The Debrecen articles sharply reprimanded anyone who turned their church into a 'pigsty', or who used the building for any inappropriate or profane purposes. The articles also issued instructions on where the faithful could bury their dead, utterly rejecting Catholic burial customs and ideas that some places were 'more holy' than others for burying the dead. The articles insisted that burials should take place in ground outside towns or villages, following the example of Christ, rather than inside church buildings or in the 'Pope's enchanted ground'.[6]

The *Confessio catholica* and 1567 Debrecen articles issued guidance to clergy on how true religion ought to be represented through the material objects which were visible during church services. Concern both clearly to distance the Reformed church from the Catholic past and to avoid any unnecessary ostentation and luxury informed advice given about the administration of communion services. The Debrecen articles insisted that clergy must abandon wearing traditional vestments which were described as 'Aaronic and Papist apparel'. They were not to 'sparkle in gold, silver or expensive apparel' but instead to dress in respectable, everyday clothing when they administered the sacrament.[7] Ministers were instructed to distribute the bread and wine from a table set among the congregation, following the example of Christ at the Last Supper. However, recognizing problems for the 'weak' among the faithful, the articles allowed that, so long as the bread and wine were distributed without any superstition, it did not matter what name was given to the table, whether it was made of wood or stone, and where it stood in the church.[8] Ministers were sanctioned to use all sorts of cups and plates to distribute the elements of bread and wine, whether made from glass, wood, earthenware, gold, silver, brass or any other sort of metal. However, they were to avoid any unnecessary extravagance, and to throw away 'the chalices and plates of the Papists' because of their association with superstition and idolatry.[9]

The founding synods of the Hungarian Reformed church therefore required that radical alterations be made to the appearance of churches, and only permitted very limited forms of decoration within church buildings. Spaces for Reformed worship

---

[5] Ibid., pp. 573, 574, 593.

[6] Ibid., p. 555.

[7] Ibid., pp. 184, 546–7, 573.

[8] Ibid., pp. 516–17: '... micsoda névvel neveztessék, és miféle anyagu legyen, kő vagy fa, a hely, melyről kiosztatik, az nem tartozik a dologra'.

[9] Ibid., p. 152: '... a pápista kelyheket, tányérokat elvetjük a babonás visszaélés miatt'.

had to be pure environments purged of idolatry and free from any profane activities. Turning to assess the impact of these decrees, evidence from surviving churches of the period confirms that wall paintings and frescoes did commonly disappear under white-wash. Empty spaces were left by the removal of objects related to Catholic ritual, objects thought to encourage idolatry, and objects which had previously been seen as appropriate adornment for church buildings. Stone altars were removed and replaced by wooden communion tables, and the focus of attention in churches shifted from the east end to the pulpit. Although walls inside churches were often white and the clergy mostly appeared in black clothing during services, all colour was not removed from Reformed religious life. Some forms of decoration persisted or were introduced into churches. There was commonly some decorative embellishment on pulpits, baptismal fonts, and on plates and cups used during communion. Images of animals, plants, and books could also be seen on embroidered Bible covers, communion table-cloths, on wooden ceiling cassettes, and in the coats of arms of noble patrons on some church walls. Other visual expressions of Reformed religious culture in churches included embroidered, painted or chiselled Bible verses. There was also a turn towards the use of symbolic imagery relating to Christ either in the figure of a lamb, holding in its front feet a flag emblazoned with a cross, or of a pelican, sacrificially wounding itself in the breast to feed its young. A similar style of symbolism was often used on the spires of churches to identify them as Reformed to the locality. Cockerels appeared on Reformed church spires from the early seventeenth century, as a sign of sin and repentance from Peter's denial of Christ. Other Reformed churches employed stars as a symbol of the advent of Christ. Some congregations in regions which were close to the frontier with Ottoman-occupied territory even displayed crescent moons in an effort to ward off destruction at the hands of Turkish raiding parties. The seventeenth-century spire of the church at Csaroda in eastern Hungary managed to cover all three options, combining a star, cockerel and a crescent moon on its spire.[10]

Further evidence about the appearance of Reformed churches during the early seventeenth century comes from the records of parish visitations undertaken by superintendents and senior clergy. Surviving records from the 1620s in the county of Zemplén reveal the determined and sustained efforts made by archdeacons to monitor both the activities of clergy and the beliefs and behaviour of congregations. Instructions on how to conduct parish visitations in Zemplén included a requirement to make an annual check of all church land in the parish, as well as to investigate the state of the church, the ministers' house and sacramental plate. There are no recorded cases in Zemplén from the early seventeenth century of any remaining images or statues inside the county's churches which were discovered and deemed a probable cause of superstition or idolatry. Given the diligent conduct of parish visitations by

[10] B. Takács, *Bibliai jelképek a magyar református egyházművészetben* (Budapest, 1986).

archdeacons, it seems very unlikely indeed that they would have ignored such abuses. Indeed, on a rare occasion in 1629 when archdeacon István Miskolczi Csulyak discovered something which he thought was inappropriate in a church he was quick to act, and parts of an altar remaining in the church at Szécskeresztúr were immediately ordered to be removed.[11]

By the early seventeenth century Reformed churches in Zemplén county at least had apparently been stripped of traditional objects of devotion while some forms of symbolic decoration had been retained or introduced. Once churches had been cleared of idols they were deemed to become appropriate spaces for saying prayers to God, for listening quietly to sermons, listening to passages from the Bible, singing hymns and Psalms, reciting catechism answers, receiving admonition from the minister, for having children baptized, for receiving bread and wine during communion, and for holding weddings and funerals. The parish visitations in Zemplén, however, illustrated a range of ongoing problems in moulding the attitudes of parishioners towards their remodelled church buildings. Above all, ministers insisted that their congregations ought to come to church more often, and some clergy particularly complained about what they perceived to be a poor level of attendance at services held during the week and on Sunday afternoons. Some individuals were reprimanded for their irregular attendance at services or for non-attendance at communion. Other clergy battled to end local customs of holding a market near the church immediately after the Sunday morning service, although this may have at least encouraged otherwise recalcitrant parishioners to come to church. When people did attend services, their conduct was not always seen as appropriate by ministers. For example, at Ricse in 1639 the minister complained that there was always shouting or noise near the church during prayers, and he wanted the congregation to depart quietly after services rather than stand around 'contending with one another'.[12]

Visitation reports also revealed complaints about the practical ways in which church buildings were used by some communities. In 1629 István Miskolczi Csulyak described the church at Polyánka as disgusting and smelly because of cured pork hanging from the beams and rafters. At Vámosújfalu, mice were found in wheat which was being kept in the church making it smelly, and meat was being stored on church benches at Újlak in 1629. Miskolczi warned both the ministers and congregations in these villages to abandon such profane uses of their churches at once.[13] Reformed ideas about the appropriate environment in which God should be worshipped had

---

[11] 'Miskolczi Csulyak István zempléni református esperes (1625–1645) egyházlátogatási jegyzőkönyvei', ed. J. Zoványi, *Történelmi Tár* 7 (1906), 75, 80, 270; G. Murdock, *Calvinism on the Frontier, 1600–1660. International Calvinism and the Reformed Church in Hungary and Transylvania* (Oxford, 2000), pp. 198–228.

[12] Ibid., p. 217.

[13] 'Miskolczi Csulyak István jegyzőkönyvei', 56–8, 71, 78, 82, 85, 285, 301, 376, 402.

clearly been enacted in the churches of Zemplén before the early decades of the seventeenth century. Clergy nevertheless remained watchful about the response of ordinary members of congregations to their churches. Ongoing warnings were issued by clergy about the dangers of idolatry, and any inappropriate behaviour inside churches was punished by disciplinary action. However, as will be suggested below there could also be some degree of negotiation between clergy and people over the appearance and uses of church buildings.

The Church at Bekecs

The parish church at Bekecs in a southern district of Zemplén county provides further insight into the design and decoration of Reformed churches during the early seventeenth century. Unlike most communities across Hungary which adapted previously-Catholic churches for their services, the church at Bekecs was built for Reformed worship during the early 1620s. Bekecs had been the daughter church of the larger community at Szerencs until 1619, when the village gained its own minister, Antal Jászai. There was a building in the village which Jászai used for services, but in 1622 work began on constructing a church on the site of an older, ruined building.[14] The new church at Bekecs was built during a turbulent period of conflict in the region when the Reformed Transylvanian prince, Gábor Bethlen, led campaigns against the Habsburgs in Royal Hungary. Bethlen claimed that his actions were inspired by a desire to defend Hungary's constitutional and religious liberties in the face of Ferdinand's attempts to impose Catholicism on the country. By the end of the summer of 1620 Bethlen's armies had advanced across most of Royal Hungary, supported by many Hungarian nobles and in alliance with Frederick V of the Palatinate and the Bohemian rebels. When the 1620 Hungarian diet offered Bethlen the crown to replace Ferdinand, Bethlen was more cautious than his ally Frederick had been in Bohemia. Bethlen's caution proved astute in November 1620 when his Bohemian allies were defeated at the battle of the White Mountain. Negotiations over terms for peace in Hungary were concluded in December 1621, with Bethlen renouncing his claims to the Hungarian crown in return for gaining control over seven counties in north-eastern Royal Hungary, including Zemplén. Although conflict between the Transylvanian prince and Habsburg forces continued during the mid-1620s, further peace treaties largely confirmed what had been agreed at Nikolsburg in 1621. Therefore, when the new church was built at Bekecs it lay in newly-won Reformed space under the rule of

---

[14] Bekecs was among villages in southern Zemplén which came under the authority of the Abaúj district archdeacon. *Református egyház-látogatási jegyzőkönyvek 16–17. század*, ed. D. Dienes (Budapest, 2001), p. 64.

Gábor Bethlen. However, Zemplén and the other six counties gained by the Transylvanian prince would revert to Habsburg sovereignty on Bethlen's death in 1629, and also remained vulnerable to attack by Ottoman forces from the south.[15]

While there are no surviving parish records or visitation records for Bekecs, details about the appearance of the parish church were recorded in a text published in August 1625 at Kassa (Košice) by Albert Szenci Molnár as *Consecratio templi novi*.[16] Molnár, one of the leading Reformed ministers of his generation, was born in 1574 at Szenc in Pozsony county in western Hungary. Molnár was then educated at the Reformed college in Debrecen, and from the 1590s spent many years working at various universities and academic centres in the Empire, including Wittenberg, Heidelberg and Herborn.[17] Molnár worked on writing and translating a number of texts during these years abroad, and published translations of the Bible, the Genevan *Psalter*, and Calvin's *Institutes of the Christian Religion*. Molnár only settled back in Hungary from 1624, working at first as a teacher at Kassa.[18] Molnár's *Consecratio templi novi* was dedicated to Miklós Monaki and to his wife Anna Csitneki, noble patrons of the church at Bekecs. Molnár's letter of dedication recalled that Monaki had been among those who offered financial support during his years in the Empire. Miklós Monaki came from a long-established noble clan in Zemplén, and from 1607

---

[15] The seven counties which were transferred were Szatmár, Szabolcs, Ugocsa, Bereg, Zemplén, Borsod and Abaúj. R.J.W. Evans, *The Making of the Habsburg Monarchy, 1550–1700: an Interpretation* (Oxford, 1979); K. Benda, 'Habsburg Absolutism and the Resistance of the Hungarian Estates in the Sixteenth and Seventeenth Centuries', in R.J.W. Evans and T.V. Thomas (eds), *Crown, Church and Estates: Central European Politics in the Sixteenth and Seventeenth Centuries* (London, 1991), pp. 123–8; J. Bahlcke, 'Calvinism and the Estate Liberation Movements in Bohemia and Hungary (1570–1620)', in K. Maag (ed.), *The Reformation in Eastern and Central Europe* (Aldershot, 1997), pp. 72–91; L. Demény, *Bethlen Gábor és kora* (Bucharest, 1982).

[16] Albert Szenci Molnár, *Consecratio templi novi, azaz, az uyonnan féléppitetett bekeczi templomnak dedicálása és megszentelésekor, sok fônépeknek, nemes uraknak, tanitoknak, és közrendeknek gyülekezetiben ez 1625 esztendônek elsô napján tetetött praedikatiok: az templom falaira es az székekre feliratott sz. irás béli könyörgések és szép mondások. Ezec mellé adattac az ott tött praedikatiockal egynihány egyenlö értelmü praedikatióc* (Kassa, 1625), pp. 3–5; J. Vásárhelyi, *Eszmei áramlatok és politika Szenci Molnár Albert életmüvében* (Budapest, 1985), pp. 88–108; J. Lugossy, 'Egyházszentelési szertartás a xvii-dik század elejéröl', *Protestáns Egyházi és Iskolai Lap* (1847), pp. 474–80.

[17] B. Varga, *Szenci Molnár Albert. A magyar zsoltárénekszerzô élete és irói müködése* (Budapest, 1932); *Szenczi Molnár Albert naplója, levelezése és irományai*, ed. L. Dézsi (Budapest, 1898), pp. 3–86; L. Dézsi, *Szenczi Molnár Albert* (Budapest, 1897).

[18] Albert Szenci Molnár, *Kis cathechismus, ... szedetöt az haidelbergai öreg catechismusbol* (Herborn, 1607); *Psalterium Ungaricum. Szent David kiralynac es prophetanac szaz ötven soltari az franciai notáknac és verseknec módgyokra most uyonnan magyar versekre fordittattac es rendeltettec* (Herborn, 1607); *Imadsagos könyveczke.... Az igaz religion valo tanitóknak és martyroknac az Sz. Irás szerint szerzett uy és ó könyveikbôl szedettec* (Heidelberg, 1621); *A keresztyeni religiora es igaz hitre valo tanitás, mellyet deakúl irt Calvinus Janos* (Hanau, 1624).

he was captain at the fortress at Ónod in Borsod county near the frontier with Ottoman-occupied Hungary.[19]

Turning to consider the appearance of the new church at Bekecs, Molnár's text does not provide a very clear impression of how the church was designed although it seems to have followed a traditional rectangular plan. Ministers who spoke during the services of consecration at Bekecs did, however, highlight different aspects of the building. Mihály Tasnadi described how, thanks to Miklós Monaki, stonemasons had been employed for two years on the church and bell-tower while carpenters worked on the pulpit and seating. András Prágai referred to the church's white-washed stone walls, to four plain internal pillars and to four windows of clear glass. Two of these pillars possibly supported a gallery at the west end of the church. The lack of any images on the church's walls and use of clear glass in the windows reflected Reformed anxiety about the potential of any imagery to foster idolatry and superstition. Albert Szenci Molnár also commented in the text that God loathes the adornment of his house with any images, silver, gold, pearls or other precious stones. However, such attitudes did not indicate any lack of care and attention to detail in the church's appearance. Clergy spoke with pride of the pristine state of the white walls, and of a pure building in which the true worship of God could take place. There were also some elements of decoration both outside and inside the church. A cockerel stood on top of the church spire. The coats of arms of both the Monaki and Csitneki families were placed on the internal east wall. During his sermon Mihály Szepsi described how a rug was placed over the front of the pulpit, with an embroidered table-cloth covering the wooden communion table. He also described a baptismal basin, and a golden cup and plate for distributing the elements of communion which, when not in use, could be covered by small pieces of cloth sewn with gold and silver thread.[20]

The most distinctive aspect of the decoration of the Bekecs church was that its internal walls were covered with painted words. Molnár recorded details of over seventy verses, the vast majority of which were from the Bible, which were visible on the walls of the church.[21] Forty-two of these verses appeared on five placards attached to the walls, which had been chosen by different members of the Monaki family. The piety of Miklós Monaki was represented by a written prayer and eighteen Bible verses, a further fifteen verses were chosen by his wife, and nine verses were placed under the names of his daughters Anna, Erzsébet and Zsuzsanna.[22] There were also more than thirty Bible verses and a quote of Augustine painted on the walls of the

[19] Vásárhelyi, *Szenci Molnár Albert*, pp. 88–9.
[20] Molnár, *Consecratio templi novi*, pp. 7–8, 31–2, 61, 77, 84, 86.
[21] Ibid., pp. 115–35.
[22] Ibid., pp. 115–27.

church. Verses had been painted on the east wall above and below the Monaki and Csitneki coats of arms, above the main arch, by windows, above the pulpit, and above the seats reserved for the Monaki family. The verse chosen for outside the church door was from Isaiah 55:1, by way of invitation to the local community at Bekecs: 'Ho, every one that thirsteth, come ye to the waters, and he that hath no money; come ye, buy, and eat; yea, come, buy wine and milk without money and without price'.

Bible verses could be seen from every vantage point in the church, and were presumably intended to aid prayer and devotion. These verses were certainly visible demonstrations that Reformed religious culture was dominated by words not images. However, not all the words on display at Bekecs were in the vernacular, and many of the most prominent places on the church's walls were covered by Bible verses in Latin. There were verses in Latin next to the minister's seat, above the church's central arch, and on the east wall.[23] A good deal of effort had gone into selecting appropriate verses for these important locations. Verses by the pulpit included Isaiah 58:1, 'Cry aloud, spare not, lift up thy voice like a trumpet, and shew my people their transgression, and the house of Jacob their sins', and 2 Timothy 4:2, 'Preach the word; be instant in season, out of season; reprove, rebuke, exhort with all long suffering and doctrine'. Albert Szenci Molnár did not offer any comment as to why Bible verses, especially those relating to preaching the word of God, were not quoted in Hungarian. This was apparently the product of a conscious decision by the church's patron with the agreement of local ministers. It can hardly have been done for the benefit of ordinary parishioners, and along with the presence of the patron's coat of arms, the five placards of prayers and verses of the Monaki family, and the special seating for the church's patrons, the Latin verses suggest that the Bekecs church was at least in part designed as an arena in which to display the piety, social prestige and intellectual endeavours of the Monaki family.

The Bible verses visible on the walls of the Bekecs church were intended to demonstrate the piety of Miklós Monaki and his family, but they also reflected themes which were prominent more broadly in Reformed church life. Almost half of the Bible verses chosen to adorn the church were selected from the Psalms, and of eighteen verses selected for Miklós Monaki's placard, eight were from the Psalms. Singing psalms was gaining an increasingly important role in Reformed church services during this period, particularly as Hungarian congregations learned the Genevan tunes which accompanied Molnár's 1607 *Psalter*.[24] Aside from the Psalms, the books of Isaiah and Job were the next most commonly-used Bible sources. The verses chosen by various members of the Monaki family featured prophetic warnings about the urgent need to acknowledge sin, to repent and to seek God's mercy. Among the verses chosen by

---

[23] Ibid., pp. 127–35.
[24] Murdock, *Calvinism on the Frontier*, pp. 166–8.

Anna Csitneki was Isaiah 1:18, 'Though your sins be as scarlet, they shall be as white as snow; though they be red like crimson, they shall be as wool', which was perhaps intended to reinforce the symbolic meaning of the appearance of the whole building. The piety on display in the church was highlighted above all by Psalm 51, which was clearly a favourite of the Monaki family. This Psalm was a lament written by David after his adultery with Bathsheba, in which David begged for forgiveness of his sins. Among the verses chosen by Miklós Monaki for his placard was Psalm 51:1–2, 'Have mercy upon me, O God, according to thy loving kindness; according unto the multitude of thy tender mercies blot out my transgressions. Wash me thoroughly from mine iniquity, and cleanse me from my sin'. Anna Csitneki chose verse 10, 'Create in me a clean heart, O God; and renew a right spirit within me', and verses 1, 4, 14 and 15 appeared on the wall above her seat in the church, while their daughter Anna selected verses 12 and 13, 'Restore unto me the joy of thy salvation; and uphold me with thy free spirit. Then will I teach transgressors thy ways; and sinners will be converted unto thee'.

The Reformed church at Bekecs was designed to permit the true, spiritual worship of God, who delighted in the presence of repentant sinners rather than in any beautiful embellishment of buildings. Albert Szenci Molnár had no sympathy for critics who found that the lack of images in the church or the lack of focus of an altar at the east end meant that the building was plain. Rather, he suggested that the pure character of the church brought 'spiritual joy' to true Christians. Although the Bekecs church had a simple appearance, it was clearly intended to be infused with spiritual meaning. The white walls and clear windows were seen as symbolic of God's grace and the effects of Christ's sacrifice. This message was reinforced by the Bible verses on the walls of the church which declared in Hungarian and Latin that the hearts of the faithful would be cleansed if they acknowledged their sins and turned back to a merciful God. The new church building at Bekecs in addition reveals much about the contribution of nobles such as Miklós Monaki in establishing and shaping the space occupied by the Reformed church, but, as we shall see, it also points to the fragility of noble Calvinism in the Hungarian countryside.

Services of Consecration

The attitudes of Reformed ministers towards the new church at Bekecs were revealed during services of consecration held on New Year's Day in 1625. These services were described as the consecration of the church building, as it was offered to God as a space in which to hear the Bible read and explained and in which to conduct the sacraments. These services of consecration were dominated by prayers and sermons, without any kind of ritual being conducted to sanctify the church or any particular part of the building. According to Molnár, celebrations had begun on New Year's Eve with a 'substantial' dinner given for invited guests who were then offered 'decent lodging' overnight by Monaki. Presumably in the freezing cold of New Year's Day, Miklós Monaki and his family, other relatives, members of neighbouring noble families, the local minister István Thuri and eleven other Reformed clergy, as well as the ordinary people of the parish attended the services of consecration. The day began with a short service held in the old building which had been used for worship in the village. When the church bell sounded, the ministers, nobles, teachers, students and community processed in song towards the new church carrying the communion cup and plate. On their arrival at the new building the congregation sang a psalm and a hymn. The first service in the new church was followed by a service of communion. Invited guests were then offered a 'beautifully prepared' lunch back at the Monaki house. Another service was held in the afternoon, and then celebratory verses were recited in Hungarian or Latin by various clergy. For example, ministers Mihály Tasnadi and Mihály Szepsi gave an oration praising the generous piety of Miklós Monaki in building the church and a manse for the minister, and in providing land for the minister's income. They also praised Monaki for building a church in which God could be truly worshipped and the sacraments rightly administered.[25] The day closed with a dinner hosted 'in a lordly manner' by Monaki, and the next morning, according to Molnár, the visiting nobles, ministers and other guests all returned to their homes.[26]

The services of consecration at the Bekecs church were dominated by the Monaki family. Their generous support for the church was celebrated, and the occasion provided the family with the opportunity to act as host to other nobles and guests. It also featured sermons given by prominent local ministers who reflected on the appearance of the new church and on the meaning of its consecration. The morning sermon was given by Mihály Szepsi, the district archdeacon and minister at Tarczal, who had been a student at Marburg and Heidelberg universities. Szepsi commended Monaki for his role in the renovation of the church, and encouraged other Reformed nobles to follow his example. Szepsi took as his text Hebrews 3:4, 'For every house is builded by some man; but he that built all things is God', which allowed him to preach on why church buildings were needed, and how they should be consecrated and used. Szepsi outlined passages from the Bible which supported the need for particular buildings to be dedicated to the worship of God. Szepsi explained that when churches were consecrated, they were being set apart from all other common uses for the particular functions of pure worship and right administration of

---

[25] 'Oratio de aedificatione templi Bekecziensis', in Molnár, *Consecratio templi novi*, pp. 93–108.

[26] Ibid., pp. x–xi; *Szenci Molnár Albert válogatott művei*, ed. J. Vásárhelyi and G. Tolnai (Budapest, 1976), pp. 423–30.

the sacraments. Szepsi stressed that churches should not be consecrated through any sort of pagan ceremony or Papist rite involving water, oil, candles, or writing letters in Hebrew.[27] A church building was rather consecrated through prayer, and Szepsi prayed that the church at Bekecs would be used to worship God without any idolatry. He gave thanks that by the mercy of God there were no images visible in the church, and that it was dedicated to God and not to any saint. Szepsi prayed for God's protection of the building from fire, for the foundations of the church to be strong and its walls secure from destruction at the hands of opponents of true religion. Szepsi also asked for God's blessing and protection to be extended over the church's patron and the local community from floods, Ottoman attacks and Catholic idolatry. At the conclusion of Szepsi's sermon, a service of holy communion was held with a prayer of blessing said for the new communion cup and plate, and a sermon given to explain the meaning of the sacrament by the minister from Szánta, András Károlyi.[28]

During the afternoon service the sermon was given by András Prágai, the minister at Szerencs who had also studied at Heidelberg university. Preaching from I Corinthians 3:16, 'Know ye not that ye are the temple of God, and that the Spirit of God dwelleth in you', Prágai suggested that God would consecrate the church at Bekecs through his presence in the hearts of the congregation. Prágai then encouraged his audience to look around the church for sources of spiritual inspiration to draw their hearts to God. Prágai drew the congregation's attention to particular parts of the building, such as the cockerel on the spire which he suggested should act as a reminder of Peter's denial of Christ and a call to remain steadfast in faith. Prágai then turned his attention to the white walls and pillars which, he suggested, represented the cleansing power of Christ's blood and the Holy Spirit to wash away the sins of repentant believers. Prágai warned his audience that just as the white-wash could become dirty, sin could sully the lives of members of the church.[29] Prágai then found other sources of inspiration in the building which the congregation could identify through the eyes of faith. Prágai spoke of the spiritual meaning of the four clear windows of the church. He suggested that the east window pointing towards the rising sun represented the bright light of true faith. Prágai then encouraged his listeners to look to the south window and feel the faith in their hearts being warmed by God's love, then turn to the west window to find hope of salvation, and then to the north to find peace and patience in suffering.[30] Prágai also spoke of spiritual qualities which

---

[27] Molnár, *Consecratio templi novi*, pp. 4–5, 27: '… legy segítséggel itt az tieidnek, mi édesség Jesusnak, kic nem Pogányoktol vött rendtartásockal, sem Papistakhoz illendő ceremoniak külső pepeczeléseckel, vizzel, olayjal, égő gyertyákkal kereszthányásockal, Sido Alphabetum le irásával nem akarjuc az Templomot felségednec consecralni'.

[28] Ibid., pp. 33–56.

[29] Ibid., pp. 84–5.

[30] Ibid., pp. 68–75.

could be associated with the four undecorated and simple pillars inside the church. In Prágai's mind, these pillars were associated with symbolic precious stones: one pillar was as a sapphire, representing virginity and cleanliness; the second pillar was amethyst, for sobriety; the third was sardonix, for humility; and the fourth was hyacinth, which Prágai wrote could bring dreams to the eyes of the faithful of their sin and of God's mercy. While churches could not contain any visual imagery as a basis for contemplation because of the danger of idolatry, András Prágai tried to assist the Bekecs congregation to find spiritual inspiration in clear glass and plain stone.[31]

From the sermons given on New Year's Day at Bekecs, it is clear that the church was not thought to have been transformed by consecration into a sacred space. Neither the building itself nor any object within the building was believed to have been made holy. The materials from which the church had been constructed remained mere stone and wood. However, through the services of consecration the church at Bekecs was declared an appropriate space in which local people could focus on God's word and in which God could be truly worshipped. The congregation could also use their eyes, inspired by faith, to perceive truth from their surroundings about the effects of Christ's redemptive sacrifice and about the life of a true Christian. These ideas made significant demands on ordinary members of the Bekecs congregation. The presence of attentive, informed believers during church services was essential for the purpose of the building to be fulfilled. The congregation had to discern the symbolic meaning of different parts of the church, and to learn about the messages conveyed by the verses on the church walls, particularly those in Latin. The people of the village of Bekecs were therefore perhaps instructed as much as invited by Miklós Monaki and minister István Thuri to come to the new church and heed the words over the church door to 'buy wine and milk without money and without price'.

The publication by Albert Szenci Molnár of the details of these services of consecration meant that the significance of events at Bekecs extended across the Hungarian church. When János Samarjai, superintendent of the Upper Danubian church province in western Hungary, wrote a service order book in 1636 he included a service of consecration which copied the pattern followed at Bekecs. This text provides a very early example of official instructions on how to hold consecration services among the Continent's Reformed churches. Samarjai's form of service did differ in some respects from the model provided in Molnár's *Consecratio templi novi*. While the services held at Bekecs highlighted the role of the nobility and clergy in church life in rural Zemplén, Samarjai's text reflected the social context for the

---

[31] Ibid., pp. 77–80. Prágai pursued similar imagery in a 1628 translation of Antonio Guevara's Life of Marcus Aurelius, which explained the virtues of a godly prince through a description of twelve gems on a clock-face. *Fejedelmeknec serkentő orája, az az Marcus Aurelius csaszarnac eleteröl az hires Guevarai Antaltol irattatot három könyvec*, transl. András Prágai (János Draskovich) (Bártfa, 1628).

Reformed church in western Hungary where many nobles had converted back to the Catholic church. Samarjai's service order book reflected his concern to retain popular support for the Reformed church and its forms of worship. Anxious about the consequences for the faith of peasant parishioners of abandoning all the familiar elements of religious life, Samarjai treated a range of questions about ritual and religious practices as matters of indifference. In advice which he issued about the appropriate appearance of church buildings, Samarjai asserted the importance of removing scandalous images and relics from sight only when there was a danger that people might kneel and pray before them. He also only recommended that new churches ought not to be as highly decorated with gold, silver or precious stones as they had previously been. Samarjai also explicitly allowed for crosses to be placed on church spires, and for people to be buried inside the church or in a graveyard around the church. Samarjai encouraged congregations to turn to the east when they prayed in church, although he made clear that members of the congregation were not restricted from access to the east end of the church. According to Samarjai's instructions to his province's Reformed clergy, communion could still be distributed from a stone altar using unleavened bread or even wafers if the minister judged that the congregation was not yet ready to move to receiving bread and wine from a communion table.[32]

János Samarjai's order of service for consecration advised the congregation to fast before gathering at the manse for prayers lead by the provincial superintendent or some other senior minister. The community was then to process to their new church carrying the church Bible and sacramental plate, accompanied by singing from a choir. On arrival at the new church, the presiding minister was to get the congregation to kneel in prayer outside the building. They could then proceed inside, and Samarjai laid out a series of set prayers for the protection of the building and for the use of the church as a place of prayer, true preaching and right administration of the sacraments. He also provided set prayers through which to consecrate the communion cup and plate, the baptismal basin and the pulpit. The clergy were also to kneel before the altar to consecrate it through prayer and by reading passages from the Bible. Samarjai then envisaged holding services which, as at Bekecs, began in the morning with a sermon which was followed by the administration of communion. The congregation were permitted to break their fast at two o'clock in the afternoon, and then return for a further service of preaching, song and prayer in the afternoon. Samarjai then allowed for people to go home and celebrate the opening of the new church so long as this did

---

[32] János Samarjai, *Az helvetiai vallason levö ecclesiaknak egyhazi ceremoniajokrol es rend tartasokrol valo könyvetske. Az eggügyüveknek rövid tanétásokra köz akaratbol irattatott Samorjai Janos Halászi predikator által* (Lőcse, 1636), pp. 8–9, 10, 11, 13, 19, 40, 188; G. Murdock, 'Moderation under Duress? Calvinist Irenicism in Early Seventeenth-Century Royal Hungary', in L. Racaut and A. Ryrie (eds), *Moderate Voices in the European Reformation* (Aldershot, 2005), pp. 178–95.

not lead to any scandalous revelry or drunkenness.[33] There were very strong similarities between events at Bekecs in 1625 and Samarjai's 1636 order for consecration services. However, Samarjai allowed for people to exhibit a more immediate and physical sense of the sacred in styles of worship and in attitudes towards parts of church buildings. These instructions both reflected Samarjai's personal beliefs and also marked an attempt to accommodate Reformed patterns of worship to the perceived spiritual needs of ordinary parishioners.

Reformed Space in Hungary

The place of the Reformed church in Hungarian society during the early seventeenth century was severely threatened as the Habsburg court steadily promoted Catholic interests and worked to overturn the legal privileges of both the Reformed and Evangelical churches. Catholic nobles and clergy tried to deprive the Reformed community of spaces in which to worship, particularly in western Hungarian counties. Reformed churches near the border with Ottoman-occupied Hungary, including southern Zemplén, also remained vulnerable to armed attacks. The construction of the church at Bekecs was a strong statement of faith by Miklós Monaki since it lay close to Ottoman-occupied territory, and was built during a contest for power in the region between the Habsburgs and the Reformed Transylvanian prince. Albert Szenci Molnár's text of *Consecratio templi novi* reflected this political context for the consecration service of 1625. Molnár included translations of two sermons by Abraham Scultetus, the Silesian preacher at the court of Frederick V. The first of these sermons had originally been given at the court chapel in Prague on the occasion of Frederick's election as king of Bohemia in October 1619. Scultetus denounced the anti-Christian idolatry promoted by the Papacy through images in churches, which he described as 'hideous monstrosities'. The second sermon translated by Molnár had been delivered by Scultetus on 22 December 1619 at St Vitus Cathedral in Prague after it had been cleansed by Frederick of its altars, images and relics. Scultetus's original sermon gave thanks that the cathedral had been made ready for Reformed worship. Molnár's translation added thanks that attempts to smash Reformed religion in Hungary had not succeeded and that the church was now claiming new ground in Upper Hungary under a Transylvanian prince who supported true religion.[34] This sense of the advance of Reformed religion was also supported by

---

[33] Samarjai, *Az helvetiai vallason levö ecclesiaknak egyhazi ceremoniajokrol*, pp. 15–27; G. Kathona, *Samarjai János gyakorlati theologiája* (Debrecen, 1939).

[34] Molnár, *Consecratio templi novi*, pp. 161–249. In 1617 Szenci had also translated and published *Postilla Scultetica: Az egész esztendő által való vasárnapokra és fő inepekre rendeltetet evangeliomi textusoknac magyarázattya* (Oppenheim, 1617); H. Louthan,

Molnár's inclusion of a sermon by Péter Alvinczi, a leading Reformed polemicist who had supported Gábor Bethlen's intervention into Royal Hungary.[35] Alvinczi's sermon had been given on the occasion of the consecration of the royal chapel at Kassa, after Gábor Bethlen occupied the town in September 1619 and expelled the Jesuits from the chapel. This sermon took as its text Isaiah 56:7, 'For mine house shall be called an house of prayer for all people', and Alvinczi prayed for the protection of the chapel under Bethlen and that idolatry would never again take place in the building.[36]

These confident sermons marking the occupation of new space for worship at Kassa and Prague formed a high-water mark for the Reformed movement in central Europe. By 1625, a greater degree of uncertainty about the future had set in, reflected by Molnár's inclusion of a 1619 sermon by Pierre du Moulin on the dangers of marrying Catholics. Moulin, who was minister to the Reformed community in Paris and then taught at the academy at Sedan, argued that the most important consideration in the choice of a partner in marriage was their religion. He suggested that if a Reformed husband allowed his marriage to be blessed by a Catholic priest then he was set on a road to idolatry, and concluded that if anyone wanted God to bless their home they should avoid marriage outside the true church. This piece was included by Molnár at a moment in 1625 when it seemed possible that Gábor Bethlen might abandon his Protestant policies and take a Habsburg princess, Cecilia Renata, for his second wife. Fears that Bethlen might be tempted to abandon the Reformed cause evaporated in March 1626 when Bethlen married Catherine, sister of the Elector of Brandenburg. The selection of this sermon by Molnár would therefore seem to be directed at Bethlen and more broadly at Hungarian nobles, encouraging them to maintain the strength and unity of Reformed noble families which was vital for the defence of the church's interests.[37]

Molnár's wider concerns about establishing and maintaining Reformed space in Hungary were directly related to events at Bekecs. In 1625 Miklós Monaki was granted the title of baron by the Habsburg king, Ferdinand. The distribution of such titles was part of a deliberate court policy to gain the loyalty of nobles, and was

---

'Breaking Images and Building Bridges. The Making of Sacred Space in Early Modern Bohemia', in Coster and Spicer (eds), *Sacred Space,* pp. 282–301.

[35] [Péter Alvinczi], *Querela Hungariae. Magyarorszag panasza* (Kassa, 1619); J. Heltai, *Alvinczi Péter és a heidelbergi peregrinusok* (Budapest, 1994).

[36] Péter Alvinczi, *Dedicatio regii sacelli Cassoviensis per ... Petrum Alvinci, Ungaricae ecclesiae Cassoviensis antistitem ac seniorem meritissimum, azaz Cassan az királyi házban valo capolnánac az abususokból isteni tiszteletre szenteltetésekor tött praedicatio, melly mostan az bekeczi templum dedicalasakor tétetött praedicatioc mellé adatott az autóránac javallásából* (Kassa, 1625), in Molnár, *Consecratio templi novi.*

[37] 'Hiuseges es idvösseges tanácz adás, az olly házasságról, melly két ellenkezö religion való személyec között leszen melyen Petrus Molinaeus franciai nyelven irott', in Molnár, *Consecratio templi novi.*

particularly used to reward those who had converted to the Catholic church. It is difficult to be certain about the degree to which the donation of this title directly affected Monaki's political allegiance. However, in 1626 while Monaki was involved in military action against Ottoman forces, he did not join Gábor Bethlen's campaign that year against Ferdinand.[38] Thus, while Molnár's publication of *Consecratio templi novi* at Kassa in the autumn of 1625 praised Monaki for building the Bekecs church, it was also intended to remind Monaki and other Reformed nobles of the need to continue to act as patrons of churches, to marry inside the church, and to be politically active in promoting the Reformed cause.

On Gábor Bethlen's death in 1629, Zemplén county reverted to Habsburg sovereignty. Reformed churches in the county initially remained relatively secure under the protection of local nobles. Indeed archdeacon István Miskolczi Csulyak continued to encourage more nobles to build new Reformed churches. He wrote letters in 1633 looking for patrons to support the desire of the villagers of Láca and Viss to rebuild their churches. Miskolczi claimed that the people of Viss wanted to follow the example of neighbouring villages in restoring their church, but lacked the resources to do so. In June 1633 he also wrote to baron Miklós Monaki, 'a most pious father and parent of the orthodox church', asking him to assist the community at Felsőmihályi. The local church had stood abandoned for around a century, and the community wanted to rebuild it. The community at Felsőmihályi requested support from Monaki either through a grant of money or by agreeing to reduce the service dues of local peasants. What response Monaki gave to this request is unknown.[39] Meanwhile, the church at Bekecs, which was a testament to Monaki's piety and a vivid expression of Reformed beliefs, proved to be a fragile construction which did not long survive its patron. Miklós Monaki is likely to have died not long after Miskolczi wrote to him in 1633, and the Monaki line died out altogether in 1643 with the death of his son János. Before then, the southern region of Zemplén had been attacked by Ottoman forces. In 1637 Bekecs was raided, houses were burned, local people were taken off into captivity, and the church was probably destroyed. The village did not recover quickly from this attack and the modern settlement at Bekecs only dates from the 1730s. By

[38] Vásárhelyi, *Szenci Molnár Albert*, pp. 88–90. See also P.G. Schimert, 'Péter Pázmány and the Reconstitution of the Catholic Aristocracy in Habsburg Hungary, 1600–1650' (unpublished Ph.D. thesis, University of North Carolina, 1990).

[39] 'Miskolczi Csulyak István esperesi naplója és leveles könyve', ed. J. Zoványi, *Magyar Protestáns Egyháztörténeti Adattár* 11 (1927), 178, 181–2, 183–4; *Református egyház-látogatási jegyzőkönyvek*, pp. 337, 345–6. Peasant unrest in the region, in part sparked by demands for greater labour service, had been crushed by nobles in 1632. L. Makkai, *A felsőtiszavidéki parasztfelkelés, 1631–1632* (Budapest, 1954).

that time the region had fallen securely under Habsburg power, and the local church at Bekecs was rebuilt for Catholic worship.[40]

The space within Hungary for Reformed religion was threatened not only by Ottoman arms but also by Catholic persecution during the early seventeenth century. The conversion of many nobles to Catholicism badly weakened the position of the Reformed church. By the time János Samarjai wrote his outline for services of consecration in 1636, Catholic nobles and councils tried hard to prevent the construction of any new Reformed church buildings. The Reformed community at Nagyszombat (Trnava) was repeatedly frustrated in their efforts to replace their old wooden church with a stone building. Only after an appeal to the diet in 1635 was permission to proceed with building work finally secured. However, the church's construction continued to be blocked by the town council with the connivance of the Catholic hierarchy and local Jesuits. The Reformed community persisted in their plans, and in 1637 Protestant noble pressure won the agreement of the Hungarian Palatine for a new Reformed church at Nagyszombat. However, threats from Catholic residents against workers on the site of the new church as well as the council's attempts to renege on a deal over the purchase of building materials forced the Reformed community to appeal again to the diet in 1638 to defend their legal rights. Although this protest was successful and a service of consecration could finally be held in the new church, the building still had to be defended from ongoing physical attacks from local Catholics. Elsewhere, many Reformed communities in western Hungary had already been denied access to their churches by Catholic nobles. In the wake of the 1645 Linz peace, Protestant nobles were able to exert sufficient pressure for the diet to agree to the restoration of some of the churches illegally occupied by Catholics. In 1647 the diet sanctioned the return of ninety churches to Reformed and Evangelical ministers, but the erosion of Protestant rights of access to a place of worship resumed shortly thereafter.[41]

From the 1560s, support had spread across Hungarian society for Reformed preaching which emphasized how the eyes of sinful men and women were only too quick to turn physical objects into idols. In efforts to reform the practice of religion, church buildings were altered to provide an appropriate physical environment for the true worship of God. Any objects in churches which were perceived to encourage superstition or idolatry were removed from sight. Reformed churches were not intended to offer any sense of the sacred in any part of the building or in any objects inside the building. Churches were, however, still to be treated with respect and were invested with a range of symbolic and spiritual meanings. The reception of these ideas by noble patrons such as Miklós Monaki

[40] Vásárhelyi, *Szenci Molnár Albert*, p. 93.
[41] E. Thury, *A dunántúli református egyházkerület története* (Pápa, 1908), pp. 440–45.

did much to shape the appearance of Reformed churches during the early seventeenth century. Reformed ideas about the importance of a pure space for worship may have also held some popular appeal and contributed to the development of a distinctive Reformed confessional identity. Nevertheless, superintendent János Samarjai felt the need to offer an enhanced sense of the sacred in church buildings in his efforts to secure the loyalty of rural communities. The attachment of many ordinary Reformed Hungarians to their pure and white churches was secured in part through the sermons and disciplinary sanctions of parish ministers and in part through the example set by local noble families. However, popular identification with Reformed church buildings was also fostered and strengthened as they became the battleground for the survival of the Reformed community against both Ottoman attacks and Catholic persecution.

Chapter 12

Rubens's *Raising of the Cross* in Context: the 'Early Christian' Past and the Evocation of the Sacred in Post-Tridentine Antwerp

Cynthia Lawrence*

Following an Italian sojourn of almost a decade, Peter Paul Rubens (1577–1640) returned to Antwerp in December 1608 and shortly afterwards began work on the *Raising of the Cross* (Figure 12.1),[1] a monumental triptych commissioned for the high altar of the Burchtkerk.[2] The triptych's interior and exterior panels were mounted in a wooden frame of a sixteenth-century design, set above a heavy stone altar table.[3] Thirty-five feet high, and twenty-four feet wide, the open triptych presents a dramatic panoramic scene of the Crucifixion.[4] In the centre panel a triumphant figure of Christ, nailed to his cross and looking upward beyond the canvas to the depiction of God in the gable, is surrounded by a group of Roman soldiers, Michaelangelesque brutes and other figures who manoeuvre his cross into an upright position. In the right wing a

* I would like to thank Barbara Haeger and David Lawrence for reading earlier drafts of this work. I am grateful to Simon Ditchfield for generously sharing his extensive knowledge of bibliography, Italian churches and early Baroque altarpieces, and to Andrew Spicer, for urging me to rethink some of the ideas in this essay.

[1] J.R. Judson, *Rubens. The Passion of Christ* (Turnhout, 2000), pp. 89–90.

[2] The church originally called the Burchtkerk was dedicated during the course of its long history to a number of different saints; I have retained the older name, rather than the more commonly used name of St Walburga's to avoid confusion.

[3] I would like to thank Valerie Hermanns for generously sharing with me her thoughts about the frame for the *Raising of the Cross*. Judson, *Rubens*, p. 91, considers that in the original programme Rubens introduced a new unification of the top and middle zones of the altarpiece, and the fluttering movements of the angels above stress the sense of action beyond the confines of the actual picture structure. He considers this to be the first display of a fully Baroque interpretation of space in a northern altarpiece; it was to become even more pronounced in Rubens's subsequent commissions.

[4] J.R. Martin, *Rubens: the Antwerp Altarpieces* (New York, 1969), p. 40.

mounted armoured soldier appears in the foreground with the two thieves being readied for their crucifixion in the background. The left wing includes figures of Mary and St John the Evangelist, with a group of weeping women and children in the foreground: both groups are directed towards the raising of the cross in the centre panel. Set in the darkened choir and dramatically lit by the lancet windows on the right, the *Raising of the Cross* appeared to fill the elevated choir, thereby contributing to an illusion that the Crucifixion was actually happening before the laity standing in the crossing and the nave.

The evocation of the Crucifixion was only a part of the iconographic scheme which defined the choir of the Burchtkerk as a sacred site. In its closed position (Figure 12.2), the exterior wings of the *Raising of the Cross* depicted SS. Amandus, Walburga, Eligius and Catherine of Alexandria, three of whom had been instrumental in bringing Christianity to Antwerp. St Amandus (584–*c*.675) had built the Burchtkerk, modelled after Old St Peter's in Rome and dedicated it to SS. Peter and Paul, around 655; only a decade earlier St Eligius (*c*.588–660) had been the first to preach Christianity in the region.[5] Around 730, St Walburga (d. 779) arrived from England and took up residence in the church's crypt for several years before moving on to Germany where, with her brothers Willibald and Winnibald, she built convents and schools for women.

At the top of the altar frame was a gable with a gilded pelican feeding her young from the blood of her pierced breast; mounted in the gable was a depiction of God the Father (now lost),[6] which was flanked on either side by monumental cut-out angels, probably painted by Rubens.[7] In the predella, between the triptych and the altar table, were three small works. An arched scene of the Crucifixion (now lost) appeared over the niche in the centre where the Host was reserved: this was an appropriate subject given the Eucharistic elements behind it, as well as the *Raising of the Cross* shown directly above, and the actual celebration of the Mass at the altar just below. It was flanked on the left by a small rectangular picture depicting *St Walburga Calming a Storm at Sea* (Leipzig, Museum der bildende Künste),[8] and in a corresponding work

---

[5] F. Prims, *De Antwerpsche Heiligen* (Antwerp, 1943), p. 13, taken from the early sixteenth-century *Chronycke van Deurne*.

[6] Although I included the more frequently-used image in the reconstructions of the altarpiece printed in 'Before the *Raising of the Cross*: on the Origins and Evolution of Rubens's Earliest Antwerp Altarpieces', *The Art Bulletin* 80 (1999), 290 (discussion of the gable painting), I have serious doubts as to whether this image of God the Father is the correct one. In the figures for this essay (Figure 12.3) I have inserted the image of God the Father and the Holy Spirit from Rubens's *The Real Presence in the Holy Sacrament* (Antwerp, St Paul's), a work from *c*.1609–10, which I think is more appropriate, if not, in fact, the image Rubens actually used.

[7] See J.R. Martin, 'The Angel from Rubens's *Raising of the Cross*', in *Rubens and his World. Bijdragen opgedragen aan Prof. R.-A. d'Hulst* (Antwerp, 1985), pp. 141–6.

[8] S. Heiland, 'Two Rubens Paintings Rehabilitated', *The Burlington Magazine* (July 1969), 421–7.

Figure 12.1 Peter Paul Rubens, *The Raising of the Cross*, 1609–10, open triptych, formerly in the Burchtkerk, Antwerp, now in the Cathedral of Our Lady, Antwerp; photo copyright: IRPA-KIK, Brussels.

Figure 12.2 Peter Paul Rubens, *The Raising of the Cross*, 1609–10, closed triptych; photo copyright: IRPA-KIK, Brussels.

Figure 12.3 Peter Paul Rubens, *The Raising of the Cross*, 1609–10; a reconstruction of the high altar (open view) in the Burchtkerk, Antwerp; copyright C. Lawrence.

on the right (now lost), a scene of the body of the decapitated Catherine carried by angels; both works refer to the two female saints to whom the altar was dedicated (see Figure 12.3).

In order to understand fully the impact and significance of Rubens *Raising of the Cross* and the altarpiece of which it was a part, it is necessary to consider the wider architectural, artistic and iconographical importance of its original setting and what was intended when it was viewed in its context not only within the Burchtkerk but within the Burcht, and even within the city of Antwerp as a whole. This examination is the first attempt to do so. Furthermore, the historical context and evocation of the sacred which lay behind its production will be considered.

The Burchtkerk

The original Burchtkerk, Antwerp's first and oldest church, was built around 655 in the 'Burcht', or fort, the core of the old city, on a man-made hillock overlooking the Scheldt. The city, which was laid out along the east bank of the River Scheldt, was punctuated by a series of elevations, the so-called 'seven hills of Antwerp', an allusion to Rome which dates from the sixteenth century.[9] While the Burcht is not among these legendary hills, it was a raised site not far from the so-called Bloedberg, a place where executions took place, which also suggested analogies to the hill of Golgotha in popular religious culture. This elevated fortified area became Antwerp's centre for the commercial activities of merchants and shippers, and many of the gifts and donations to the Burchtkerk were donated by these groups.

Following the burning of the original Burchtkerk by the Northmen in 836, a second structure, this time dedicated to SS. Eligius and Amandus was erected at the end of the ninth century.[10] With the canonization of Walburga in 893 the church was renamed in her honour. The church was re-established at the beginning of the twelfth century, as a

[9] F. Prims, 'De Stad van de zeven bergen', *Gazette van Antwerpen* (10 June 1939), 3.
[10] For the history of the Burchtkerk, see C. De Clercq, 'Eenige documenten der XIVde–XVIIde eeuw betreffende de Burchtkerk te Antwerpen', *Antwerpsch Archievenblad* 4 (1929), 296–304; P. Genard, *Verzamelingen der graf-en-gedenkschriften van de Provincie Antwerpen* (11 vols, Antwerp, 1856–1903), I, pp. 305 ff.; M. van Hoeck, *Over de oude Ste. Walburgiskerk op de Burcht voor de Nieuwe Ste. Walburgiskerk in the Volkstraat* (Antwerp, 1937); F.H. Mertens, *De kroft van Ste. Walburgis te Antwerpen* (Antwerp, 1864); F. Prims, 'De Bewoners onzer burcht', *Antwerpiensia* 1928, 155–161; F. Prims, 'De pilgrimage naar de Burchtkerk', *Antwerpse Courant* (26 March 1939), 4; A. van Valckenisse, 'Beschrijving van den Borcht en Borggraefschap van Antwerpen', *Antwerpsch Archievenblad* 18 (1864), 1–162; J. de Wit, *De Kerken van Antwerpen. (Schilderijen, beeldhouwwerken, geschilderde glasramen, enz., in de XVIIIe eeuw beschreven door J. de Wit.) Met aanteekeningen door J. de Bosschere en grondplannen* (Antwerpische Bibliophilen 25, Antwerp, 1910).

chapel within the parish of the Cathedral of Our Lady. Around 1249 a new church and crypt were built, possibly in the Romanesque style, to accommodate the growing parish. At the same time, Catherine of Alexandria was named as co-patron (with Walburga) of the church;[11] they were paired because their bones were both considered to produce an oil with curative properties. Because of the larger number of pilgrims attracted by their cult, the small Romanesque church was replaced by a larger Gothic structure in 1499–1509 that was more commensurate with the Burchtkerk's new status as one of the five parish churches of Antwerp. The raised choir, with an underpass beneath it, probably dates from this period, although – as was the case with several other churches in Antwerp – the choir was probably not completed until considerably later.

Following the iconoclasm of the 1560s and 70s, the Burchtkerk was in need of restoration and renovation. Both the church and its yard were resanctified in September 1585; the high altar was rededicated to SS. Walburga and Catherine of Alexandria, and the relics of St Ambrosius and the 10,000 Virgins were placed inside. The following month, the Chapel of the Holy Sacrament was also dedicated. By 1602, services at the Burchtkerk were again flourishing; fourteen chaplaincies were maintained, with a schedule of forty masses each week. The revival in the church's fortunes culminated in 1615 in a visit by the Habsburg Archdukes Albert and Isabella, who prayed in the crypt, where Walburga had presumably lived, and kissed her recently recovered relics.

Also of significance was the Twelve Years Truce, agreed in 1609, which established a period of relative peace and stability between the Northern and the Southern Netherlands and thus allowed the Archdukes and their advisers to introduce an ambitious programme to re-establish the Church, both physically and institutionally, in the Catholic southern provinces.[12] While this initiative was consistent with the objectives of the Catholic Reformation, as set down in the resolutions of the Council of Trent,[13] it also served the Habsburgs's nation-building agenda which was based on the concept of 'one country, one faith'.[14] This campaign included not only the

---

[11] Judson, *Rubens*, p. 114.

[12] See P.C. Sutton, 'The Spanish Netherlands in the Age of Rubens', in P.C. Sutton, M.E. Wieseman *et al.* (eds), *The Age of Rubens* (Boston, 1993), pp. 106–30.

[13] F. Baudouin, 'Altars and Altarpieces Before 1620', in J.R. Martin (ed.), *Rubens before 1620* (Princeton, 1972), pp. 45–92.

[14] T.G. Corbett, 'The Cult of Lipsius: a Leading Source of Early Modern Spanish Statecraft', *Journal of the History of Ideas* 36 (1975), 139–52; H.J. Elias, *Kerk en Staat in de Zuidelijke Nederlanden onder de Regeering der Aartshertogen Albrecht en Isabella (1598–1621)* (Antwerp, 1931), pp. 47–60. In a reference to heresy, one historian makes clear that the concept of 'one faith, one country' was promoted by the Jesuits. J. Andriessen, *De Jezuieten en het samenhorigheids bereft in Nederlanden, 1585–1648* (Antwerp, 1957), pp. 156–8. See also S.

implementation of doctrinal and liturgical reforms, but also sought to restore the physical fabric of the Church through the building (or restoration) and decoration of churches, monasteries, convents and schools. This included the commissioning of new works to replace those destroyed by the iconoclasts. The *Raising of the Cross* was part of this programme of Catholic renewal, represented in the Burchtkerk particularly through the depiction of the saints on the reverse of the wings of this triptych. The pairing on the left of SS. Amandus and Walburga reflected the building of churches (and other ecclesiastical structures), while preaching and proselytizing, which led to many conversions, were symbolized by SS. Eligius and Catherine on the right.[15]

The Triptych *in situ*

By reconstructing the Burchtkerk and its site we can for the first time better understand how Rubens's *Raising of the Cross* related to the space for which it was commissioned. For the triptych was not only an element in the programme of Catholic renewal but it was also part of an artistic and architectural attempt to define the Burchtkerk as a sacred site with references to the city's Early Christian past, while also making allusions to the sacred cities of Rome and Jerusalem.

Unfortunately, it is difficult to imagine a more challenging candidate for a contextual investigation than the Burchtkerk: so much of the site in which the triptych was originally presented has now disappeared, and, in many cases, it has not even been documented (either visually or in writing). Not only was the Burchtkerk and its surrounding neighbourhood razed in the early nineteenth century, but also the triptych's original frame, and the pictures and painted decoration mounted within it, were auctioned off in 1737 to subsidize a new one. Furthermore, there are fewer than half a dozen depictions (painted, drawn, or printed) of the church's exterior or interior which can provide us with reliable evidence as to how Rubens and his contemporaries might have seen or understood the relationship between the *Raising of the Cross* and its intended location, and not all of them include the altarpiece.

Only two depict the choir in detail.[16] The earliest view of the interior of the Burchtkerk choir appears in Ambrosius Francken's *St Eligius Preaching in the Burchtkerk* painted in 1588, the centre panel of a triptych commissioned by the

---

Zurawski, 'Reflections on the Pitti Friendship Portrait of Rubens: in Praise of Lipsius and in Remembrance of Erasmus', *SCJ* 23 (1992), 730.

[15] C. Lawrence, 'Rubens's Antwerp Saints: History, Heresy and Hagiography,' unpublished paper delivered to the College Art Association, Annual Meeting, 1995.

[16] Another by Arnoldus Bouttats (see fn. 21 below) shows the choir in the midst of a major restoration, and is thus of only limited use.

Figure 12.4 Ambrosius Francken, St Eligius Preaching in the Burchtkerk, 1599, Antwerp, Koninklijke Museum voor Schone Kunsten; photo copyright IRPA-KIK, Brussels.

Antwerp Guild of Metalsmiths (Figure 12.4).[17] Painted some twenty years before Rubens's *Raising of the Cross*, Francken's painting depicts the Burchtkerk's choir and nave as it looked three years after Antwerp was reconquered by Alexander Farnese and Catholicism restored. In an elevated pulpit on the south side of the nave, St Eligius, wearing his bishop's regalia, preaches to an audience comprised of guild members and their families (recognizable as portraits). To either side of the broad central staircase behind them, which leads up to the choir, are two recesses framed by rounded arches outlined by segmented moulding: that on the left is the Chapel of Our Lady, and that on the right the Chapel of the Holy Sacrament.

At the top of the choir is a cast-iron gate with a cross rising from the centre: while this gate may have been an actual detail of the choir, its materials were perhaps intended as a symbolic reference to Eligius, patron of the metal workers' guild, and to the guild members. To each side of the gate is a smaller altar; on that on the right is a figure of what appears to be a bishop (probably Eligius), behind which is a painting of the Adoration of the Magi.[18] The work above the high altar, somewhat square in format, is possibly an Ascension of Christ, or an Assumption of the Virgin. It may once have been the centre panel of a triptych that is now missing its wings.

The striking height of the choir, some twenty feet (approximately six metres) above the floor of the church, is a consequence of the vaulted-over street-level passage just below.[19] Anthon Gunther Gheringh's 1661 picture (Figure 12.5) records Rubens's triptych *in situ*, showing two parallel flights of stairs which are joined midway to form a single flight to the choir, while an additional four steps lead to the foot of the altar; the total number of steps is nineteen, a point of some significance, as we shall see

[17] See E. Vandamme (ed.), *Catalogus Schilderkunst Oude Meesters. Ministerie van de Vlaamse Gemeenschap. Koninklijk Museum voor Schone Kunsten – Antwerpen* (Antwerp, 1988), Cat. No. 576–90.

[18] This painting may be that listed in De Wit: 'Daer nevens nog een Ander, synde eene Aenbiddinghe der Koninghen, door een oudt meester geschildert', *De Kerken van Antwerpen*, p. 139. The picture somewhat resembles Joos van Cleve's painting of the same subject in Brussels, H. Pauwels (ed.), *Koninklijke Musea voor Schone Kunsten van België Department Oude Kunst. Inventariscatalogue van de Oude Schilderkunst* (Brussels, 1984), Cat. No. 566, 61.

[19] See F. Baudouin, 'Vier afbeeldingen van het interieur der verdwenen Sint-Walburgiskerk te Antwerpen', in *Miscellanea Philippe Roberts-Jones. Bulletin van de Koninklijke Musea voor Schone Kunsten van België* 34/37 (1985–88), 181–94, at 184. Baudouin cites Genard, *Verzameling*, II, pp. lxviii, lxxx, where it is also noted that the 'high choir' (Hooge Koor) church is situated twenty feet above: 'the twintig voeten boven de overige gedeelte der Kerk gelegen is, d.w.z. 5m. 73.6 cm'. A stone vault was added in 1664, probably by Jan van den Eynde, architect of the church in Averbode.

Figure 12.5 Anthon Gheringh, *View of the Interior of the Burchtkerk, Antwerp*, 1661. Antwerp, St Paul's; photo copyright: IRPA-KIK, Brussels.

below.[20] Between the two flights is the entrance to the Romanesque crypt. The commemorative engraving of 1676 by Arnoldus Bouttats depicts numerous splendidly-dressed visitors to both chapels as well as to the crypt. It also indicates two landings, one located midway to the high altar, and a second only four steps or so from it.[21] Above the altar, supported by a double predella, was Rubens's triptych.[22]

When closed, the depiction of St Walburga on the outside of the triptych reminded the viewer of the modest cell in the Romanesque crypt beneath the choir where the saint was thought to have lived for several years. The cell was destroyed sometime in the last quarter of the sixteenth century, but in 1612 Rubens's friend and supporter, the wealthy merchant Cornelis van der Geest, conducted an archaeological 'dig' in the Burchtkerk's crypt, hoping to find artefacts of Walburga which would confirm her sojourn in Antwerp.[23] Although van der Geest's recovery of several bones and other implements did not resolve the issue, he apparently remained convinced of her presence. The following year, van der Geest began the process of rebuilding the crypt; it was completed two years later in time for the visit of the Archdukes Albert and Isabella.[24]

When viewed from the nave below, in its original frame, Rubens's opened *Raising of the Cross* (Figure 12.1) must have created a life-like tableau that filled the space of the Burchtkerk's narrow choir, virtually redefining it as the site of the Crucifixion. Certainly the verisimilitude of the work was enhanced by the natural light that streamed through the lancet windows on the south side of the choir, where it merged

---

[20] Anthon Gheringh, View of the Interior of the Burchtkerk, Antwerp. 1661. Antwerp, St Paul's (Photo: IRPA-KIK, Brussels). Peter Eyskens, 'Het Interieur van de Sint-Walburgiskerk door Anthon Gunther Gheringh', *Sint-Paulus Info* 60 (Spring 1995), 1142–4; Baudouin, 'Vier afbeeldingen'.

[21] Arnoldus Bouttats, *The Celebration of the 900th Anniversary of the Death of St Walburga*, 1676. Engraving, 60 x 42 mm. Antwerp, Vleeshuis Museum.

[22] Note Cardinal Borromeo's injunction for the main altar: 'If there is sufficient space at the sides and front of the altar, three steps should be prepared; that is one consisting of the predella itself, and two others lower than this predella. The two lower steps ought to be made of marble or of solid stone, or, if this is not possible, of brick.... The third step, however, which consists of the predella itself, is to be made of wooden boards': E. Cecilia Voelker, 'Borromeo's Influence on Sacred Art and Architecture', in J. M. Headley and J. B. Tomaro (eds), *San Carlo Borromeo. Catholic Reform and Ecclesiastical Politics in the Second Half of the Sixteenth Century* (Washington, 1988), p. 175.

[23] G. van Cauwenbergh, *Gids voor Oud Antwerpen* (Antwerp, 1990), pp. 39–44.

[24] For the crypt, see J.C. Diercxsens, *Antwerpia Christo Nascens et Crescens* (Antwerp, 1613), p. 82; D. Papebrochius, *Annales Antwerpienses ab Urbe condita ed annum MDCC* ed. F.H.Mertens and Ern. Buschmann (5 vols, Antwerp, 1845), I, pp. 49–52, 65; F.H. Mertens, *De kroft van Ste. Walburgis te Antwerpen* (Antwerp, 1864); F.H. Mertens and K.L. Torfs, *Geschiedenis van Antwerpen* (8 vols, Antwerp, 1845–53), V, pp. 425–7; Genard, *Verzameling*, II, p. 372; Hoeck, *Over de oude Ste. Walburgiskerk*, p. 21.

with the fictive light of the altarpiece. This was made possible by the manipulation of the windows through which light entered the choir. If Francken's *St Eligius Preaching* accurately records the choir, it appears that around 1588 the lancet windows on the east and north of the choir were only partially filled in, with small *oculi* retained near the top; by the time of Gheringh's view in 1661, it seems that those same windows were completely blocked, perhaps to prevent glare. This would have created a totally darkened space, against which the brighter triptych, struck by light from the lancet windows on the south, must have shown to good effect. The differences in the lighting of the different stages in the narrative recorded in the triptych's three panels is enhanced by the manipulation of light entering the choir. Since the scene in the panoramic view was lit by natural light from the right, it seems consistent that the depiction of the nailing of the bodies of the thieves to their crosses on the far right receives the most light, with decreasing amounts relegated to the title scene, in the centre panel, and even less to that with John and Mary, with the wailing women and children, on the far left. Thus darkness falls across the scene moving from left to right.

While the subject of the *Raising of the Cross* is unusual in Flemish art, its Eucharistic references are eminently suitable as a backdrop for the celebration of the Mass. In the context of the Burchtkerk, the elevation of the cross provided an appropriate pictorial parallel for the ritual of *elevatio* performed by the celebrant at the altar just below as he held up the consecrated host before the congregation. At the same time, the raised choir, which naturally assumes the role of the Hill of Calvary or Golgotha in this context, is an ideal setting for a scene of the Crucifixion, since it increases the viewer's sense that the scene is actually taking place on the 'hill' in front of him.

The cross itself is an exceptionally polyvalent form; thus, in this context, it would seem to recall any number of significant references which served to define the church as a sacred site. One concerns the cross as signifying the presence of Christians. According to the Counter-Reformation scholar Giacomo Bosio, uncle of the famed archaeologist Antonio, the custom of raising crosses on the sites where churches were to be built was introduced by the apostles. This was done in imitation of the Patriarch Jacob who wanted to consecrate the place where he saw the ladder (a prefiguration of the cross).[25] Thus the erection of crosses as claims or signs was long observed in ancient times. Crosses might also indicate houses given over to divine worship; thus Cardinal Baronio, wishing to emulate the earliest Christians as closely as possible, raised a cross near the spot where he was restoring a building dedicated to God in 1596–97.[26] Furthermore, during the later part of the sixteenth century, rood screens

[25] A. Herz, 'Cardinal Cesare Baronio's Restoration of SS. Nereo ed Achilleo and S. Cesareo de' Appia', *The Art Bulletin* 70 (1988), 597.
[26] Ibid.

throughout Flanders were systematically demolished so that they would not obscure a clear view of the high altar (the site where the host was now reserved). This meant, as well, that roods – mounted or hanging sculpted figures of the crucified Christ – were also effectively eliminated from the church interior. Rubens's *Raising of the Cross* circumvents this problem by depicting the Crucifixion taking place in the altarpiece, directly above the altar table, in a clear and unobstructed view.

The significance of the number of steps leading from the Burchtkerk's nave to its high altar has not so far been observed. Nineteen steps are also found in the Upper Chapel of Calvary (the hill of Golgotha) in the Church of the Holy Sepulchre in Jerusalem, as described in contemporary guide books and other sources for pilgrims visiting the Holy Land. This would have also been familiar for those undertaking only a 'virtual' pilgrimage to Jerusalem without leaving home,[27] a journey based solely on the information available from a guide book illustrated with views, portraits of buildings, maps and diagrams, a descriptive text and (sometimes) passages from the Scriptures and/or prayers which were to be read at particular sites. The vibrant tradition of these guides in the Southern Netherlands from the beginning of the sixteenth century, especially in Antwerp where many of them were printed, culminated in Antonius Gonzales's *Hierusalemsche Reyse* (1664), which is one of the most detailed and richly illustrated.[28] These nineteen steps to the Upper Chapel of Calvary were, in many guides, accompanied by a prayer to be said on each step. The steps therefore link the Burchtkerk's raised choir to the Church of the Holy Sepulchre, and, indirectly, to the large number of churches built in Western Europe by returning

---

[27] F. Prims, 'Jerusalemsche Pelgrims', *Antwerpiensia* 2 (1928), 336–9.

[28] For Dutch-language guides to the Holy Land published in the early modern period, see: R. Jansen-Sieben, *Repertorium van de Middelnederlandse Artes-Literatuur* (Utrecht, 1989); R. Lindeman, Y. Scherf and R. Dekker, *Reisverslagen van Noord-Nederlanders uit de zestiende tot begin negentiende eeuw. Een chronologische lijst* (Haarlem, 1985); J. van Herwaarden, 'Geloof en geloofsuitingen in de late middeleeuwen in de Nederlanden: Jeruzalembedevaarten, lijdensdevotie en kruiswegverering', *Bijdragen en Medelingen betreffende de Geschiedenis van Nederlanden* 98 (1963), 400–26; J. Staes, *Antwerpsche reizigers van de vroegste tijden tot op heden* (Antwerp, 1883). Works of particular interest are: Jan van Cotwyck, *De loflyche reyse van Jerusalem en de Syrien (...). Antwerpen, Hieronymus Verduffen* (1620), pp. 178–9, 204–11; H.W. Davies, *Bernhard von Breydenbach and his Journey to the Holy Land, 1483–84. A Bibliography* (London, 1911), p. 43; Anthonius Gonzales, *Hierusalemsche reyse (...)* (Antwerpen, 1673); Jan Pascha, *Een devote maniere om gheestelyck Pelgrimagie te trecken tot den heylighen lande als te Jherusalem, Bethleem, ter Jordanen (...) met die rechte gheleghentheyt der heyligher plaetsen (...) ghmaect bijwijlen Heer Jan Pascha int licht gebrocht door Peeter Calentijn* (Leuven, 1563); A. Viaene, 'Vlaamse Jerusalemvaarders in de Bourgondische Eeuw', *Biekorf* 65 (1965), 5–16, 119–22; A. Viaene, *Vlaamse Pelgrimstochten* (Bruges, 1982), pp. 18, 183–4. On Gonzales's work, see B. Wasser, *Nederlandse pelgrims naar het heilige land* (Zutphen, 1983), pp. 158–9; an engraving of the climb to the Upper Chapel of Calvary appears ibid., p. 72.

crusaders, pilgrims and grateful merchants, in imitation of either the whole church, or of just the Upper and Lower Chapels of Calvary.

The association of the flight of nineteen steps that links the nave to the top of the raised choir in the Burchtkerk with the flight of steps linking the Upper and Lower Chapels of Calvary in the Church of the Holy Sepulchre in Jerusalem helps to define the former's space. The configuration in the Burchtkerk of the raised choir, the stairs and the crypt corresponds to the same arrangement; therefore, it would appear that at some point the east end of the Burchtkerk had been intended as a Jerusalem church. If the scene in Rubens's open triptych encourages an analogy with the Upper Chapel of Calvary, it also reflects the contemporary enthusiasm in the Southern Netherlands for heroes like Godfrey de Bouillon (who died in the First Crusade) and his brother Baldwin, Count of Flanders, both of whom were buried in the Lower Chapel of Calvary in the Church of the Holy Sepulchre.[29] Likewise, it should be noted that the Upper and Lower Chapels of Calvary at the Church of the Holy Sepulchre, and those churches built in imitation of them in Western Europe, had long been part of an elaborate Good Friday and Easter Sunday ritual, one which might also have been observed at the Burchtkerk.[30]

If the open altarpiece, with its scene of the *Raising of the Cross*, contextualizes the Burchtkerk's raised choir as the Mount of Calvary, the site also contributes to the scene presented by the closed triptych. In this context, with the four Antwerp saints mounted above the altar, the raised choir could be interpreted as a pseudo-'Burcht', that raised hillock on which Eligius first preached Christianity in Antwerp, and on which Amandus built the city's first church.

The final element in defining this setting for the celebration of the Mass was a series of commemorative epitaphs supporting monumental sculpted figures of apostles, each holding the instrument of his martyrdom, which were mounted on the columns of the nave arcade between the 1620s and 1660s.[31] The impact of this programme, as suggested in Gheringh's painting, is that the apostles (as martyrs) provide a parallel to the figure of Christ, nailed to his cross, the instrument of his Passion. Christ's sacrifice for mankind, as originally preached by the 'Antwerp saints', was revealed to the laity of Antwerp on the exterior of the triptych. The significance of these saints to the worshippers in the nave, established through the iconography of the altarpiece, was

[29] Godfrey de Bouillon was the legendary founder of the Chapter of the Church of Our Lady in Antwerp and a stained glass window was erected in cathedral in 1616 depicting this. W. Aerts (ed.), *The Cathedral of Our Lady in Antwerp* (Antwerp, 1993), p. 24.

[30] B. Lane, '"*Depositio et Elevatio*": the Symbolism of the Seilern Triptych', *The Art Bulletin* 57 (1975), 21–30.

[31] C. Lawrence, *Flemish Baroque Commemorative Monuments, 1566–1725* (New York, 1977), pp. 132–51, 290–95.

reinforced by the monumental sculpted apostle-martyrs. Although Rubens would have been familiar with other examples of apostle programmes in Flemish churches, there was, as we shall see, an Italian example that was even more significant as an inspiration for his creation.[32]

This investigation differs significantly from other considerations of Rubens's altarpieces in context (and those of early modern Flemish altarpieces more generally) in that it holds open the possibility that the *Raising of the Cross* may have figured in a larger and more comprehensive programme, one in which the triptych may have been more integrated into the interior beyond just the altar and choir, perhaps including the church exterior as well. Consequently, as indicated in Gheringh's view, a programme of monumental sculpted apostles, each holding the instrument of his martyrdom, leads the eye directly to the high altar with its depiction of Christ's death on the Cross. Rubens appears here to have anticipated both Bernini's use of *gesamtkunst* (defined here as a harmonious unity created from works executed in diverse media), as well as, as we shall see, the Italian artist's propensity to link or relate disparate units along a linear axis.[33]

The Triptych in its Wider Context

Between the Burchtkerk and the Scheldt was the *Werf* (or *Werp*) or *Werfplein*, Antwerp's principal wharf or dock. Known since the thirteenth century for its commercial activity,[34] it was the principal point for the arrival and departure of travellers (including pilgrims to and from Rome and the Holy Land).[35] The *Werf* was recorded in a number of pictures,[36] but the amateur drawings by Johannes Scheffer (Figures 12.6 and 12.7) offer some new and potentially useful evidence regarding the

---

[32] See p. 271-73.

[33] C. Scribner, 'Rubens and Bernini', *The Ringling Museum of Art Journal* (1983), 164–77.

[34] For basic works on the commercial activity of Antwerp in the late sixteenth and seventeenth centuries, see G. Asaert, *De Antwerpse scheepvaert in de XVe eeuw (1394–1480); bijdrage tot de ekonomische geschiedenis van de stad Antwerpen* (Brussels, 1973); G. Asaert, 'From Wharf to Commercial Metropolis', in *Antwerp, a Port for All Seasons* (Antwerp, 1986), pp. 13–164; Ph.M. Bosscher, *Zeegeschiedenis van de Lage Landen* (Bussum, 1975); E. Scholliers, *De Levenstandaard in de XVe en XVIe eeuw te Antwerpen* (Antwerp, 1960); H. van der Wee, 'De Antwerpse economie ten tijde van Rubens', *Academische tijdingen* 11 (1977), 6–7; H. van der Wee, *The Growth of the Antwerp Market and the European Economy (Fourteenth-Sixteenth Centuries)* (3 vols, The Hague, 1963), II, pp. 1443–520.

[35] Wasser, *Nederlandse pelgrims*, pp. 95–8.

[36] See, for example, Frans Francken's *View of the Werf*, 1616–18, Koninklijke Museum voor Schone Kunsten, Antwerp; Jan Wildens, *View of Antwerp*, c.1631; Brussels, Koninklijke Musea voor Schone Kunsten van België, Cat. No. 3068; see in Baudouin, 'Vier afbeeldingen'.

Figure 12.6 Johannes Scheffer, *The Burchtkerk from the West with the Werfpoort and Wharf*. Nd Antwerpen, Statsarchief, 52/26; photo copyright: Stadsarchief, Antwerp.

Figure 12.7 Johannes Scheffer, *The Burchkerk and its Yard, from the South with the Churchyard and a View from the Werfpoort*. Nd Antwerpen, Statsarchief, 52/27, photo copyright: Stadsarchief, Antwerp.

relationship between the Burchtkerk, the *Werf* (wharf), the *Werfpoort*, and the churchyard. Figure 12.6 contains one of the most detailed renditions of the *Werfpoort*, the monumental portal through which one reached the *kerkplein*; this space, in front of the Burchtkerk's square Norman tower with its soaring spire, appears in most depictions of the Antwerp waterfront.

Although there is no date for the *Werfpoort*, the distinctive vertical imposition of *chaînes* (piers), with their alternation of long and short stones,[37] indicates it is from the early modern period, perhaps from the mid-sixteenth century when Antwerp was the centre of European trade and commerce. Directly above the arch, outlined with rusticated stones, was a triangular pediment, on which was mounted Antwerp's coat of arms, set in a cartouche.[38] At the apex, mounted on a low soccle, is a figure, holding up an object in his right hand; this is probably Silvius Brabo, a youthful relative of Julius Caesar, who, according to legend, had delivered the city of Antwerp from the tyranny of the giant Druon Antigonus who severed the hands of the Scheldt shippers who failed to pay him tribute.[39] These hands, which appear in the city's shield, are perhaps a reference to the origin of its name – *handwerp*, meaning to throw a hand.

Scheffer's drawing (Figure 12.6) is perhaps unique in that it presents the *Werfpoort* almost perfectly aligned with the church tower so that they appear as a unit: if he had composed his picture from a point slightly more to the left, one would have seen (as did travellers arriving or departing) both the coat of arms and the historic hero – with the tower and spire of the Burchtkerk rising above them. In Netherlandish cityscapes, dating from the mid-seventeenth century, church towers juxtaposed to civic buildings have been considered as an affirmation of the power of religion over secular politics.[40] That would seem to be what is intended here, with the taller church as an indication of religion's dominance. Scheffer's view also suggests another important aspect, the establishment of a visual axis linking the *Werfpoort* to the Burchtkerk.

Later, in his programme for St Peter's, Gian Lorenzo Bernini created a visual axis running from the piazza, with its central obelisk, into the basilica and down the nave to the *baldacchino* (1624–33), eventually leading to the high altar with the *Cathedra Petri*

---

[37] P. Lavedan, *French Architecture* (London, 1944), p. 29.

[38] A similar but much smaller portal appears in a view of Antwerp, with the Werf in the foreground, included in *Unio pro conservatione rei publice (Tribute to the Emperor Maximilian I)*, 1515. See Jan van der Stock, *Antwerp, History of a Metropolis* (Antwerp, 1993), Cat. No. 10.

[39] M. van den Berg, 'De oorsprong van de Brabosage: de ridder en de reus', in E. Warmenbol (ed.), *Het onstaan van Antwerpen, feiten & fables* (Antwerp, 1987), pp. 81–92.

[40] C. Lawrence, *Berckheyde* (Doornspijk, 1991), pp. 52, 53. See also G. Schwartz, *The Dutch World of Painting* (Maarsen, 1976), p. 43; S. Schama, *The Embarrassment of Riches* (New York, 1977), pp. 118–19; R. Fuchs, *Dutch Painting* (New York, 1978), p. 129.

(1657–66).[41] This is similar to the progression in the Antwerp Burchtkerk: here the visual axis, initiated by the *Werfpoort*, ran through the Norman tower, the oldest part of the extant church, down the nave flanked by the figures of the apostles mounted on the columns of the arcade, to the crossing and the entrance to Walburga's crypt, and from there up the two flights of steps to the altar, above which was mounted Rubens's triptych. While the earliest recorded plans of the Burchtkerk, probably dating from its rebuilding in the Gothic style (1499–1509), indicate that there were entrances opening into the side aisles on the south and north sides of the church, there is no indication that an entrance was ever cut in the tower, either from the *kerkplein* (the church square) or from the tower interior into the narthex or nave, so that the visitor might take in the view recorded in Gheringh's picture. Nevertheless, the conceptual (and perhaps even visual) resemblance between the unification of the parts of the Burchtkerk and those of St Peter's along a linear axis presents an intriguing comparison which calls for further consideration.

The Tripych's Ideological Context

If Christianity was the basis of the formation of the religious state, the imposition of the objectives of the Catholic Reformation marked the introduction of proto-nationalistic sentiments in the Southern Netherlands; that programme initiated in 1585 with the victory of the Catholic leader Alexander Farnese, and reintroduced in 1609 at the beginning of the Truce, to build, restore and redecorate Flemish churches was a statement of the Church's newly found confidence and authority. During this period, Rome was redefining itself as the capital of the first world religion, as reflected in programmes of extensive building and decorating activity. This endeavour focused on the reclamation of the material culture of early Roman Christianity as the means of setting in motion a comprehensive mental and spiritual reimagining of Early Christian devotional practices more generally. Likewise, during the Truce the Church set about converting Antwerp into a bastion of reformed Catholicism:[42] realizing the strategic and symbolic value of transforming what was now the seat of a new bishopric, as well as the northernmost Catholic city and a virtual beacon shining out on Protestant northern Europe, the state became an active participant in the fight against heresy, a struggle which had not only religious but also political significance.

---

[41] I believe that both Rubens and Bernini were inspired by the example of the visual axes in Baronio's restored Early Christian churches (and others as well). Herz occasionally alludes to Bernini's similar inclinations: 'Cardinal Cesare Baronio's Restoration', 594.

[42] A.K.L. Thijs, 'De Strijd van kerk en overheid om de controle over de cultuurproduktie en-beleving in contra-reformatorisch Antwerpen (1585–ca. 1700)', *De Zeventiende Eeuw* 8 (1992), 3–11.

This sense of forging a new Catholic nation, a virtual citadel or a bulwark in the religious wars, may have been of particular significance for pilgrims departing for Rome or for the Holy Land, from the wharf adjacent to the Burchtkerk. It was the last sight of the city church pilgrims had prior to leaving Antwerp, and, at the same time, it was the first they encountered on their return, where they could give thanks for a safe journey. The association of the *Werf*, the Burchtkerk and even Antwerp with Jerusalem may have had special meaning, both historically and again around the time of the Truce: Antwerp, once again safely under the control of the Church, had been characterized as a 'new Jerusalem', a virtual *Civitas Dei* (City of God).[43] Thus it is not surprising that Rubens may have recognized and even reinforced the Burchtkerk's references to the Church of the Holy Sepulchre in Jerusalem.

When Rubens's *Raising of the Cross* is considered *in situ*, it becomes clear that the iconographic plan evoking the sanctity of the Burchtkerk was influenced by two of the most important Early Christian churches – not only the Church of the Holy Sepulchre, but also Old St Peter's (and those many early churches based on it) in Rome. Rubens could have known the Upper and Lower Chapels of Calvary in the Church of the Holy Sepulchre from the many illustrated guides to the Holy Land that were available in Antwerp.[44] The configuration of these chapels is analogous to that created by the Burchtkerk's raised choir (especially with his panoramic view of Golgotha in place) together with its subterranean crypt. Given his commission for the Chapel of St Helena in Santa Croce in Gerusalemme in Rome (the floor of which was covered with earth from Golgotha that Helena had brought back), his awareness and knowledge of both the Church of the Holy Sepulchre and the Mount of Calvary were probably considerable.

Likewise, there is evidence that Rubens also knew first-hand several other Early Christian churches in Rome: these included SS. Nereo and Achilleo (dating from the eighth century) and San Cesareo de' Appia (built in the sixth century), both of which had been carefully restored by Cardinal Cesare Baronio (1538–1607) at the end of the sixteenth century. Their chancels, like the Burchtkerk's raised choir and subterranean crypt, had elevated presbyteries and subterranean *confessiones*.[45] Several features of Baronio's restoration of SS. Nereo and Achilleo were later reflected in the iconographic programme for the Burchtkerk. Although it has not previously been recognized, one of the so-called 'victory angels' Baronio commissioned Pomarancio (Cristoforo Roncalli) to paint in the spandrels of the nave arcade in SS. Nereo ed

---

[43] Michael Grisius, *Honor S. Ignatio de Loiola Societatis Jesu fundatori et S. Francisco Xaverio ... habitus a patribus domus professae & collegij Soc. Iesu Antverpiae 4 Julij, 1622* (Antwerp, 1622), p. 13.
[44] See fn. 28 above.
[45] Herz, 'Cardinal Cesare Baronio's Restoration', 590–620.

Achilleo was probably the model for the cut-out angel (Flint, The Flint Art Museum) to the right of the gable in the *Raising of the Cross*'s original frame (as in Figure 12.3). There were also echoes of this angel in the monumental sculpted apostle-martyrs commissioned for the nave of the Burchtkerk.[46] Furthermore, as Herz has pointed out, Baronio did not create the little piazza in front of SS. Nereo ed Achilleo, but instead, as always, made excellent use of pre-existing circumstances (such as the open atrium) and materials: by placing a column in the centre of the piazza, he not only established a visual axis that ran through the entire church, but he also set up a situation much like that found later in the *Werfpoort* and the Burchtkerk.[47] Not only were Philip Neri, Baronio and others associated with the Oratory inspired by all things Early Christian, but they, like many others, sought 'to revive the Church on the basis of a return to its origins'.[48] Catholics as well as Protestants also hoped to reform the decaying Church by returning to the simpler faith of Christ, the Apostles and the Church Fathers.[49]

There is no firm evidence that Rubens knew Baronio, who died the same year the artist received the commission for the high altar of the Chiesa Nuova, the Oratorian new church in Rome.[50] He might well have been informed of the scholar's knowledge of Early Church architecture from other members of the Oratory, or through the *Annales* or perhaps, most importantly, from the churches which Baronio had restored. But it should be noted that the Burchtkerk was recast as a 'Merovingian' church, originally dating from the eighth century, roughly the same period as SS. Nereo ed Achilleo (which was restored in 1596–97), or San Cesareo de' Appia (restored in 1597–1603). Rubens's new familiarity with the Early Christian churches of Rome perhaps made him more aware of the Burchtkerk's Early Christian characteristics and their iconographic significance. Furthermore, Rubens may have seen in these references the equivalent of an Early Christian past for Post-Tridentine Antwerp. There is certainly evidence that Rubens's interests in Early Christian Antwerp were not unique. Around the time of his return from Rome several amateur archaeological excavations were underway in the Burcht: these endeavours unearthed artefacts of the gods Thor and Freya and a male fertility figure ('Papa Semini') dating back to the Norse occupation in the ninth century. In the early eighteenth century, the French scholar Bernard de Montfaucon, in his richly-illustrated overview of classical antiquity, *Antiquity Explained* (1721–22), noted the discovery of several urns and monuments in Antwerp in 1610.[51]

---

[46] For a 'victory angel' from Pomarancio's programme, see ibid., Fig. 14.

[47] Ibid., 594, 596.

[48] Ibid., 590.

[49] Ibid., 591 (paraphrased).

[50] Although there is no documented proof that Rubens knew Baronius, he would certainly have known about the cardinal's role in the restoration of SS. Nereo ed Achilleo and S. Cesareo de' Appia, either from verbal reports by other Oratorians, or from Baronius's *Annales ecclesiastici*.

[51] B. de Montfaucon, *Antiquity Explained and Represented in Sculptures* (5 vols, London,

Rubens was also surely aware of the other similarities between the Burchtkerk and Santa Croce in Gerusalemme, which he had worked on earlier in Rome.[52] Although it has frequently been noted that his Antwerp *Raising of the Cross* is iconographically related to the *Raising of the Cross* he painted in 1601 as part of the tripartite programme for the Chapel of St Helena – now lost and known by a copy (Grasse, Cathédral Notre-Dame) – it has not previously been considered that both the Burchtkerk and Santa Croce attracted large numbers of pilgrims.[53] Santa Croce, which was founded by St Helena from one of the wings of her palace (the Sessorian) in the fourth century following her return from Jerusalem, was one of Rome's seven great pilgrimage churches.

All seven of these early churches could be seen in the course of a day's walk: Neri and the members of the Oratory considered them to be an important catalyst in stimulating the public's interest in the catacombs, ancient churches and other Early Christian monuments;[54] their great age demonstrated the continuity of faith and practice. However, Santa Croce was, above all, a pilgrimage church, with a large collection of important relics (e.g., a Thorn from the Crown of Thorns, Nails by which Christ's hands were attached to the Cross, a piece of the Cross) which attracted many visitors. Not only did Helen bring back with her large portions of the Cross (including a portion of the *titolo*), but, as noted earlier, also a vast amount of earth from the Mount of Calvary which she had distributed over the floor of the chapel later named for her; in so doing, she created a virtual 'piece of Jerusalem', a metaphor sometimes employed by those who wished to characterize the Eternal City as a 'New Jerusalem'.

The Burchtkerk was similarly an important centre of pilgrimage (as in Figures 12. 6 and 12.7). Its location meant that the church was assured a constant lucrative income: adjacent to Antwerp's primary wharf, it was the last church one might visit before setting off on a journey, and the first one would encounter on one's return. Walburga, whose trip across the storm-tossed Channel from England was the subject of one of the panels Rubens painted for the predella (as in Figure 12.3), attracted a considerable following in her adopted city, especially among the seamen of the Burcht: according to the legend, she had lived in the church's crypt for several years, praying

1721–22), V, Book 5: Tombs, pp. 551–2. Also see above, p. 262.

[52] For the Church of S. Croce in Gerusalemme, see E. Michel, 'Les Rubens classés de l'hospice de Grasse', *Bulletin Monumental* (1941), 294–314; J. Müller Hofstede, 'Rubens in Rom 1601– 1602; die Altargemälde für Sta. Croce in Gerusalemme', *Jahrbuch der Berliner Museen* 12 (1970), 61–110; S. Weppelmann, *Die Altarbilder für Santa Croce in Gerusalemme in Rom* (Münster, 1998), pp. 58–67.

[53] Wasser, *Nederlandse pelgrims.*

and effecting conversions, before setting off for Germany to join her missionary brothers.[55] Together with St Catherine of Alexandria, she was extolled in Antwerp for the healing oil her bones secreted. Printed images of the two female saints were popular souvenirs of the church; in addition to the sale of the holy oil supposedly extracted from their bones, and donations from arriving and departing travellers, the tangible veneration of these saints was a lucrative endeavour.

Unlike the Roman churches restored by Baronio, the Antwerp church was not stylistically homogenous: it had been built and then rebuilt, decorated and redecorated in a series of period styles. On one hand, this might have seemed unfortunate; however, on another, the Burchtkerk's architecture was an indication of its history, and thus the history of faith in the region. If the origins of the Burchtkerk are 'Merovingian' (pre-Carolingian), the church also referenced a broad range of period styles in terms of the ninth-century 'Norman tower'; the early Medieval crypt; the Romanesque nave and crypt; the late Gothic choir; the late Renaissance altar frame; the early Baroque triptych; and, somewhat later, the High Baroque apostle figures. Rubens's understanding of the Burchtkerk's architecture, its historical role in the introduction and proliferation of Christianity in Antwerp beginning in the mid-seventh century, and of how its agglomeration of period styles attested to the continuity of faith and practice in Antwerp and the Scheldt basin from the seventh to the seventeenth centuries, is also derived from his familiarity with the early churches of Rome. San Cesareo de' Appia and SS. Nereo ed Achilleo both included chancel areas with raised presbyteries and subterranean *confessiones*,[56] just like that in the Burchtkerk. Like the Upper and Lower Chapels of Calvary in the Church of the Holy Sepulchre, the arrangement of the chancels in the Roman churches (which are also based on Old St Peter's) is analogous to the vertical programme in the Burchtkerk: here, as noted above, the altar and altarpiece are placed at the summit of the raised choir, above the flight of nineteen stairs, and over a subterranean crypt.[57]

Thus, following his activity in Rome, Rubens may have come to understand and appreciate the way in which period styles in architecture (and probably in art more generally) were linked to the concept of time and its passage: different stylistic vocabularies, signifying different periods, represented the vast block of time from the seventh to the seventeenth centuries – and, consequently, the history of the (Catholic)

---

[54] Herz, 'Cardinal Cesare Baronio's Restoration', 593.

[55] For Walburga and Catherine of Alexandria as a pair of saints, sacred to the Burchtkerk, see C. Stroo, 'De Iconographie van de heilige Walburga in Vlaanderen', *Jaarboek Koninklijke Museum voor Schone Kunsten, Antwerpen* (1985), 189–276.

[56] Herz, 'Cardinal Cesare Baronio's Restoration', 597–601, Figs 5, 7, 9.

[57] Ibid., 594–7. Baronio's inclusion of a column in the centre of the open atrium before the west facade of SS. Nereo and Achilleo has no precise analogy; thus, the role of the *Werfpoort* in establishing the vertical axis leading to the choir is perhaps significant.

Church and of Christianity in northern Europe more generally. It is important to consider Rubens's *Raising of the Cross* against this background and to recognize the significance of the several levels of meaning in the triptych's evocation of the sacred when considered *in situ*. In an atmosphere characterized in terms of repeated Protestant challenges to the institution and teachings of the Church, which recalled the confrontations of earlier heretics in Antwerp, the Catholic-Christian heritage of the northernmost Catholic capital was a timely issue: this was stated (obliquely but emphatically) in the architecture of the Burchtkerk with its allusions to the ancient origins of Christianity in the city and in the Scheldt basin. However, at the same time, the church's architectural diversity also suggested another important aspect of the Church's message – which was concerned not only with the early origins of Christianity, but also with its renewal in the early seventeenth century.

Chapter 13

The Consecration of the Civic Realm

Judi Loach

In the sixteenth century, the territory of the civic realm of Lyons was contested by opposing religious groups. The Catholics and Protestants appropriated in turn this secular sphere, and after the Roman Catholic party triumphed definitively, it 'refounded' the city as an avowedly Christian – that is, Catholic – one. Nevertheless economic exigencies delayed its physical reconstruction, so that urban redevelopment was not accomplished until a century later. The new civic centre became the setting for a series of rites – notably its own foundation and consecration, culminating at the centenary of the Catholics' victory – which exploited vivid and dramatic imagery so as to impress the city's refoundation into the collective imagination and memory of the citizenry. These ceremonies evoked the religious practices of their pagan forebears in Roman antiquity: their temples and altars with their attendant rites, notably public vows and secular games. The exceptional, and unexpected, aspect of all this is that civic rituals were presented in terms of pagan rites, by Counter-Reformation priests – Jesuits – who, moreover, claimed to do so specifically to affirm the Christian nature of the city's refoundation.

The Civic Realm of Lyons

Lyons, one of Europe's most prosperous and cosmopolitan trading centres since Roman times, was France's second city, in secular terms. Yet it had long served for Catholics as the nation's first city, possessing as it did the Primacy of Gaul. In the early sixteenth century, however, it was both the city in France closest to the capital of Calvinism, Geneva, and also the national – indeed an international – centre for printing and publishing. Consequently it found itself under heavy attack from Reformers, subject to illicit missionaries and inflammatory propaganda, with several Protestant congregations provocatively establishing temples in its *fauxbourgs* and even psalm singing outdoors in the city centre itself.[1]

The civic realm thus became contested territory, the two conflicting religious parties competing to appropriate its space for themselves. On the night of 29–30 April 1562 Calvinists captured the city, which they then held for over a year (until 9 June 1563). During this time they systematically purged the Church of Rome's capital in Gaul of all evidence of Catholicism: they prohibited the Mass and other religious rites; expelled priests, monks, nuns and friars; and closed church property, demolishing or defacing much of it.[2] Since many of the city's educational or welfare institutions had been Catholic establishments, these became the object of attack as much as did churches, monasteries and convents. Within little more than a year most of the city's public buildings had therefore been severely damaged, if not altogether destroyed. Although Catholic institutions suffered a similar fate in other towns across France, those in Lyons were subjected to the most thoroughgoing campaign of effacement. The propaganda value of so vividly turning the Primacy of the Gauls into a 'second Geneva' was obviously quite unique.[3]

The reversal of power at the Catholics' recovery of the city led to a comparable effacement of evidence of any Protestant presence. Catholics perceived the Calvinist occupation of Lyons as a defilement, and the consequent destruction of Huguenot temples and burning of Protestant books were viewed as purification rites.[4] The Catholic party now wished to rebuild the city, for obvious, practical reasons and also to represent, in the most vivid and tangible way, the change in religious allegiance and related authority – or, as it was stated at the time, the re-

---

[1] Jean de Saint-Aubin, S.J., *Histoire de la Ville de Lyon* (2 vols, Lyons, 1666), I, pp. 206, 243, 249.

[2] Claude de Rubys, *Histoire véritable de la ville de Lyon* (Lyons, 1604), pp. 394–6; Saint-Aubin, *Histoire*, I, pp. 200–206, 208–12.

[3] P. Hoffman, *Church and Community in the Diocese of Lyon, 1500–1789* (New Haven, 1984), p. 31. Examples of anonymous Calvinist propaganda from 1562 include: *Le Prinse de Lyon*, *Le Pitieux Remuëment* and *La Juste et Saincte Défense*.

[4] Jean Guéraud, *Chronique lyonnaise (1536–1562)*, ed. J. Tricou (Lyons, 1929); Gabriel de Saçonay, *Discours catholique des miseres et mal-heurs de ce temps* (Lyons, 1568); *Apologie pour la ville de Lyon* (Lyons, 1569); Guillaume Paradin, *Mémoires de l'histoire de Lyon* (Lyons, 1573); de Rubys, *Histoire*; Saint-Aubin, *Histoire*, I, Lib. V. See also J. Loach, 'The Restoration of the Temple de Lyon in the Seventeenth Century' (unpublished Ph.D. thesis, University of Cambridge, 1987), I, pp. 20–21, 45; Hoffman, *Church and Community*, p. 32.

establishment of the city's ancient religion.[5] Such a commitment to restoring primordial dogmas and practices was common to both sides during the Wars of Religion throughout Europe. In Lyons, however, Catholics additionally evoked such sentiments for the defence of their see's primacy over other French dioceses, a contested issue at this time.[6]

The Calvinists' downfall had derived not only from their minority presence within the local population but, increasingly, from discontent engendered by the economic consequences of their occupation: Lyons's famous fairs ceased, and in their wake all international trade, the city's economic base; foreign merchants and bankers left town; and the famous printing and publishing industry collapsed. Subsequently the city's economy would take nearly half a century to return to a level where any physical reconstruction of the city could even be considered.

The period of reconstruction coincided with that of the establishment and ascent of the Neufville-Villeroy dynasty, which governed Lyons through almost two centuries, until the Revolution. In 1607 Charles de Neufville (1566–1642), marquis of Villeroy, became lieutenant and in 1625 governor, both offices remaining in the family thereafter. Under his governorship the city was modernized through a coherent programme of public works, creating or upgrading ports, quaysides and thoroughfares, and bringing fresh water into all districts. This period also saw the construction of two major civic institutions, the hospital of the Hôtel-Dieu and the Charité (a home for poor of all sorts), consolidating the multiplicity of existing welfare institutions, largely sustained by a variety of Catholic orders and societies, by absorbing them into these secular ones: both were run by explicitly secular (rather than ecclesiastical) committees, albeit consisting exclusively of devout Catholics, for whom the Governor effectively served as model.[7] Both were erected along the bank of the Rhône, on the very edge of Lyons's *presqu'île* (peninsula), their elegant facades thus presenting the city's new self-portrait at once to largely Calvinist Dauphiné (whose territory extended to the opposite bank) and to the road from Rome; under Charles's sons this facade was extended, through a new building for the town college, the Collège de la Trinité

---

[5] Juan Perpiñen, S.J., 'De retinenda veteri religione et falsa recentium hoereticorum rejicienda ad Lugdundenses', in *Opera*, ed. P. Lazéri (3 vols, Rome, 1749), I, pp. 228–69.

[6] For example, see Saint-Aubin, *Histoire*, II, p. 133. Challenges to Lyons' primacy led to several treatises, including Théophile Raynaud's 'Assertio Primatus Sedes Lugdunensis' published within his *Indiculus sanctorum Lugdunensium* (Lyons 1629; repr. 1662); Pierre de Marca's *De primatu Lugdunensi et ceteris primatibus* (Paris, 1644).

[7] André Clapasson, *Description de la Ville de Lyon avec des recherches sur les hommes célèbres qu'elle a produits* (Lyons, 1741), pp. 9–14, 48–52; Claude-François Menestrier, S.J., *Eloge historique de la Ville de Lyon* (3 vols, Lyons, 1669), II, pp. 43, 75–81.

(today's Lycée Ampère), and the town's first purpose-built town hall, contemporary engravings of this view confirming the propagandist intentions underlying the urban redevelopment scheme. Simultaneously vast numbers of churches, monasteries and convents were reconstructed, or in the case of the new, Counter-Reformation orders, built from scratch; such programmes were often financed by Consular and other patrician families, including the Neufville-Villeroys.[8]

In 1642 Charles's more eminent son, Nicolas de Villeroy (1598–1685), already recognized as a brilliant military strategist, succeeded him as governor, and three years later his younger brother, Camille de Neufville, abbot of the royal abbeys of St Martin d'Aînay in the town and of Ile-Barbe just upriver from it, became lieutenant. The brothers had even higher ambitions for their town (and their family), which are reflected in the series of monumental civic buildings they constructed over the next decades. Following Nicolas's promotion to *maréchal* and appointment in 1646 as governor (in this context meaning tutor) to the young Louis XIV, all executive powers over the city effectively passed to a single individual, Camille, who would add sacred to secular control on becoming archbishop (and thus national primate) in 1653; the following year he appointed his bastard brother Antoine as vicar general, and thus effectively the official censor of the Lyonese press. This ultramontane family's ascent, coinciding as it did with a period of economic renewal, ensured that the conditions for a Catholic reconstruction – or, rather, refounding – of the city were at last in place.

Under Camille these developments deliberately evoked Roman parallels and precedents in order to present Lyons as a Roman community, a *colonia* or *municipium*. Memories of the previous, supposedly foreign (Genevan), regime were to be effaced by supplanting them with more striking imagery recalling the city's native heritage, the Roman Temple de Lyon, symbolic of Lyons's capital status – in worship, commerce and government – within the Roman Empire.[9] As a *colonia* or *municipium* the city had entered an alliance with Rome, retaining full autonomy apart from foreign policy, in return for which citizens gained civil liberties (*conubium* and *commercium*); the official interpretation of the Grande Salle's ceiling decoration made explicit this reciprocity between Rome as Europe's mind and Lyons as its heart.[10]

---

[8] F.Z. Collombet, 'Les Eglises de Lyon', *Revue de Lyonnais* 17 (1890), 447; Menestrier, *Eloge*, II, pp. 43–6; Samuel Chappuzeau, *Lyon dans son lustre* (Lyons, 1656), p. 75.

[9] De Rubys, *Histoire*, p. 49. See also Claude-François Menestrier, S.J., *Histoire civile ou consulaire de la ville de Lyon* (Lyons, 1696), p. 72.

[10] Menestrier, *Eloge*, III, Chapter V, pp. 36–8.

Refoundation

In Imperial Roman practice, a city's refoundation implied a significant change in its power base and allegiances. Roman practice thus resonated with the political situation experienced by the Lyonese in the mid-sixteenth, and celebrated by them in the mid-seventeenth, centuries. A city's refoundation required a new founder (or *conditor*), supplanting – whilst inevitably recalling – the original founder, in this case the legendary Roman 'knight' (literally *chevalier*), Plancus.[11] Under the Roman Empire this figure was always summoned from the mother city, Rome itself, and then exercised complete control over the new colony until its foundation had been fully established. Camille de Neufville, simultaneously exercising secular and ecclesiastical authority, fulfilled the founder's role so-defined; in addition, although now resident in Lyons, he had initially come from Rome, where he was born during his father's embassy, and had returned there to study. Moreover, he was named after his godfather, Camillo Borghese, who as Pope Paul V had seen himself as a refounder of Rome in the wake of its sack in 1527. Rome's subsequent refoundation as a Christian capital – exploiting its antique heritage to support its claims of venerability – first found physical expression under Sixtus V (1585–90), with the piercing of thoroughfares through the historic urban fabric to link its seven pilgrimage churches, simultaneously proclaiming the city's modernization; this scheme seems to have inspired early seventeenth-century developments in Lyons.[12]

Camillo Borghese saw himself as a Christian version of the legendary Camillus in Roman antiquity, Marcus Furius Camillus, commemorated by Livy as 'parens patriae conditorque alter urbis',[13] the saviour of Rome after the Gallic invasion (387/6 BC) and then its second founder. Camille de Neufville was similarly depicted by his Lyonese contemporaries in these roles. In 1657 the decorations devised for the Trinity Sunday celebrations – the annual festival at the town's college dedicated to the Trinity, organized by its Jesuit teachers for the city fathers – centred on emblems of the theological virtues, Faith, Hope and Charity. The painting for Hope – more precisely here the hope of the Lyonese ('Spes Lugdunenses') – showed a ship led by cupids across a stormy sea (with the sky riven by lightning), its oars marked with the consuls' arms whilst its anchor, held by Hope herself, took the form of a heraldic anchor cross 'des armes de Monsieur l'Archevesque', in fact the arms of the Neufville-Villeroy family. The emblem's

---

[11] Paradin, *Mémoires*, p. 29; Menestrier, *Eloge*, I, pp. 12–13.
[12] J. Loach, 'The Hôtel de Ville at Lyons: Civic Improvement and its Meanings', *Transactions of the Royal Historical Society*, 6th ser., 13 (2003), 261.
[13] Livy, 5. 49. 7: 'another father of the fatherland and founder of the city'.

motto read 'Dabit Anchora sacra salutem' [The sacred anchor will give safety], alluding to Lyons's wise government during the nation's recent *troubles* (the Fronde). The accompanying explanation explicitly drew a parallel between the Archbishop and 'Camille, qui delivra Rome'.[14]

Lyons's latter day Camillus turned towards Roman art and architecture – both the antique and the baroque inspired by it – to express most appropriately the character of his own city's refoundation. First, it alluded to the venerability of his *patria*, whose capital status in Roman Gaul was increasingly coming to light, as a result of digging the foundations for the city's physical reconstruction.[15] Second, Camille's building programme sought to differentiate Lyons's religious allegiance not only from that of the Protestants but also from other kinds of Catholics, such as Gallicans or Jansenists, using evocations of ancient and modern Rome to emphasize the *Roman* nature and the venerability of its Catholicism.[16]

Under Camille's rule a new civic centre – or capitol[17] – was created around the 'twin' buildings of the town college and town hall, so-called because they were 'born' (built) at the same time and of the same 'parent' (donor).[18] The town college, the Collège de la Trinité, originally set up by a confraternity, had been taken over by the city fathers in the early sixteenth century to provide humanistic education free for all citizens' sons. As in many other towns, financial exigencies had led the Consulate to investigate delegating teaching to a religious order and in the aftermath of the Calvinist occupation its management was acquired by the Jesuits.[19] They thus became the dominant intellectual group in town, and consequently assumed responsibility for arranging all civic festivals and decorations. In 1644 a fire largely destroyed the college buildings, forcing its rebuilding. Meanwhile Lyons, despite being France's second city, lacked any purpose-built town hall, effectively using the church of St Nizier – notably its

---

[14] Claude-François Menestrier, S.J., *L'Art des emblemes* (Lyons, 1662), p. 82; Germain Guichenon, *La Vie d'illustrissime et reverendissime Camille de Neufville* (Trévoux, 1695), pp. 245–6.

[15] See Menestrier, *Histoire*.

[16] See Loach, 'The Hôtel de Ville', 273–7.

[17] Archives Municipales de Lyons (hereafter AML) BB208, p. 271 [Joseph Gibalin's sermon]; Saint-Aubin, *Histoire*, I, p. 340; Menestrier, *Eloge*, III, Chapter IV (unpaginated), entry for 1655.

[18] Jean de Bussières, S.J., *Basilica Lugdunensis* (Lyons, 1661), p. 7. See Loach, 'The Hôtel de Ville', 261, fn. 23.

[19] G. de Groër, *Réforme et Contre-Réforme en France: le college de la Trinité au XVIe siècle à Lyon* (Paris, 1995), pp. 9–12, 74 ff.

Chapelle de Saint-Jacquême – for all its ceremonial functions, whilst fitting its administrative ones into a variety of converted private houses.[20] A building was therefore designed specifically to equip Lyons with a town hall 'commode, belle et bien séant à ceste ville'.[21] A decorative scheme presenting them together as the 'Temple de Lyon' was then executed in their principal public spaces, the town hall's Grande Salle and the college's Grande Cour.[22]

The monumental 'twin buildings' were erected in the Terreaux district, removing the civic focus from the heart of the city's *presqu'île* to its eastern boundary, away from the churches of St Bonaventure, the city's guild church (in the care of the *Cordeliers*, or Franciscans), and, above all, of St Nizier. The latter was the largest and most important of the three oldest churches in Lyons, those which could trace their origins back to underground oratories established during Roman antiquity. As such it was more venerable than the city's cathedral, and indeed had been the original cathedral, in which Lyons's first bishop, St Pothin, had consecrated the first altar dedicated to the Virgin Mary in Gaul, setting up an image of her which he personally had brought back from the Middle East. The church then built above this was initially dedicated to the Holy Apostles, commemorating SS. Peter and Paul together with the first forty-eight Martyrs of Lyons. The dedication was changed to that of a subsequent archbishop of Lyons, St Nizier, when his shrine acquired a reputation for working miracles; the current, early medieval building being erected to cater for the crowds of pilgrims attracted by this shrine. Ever since the early fourteenth century, when the citizens had gained their independence from the archbishop (hitherto their feudal overlord), this church served not only as their principal meeting place but also as symbol of their legal independence. The church's continuing success, largely due to its accommodation of numerous confraternities, is demonstrated by its Western porch, an outstanding example of Renaissance architecture.[23]

Nevertheless, the treatises on 'Lyonese saints' (*hagiologium Lugdunense*) sponsored by the Consulate in the mid-seventeenth century and authored by an eminent Jesuit theologian at the Collège de la Trinité, Théophile Raynaud, signally omit St Nizier, and indeed any of the other saints from the Early Church of Lyons. These are displaced by saints more widely known but with more tenuous local

---

[20] Menestrier, *Eloge*, III, Chapter V, pp. 1–2; V. de Valous, *Les Anciens Hôtels de ville de Lyon* (Lyons, 1882).
[21] AML, BB200, f. 9v. See also de Bussières, *Basilica Lugdunensis*, p. 13.
[22] Loach, 'The Restoration of the Temple de Lyon'.
[23] Menestrier, *Eloge*, II, pp. 44, 46; Clapasson, *Description*, pp. 105–6; Loach, 'The Hôtel de Ville', 253–4.

connections; furthermore, their relevance to the city is now proclaimed in terms of guardians of cities in Roman antiquity, and thus pagan religion: St John Benezet Berger as the city's *pontifex* [high priest], St John the Evangelist as its *atavus* [ancestor], St George as its *indiges* [deified hero], St Anthony as its *praeses* [presiding deity] and, last but not least, St Ignatius of Loyola as its *praestes* [guardian deity].[24]

It is far from coincidental that it was a Jesuit who wrote, and that the civic authorities sponsored, this propagandist work – overtly culminating in the founder of the Company of Jesus and more subtly downplaying the civic role of St Nizier – at the same time as the Consulate financed building the new civic centre in the Terreaux district. For the formal transfer of civic activities from St Nizier into the new Hôtel de Ville followed the spontaneous departure of devout laity, deserting this parish church and the confraternities which met in it for the churches of religious orders with the confraternities run by them, most notably the Jesuit church at the Collège de la Trinité and the *congrégations* attached to it. In the late 1660s the city's official *Eloge historique* (admittedly authored by a Jesuit, but nevertheless sponsored by the Consulate) claimed that Lyons had ten lay – but Jesuit-directed – *congrégations* (with around three thousand members) and five *societez* of penitents, plus more than fifty confraternities dedicated to various devotions, and further, over eighty specialist devotional bodies (*corps*) for merchants and craftsmen, also outside the authority of parish priests.[25] Meanwhile the pre-eminent confraternity of penitents (*confalons*) met at the Franciscan church (*Cordeliers*), that of the *tireurs d'or* at the Jacobins, and the Penitents de la Miséricorde at the Carmelites (*Carmes*); at the same time major families set up chapels in churches of religious orders rather than in parish churches, most notably the Villeroys at the Carmelites, but also the Gadagnes at the Jacobins (Notre-Dame de Confort), the Groliers at the Cordeliers de l'Observance at Vaise, the Pazzis at the Celestins, the Scarrons at the Feuillans, and the Savarons at the Augustins Déchaussés on the Croix Rousse.[26] This movement away from parish churches reflected a phenomenon at that time affecting much of Catholic Europe.[27] Through the creation of the new civic centre, propaganda – built, enacted and printed – helped to divert attention from the fact that the authority and popularity of long-

---

[24] Théophile Raynaud, S.J., *Hagiologium Lugdunense* (Lyons, 1662).

[25] AML, BB223, p. 272, BB224, p. 34; Menestrier, *Eloge*, II, pp. 44, 46.

[26] Hoffman, *Church and Community*, p. 39; Clapasson, *Description*, pp. 35, 41–4, 68–74, 132, 138, 156–61, 167–8,180.

[27] L. Châtellier, *L'Europe des devôts* (Paris, 1987).

established, lay-run confraternities was now being usurped by clergy-controlled equivalents, especially new, post-Tridentine ones, of which the Jesuit *congrégations* were most successful.

Temples and Altars

The Terreaux was far from self-evident as a site for Lyons's prestigious new civic centre, since it was peripheral and insalubrious, marshy ground hitherto used only for the pig market and gibbet. To justify this relocation of civic centre and then persuade citizens of its validity, powerful rhetoric was required, and the Consulate turned to the Jesuits to provide this. The town hall was being built over the site of the Huguenot 'Temple de Lyon'; the city's history, as retold by Catholics over the previous century, left citizens well aware of this fact.[28] Meanwhile the college, in being rebuilt on its previous site, was likewise asserting Catholic conquest over Protestants, this time effacing memories of a building portrayed by the same authors as having harboured Calvinist ferment.[29] By presenting the new civic centre in terms of a 'Temple de Lyon' the Jesuits thus implied the Catholic victory over the Huguenots, without any need for further explanation.

This nomenclature was not, however, just an allusion to physical and moral destruction, but also a deliberate erasure from history,[30] a civic purification. Yet, being essentially negative, it was neither likely to engender the kind of enthusiasm required to rebuild the civic community as a fervently Catholic one, nor to communicate the specifically Roman Catholic character of the refounded city to outsiders. The context of the Terreaux district, however, simultaneously offered an alternative reading of the title 'Temple de Lyon', reconnecting the city with its antique heritage, since it contained the supposed site of the city's Temple of Vesta.[31] In Rome itself the Temple of Vesta had been considered the holiest place in the city, and subsequently temples dedicated to this goddess had acquired comparable status in cities throughout the Empire. Moreover, Vesta's Greek

---

[28] The site was actually referred to as 'en la place du Temple', AML, BB200, f. 9v. Terreaux was also well known for Huguenot martyrs being burned at the stake there in the 1550s: Théodore Agrippa d'Aubigné, *Les Tragiques: les feux* (Paris, 1995), ll. 441–52; Saint-Aubin, *Histoire*, I, p. 243.

[29] Groër, *Réforme et Contre-Réforme*, pp. 49–68.

[30] In the mid-seventeenth century the phrase 'et falsa [religione] recentium hoereticorum rejicienda' was dropped from the title of Perpiñen's oration of 1567. Menestrier, *Eloge*, II, p. 84.

[31] Menestrier, *Histoire*, pp. 31–2.

predecessor, Hestia, had been the deity most closely associated with *prytaneia*, the 'town halls' of Greek antiquity, thus justifying the Terreaux as the most appropriate location for the new town hall. Jesuit schoolmasters used ballets which they mounted in the course of the Terreaux redevelopment to signal the new, Roman Catholic civic centre's identification with its pagan forebear in Roman antiquity; this was made most explicit in 'L'Autel de Lyon', where a personification of 'the town of Lyons' appeared as 'a Vestal of Louis Augustus, in order to conserve the sacred fire on his Altar'.[32] In antiquity the city's hearth was situated at the Temple of Vesta, which was therefore considered 'le temple de la communauté'; accordingly the Chief Pontiff resided there. Whilst free-running water symbolized civic liberties, ever-active fire represented corresponding responsibilities, symbolized by the sacred flame in the civic hearth, whose conservation depended upon citizens replenishing it, and thereby representing the citizens' need of mutual support.[33]

Although the new civic centre at the Terreaux was erected on the site of the sacred Roman Temple of Vesta, it referred to the 'Temple de Lyon' in antiquity, dedicated to Augustus and Rome, which had stood at Aînay, at the opposite extreme of the *presqu'île*, at the confluence of the rivers Rhône and Saône.[34] For the Temple of Augustus and Rome was explicitly identified through allegories chosen by Jesuits from the Collège de la Trinité, both in the decorative scheme they devised for the town hall and town college together, and in the complementary tragedies and ballets performed (usually at the annual Trinity Sunday celebrations) to celebrate each stage of its execution. In 1658, the completion of the ceiling decoration in the town hall's main reception room, the Grande Salle − as the 'Temple d'Auguste' − was celebrated with pupils from the town college performing ballets devised by Claude-François Menestrier, 'Les Destinées de Lyon' on Trinity Sunday and 'L'Autel de Lyon' later, during Louis XIV's visit; the latter ballet alluded simultaneously to the altar erected at Lyons in Roman antiquity by the sixty Gallic tribes in honour of Augustus, and − exploiting a pun − to the

[32] According to Menestrier's later treatise on ballets, this figure appeared in Menestrier's 'L'Autel de Lyon', part 1, 6th entry [Menestrier, *Des Ballets anciens et modernes selon les regles du theatre* (Paris, 1682), Preface]; but it is not actually mentioned in the *relation* for that ballet: Menestrier, *Autel de Lyon* (Lyons, 1658).

[33] Menestrier, *Histoire*, Dissertation (separate pagination), pp. 30 ff.

[34] Paradin, *Mémoires*, p. 16; Guillaume du Choul, *Discours de la religion des Anciens Romains* (Lyons, 1581), p. 269; De Rubys, *Histoire*, p. 49; De Marca, *De primatu Lugdunensi*, p. 273; Saint-Aubin, *Histoire*, I, p. 15; Menestrier, *Histoire*, pp. 71–2.

new 'Hôtel de Lyon', as the town hall was often called.[35] Likewise, in 1663, the completion of the painting of the college's own Grande Cour was celebrated by the pupils performing 'Le Temple de la Sagesse', the theme of the scheme covering the courtyard's walls; this alluded to the other half of the antique dedication, to Minerva, the Roman goddess of wisdom, whilst also hinting at an alternative dedication, to Rome, reflecting the Jesuits' unique vow of allegiance to the papacy.[36] In 1667 the completion of the entire civic centre was celebrated by the tragedy 'Lyon rebâti, ou les destins forcés'.[37]

The analogies drawn between the new civic centre at the Terreaux, erected on the site of the sacred Roman Temple of Vesta, and the antique 'Temple de Lyon' dedicated to Augustus and Rome, which had stood at Aînay, reflected modern political realities. In the seventeenth century the virtually pastoral district of Aînay, in the hardly developed southern part of the *presqu'île*, was best known for the abbey of St Martin, the only royal abbey in Lyons. The abbey was subject to the authority of its abbot, none other than the ultramontane archbishop, Camille de Neufville. This abbey thus provided an exemplary image of the centralization of ecclesiastical control, marginalizing parish clergy, as promulgated by the Council of Trent, but portrayed as growing from ancient roots.

This church, by being built over a Roman temple, provided material expression of Christianity's triumph over paganism; one account stressed the deliberate destruction of the temple, by 'princes catholiques, & saincts prelats', in order to abolish 'l'idolatrie & paganisme', as a prerequisite for building the church.[38] Like St Nizier's, St Martin's had claims to sanctity, having supposedly begun, in the fourth century, as the chapel (or 'grotto') around the tomb of St Blandine and other Christians martyred by the Roman authorities in the arena at Lyons. The current building, however, dated from the eleventh century, erected after its predecessor

---

[35] AML, BB213, p. 293, CC2091, piece 24; Menestrier, *Eloge*, III, Chapter V, p. 16; Claude-François Menestrier, S.J., *Ballet des destinées de Lyon* (Lyon, 1658); Paradin, *Mémoires*, pp. 15–16; de Rubys, *Histoire*, p. 51; De Marca, *De primatu Lugdunensi*, p. 273; Saint-Aubin, *Histoire*, I, p. 15; Menestrier, *Autel de Lyon*, p. 47; Claude-François Menestrier, S.J., *Le Temple de la Sagesse ouvert à tous les peuples. Dessein des peintures de la Grande Cour du College* (Lyons, 1663), p. 3; Menestrier, *Histoire*, pp. 66–85. The craftsman François Basset's account submitted to the Consulate for his work on the town hall refers to it as the 'Autel de Lyon' (AML, CC 2049, pièce 51).

[36] AML, BB217, p. 452, CC2155, No. 3; Archives Departmentales de Rhône, D10; Menestrier, *Temple de la Sagesse*, p. 3 and *passim*.

[37] Gaspar-Joseph Charonier, S.J., *Lyon rebâti, ou les destins forcés* (Lyons, 1667). See J.Loach, 'Charonier's Medal for "the City's Eternity" – Ephemeral Jeton or Foundation Monument?', *The Medal* 9 (September 1986), 54–78.

[38] Paradin, *Mémoires*, p. 16.

was destroyed by the Huns (significantly referred to in the seventeenth century as 'Sarasins'); the demolition of its cloisters during the Wars of Religion encouraged parallels with the destruction wrought by infidels in the Middle Ages and by Huguenots just a century earlier.[39] In the seventeenth century, interest in the church centred upon the columns supporting its crossing dome, supposedly the pair flanking the Roman Autel de Lyon, each now sawn in half. Whilst the rest of the temple had utterly disappeared, it was believed that its masonry had largely been incorporated into various church buildings including the abbey now standing on its site, where antique Roman fragments were clearly incorporated into the walls.[40]

The construction of a new capitol for Lyons, on the site of one of its major antique temples – the Terreaux being that of Vesta – yet designed to refer to another – that of Augustus and Minerva, at Aînay – implied an inherent relationship between these two temples, and between their respective sites. Moreover, a long-standing tradition equated the title of 'Athenée' (or 'Athenaeum') with the temple at Aînay,[41] thus leading to its association with the role now fulfilled by the town college,[42] situated at the Terreaux. Furthermore, in antiquity the chief pontiff resided at the Temple of Vesta, by the Terreaux,[43] whilst the town's seventeenth-century religious leader, Camille, built a residence at Aînay. Reciprocity is apparent between the secular – commercial and governmental – focus at Terreaux and its ecclesiastical counterpart at Aînay. Such reciprocity between the two temples, as projected onto the evidence extant in the seventeenth century, reflects authentic origins in antiquity. For it was the loyalty to Rome shown by the sixty Gallic tribes in establishing the Temple to Augustus at Aînay which led Augustus to erect the Temple of Vesta at the Terreaux, specifically to express the status of *colonia* (or *communauté*), which he had given to the city.[44] The reciprocity between Lyons and Rome was reiterated in the ceiling

---

[39] Saint-Aubin, *Histoire*, I, pp. 156–7; Menestrier, *Eloge*, II, p. 53; Clapasson, *Description*, pp. 25–7.

[40] Du Choul, *Discours*, p. 269; Menestrier, *Histoire*, pp. 6–7, 53, 69–71 & pl. opp. p. 69.

[41] Paradin, *Mémoires*, pp. 16, 17; De Rubys, *Histoire*, p. 53; De Marca, *De primatu Lugdunensi*, p. 285. The force of Menestrier's refutation of this tradition indicates its strength (Menestrier, *Histoire*, p. 85). See also Anon., *L'Athenée rétabli et consacré à Louis le Grand* (Lyons, 1691), p. 8.

[42] Saint-Aubin, *Histoire*, I, pp. 13–14, 23; Menestrier, *Eloge*, I, pp. 55ff. This was most developed in the Trinity Sunday ballet of 1691, *L'Athenée rétabli et consacré à Louis le Grand*. The foundation stone to the college building erected in 1607 read 'Hoc saxum veteri Athenae Soc. Jesu omnibus artibus renovando' (AML, DD369 Inventaire Chappe, 18).

[43] Menestrier, *Histoire*, Dissertations (separate pagination), pp. 30 ff.

[44] Ibid.

decoration of the Grande Salle, officially interpreted as representing Europe as a body, with Rome as head and Lyons as heart.[45]

By referring through its decorative scheme to the Temple of Augustus and Minerva, the new capitol at the Terreaux expressed the contemporary political situation in visual terms. For the Gallo-Roman temple paid for by all sixty Gallic nations, who used it each year for their communal sacrifices, was the symbol of Lyons's capital status; the resonance with contemporary political ambitions was made clear through writings and performances.[46] In noting that the antique Temple d'Auguste had been built because of that emperor's sojourn in Lyons, and moreover specifically after he had 'appaisa les tumultes',[47] a parallel was inferred between it and the building and decoration of the town hall: undertaken in view of Louis XIV's anticipated visit,[48] likewise taking place in the shadow of civil unrest, the Fronde.

Temple Rites

According to the seventeenth-century Jesuit authors, the Roman Temple de Lyon was intended for communal participation in sacred rites: sacrifices, but also games (*jeux*) and performances (*spectacles*).[49] These games preceded, accompanied or followed sacrifices, and were therefore deemed sacred, to be supervised by princes and high-ranking magistrates or by pontiffs and priests.[50] Priests (*Augustales*) exercised especial responsibilities, and they alone were responsible for recording and publishing the games and spectacles. In antiquity Lyons had appointed six Augustales (*seviri Augustales*), and so in the seventeenth century the Consuls were sometimes identified as their successors; yet the Augustales' function implied that they must be priests, so that Jesuits, as organizers of civic festivities, were sometimes perceived as fulfilling this role; moreover Jesuits wrote the published accounts of such 'games'. Overall the role performed by Augustales in antiquity

---

[45] Menestrier, *Eloge*, III, Chapter V, pp. 36–8.
[46] Menestrier, *Histoire*, pp. 71, 72; J. Loach, 'Lyons *versus* Paris: Claiming the Status of Capital in the Middle of the Seventeenth Century', in G. Sabatier and R. Costa Gomes (eds), *Lugares de Poder* (Lisbon, 1998), pp. 260–85.
[47] Menestrier, *Histoire*, p. 73.
[48] Menestrier, *Factum Justicatif* [Paris, 1694], p. 67.
[49] Paradin, *Mémoires*, p. 17; de Rubys, *Histoire*, pp. 54–7.
[50] Menestrier, *Histoire*, pp. 72, 77.

seems to have been understood in the seventeenth century as being undertaken by consuls and priests acting together.[51]

Naturally the Catholic Mass was considered as having superseded the temple's pagan sacrifices. The renown of the games held at the Temple de Lyon had been assured by antique writers. These 'Jeux Gaulois' – national games – were contests of eloquence (and poetry), in both Greek and Latin, instituted by the Emperor Caligula and with infamous penalties for losers.[52] Although antique sources indicated that they had been accompanied by 'spectacles', less detail about these had survived. Seventeenth-century Jesuits surmised that these games had consisted of a mixture of musical and sporting events,[53] perhaps partly influenced by the ambiguity inherent in the Latin term, *ludi*, meaning both games and plays. Within a context of rising *politesse* and *honnêteté* some felt it necessary to distinguish between the 'public games' in theatres and amphitheatres (comedies and tragedies, and 'jeux sanglants') and the more *honnestes* 'mixed games' at the Temple d'Auguste – various sorts of recreation and exercise undertaken by youths, horse racing, wrestling and singing,[54] but perhaps also dramatic performances.[55] Such a definition reflects the contemporary understanding of the games at sacred festivals in antiquity, the *agones*, which included not only athletics and gymnastics but also singing.[56]

[51] De Rubys, *Histoire*, p. 50; Menestrier, *Histoire*, pp. 74, 76, 77, 98–9; Menestrier, *Eloge*, I, pp. 55 ff.; du Choul, *Discours*, pp. 269–70; Menestrier, *Ballet des Destinées*; Menestrier, *Autel de Lyon*; Menestrier, *Temple de la Sagesse*; Charonier, *Lyon rébâti*.

[52] Paradin, *Mémoires*, p. 17; De Rubys, *Histoire*, pp. 56–7; Saint-Aubin, *Histoire*, I, pp. 18, 23; Menestrier, *Autel de Lyon*, p. 47; Menestrier, *Ballets anciens et modernes*, Preface; Anon., *L'Athenée de Lyon*, pp. 8, 16; Menestrier, *Histoire*, pp. 68, 99, 100.

[53] Menestrier includes dances, gladiatorial combats and horse races: *Histoire*, p. 99. Saint-Aubin includes 'diverses sortes de d'exercices, de Musique, de manege, de courses, de luttes, de ioûtes': *Histoire*, I, p. 18.

[54] De Rubys, *Histoire*, pp. 54–5. The leading writer on public entertainments in Roman antiquity, the Jesuit Jules-César B[o]ulenger, likewise differentiated between games explicitly according to their location and implicitly to current acceptability, but divided them between the circus or amphitheatre (for sport and combats) and theatres (for dramatic performances), allocating one treatise to each: *De circo romano ludisque circensibus, ac circi et amphitheatri venatione* (Paris, 1598), and *De theatro, ludisque scenicis libri duo* (Tricasses, 1603).

[55] Paradin thought the temple festivities consisted of 'grandes resiouissances publiques, comme des ieux de theatre, meslez de divers passetemps': Paradin, *Mémoires*, p. 17.

[56] Petrus Faber, *Agonosticon, sive de re athletica ludisque veter, gymnicis, musicis et circensibus tractatus* (Lyons, 1592). See N.G.L. Hammond and H.H. Scullard (eds), *The Oxford Classical Dictionary* (Oxford, 1970), p. 28.

In antiquity these games and spectacles had been held annually, when the sixty Gallic tribes gathered together to sacrifice at the Temple de Lyon.[57] The Temple de Lyon 'reconstructed' in the seventeenth century comprised the town hall and college, with the latter's Grande Cour representing a 'Temple de la Sagesse' specifically defined as being 'open to all peoples', thus implying superiority over its antique predecessor, open to the sixty Gallic nations.[58] The annual celebrations mounted at the town college on Trinity Sunday – organized, like those in antiquity, by priests – therefore substituted for the sacrifice and associated games at the original Temple de Lyon. A festal mass in the morning was followed by a banquet, during which prize-winning speeches or poems in a variety of languages (known as *affiches*, a speciality of Jesuit-run colleges)[59] were recited by their schoolboy authors; then in the afternoon boys from the Rhetoric year performed a tragedy, with boys from the year below, Humanities, performing a ballet, interpolated act by act, both usually being devised by the respective year masters. The *affiches* thus represented antiquity's games – its contests in eloquence and poetry (now in a larger number of languages than in antiquity, again insinuating Catholicism's superiority over its pagan forebear)[60] – whilst the dramatic performances represented its spectacles. The parallel between the antique games and seventeenth-century contests in composition was reinforced by comparing them with the Académie Française's biennial prize for a speech in the French language.[61] As for the dramatic performances, their Jesuit organizers regarded ballet not as mere entertainment, nor even as an allegorical medium for enlivening instruction, but as 'une espece de mystere & de ceremonie'; moreover they asserted that its sacred character had been accepted by Jews and Early Christians, both of whom had accorded dance a central role in their liturgies.[62]

During the period of the Catholic refoundation of Lyons, the single annual temple rite seen as continuing from antiquity was that of public vows (*Vota*

---

[57] Menestrier, *Histoire*, p. 68.

[58] Menestrier, *Temple de la Sagesse*, full title and pp. 3–5.

[59] Bibliothèque Municipale de Lyon, MS 1514, Claude-François Menestrier, S.J., 'Pompe des Colleges', f. 70; Dupont-Ferrier, *Du Collège de Clermont au Lycée Louis-le-Grand* (Paris, 1921–25), I, p. 270.

[60] In the ballet *L'Athenée de Lyon*, the section 'L'Athenée ouvert à tous les peuples' elaborates upon how the seventeenth-century Athenée, the Collège de la Trinité ('open to all peoples'), outdoes its antique forebear ('open to the sixty Gallic nations'): in the third *entrée* Louis XIV outdoes Augustus, in the fourth, eulogies are delivered in half a dozen languages (i.e. as *affiches*) as opposed to the two in antiquity, and in the fifth the games are revived (*L'Athenée de Lyon*, p. 16).

[61] Menestrier, *Histoire*, p. 100.

[62] Menestrier, *Ballets*, pp. 8, 9 ff., 13.

publica, or *Voeux publics*).[63] In antiquity this was the rite articulating both mutual duties of gods and men, empire and individual citizen, and the passage from one year to another, from past to future. The people, through their senate and republic, confirmed their recognition of, and allegiance to, their emperor; the emperor thanked the gods for having protected the empire since the previous vows were taken; and the magistrates, on behalf of the people, took new vows for the forthcoming year,[64] promising to offer the gods sacrifices, games, the building or maintenance of temples and the dedication of altars in return for divine support. These vows could all be said to be for conservation, primarily of Rome and the empire, then for the current emperor and citizens.[65] The rite exemplified the reciprocity inherent throughout the Temple de Lyon as 'refounded' in the seventeenth century, in the town hall and new town college.

The continuation – or appropriation – of this rite by Christian emperors was evoked by Lyonese Jesuits, thus justifying their own re-enactment of it. In addition evidence was provided for the continuity between this pagan ceremony and current Catholic rites through the credence table beside the High Altar in the cathedral, comprising two fragments of antique masonry and originally used for public vows; indeed, it was supposed that its initial function had led to its appropriation for its current one, both serving to 'recevoir les oblations sacrées'. Jesuits overtly applied the term 'Voeux publics' to civic or state festivities which they organized, such as those celebrating the erection of the statue of Louis XIV in front of the town hall in Paris (in 1689), thus attributing to him the status formerly enjoyed by a Roman emperor.[66]

In antiquity public vows had been commemorated in coins and medals, where the words defining the duration of the vows appeared within laurel crowns, or on shields, held by Victories. In seventeenth-century Lyons such Victories bearing laurel crowns immediately recalled those flanking the Autel de Lyon in antiquity.[67] By implication, since the town hall and college constituted the new Temple de Lyon, these became the new sites for public vows.

[63] Du Choul, *Discours*, p. 274.
[64] Menestrier, *Histoire*, p. 156.
[65] Du Choul, *Discours de la Religion*, pp. 274, 281; Menestrier, *Histoire*, pp. 156–7.
[66] Menestrier, *Histoire*, pp. 157–8; Claude-François Menestrier, S.J., *Décoration de la cour de l'Hôtel de ville de Paris* (Paris, 1689); *La Statue de Loüis le Grand, placée dans le temple de l'Honneur* (Paris, 1689); [Pierre Jurieu], *La Religion des Jesuites* (The Hague, 1689); Claude-François Menestrier, S.J., *Lettre à Mr. *** sur ... l'Hostel de ville* (Paris, 1689); Claude-François Menestrier, S.J., *Seconde Lettre pour iustifier ... Temple de l'Honneur* (Paris, 1689); Claude-François Menestrier, S.J., *Les Respects de la ville de Paris, en l'érection de la statüe* (Lyons, 1690).
[67] Du Choul, *Discours*, pp. 269, 274, 277, 281; Menestrier, *Histoire*, pp. 69–71, 156 and pl. opp. p. 69.

Although these vows had originally been taken by secular officials – higher magistrates, such as consuls, praetors and censors – their efficacy depended upon priests, who alone could offer the associated sacrifices. Indeed, once the magistrates had pronounced their vows, the priests effectively took over, taking charge not only of the sacrifice but also of related fires, dances and banquets,[68] in other words, precisely the role assumed by the Jesuits, notably on Trinity Sunday. It seems more than coincidental that these Jesuits were aware that Christian emperors had performed public vows on the Church's holy days, notably – and appropriately – at Epiphany, 'la fête des Rois'.[69] Further correspondences between the pagan priests in antiquity and Catholic ones in the seventeenth century were implied in Lyonese descriptions of the Romans' *Soteria*, the games and sacrifices likewise mounted for the conservation of the emperor. The *Galli*, the priests responsible for these *Megalesia*, or *grands ieux*, were 'sacerdotes de la Mere des Dieux', a title equally applicable to Jesuits, as directors of Marian congregations. Not only parallels but continuity was seen between the *Galli*'s processions, with their portable statues and their altars of repose, and those used to celebrate Corpus Christi in Catholic France.[70]

Secular Games

Under the Romans public vows were pronounced at regular intervals, not only annually but also at the conclusion of lustrations (*lustra*), or purification ceremonies, usually every five years. They likewise were performed after ten years (*Vota decennalia*) or twenty years (*Vota vicennalia*), and at the conclusion of each *saeculum* (era), where they were accompanied by secular games (*ludi*, a word equally meaning plays).[71] Although the duration of a *saeculum* had originally been defined as that of a human life, under the Republic it became fixed as a century.[72] Seventeenth-century Jesuits throughout northern Europe accepted this latter

[68] Du Choul, *Discours*, pp. 276, 281.
[69] Menestrier, *Histoire*, p. 156. It was also commonly believed, albeit without proof, that the *Amburbium*, or annual lustration of cities, had been superseded by Candlemas (Hammond and Scullard, *Oxford Classical Dictionary*, p. 51).
[70] Du Choul, *Discours*, pp. 271–2.
[71] Ibid., pp. 282–4.
[72] Menestrier, *Histoire*, p. 156; Gaspar-Joseph Charonier, S.J., *Le Temple de la Gratitude* (Lyons, 1666), pp. 1–2; Hammond and Scullard, *Oxford Classical Dictionary*, p. 969.

duration.[73] Indeed, the Flemish Jesuits presented part of their college's celebrations as 'Secular Games'.[74]

In 1667 the Jesuits presented their Trinity Sunday celebrations in Lyons as Secular Games, commemorating that year's festivities – uniquely – by striking a bronze medal. According to the inscription around its reverse, it referred to 'ludis solemn[ibus]'[75] – solemn plays, or games, but in either case in the plural – performed by the boys in the Rhetoric class that day. All major Jesuit-run colleges, including that at Lyons, usually mounted two interpolated performances for such occasions: a historical tragedy performed by the Rhetoricians and an allegorical ballet or opera performed by the Humanists. Yet the extant records imply that a single performance was presented at Lyons on this Trinity Sunday, 'Lyon rebâti ou le destin forcé', and although this was qualified as a 'tragedie',[76] and performed by the Rhetoricians, it took instead the form of an allegorical performance.[77] The deliberate use of the plural form (*ludis*) is thus most likely intended to allude to antique usage, where the plural designated public games, such as those given in honour of the gods, or stage plays (as opposed to the games held in the circus); the apposition of the adjective 'solemnibus' supports this interpretation.[78]

The tragedy took as its theme 'le rétablissement de cette Ville, apres son incendie arrivé sous l'Empire de Neron'.[79] In historical terms this referred to the famous Fire of Lyons which had entirely destroyed the town, including its famous temple, and was known from Seneca's letter which reassured his distraught friend, a native of Lyons, that the city would 'rise more glorious than before'.[80] Seventeenth-century citizens of Lyons understood this story allegorically, local historians having used it as a metaphor for the city's spiritual destruction a century earlier, when captured by Huguenots.[81] The decorative scheme for the town hall's

---

[73] As is evident from the title of the work produced by the Flemish Jesuits to celebrate the Society's centenary: *Imago primi saeculi Societatis Iesu* (Antwerp, 1640).

[74] *Ludis Saecularis de Ortu et Progressu Societatis Jesu* (Antwerp, 1640).

[75] Charonier, *Lyon rebâti*, p. 14; Claude-François Menestrier, S.J., *La Philosophie des images* (Lyons, 1682), I, p. 322. For numismatic details of the medal, see J. Tricou, 'Médailles religieuses de Lyon du XVIe au XVIIIe siècle', *Revue Numismatique*, 5th series, 13 (1951), 119–22; J. Tricou, *Médailles Lyonnaises* (Lyons, 1958), Pl. X, No. 112.

[76] Menestrier, *Philosophie*, I, p. 322.

[77] Charonier, *Lyon rebâti*.

[78] Concerning the Autel de Lyon, 'ces grandes ceremonies étaient accompagnées des jeux solemnels' (Menestrier, *Histoire*, p. 72).

[79] Menestrier, *Philosophie*, I, p. 321.

[80] Seneca, *Moral Letter* 91.

[81] 'Introduction', Charonier, *Lyon rebâti*.

ceremonial Grand Escalier took as its theme 'L'Incendie de Lyon',[82] and its principal painting, depicting the burning temple, was supplied with a title, lifted from Seneca's letter. In 'Una nox interfuit' ('a night intervened'), seventeenth-century visitors would have understood this single night as referring to the night intervening between Lyons's glory as Roman Gaul's capital and her physical disappearance, but equally to that between her Renaissance apogee and its collapse engendered by the Huguenot occupation.

The tragedy's title – 'Lyon rebâti ou le destin forcé' – simultaneously refers back to earlier decorations and performances, notably the first ballet in the sequence, that 'des destinées de Lyon' (1658). This had enunciated the decorative scheme of the Grand Escalier, both narrating the Fire and its aftermath, notably the battle between good and evil destinies over the city's subsequent future. This ballet consisted of four acts – 'Lyon Basty', 'Lyon Retably', 'Lyon Chrestien' and 'Lyon François' – so as to emphasize the Christian character of the city's refoundation, an aspect reiterated in details elsewhere in the larger scheme. The tragedy performed in 1667 likewise begins with the Fire's aftermath, this time with the city's and the province's protecting *genii* – evidently representing the current governor and lieutenant, the Neufville-Villeroy brothers – pleading with Apollo (a thinly veiled Louis XIV) to influence Destiny. Lugdus, the city's *genius* (*alias* Camille de Neufville) rebuilds the town, but in so doing moves it from the top of the Fourvière Hill, where the Roman theatres stood, down to the *presqu'île*, encompassing Terreaux and Aînay. Meanwhile Pallas, the province's *genius* (Nicolas de Villeroy), persuades Apollo to send Art to ensure that the new city will be even more beautiful than its predecessor.

The programme printed for the performance included an extensive 'Explication de l'Allegorie', detailing how Destiny had been influenced – and thus the town restored – thanks to a rare, but 'admirable', 'union … entre l'Eglise Romaine & nos Roys', tacitly represented by their respective agents Camille and Nicolas. Louis's part in this alliance, and hence his title 'Catholic', was demonstrated by his 'démolition d'une infinité de Temples, où l'heresie triumphoit avec insolence'.[83] At one level this referred to a topical situation of which his audience would have been well aware, since just a few years earlier – in the early 1660s – Louis XIV had demolished 152 Huguenot temples in Bas Languedoc, Provence and the Haute Cevennes, in other words those within the Jesuit Province de Lyon, whose administrators were based in the Collège de la Trinité. At another level this simultaneously alluded to the demolition of the Huguenot temples in Lyons exactly

---

[82] Saint-Aubin, *Histoire*, I, pp. 335–6; Menestrier, *Eloge*, III, Chapter V, pp. 9–16.
[83] Charonier, *Lyon rebâti*, pp. 30–31.

a century before,[84] an event which the play – and thus the 'Secular Games' – celebrated.

The medal struck to commemorate these *ludi* depicts a figure of Eternity on its reverse, seated on a globe and wearing a helmet,[85] her extended right hand holding a blazing bird, evidently a phoenix. The obverse carries the names and arms of the current Consulate, the king, his *intendant*, and the governor and lieutenant, all of whom are thus implicitly credited on the reverse with the 'restoration' being celebrated. Research has shown that this medal did more than celebrate Lyons's recent phoenix-like rising from its own ashes. It also alluded to Eternal Rome, thereby commemorating Lyons's refoundation as a second Rome, a second eternal city, its posterity now guaranteed through its rededication to Christ.[86] Those receiving the medal, together with others composing the ballet's audience, were by now all familiar with the decoration of the town hall's Grande Salle, the setting for council meetings since its completion several years earlier. Here the painting above the chimneypiece depicted Plancus, Lyons's Roman refounder (representing Camille de Neufville), raising a nymph (representing the city) from the ground, so that he 'Iette les fondemens d'une seconde Rome'.[87] Its composition recapitulated, and thus alluded to, the frontispiece of *Icones et Segmentae*,[88] a mid-seventeenth-century book by an artist well known in Lyons, François Perrier;[89] here a citation from Claudian addresses Rome, encouraging her restoration specifically on the basis of her Christian faith,[90] a sentiment evidently inferred in the Lyonese painting.

Critically, the representation of 'secular games' at Lyons in 1667 fell exactly a century after the Catholics' final victory over the Protestants; above all the town – let alone the Consulate – had been purged of Protestants from late 1567 (following the Huguenots' attempted recapture of Lyons), and a permanent contract had been granted to the Jesuits for assuring education in the town college.[91] Evidently the centenary celebrations tacitly adopted as the theme that of the oration delivered a century earlier, by the eminent Spanish Jesuit Pedro Juan Perpiñen, brought from

---

[84] Saint-Aubin, *Histoire*, I, p. 243.

[85] Charonier, *Lyon rebâti*, p. 14.

[86] See Loach, 'Charonier's medal', 64–78.

[87] Menestrier, *Eloge*, III, Chapter V, pp. 21–2; Saint-Aubin, *Histoire*, I, pp. 336–7. For an engraving, see Menestrier, *Eloge*, header to Pt. I.

[88] François Perrier, *Icones et Segmentae* (Rome, 1644); L. Galactéros de Boissier, 'Thomas Blanchet: la Grande Salle de l'Hôtel de Ville de Lyon', *Revue de l'Art* 47 (1980), 33.

[89] Daniel Ternois, 'François Perrier et Lyon', in J. Jéhasse (ed.), *Mélanges offerts à Georges Couton* (Lyons, 1981), pp. 223–35.

[90] Loach, 'Charonier's medal', 72.

[91] Groër, *Réforme et Contre-Réforme*, pp. 94, 114.

Rome especially for the purpose of celebrating this Catholic, and Jesuit, victory in Lyons; his oration was referred to in the 1660s as 'De veteri religione retinenda ad Lugdunenses', an address to the Lyonese on preserving their ancient religion.[92]

Conclusion: the Consecration of the Civic Realm

Although the intention to refound Lyons as a Christian city was apparent from 1567, financial exigencies delayed the materialization of this ambition, unfulfilled until the following century, and then only in stages. The long-drawn-out nature of its realization was implicitly justified by antique precedent, where an intention to build a temple led to choosing a site, preparing materials, and then construction.[93] The laying of the foundation stone for the Hôtel de Ville was evidently conceived as the foundation rite for the new Temple de Lyon. The ceremony was presided over by Camille de Neufville, as Primate of the Church of Gaul, and thus the contemporary equivalent of Drusus, the Augur responsible for this in Roman antiquity. An auspicious date was selected, 5 September 1646,[94] the birthday of 'Louis Auguste', its dedicatee, thus again recalling Lyons's foundation in Roman antiquity, likewise celebrated on the birthday of its dedicatee, the Emperor Augustus.[95] In this it also paralleled another city's foundation, in this case at once Roman and Christian, namely Constantinople (whose basilica of Hagia Sophia – holy wisdom – was depicted in the Grande Cour as a precedent for Lyons's 'Temple de la Sagesse'),[96] on the birthday of Constantine; in this case the foundation was explicitly as a 'second Rome'.[97] In the decoration of the Grande Salle as the 'Temple d'Auguste', Lyons's refoundation was explicitly presented as that of a second Rome.[98]

---

[92] Menestrier, *Eloge*, II, p. 84.

[93] Menestrier, *Histoire*, p. 73.

[94] Inscription recorded AML, DD369 Inventaire Chappe, 18; Menestrier, *Eloge*, III, Chapter IV (unpaginated), entry for 1647.

[95] Menestrier, *Histoire*, pp. 72–3.

[96] Menestrier, *Temple de la Sagesse*, pp. 2, 12 (cit. Raynaud, *Hagiologium Lugdunense*, pp. 440 ff.); Saint-Aubin, *Histoire*, p. 345; 'Recueil de Dessins de Paul Sevin, 1650–', Ecole National Supérieur des Beaux-Arts, Paris, Collection Chennevières, inv. no. B.1000.1518, pls. 17b, 18b, 17bisa, 17bisb, 17a.

[97] G. Dagron, *Naissance d'une capitale: Constantinople et ses institutions de 330 à 451* (Paris, 1974), p. 38.

[98] Menestrier, *Eloge*, III, Chapter V, p. 23.

Only after construction was completed, in spring 1655,[99] could the capitol's symbolic function be made manifest, through the decoration of the town hall's Grande Salle as the Temple d'Auguste: between spring 1655 and summer 1658 its ceiling was painted, and from then to summer 1660 its walls.[100] Next, between summer 1661 and winter 1664,[101] the ceremonial staircase to the Grande Salle was decorated as 'The Fire of Lyons', extending the theme to cover the Temple de Lyon's dual dedication.[102] Finally the Grande Cour of the town college was decorated as the Temple de la Sagesse, its walls during the summer vacation of 1662 and its paving over the summer of 1667.[103] These stages were articulated by dramatic performances, devised not to be merely didactic, but also persuasive. Moreover several of them overtly evoked sacred rites, from the foundation in 1646 to the Secular Games of 1667, with the ballet performed before Louis XIV in 1658 presented as the altar's consecration.

The primary aim of this process was the city's refoundation, understood principally in spiritual terms; it therefore depended more upon transforming its citizenry than its built fabric. Civic monuments were certainly accorded symbolic roles as well as functional ones, but only supporting ones in this strategy for changing hearts and minds; they provided the complementary backdrop for a variety of orations, dramatic entertainments and civic rites used to touch and move a mass of individuals. The tragedies and ballets devised to mark each stage in the city's physical reconstruction were delivered by schoolboys – tellingly those known as 'Rhetoricians' – at once sons of citizens and on the verge of becoming citizens themselves; those taking part as witnesses to these civic rites equally did so as citizens, led by the Consulate and other official representatives but, through the parents of the performers, representing a wide range of the population. A sense of audience participation was inculcated through the festal context, initiated by the Mass, the Church's ritual sacrifice, partaken by pupils and adults together, and whose priestly administrators then joined their fellow citizens to form the audience. The theatrical modes invariably selected – tragedy and ballet – were those then understood as being innately sacred in character.

The ritual character accorded to these performances becomes clearest from the ballet danced before the king, entitled 'L'Autel de Lyon consacré à Louis Auguste', effectively serving as the new temple's rite of consecration. Occurring in

---

[99] Inscription in garden facade of Hôtel de Ville (Menestrier, *Eloge*, III, Chapter IV (unpaginated), entry for 1655).
[100] AML, BB213, p. 293, CC2091, piece 25, BB215, p. 189, CC2123, piece 7.
[101] AML, CC2137, piece 8, BB219; CC2197, pieces 5, 6.
[102] Menestrier, *Eloge*, III, Chapter V, p. 8.
[103] AML, BB217, p. 452, BB222, f. 211, CC2155, No. 3, CC2256, ff. 357v–358; Archives Departmentales de Rhône, D10.

1658, it literally occupied a central position within this sequence of largely annual rites, appropriate since it marked the crucial moment when the site was transferred from the profane sphere to the secular. In Roman antiquity consecration (the act of rendering an object or place a *res sacra*, a holy thing) had involved a dedication authorized by the state, on ground which was the property of the state, and only priests could perform such rites, at which their entire college was to be present; the Lyonese consecration of 1658 tacitly alluded to such parallels in antique practice, thus investing the new capitol with *numen* in the minds of its citizens.

Furthermore, consecration was the rite which most epitomized the reciprocity inherent throughout the process of refounding the city, depending as it did equally upon magistrates, representing the secular authorities, to dedicate the temple to a quasi-deified ruler (an Augustus), and upon priests, representing the ecclesiastical authorities, who alone could effect its consecration. In the ballet of 1667 – 'Lyon rebâti ou le destin forcé' – the fulfilment of the city's destiny depends upon her fidelity to both monarch and papacy. She was to act as a second Rome, in France, as was evoked by reference to the ancient legend of a mirror on the summit of Fourvière, reflecting light from Rome.[104] The entry mounted for the papal legate, Cardinal Chigi, in 1664, stated that Lyons's supremacy in Gaul – both commercial and religious – had been due to her 'alliance avec Rome'. It then proceeded to state that 'Rome Chrestienne a conservé à Lyon les avantages qu'elle avoit receus de Rome Payenne'.[105]

Following its desecration and destruction by the Huguenots, Lyons – once allegorically purified by fire – had been re-established, as a second Rome, under an ultramontane ruler, who exercised authority over it in sacred and secular domains alike. The fact that Secular Games were re-enacted as the means of marking the completion of the city's physical reconstruction signals that this moment was perceived not so much as an end as a beginning, inaugurating a golden age for this phoenix city. The citizenry was being transformed into a Catholic one, a living exemplar of the post-Tridentine model, by transforming its collective understanding, imagination and memory, so as to effect a conversion of its collective will.

No change of urban scenery alone would suffice in such an endeavour, that of persuading citizens to act in such a radically new way. Rather the renewed urban fabric had to be invested with divine authority – through consecration – and all citizens had to be brought into this rite, so that their individual understandings, imaginations and memories of their city were transformed, and thence their wills.

---

[104] Menestrier, *Eloge*, I, pp. 12–14.
[105] Menestrier, *Relation de l'Entrée de Monsigneur l'Eminentissime Cardinal Flavio Chigi* (Lyons, 1664), pp. 22–4.

The materiality of their transformed city – epitomized by its new town hall and college – would then stand as daily reminders to them of their new vocation. These rites of consecration thus instigate a construction of sacred space, but one which exists as much within the collective mind of the citizenry as in the stones and mortar of the rebuilt city. Neither this mental nor this material space, however, can exist without the other.

Chapter 14

The Priest, the Quakers and the Second Conventicle Act: the Battle for Gracechurch Street Meeting House, 1670

Simon Dixon

On 3 July 1670 George Alsop, the recently appointed rector of Chipping Ongar in Essex, was sent by Humphrey Henchman, the Bishop of London, to read from the Book of Common Prayer in the Quaker meeting house in Gracechurch Street in the City of London. According to Alsop's account he was attacked by the Quakers, who called him names such as 'Popish Priest' and 'Jesuit'.[1] The Quaker version of events is somewhat different, describing how Alsop arrived with a band of drunken soldiers, only to withdraw 'without mollestation'.[2] The incident itself was just one part of a concerted effort by the authorities in London to clamp down on religious dissenters in the immediate aftermath of the Second Conventicle Act (1670). It has been cited by historians of the Restoration period as an episode in what has been characterized as a 'battle of London' between the City authorities and religious dissenters, who were said to have flooded the capital in an effort to head off the threat posed by the new legislation.[3] The aim of this paper is to focus upon a series of incidents occurring at Gracechurch Street meeting house and elsewhere in the

---

[1] NA, SP29/277/14. See also, *Extracts from State Papers Relating to Friends 1654 to 1672*, ed. N. Penney (London, 1913), p. 314. I first discovered some of the events discussed in this paper while researching an MA dissertation, 'Early Quaker Meeting Houses in London, 1654–1688' (University of York, 2001). I remain indebted to Bill Sheils for his encouragement at that time. I am also grateful to Justin Champion and Andrew Spicer for discussing earlier drafts with me. All dates in the text have been modernized.

[2] Library of the Society of Friends (hereafter LSF), Great Book of Sufferings, 44 vols, II, p. 102.

[3] G.S. de Krey, 'The First Restoration Crisis: Conscience and Coercion in London, 1667–1673', *Albion* 25 (1993), 570; R.L. Greaves, *Enemies Under His Feet: Radicals and Nonconformists in Britain, 1664–1677* (Stanford, 1990), pp. 157–9.

summer of 1670, and to consider the extent to which they illustrate the role played by notions of religious space in the conflicts of the Restoration period. In attempting to take possession of the Quaker meeting house for use by the established church, the secular and ecclesiastical authorities were seeking to conduct a structured form of worship within a space designed for a very different exercise of religion. The challenge to authority represented by groups such as the Quakers was physically manifested by the presence of meeting houses and dissenting chapels in and around London. In their efforts to assert the authority of the established church the Lord Mayor and the bishop of London employed a variety of tactics to disrupt dissenting activities by seeking to take control of the premises within which they conducted worship. In turn, the Quaker resistance of such efforts highlights the limitations of the capacity of the local authorities to exercise power over intransigent dissenting groups.[4]

Quaker Attitudes to Sacred Space

It may seem strange in a volume concerned with the notion of sacred space to have any discussion of Quaker meeting houses. The Quaker belief system has been interpreted as a 'largely logical development' of Puritanism. While the Puritans contended that the Holy Spirit indwells only in the converted, the Quakers believed that it indwells in all men, the converted completely and the unconverted incompletely.[5] Leaving this difference aside, it is possible to find some similarities between the Quakerism of seventeenth-century England, and the Reformed churches of sixteenth-century Europe. In terms of locating the holy in Quaker belief, the internalization of the sacred that can be found in Quaker doctrine can be compared with the teachings of Jean Calvin. Calvin rejected the notion that the sacred was localized within churches, and told his readers not to attribute 'any secret holiness' to them. He wrote that the divine was located within the believer, and was not confined to the church building since, 'if we are the real temples of the Lord, we must pray to him within ourselves if we wish to invoke him in his real temple'.[6] Thus both for Calvin, and for other reformers, the church building held

---

[4] On power relations in early modern Britain, see M.J. Braddick and J. Walter, 'Introduction. Grids of Power: Order, Hierarchy and Subordination in Early Modern Society', in M.J. Braddick and J. Walter (eds), *Negotiating Power in Early Modern Society: Order, Hierarchy and Subordination in Britain and Ireland* (Cambridge, 2001), pp. 1–42.
[5] G. Nuttall, *The Holy Spirit in Puritan Faith and Experience* (Oxford, 1947), pp. 14, 161–2.
[6] C. Grosse, 'Places of Sanctification: the Liturgical Sacrality of Genevan Reformed Churches, 1535–1566', in Coster and Spicer (eds), *Sacred Space*, pp. 60–80; Jean Calvin, *Institutes of Christian Religion*, quoted by Grosse, p. 64.

no special sacred status in its own right, and was only made holy through its use as an arena for the conduct of religious worship.[7]

A similar interpretation of the space necessary for religious worship can be found in the writings of some early Quakers. In *Concerning the Worship of the Living God*, Isaac Penington considered the question, 'Which is the place of worship?' From here, Penington develops the idea of the internalization of the sacred:

> The only place of Worship in the New-Testament, is where the Spiritual Worshippers meet together. The place is spiritual. As the Worship is spiritual, so is the place where it is to be offered. It hath a spiritual consideration, not outward, as under the Law. It is to be offered in the Spirit; that's the place. Where doth my soul offer its private Worship to God? Hath it relation to any outward place? Or is it in the building, which God hath reared up in my heart by his Spirit.

Thus the appropriate location for worship is not in outward buildings, but in the inward building constructed by God, a metaphor which illustrates the Quaker notion of the internalization of the Holy Spirit and the existence of a direct and unmediated relationship between the believer and God. Penington expands this idea by describing Quaker worship as the joining together of 'Divers living Stones' meeting 'in one and the same place, in one and the same Power, in one and the same fountain of Life'.[8]

The word 'sacred' appears seldom in early Quaker texts, and in the case of Penington's writing has been supplanted by the word 'spiritual'.[9] The Quaker interpretation of the location of the spiritual owes much to the exhortations of St Paul and St Stephen that God 'dwelleth not in temples made with hands' (Acts 7:48, 17:24). These citations appear both in George Fox's writings on churches, and in those of the Genevan reformers of the sixteenth century.[10] Furthermore, Penington appears to be alluding to other parts of the New Testament comparing the church to a building, with believers being the individual stones that comprise the whole church (for example, Eph. 2:20–22). This interpretation of the scriptures

---

[7] Grosse, 'Places of Sanctification'; A. Spicer, '"What Kinde of House a Kirk is": Conventicles, Consecrations and the Concept of Sacred Space in Post-Reformation Scotland', in Coster and Spicer (eds), *Sacred Space*, pp. 60–103.

[8] Isaac Penington, *Concerning the Worship of the Living God* (s.l., s.d.), p. 2.

[9] K. Thomas, *The History and Significance of Quaker Symbols in Sect Formation* (Lampeter, 2002), pp. 23–4.

[10] George Fox, *A Paper Sent Forth into the World from them that are Scornfully called Quakers* (London, 1654), p. 3; George Fox, *To all the People who meet in the Steeple-Houses in England, and Elsewhere* (London, 1657), pp. 1–2, 5; Robert Barclay, *An Apology for the True Christian Divinity* (London, 1678), p. 268; Grosse, 'Places of Sanctification'.

helps to explain the Quaker attitude to the sacred and the notion of sacred space. The Holy Spirit dwells within humankind, and is not localized within a specific building. Thus the building inside which religious worship takes place is of no especial theological significance. It does not need to be consecrated or to have any specific geographical orientation. Internal furnishings are required only to the extent necessary to accommodate those worshipping within it. How we interpret the meeting house as a physical embodiment of Quaker doctrines is therefore open to debate.

In theory, then, Quakers did not need any special premises to worship within. However, in practice it took London Friends very little time to obtain their first permanent meeting places in the capital. Writing to Margaret Fell in 1654, the 'first publisher' Francis Howgill lamented the lack of a fixed meeting place in the city, complaining to Fell that 'our trouble is wee know not what to doe for a place larg enough to meett in' and stating that 'wee would gladly hire any great place for publick meetings if we could'.[11] Howgill's comments indicate the importance of acquiring a permanent physical space to the success of his and Edward Burrough's missionary endeavours in London. Thus in 1655 part of 'an ancient great house' in Aldersgate was hired as a meeting place. This became known as the Bull and Mouth meeting after the sign of the inn which occupied the same building.[12] While throughout the 1650s and 1660s London Quakers continued to hold meetings in private homes, by 1670 eight permanent meeting places were in use in the City of London and outlying districts. Some of these, such as Gracechurch Street, Horsleydown and Ratcliff were built specifically for use as Quaker meeting houses. Others, such as Devonshire House in the City, and Aldersgate and Almonry in Westminster, were existing structures leased by Friends.[13]

While the acquisition of permanent meeting places had no specific grounding in Quaker doctrine, there were a number of reasons why Friends might have felt the need to establish them in the capital as quickly as possible. The establishment of a church or meeting house is an important statement of permanence within society, fostering a sense of community while offering hope of survival. The acquisition or construction of a fixed place of worship presented a perception of permanency and stability, while from a missionary perspective such premises provided a 'visible

---

[11] LSF, Caton MS, vol. 3, 66, pp. 155–8, Francis Howgill to Margaret Fell.

[12] W.C. Braithwaite, *The Beginnings of Quakerism* (Cambridge, 1955), p. 182.

[13] D.M. Butler, *Quaker Meeting Houses of Britain* (2 vols, London, 1999), I, pp. 372–436. This figure includes premises built or leased for religious worship and in use in 1670. It does not include settled meetings held in private homes, unless a meeting house was subsequently built on the same site. The Bull and Mouth meeting house is excluded, since this was burnt down in 1666, and not rebuilt until 1671. Another meeting place, the Savoy in Westminster, was destroyed by fire in 1669 and rebuilt in 1672.

and physical rallying point that both motivated and united a community in the furtherance of a common religious cause'.[14] Given the instability of the political and religious climate in mid-seventeenth-century England, and in London in particular, the early establishment of regular places of worship was of considerable evangelical importance to the Quaker mission in the capital. Moreover, for a group such as the Quakers who sought to challenge the authority of the established church, obtaining permanent and public meeting houses could be seen to represent a self-conscious effort to challenge the monopoly of the parish church in the public sphere. In this respect, the behaviour of the Quakers was at variance to that of other dissenting groups in early modern Europe. For example, while the *schuilkerken* of Dutch dissenters were concealed from the public gaze in an effort to maintain a semblance of religious unity, the Quakers made no such allowances in the acquisition of their meeting places.[15] The plainness of their premises was a manifestation of their religious principles, and not part of a strategy for survival.

Therefore, there were plenty of practical and tactical reasons why the establishment of permanent meeting places was desirable to the early Friends. However, this still does not answer the question of whether the Quaker meeting house can, in any sense, be interpreted as a sacred space. The exact form and content of the early London meeting houses is unclear but would have been basic and functional. When meeting houses at Ratcliff in Stepney and Horsleydown in Southwark were raided in 1670, the principal items taken were benches, forms and tables. When the Horsleydown meeting house was restored a few years later, there is evidence of some degree of comfort being taken into consideration, with the record of payment of £2 7s 6d for curtains and carpets for the meeting house.[16] The outward appearance of the buildings is simply not known, although some indication can be drawn from the description of the Gracechurch Street meeting house by William Leybourne on a plan from the 1680s as 'a large shedd where ye Quakers did convene'.[17] From this fragmentary evidence, it would seem that Quaker meeting houses in London were largely as could be expected, both in terms of form and content. In the context of the Quaker interpretation of Christianity,

---

[14] V. Bennett, *Sacred Space and Structural Style: the Embodiment of Socio-Religious Ideology* (Ottawa, 1997), pp. 32, 36, 74, 75.

[15] B.J. Kaplan, 'Fictions of Privacy and House Chapels and the Spatial Accommodation of Religious Dissent in Early Modern Europe', *American Historical Review* 107 (2002), 1036.

[16] Joseph Besse, *A Collection of the Sufferings of the People Called Quakers* (2 vols, London, 1753), I, pp. 416, 696; George Whitehead, *The Christian Progress* (London, 1725), p. 342; LSF, Horsleydown Monthly Meeting Minutes (1666–1677), 19 February 1673.

[17] The plan is reproduced in P. Metcalf, 'Seven Centuries in White Hart Court', *Guildhall Studies in London History* 4 (1979), 14–15, Fig. 1.

these premises can be seen within the framework of alternative definitions of the sacred and sacred space.

Two explanations can be offered as to how the Quaker meeting house can be viewed as a response to, and manifestation of, conflicting definitions of sacrality in seventeenth-century England. The first interpretation has already been mentioned, and is not particularly unique to Quakerism. This is the argument that the church was made holy only through its use, and did not possess an inherent sanctity of its own. The Quaker mode of worship, of sitting in silence to wait upon the Holy Spirit, can be perceived as a sacred act. While the primacy of the relationship between the individual and the divine should not be overlooked, Quaker worship also reflected the high value placed upon the unity of the Spirit within meetings.[18] This concept is reflected in Robert Barclay's discussion of Quaker worship, in which he wrote that meeting together was necessary to 'encourage and refresh the saints'.[19] Penington's metaphor of each believer as a 'living stone' is also instructive. A stone on its own has no meaning in itself, and only obtains meaning in the company of other stones in the form of a building. Thus for the early Quakers, communal worship both transcended and nurtured the relationship between the individual and the Holy Spirit. The meeting house, or meeting place that facilitated this act of worship, thus became sanctified for the duration of the meeting not by virtue of any inherent special quality of its own, but through the sacred act taking place within it.

The second explanation that has been offered has been based on a reading of the symbolism associated with Quakerism in terms of Durkheim's definition of religion. This model seeks to measure the extent to which Durkheim's interpretations of sacred and profane are applicable to Quaker beliefs.[20] Rather than seeing Quaker meeting houses as devoid of religious symbols, in fact they are laden with symbolism. In using very simple buildings with no ornamentation or grandeur Friends were expressing their view that God dwelt not in the outward world of buildings and religious imagery, but internally, as manifested in the inward light. To Quakers, churches were 'steeple-houses' invested with superstition and were the physical embodiment of the errors of the established religion. By worshipping in premises bearing none of the physical characteristics of the parish church, Friends were stripping away all that they considered to be profane in such buildings. In worshipping behind plain edifices in such basic accommodation Quakers created an environment that reflected their interpretation

---

[18] R. Bauman, *Let Your Words be Few: Symbolism of Speaking and Silence Among Seventeenth-Century Quakers* (Cambridge, 1983), pp. 121–2.
[19] Barclay, *Apology*, p. 245.
[20] Thomas, *Quaker Symbols*, pp. 7–9.

of the sacred. Whilst the building itself was not perceived as sacred, for those who met inside it, it represented a separation from the profane world outside. Before the Act of 1689 forbade this, the world outside was shut out through the closing of the meeting house door during worship.[21] If necessary, unsavoury elements were to be kept out of the meeting house by force. A note from George Fox dated 1668 directed each monthly meeting in London to choose six 'substantiall men Freinds', so that two of them may 'be about the doore' every day, so that the meetings be kept 'Civill from all rudeness through boyes or children or unruly persons'.[22]

The Impact of the Conventicle Acts on Quaker Worship

The radical departure from the established church that Quakerism and other dissenting sects represented brought about a series of bouts of sustained persecution of nonconformists during the Restoration period. In terms of the number of convictions of Quakers in London and Middlesex, the most intense of these occurred in the aftermath of the First Conventicle Act (1664). The events described in this paper concern the second most intense period of persecution, namely the six months following the passage into law of the Second Conventicle Act (1670).[23] The Act of 1670 augmented existing legislation equipping local authorities with extensive powers to disrupt nonconformist meetings, and to fine and imprison those guilty of preaching or worshipping at them.[24] It allowed for local officials and militia to take all necessary means to prevent and disperse illegal assemblies. The Act was used to justify locking dissenters out of their meeting houses, removing pulpits and pews from dissenting churches, and even their requisitioning for alternative uses.[25] In the hands of the right local officials, it provided almost limitless potential for the disruption and persecution of nonconformists.

The impact of the Second Conventicle Act on dissenters in London was instant. The Act came into force on 10 May 1670, and on 11 May a guard of watchmen with halberts were appointed to stand watch outside the Quaker meeting house in Gracechurch Street and prevent anyone from entering. The meeting house was

---

[21] Ibid., pp. 137–9.

[22] LSF, Southwark MS vol. 1, 31, George Fox, Epistle, 1668.

[23] The number of convictions for attending Quaker meetings in 1664 was 1729. In 1670 the figure was 515. C. Horle, *The Quakers and the English Legal System, 1660–1688* (Philadelphia, 1988), p. 284.

[24] For an account of legislation effecting Quakers in the Restoration period see Horle, *Quakers and the English Legal System*, pp. 46–55.

[25] Greaves, *Enemies*, pp. 159–64.

located at White Hart Court, in the City of London, and would have been
accessible from both Gracechurch Street and Lombard Street.[26] Access to the
building could be obtained through passages from Lombard Street and
Gracechurch Street, and it would only have been necessary to blockade these two
openings to prevent access to the meeting house. The Quakers responded to this
incursion by holding their meeting in the courtyard. Four days later, the appointed
guard kept the Quakers out of the meeting house, and out of the court outside.
George Fox, who was present, began to speak, only to be hauled off to appear
before the Lord Mayor and subsequently fined £20. The next month saw these
actions repeated, with Quakers turning up to hold their weekly meeting for
worship, only to be kept out in the street and, in some cases, arrested and taken
before the Lord Mayor and subsequently bound over to appear before the Sessions
of the Peace.[27] Quakers were by no means alone in suffering under the terms of the
Act. On 15 May the Congregationalist Anthony Palmer was among a number of
dissenters fined £20 for preaching, while one Doctor Anslow was convicted the
following week. On 23 May, Sir John Trevor, a principal secretary of state,
reported an unsuccessful attempt to break up three large presbyterian meetings,
involving 3,000 or 4,000 people.[28] On a weekly basis dissenters were being locked
out of their meeting houses, arrested, convicted, fined and imprisoned. The
principal actors in this campaign against the London dissenters were the Lord
Mayor, Sir Samuel Starling, and the Lieutenant of the Tower, Sir John Robinson.
Starling was 'a staunch churchman and advocate of coercion', while Robinson
happened to be the half-nephew of William Laud and was described variously by
Pepys as 'a talking, bragging bufflehead', a 'fool', and 'a heavy-headed
coxcomb'.[29]

Enforcement of the Second Conventicle Act in London was influenced by the
specific local context of the aftermath of the Great Fire of 1666. The fire had
destroyed no fewer than 87 parish churches. The question of how many of these
should be rebuilt was much debated, and only resolved in April 1670. The
administrative and logistical difficulties involved in the rebuilding of the churches
made this a slow process that would continue in some parishes into the early

---

[26] On Gracechurch Street meeting house, see Butler, *Quaker Meeting Houses*, I, pp. 395–400; Metcalf, 'Seven Centuries', 1–18.

[27] Besse, *Sufferings*, I, pp. 408–10; LSF, Great Book of Sufferings, II, pp. 101–2; Corporation of London Record Office (hereafter CLRO), Conventicle Box 1.2, Justices convictions of conventiclers May–August 1670.

[28] *Calendar of State Papers, Domestic Series, 1670*, ed. M.A. Everett Green (London, 1895), pp. 221, 226–34; NA, SP29/275/135, 173, 174; Greaves, *Enemies*, pp. 158–9.

[29] De Krey, 'First Restoration Crisis', 568–9; *The Diary of Samuel Pepys*, ed. R. Latham and W. Matthews (11 vols, London, 1970–83), IV, p. 77, V, p. 307, VI, p. 299.

eighteenth century. In order that the returning populace should have somewhere to congregate for worship, the commission charged with overseeing the reconstruction work sought to fill the void by ordering the building of some thirty temporary 'tabernacles' throughout the City.[30] Yet even this was a slow process. By February 1670 a sufficient number of parishioners had returned to All Hallows Lombard Street for the vestry to begin discussing what measures to take, so that inhabitants may 'congregate & Meet together About the worshipp of god'.[31] On 1 June 1670 the minister, John Archer, suggested that a service be held in the nearby church of St Martin Outwich. The same vestry meeting also determined that a greater effort should be made to build within the parish of All Hallows, and that the assistance of the younger parishioners be sought to this end. However, even this temporary structure does not appear to have been ready for use until some time in 1673, since in January and February of that year the vestry was still arranging for the furnishing of the tabernacle, while in March the Churchwardens and 'Antients of the Parish' were empowered to allocate pews.[32] The absence of a church in the neighbouring parish of St Benet Gracechurch Street was also proving to be a cause of concern, not least to the incumbent, John Cliff. In May 1671 he complained to the vestry that he had not received payment for 'certaine sermons to bee preached by him in the church; wch sermons cannott be preached by reason the church is not yett built'.[33]

The slow progress made in the provision of places for worship clearly worried both the secular and religious authorities. This was compounded by the fact that the various dissenting groups in the City had been somewhat quicker in establishing new places of worship after the fire. Thus a number of London parishes found themselves the home to one or more dissenting meeting places, but no parish church. In an effort to rectify the situation, a command from the king in Council ordered that the bishop of London, Humphrey Henchman, appoint Church of England ministers to conduct prayer-book services in eight meeting houses, 'for the benefit of the Inhabitants of the Parishes near adjoyning respectively, where the

---

[30] *The Statutes of the Realm*, ed. A. Luders *et al.* (12 vols, London, 1810–28), V, pp. 665–82; T.F. Reddaway, *The Rebuilding of London After the Great Fire* (London, 1940), pp. 122–6; S. Porter, *The Great Fire of London* (Stroud, 1996), pp. 112–15; W. Page (ed.), *VCH: London* (1 vol., London, 1909), I, p. 340. The first temporary structure appeared in the parish of All Hallows the Great, Thames Street in 1669, but the wider effort did not begin until the following year.

[31] Guildhall Library Manuscripts Section [hereafter GL], MS 4049, All Hallows Lombard Street, Vestry Minutes, II (1667–1703), p. 8, 15 February 1669/70.

[32] GL, MS 4049, II (1667–1703), pp. 10 (1 June 1670), 13 (24 February 1671–2), 14 (15 January 1672–3), 16 (26 February 1672–3, 31 March 1673), 17 (9 April 1673).

[33] GL, MS 4214, St Benet Gracechurch Street, Vestry Minutes, I, 1607–1758, f. 95.

Parish Churches have been consumed by the fire'. On the same day, the king also ordered that the seats and pulpits in all meeting houses in London, Bristol and elsewhere were to be removed.[34] If the survival of the dissenting places of worship had been threatened by the rigorous enforcement of the Conventicle Acts across London prior to this point, this new tactic turned the meeting houses into contested religious spaces. The aims of the order were twofold. Firstly, it was designed to augment existing tactics of persecution by destabilizing the physical and cultural space of the dissenters.[35] This intention indicates an appreciation of the importance of permanent places of worship to the stability and longevity of the sects. Secondly, it indicates a feeling among the religious and secular authorities that the negative tactic of persecution was insufficient to win the battle against the nonconformists. A renewed effort to assert the supremacy of the established church was also required.

Despite the lack of church buildings in All Hallows Lombard Street and surrounding parishes, it does not appear to have been a local clergyman who was appointed by Humphrey Henchman to conduct prayer-book services in the Quaker meeting house in All Hallows parish, and the reasons for this are not recorded. Nonetheless, what has been recorded is that on each Sunday between 26 June and 24 July 1670, a minister, accompanied by soldiers, attended the meeting house to preach and read from the Book of Common Prayer. On at least one of these occasions, the minister appointed was George Alsop, rector of Chipping Ongar in Essex from 18 June 1670 until 1673.[36] It seems likely that this man was the author of at least two of three known printed works attributed to a certain George Alsop. The first of these, *A Character of the Province of Mary-land*, can be classified within the genre of colonial promotional literature produced by early settlers in America, and was published in London in 1666.[37] A second pamphlet, *An Orthodox Plea for the Sanctuary of God, Common Service, White Robe of the*

[34] *London Gazette* 478, Monday 13 June to Thursday 16 June 1670; *Historical Manuscripts Commission, Reports 25, S.H. Le Fleming, esq.* (London, 1890), p. 71; *Calendar of State Papers and Manuscripts Relating to English Affairs existing in the archives and collections of Venice*, ed. R. Brown *et al.* (London, 1864–), XXXVI, pp. 215–16; Greaves, *Enemies*, pp. 159–60.

[35] C. Wall, *The Literary and Cultural Spaces of Restoration London* (Cambridge, 1998), pp. 186–7.

[36] Richard Newcourt, *Repertorium ecclesiasticum parochiale Londinense* (2 vols, London, 1708–10), II, p. 451; GL, MS 9531, Diocese of London, Bishops Registers, XVI, 1660–1675, ff. 148, 170.

[37] George Alsop, *A Character of the Province of Mary-land* (London, 1666).

House, was printed in London in 1669, and makes interesting reading in the context of issues of sacred space.[38]

An Orthodox Plea is an eighty-six-page polemic extolling the virtues of religious worship conducted according to the Book of Common Prayer in a church building, and by a minister wearing the 'White Robe of the House' or surplice. The longest section deals with the importance of worshipping in churches, opening by stating that, 'GOD from the very beginning hath always had a Place set apart for his Divine Worship and Service to be performed in, where the Reverence and Obedience the Creatures acknowledgements were still offered up to the Creators acceptance'.[39]

During the course of his polemic, Alsop argues that the rejection of churches involves an undermining of the entire principles of Christian worship. Whilst he generally avoids mentioning specific nonconformist sects by name, at least some of his comments seem to be aimed at Quakers. He writes that those who object to the church building then come to reject the church ornaments and the church bells. From there it is a short distance to dismissing the scripture as 'but a dead Letter'. He also condemns those 'wretches' that claim to have, 'a quickening spirit within them that informs them in all things', an apparent reference to the Quaker doctrine of the inner light.[40] He goes on to launch an attack on those who conduct religious worship in houses not set aside specifically for that purpose, citing St Paul's chastisement of the Corinthians for eating and drinking in the same house as they used to worship God. Those who do not build churches within which to worship God do not do so out of reverence, but because they seek to avoid the expense of building and repairing churches, and paying for the maintenance of a minister.[41]

The relationship between the church building and the location of the sacred in Alsop's thought is not always explicit. The exact form of church building he is advocating is unclear. He takes care not to engage in any language that might be interpreted as being overly popish. However, there is some indication that he believes that the building should represent a physical expression of God's glory. He writes that, 'If there be a God and Religion, then there must be a Worship; and if a Worship, then a Tabernacle or Temple; and if so, then it must be answerable to

---

[38] George Alsop, *An Orthodox Plea for the Sanctuary of God, Common Service, White Robe of the House* (London, 1669). On Alsop see J.A.L. Lemay, *Men of Letters in Colonial Maryland* (Knoxville, 1972), pp. 48–69, 343–5. Lemay suspects that *An Orthodox Plea* was the work of a different George Alsop. However, a close examination of the two works shows considerable stylistic similarities that suggest that *A Character* and *An Orthodox Plea* were indeed the work of the same author.

[39] Alsop, *An Orthodox Plea*, p. 1.

[40] Ibid., pp. 7–10.

[41] Ibid., pp. 16–17, 31–2.

his glory in a comely manner'.[42] Churches, then, should be physically splendid, distinct from all other buildings in both their usage and their grandeur. Yet, in the final part of the section on the 'Sanctuary of God' he makes clear that the church is literally God's house. He writes of 'mad and perverse Rake-hels' that 'will not allow God the same benefit they have themselves to dwell in a house' and 'aim as destructively as ever they can against the Dwelling of the Lord'. Thus, 'God hath, and shall for ever have a House for his Honor to dwell in'. Alsop pursues this argument with vigour, writing that, 'Holy and Religious men makes Gods House a place of Fear and Reverence', comparing such men to those who see no difference between the House of God and the marketplace.[43] Thus for Alsop, the church is more than simply a convenient place within which to worship God. It is a physical manifestation of His presence on earth, and those whose words and actions deny God's presence within the church are beyond contempt. The remainder of the pamphlet is devoted to a defence of the prayer-book and the surplice. While we cannot be sure that the author of the pamphlet was the man who became rector of Chipping Ongar, the views expressed in it would seem to be consistent with a man who would be prepared to walk into a Quaker meeting house dressed in a surplice and armed with the Book of Common Prayer. This may also help to explain why the bishop of London chose Alsop for this task.

The Battle for Gracechurch Street Meeting House

The incursions of the Church of England into the Quaker meeting house in Gracechurch Street in June and July 1670 are well documented in the records of Quaker sufferings. These events illustrate a competition over the use to which a space set aside for the purpose of religious worship was put. Through requisitioning dissenting meeting houses for use by the established church, the London authorities were tacitly acknowledging the existence of alternative forms of religious space in the capital. The clashes at the Quaker meeting house in the parish of All Hallows Lombard Street create a fascinating image of religious conflict, with both sides attempting to define the nature of the physical space as an arena for a different mode of religious worship. The first incident occurred on 26 June 1670, on which occasion the identity of the minister concerned is unknown. The autobiography of the Quaker George Whitehead provides a full account. Whitehead notes that the minister entered the meeting house and read common

---

[42] Ibid., p. 11.
[43] Ibid., pp. 27, 30.

prayer and preached in the gallery, 'seeming to preach up, and excite to *Love*'.[44] The positioning of the minister in the gallery is the first indication of an attempt to redefine the use to which the meeting house was put. There were two types of galleries in Quaker meeting houses. One type was simply to accommodate those attending the meeting. The other type – the 'ministers' gallery' or 'ministers' stand' – accommodated those 'public Friends' deemed most likely to speak during meeting for worship. This second type appears to have been commonplace during the later seventeenth century, but it is unclear how widespread it was as early as 1670.[45] Therefore, it seems likely that the gallery referred to was of the first type, but its use by the Anglican priest indicates an attempt to elevate himself above the assembled crowd.

As the minister taught 'The Commendation of Love' to those assembled, the soldiers accompanying him disturbed the Quakers who were present to conduct their own worship. In an action contrary to the words of the sermon, the soldiers committed acts of 'Rudeness and Violence to our Friends, Women, as well as Men'. A great crowd gathered inside the meeting house, 'for it seemed a very strange Thing, to see a Minister, or Priest of the Church of England, stand up, and read Common-Prayer, Say, or Sing their Service, and Preach in a Quakers Meeting, deem'd an Unlawful Conventicle'. After the sermon was over, Whitehead stood up and began to preach 'the Gospel of Peace and Love' for a while, until 'two rude Fellows, with the Soldiers following them, violently pulled the said G.W. down', and carried him before the Mayor. According to Whitehead the occasion was attended by 'a Concourse of People of all Sorts, many not being our Friends'.[46]

The description of this event illustrates the importance of religious space within early modern communities. In the context of an ordinary parish, the parish church represented a key agent of social integration and cultural homogeneity. The church building was not just a place of religious worship, but an arena of social interaction within the local community. As Benjamin Kaplan has recently argued, this relationship of the civic with the sacral was undermined by the very existence of religious dissent. When nonconformist worship could be confined to small gatherings in private houses, pretence of religious uniformity could be maintained. When dissenters chose to conduct their worship in publicly accessible meeting places, they posed a direct challenge to the established order. This challenge tended to be perceived as particularly serious at times of social or political crisis.[47] Thus

---

[44] Whitehead, *Christian Progress*, pp. 330–33.
[45] Butler, *Quaker Meeting Houses*, II, pp. 887, 892; R. Vann, *The Social Development of English Quakerism 1655–1725* (Cambridge, MA, 1969), p. 100.
[46] Whitehead, *Christian Progress*, pp. 330–31.
[47] Kaplan, 'Fictions of Privacy', 1036–9.

the existence of a Quaker meeting house in the parish of All Hallows Lombard Street in 1670, when the church still lay in ruins, represented a crisis for the Church of England in the parish. It has been argued that 'when a religious group enacted its beliefs in a public space, it was claiming possession not just of that space but of the entire community, appropriating the authority to speak and act for everyone, and making those of other faiths accomplices in rituals they rejected or even abhorred'.[48] Thus by appointing a representative of the established church to conduct a service in the Quaker meeting house, and in other dissenting chapels and meeting places, the secular and religious authorities in London were seeking to both restore the authority of the established church within the local community, and to suppress the threat posed to that authority by religious nonconformity.

The week following the first attempt to hold a prayer book service in Gracechurch Street meeting house was the occasion of the incident involving George Alsop noted above. Alsop's report back to the Lord Mayor that the Quakers had physically assaulted him casts him in a rather different light to the Quaker account of events.[49] This records how he approached the meeting house with a guard of soldiers who had been drinking in a nearby alehouse. Before they could enter the meeting house, Alsop 'suddenly shrunk from his guard & hudled away into the street'. Shortly after this, he returned 'with a double guard to the doore & shrunk again saying there was no entrance for him, & so being in a maze turned about haire & last went away, being derided by the people without'. Meanwhile, William Bailey had begun speaking inside the meeting house, only to be pulled down by the attendant soldiers and committed to Newgate for abusing Alsop. Appearing before Lord Mayor Starling with his hat on, Starling reportedly pulled Bailey's hat from his head, 'saying he gave no honour to Governours'. Bailey retorted, 'doth thy honour stand in taking off the hatt', to which Starling replied yes and stamped on the hat causing Bailey to remark, 'then he trodd on his honor'.[50]

Again, this incident raises several interesting points concerning the relationship between religious space and the politics of early modern religion. The presence of the Quaker meeting house represented a challenge to both the spiritual authority of the church, and also to London's civic authorities. Alsop's presence at the meeting house represented an attempt to exert the spiritual authority of the Church of England as vested in him by his appointment by the bishop of London. As had been the case the previous week, he had been provided with the physical means to

---

[48] Ibid., 1038.

[49] For Alsop's account see NA, SP29/277/14 reproduced in Penney, *Extracts*, p. 314.

[50] LSF, Great Book of Sufferings, II, p. 102; Besse, *Sufferings*, I, p. 412; CLRO, City of London Sessions Records, Sessions File 203, Calendar of Gaol Delivery Papers.

obtain entry in the form of the trained bands that accompanied him (civic authority). However, he was unable to enter the building, as the Quakers present refused to accept both Alsop's spiritual authority, and the secular authority of the bands of soldiers with him. In protecting their meeting house from invasion by Alsop the Quakers indicated a reluctance to countenance the use of their own religious space as an arena for an alternative form of worship. This contestation of religious space presents a picture of the complexity of early modern power relationships as both sides in the dispute sought to exercise their authority over the meeting house. In doing so, as stated above, they were seeking to appropriate the authority to speak and act for the entire community. Thus events such as those that occurred at Gracechurch Street illustrate the capacity of Quaker belief and practice to undermine established systems of power and subordination. In this respect, the advent of new dissenting sects during the seventeenth century brought new concepts of authority that add a further dimension to what has been described as the 'early modern power grid'.[51]

The next three weeks saw similar dramas acted out involving trained bands forcing entry into the Gracechurch Street meeting house, and a priest being enlisted to conduct a service and preach inside the meeting house. On each occasion the Quakers were prevented from entering, and defiantly assembled outside in the street where they held their own meeting for worship. Efforts were made by the soldiers to interrupt the Quaker worship by beating drums to drown out the ministering Friends. This act would also have served to disrupt the silence of the Quaker worship.[52] Recalling such incidents in his autobiography William Crouch noted that it was common practice for Quakers kept out of the meeting places to gather in the street, 'as near to the Meeting-Houses, as the Guards would suffer them to come'.[53] This practice underlines the point that Quaker worship could take place anywhere, and illustrates that whilst attempts to requisition the meeting house for alternative uses were disruptive to the exercise of Quaker worship, they did not prevent it from taking place. This in turn indicates a cultural disparity between Quakerism and the established church. While the rector of St Benet Gracechurch Street complained that he was unable to deliver his sermons because of the destruction of the parish church, depriving the Quakers of their place of worship did not have similar effects. Thus while the existence of a parish church was a vital ingredient for the functioning of the Church of England, for Quakers and other nonconformists a meeting could be held as well in the street as it could in the meeting house.

---

[51] Braddick and Walter, 'Introduction', pp. 38–42.
[52] LSF, Great Book of Sufferings, II, pp. 102–3; Besse, *Sufferings*, I, pp. 412–15.
[53] William Crouch, *Posthuma christiana* (London, 1712), pp. 95–6.

That the lack of a building was not an impediment to Quaker worship is underlined by the behaviour of Quakers whose meeting houses were demolished in the late summer of 1670. Clearly, keeping the Quakers out of their premises had not had the desired impact, and in August and September a new tactic was adopted – the demolition of the buildings themselves. By this time, Sir John Robinson was becoming particularly exasperated by the persistence of the Quakers in Tower Hamlets. He wrote to Lord Arlington that public meetings of dissenters had ceased, with the exception of those of the Quakers. 'If I ridd not my Quarters of them', he raged, 'I'le pull downe their house'.[54] On 2 September 1670, Robinson finally lost patience and ordered the demolition of Ratcliff meeting house, where soldiers worked all night, 'and carryed away twelve cart loads of doores windows and floores, wth other materialls as glass windowes casements & leade all the tyles being broken too peeces some of the materialls they sold for strong drink and money at the place'. However, even this failed to dishearten the Quakers, as the following week they returned to the site of the meeting house and attempted to hold their meeting on the ruins of the building, only to be prevented from doing so by the local constable.[55] In Southwark, the Horsleydown meeting house was badly damaged following an order by Wren for its demolition, Whitehead describing it as having been 'very much spoiled'. Again, the Quakers responded by holding their meetings on the ruins of the building, often in the face of savage persecution.[56] In publishing an account of the beatings suffered by Friends who gathered on the site of the meeting house, the Southwark Quakers claimed that their intransigence in so doing was, 'not in Stubbornness, nor in contempt to Magistracy, but in tenderness of Conscience to God'.[57] However, the fact that they continued to hold meetings on the site for four successive Sundays suggests both an element of defiance and a continuing desire to challenge the authority of the soldiers whose brutality appeared to know no bounds. On 9 October 1670 over fifty people were injured by troops, including a pregnant woman who suffered a miscarriage after being struck twice in the stomach with a musket. The following week the soldiers attacked the Quakers with such ferocity, 'as if they would have killed all in the place'.[58]

On 8 September 1670 an order from Lord Mayor Starling was fixed to the door of Gracechurch Street meeting house declaring it 'an irregular building' under building regulations introduced in the aftermath of the fire of 1666, and threatening

---

[54] NA, SP29/278/113i; *Calendar of State Papers Domestic 1670*, p. 409.

[55] LSF, Great Book of Sufferings, II, pp. 105–6; Besse, *Sufferings*, I, p. 429.

[56] Whitehead, *Christian Progress*, pp. 342–5; Robert Allen, *The Cry of Innocent Blood* (s.l., 1670); Horle, *Quakers and the English Legal System*, pp. 127–8; W. Beck and T.F. Ball, *The London Friends' Meetings* (London, 1869), pp. 216–18.

[57] Allen, *Cry of Innocent Blood*, p. 3.

[58] Ibid., pp. 4–5.

its demolition. At the same time, a similar threat was made against another dissenting meeting place in Petty France. However, there is no evidence of the Gracechurch Street meeting house having been demolished. It is possible that the order was a little premature, since the contention that the building was irregular was made without proper inspection by the surveyors of new buildings. That this was the case is demonstrated by the fact that the Court of Aldermen did not order the surveyors to view the house until a week after issuing the threat to destroy it.[59] Moreover, Starling's term as Mayor was nearly up and his successor, Sir Richard Ford, did not share in his attitude towards the dissenters. Ford seems to have suspended the persecution of nonconformists during his mayoralty, and there was a dramatic drop in the number of Quakers convicted in 1671 compared with the previous year.[60] This negligence was criticized by the chamberlain of London, Sir Thomas Player, who complained that 'the laws against Conventicles have binne layd asleepe'. Meanwhile Secretary of State Williamson observed that Ford endeavoured to 'ingratiate himselfe wth [the] Phanaticks'.[61]

The attempts to demolish Quaker meeting houses in London, and the Quaker reaction to them provide one final insight into differing attitudes to religious space and the location of the holy. For Church of England clerics such as George Alsop, the church was 'The sanctuary of God', God's dwelling place on earth. As indicated in the attitude of the rector of St Benet Gracechurch Street, Church of England worship could not take place in the absence of a parish church. Such attitudes help to explain why it might seem desirable to the church authorities to attempt to demolish Quaker meeting houses. This attitude is summarized by Alsop in a single sentence: 'If there be a God and Religion, then there must be a Worship; and if a Worship, then a Tabernacle or Temple'.[62] Applying this logic to the subject of religious dissent and religious persecution, then the destruction of meeting places could be seen as an effective method of inhibiting the capacity of the Quakers to meet publicly in a fashion that would challenge the authority of the established church. However, to the Quakers, their meeting places held no special theological importance. Though useful as a space within which they could meet together to the exclusion of the world, they were not essential for the conduct of Quaker worship. Lock them out of their meeting places, and they would meet in the street; demolish their meeting places, and they would meet on the ruins.

---

[59] CLRO, Repertories of the Court of Aldermen, 75, ff. 296–7, 8 Sept. 1670, ff. 305–6, 15 Sept. 1670; Besse, *Sufferings*, I, p. 429.
[60] Metcalf, 'Seven Centuries', 12–13; A.B. Beaven, *The Aldermen of the City of London* (2 vols, London, 1908–13), II, p. 187; Horle, *Quakers and the English Legal System*, p. 284.
[61] NA, SP 29/291/143; 29/293/222; *Calendar of State Papers, Domestic Series, 1671*, ed. F.H. Blackburne Daniell (London, 1895), pp. 368, 554.
[62] Alsop, *An Orthodox Plea*, p. 11.

Conclusions

That Quakers did attempt to meet on the physical ruins of the Ratcliff and Horsleydown meeting houses suggests that, as time passed, the meeting houses did come to contain some special symbolic importance to Friends. It may require a very loose definition of the term 'sacred' to perceive Quaker meeting houses as 'sacred space'. Nonetheless, the disputes surrounding the London meeting houses in 1670 do indicate that they held a strong degree of symbolic potency from the perspective of both the ecclesiastical and civic authorities, and the Quakers themselves. In the unique context of post-fire London the presence of Quaker and other dissenting meeting places presented a serious challenge to the authority of the established church. In a sense, the Gracechurch Street meeting house, the large shed described by Leybourne in the 1680s, was a mundane and unexceptional building. However, this plainness represented a challenge to the conventions of ecclesiastical architecture that would be employed in the rebuilding of the City churches. Moreover, the requisitioning of the premises by the established church almost validated the functioning of the building as a dedicated religious space within the parish of All Hallows Lombard Street. Thus for both the Quakers who sought to protect their meeting houses, and their opponents who sought to requisition and demolish them, these buildings were an important feature in the religious topography of post-Restoration London. The reaction to their existence enables us to reconstruct the boundaries of debate over the location of the holy in later seventeenth-century England.

Chapter 15

La Ville Sonnant: the Politics of Sacred Space in Avignon on the Eve of the French Revolution

Eric Johnson

Avignon is remarkable for the number seven; having seven ports, seven parishes, seven colleges, seven hospitals, and seven monasteries; and I may add, I think, seven hundred bells, which are always making a horrid jingle; for they have no idea of ringing bells harmoniously in any part of France.

Philip Thicknesse, *A Year's Journey through France and Spain*, 1777

Thicknesse's impression of the southern French city of Avignon and its noisy bells was quite typical of the many foreign travellers who visited the city in the late eighteenth century.[1] Avignon had a widespread reputation for its exuberant public rituals, and was even described as a 'perpetual festival' by Madame de Sévigné.[2] Bells and festivals figured prominently in descriptions of Avignon from the late eighteenth century because for a city of its size of population (approximately 25,500 in 1781),[3] it had a remarkable number of religious institutions. According to one reliable estimate, the city contained thirty-five churches, forty-eight chapels, forty convents, seven penitential confraternities, twenty-eight corporations, five hospitals, and seven almonries on the eve of the French Revolution.[4] Religious

---

[1] A. Viala, 'Les Avignonnais vus par des étrangers au XVIIIème siècle', *Mémoires de 'Académie de Vaucluse* 6 (1968), 113–22. The title for this paper, which translates as 'the chiming city', comes from a description of Avignon attributed to Rabelais. I am grateful to the Department of History at the University of California, Los Angeles, for a travel grant to deliver an earlier version of this paper at the University of Exeter and to the Camargo Foundation for their support while I wrote this article during Spring 2004.
[2] Letter to Madame de Grignan, 12 June 1689. Bibliothèque Municipale d'Avignon (hereafter BMA) 8° 50.471.
[3] Archives Départementales de Vaucluse (hereafter ADV) 1G23, no 5, f.19.
[4] L. Duhamel, 'Avignon au XVIIIe Siècle', *Annuaire de Vaucluse* (1911).

institutions filled the urban landscape, which was described by a contemporary of Thicknesse as 'bristling' with steeples, spires, and belfries.[5]

With such a high number of churches, chapels, convents and monasteries within its walls, Avignon was a city with many sacred spaces. The reason for this is that Avignon, together with most of the territory that today makes up the *département* of the Vaucluse, was a papal enclave until the French Revolution, and centuries of patronage from the papal court had left the city with a higher concentration of religious centres than many French cities.[6] As a centre of papal power and influence north of the Alps, Avignon was a point of entry into France for new forms of Catholic piety from Rome. Many new religious orders, such as the Ursulines, first appeared in Avignon before spreading to the rest of France.[7] Avignon's proximity to the Protestant strongholds around Nîmes and Orange gave it additional importance during the Catholic Reformation, as it was a base of operations for the Society of Jesus and other missionary establishments in southern France.

Avignon's unique history and its relationship with Rome were an important part of how its inhabitants represented their city in the eighteenth century. The inscription 'altera Roma' (the other Rome), which appeared on dozens of urban monuments, alluded to Avignon's past as the capital of Christendom during the fourteenth century and the fact that it continued to be governed by papal officials until 1790. The prominence of the number seven in its geography, which many other visitors besides Thicknesse noted, further underscored the city's association with Rome. Avignon's number of ports, parishes, monasteries and colleges corresponded with the seven hills of the Eternal City. This in turn had a spiritual meaning because seven was one of the most important numbers in Catholic liturgy and cosmology.

This chapter will examine Avignon's three most important sacred spaces, focusing on their associations with political authority and the ways they were used at the end of the *ancien régime* to navigate within the city's overlapping spheres of political influence. Because Avignon was a pocket of papal sovereignty in the heart of the French Midi with a francophone population and an Italian ecclesiastic for a governor, there were several competing identities and interests in the city that were balanced through the use of the city's ritual geography and the location of sacred objects in urban space. Through their association with sacred sites in the city, papal, royal and local authorities were each presented in a hierarchical relationship with

---

[5] M. Bérenger, *Les Soirées Provençales ou Lettres de M. Bérenger écrits à ses amis pendant ses voyages dans sa patrie* (Paris, 1786).
[6] On the history of papal rule over Avignon and the Comtat Venaissin, see R.-L. Mouliérac-Lamoureaux, *Le Comtat Venaissin Pontifical, 1229–1791* (Vedène, 1977).
[7] R. Po-Chia Hsia, *The World of Catholic Renewal, 1540–1770* (Cambridge, 1998), p. 112.

one another. This politico-religious nexus could be, and often was, manipulated to reflect and effect changes in urban power.

Avignon was by no means unique in early modern Europe for having such a complex interconnection between urban authority, identity, and sacred space, although its status as a contested space between the papacy and the monarchy presents a unique case study. Sacred geography provided an arena in which papal, royal, and local authority were continuously negotiated, defined, and redefined on the eve of the Revolution. What I am seeking to demonstrate is that the defining and use of sacred space could still be an important part of urban political discourse at the end of the eighteenth century, a time that historians normally characterize as 'dechristianized' and when political authority was becoming increasingly based on secular ideologies.[8] Traditional notions of the sacred and their relationship to urban political geography still resonated in cities like Avignon on the eve of the Revolution, and still had enough vitality that they could be co-opted to facilitate changes in political power.

The Cathedral and the Place du Palais

Avignon's most important sacred space was its cathedral, which was named Notre Dame des Doms but was more often called the *Métropolitaine*. Although it was not the most frequently used sacred space in the city, it was where Avignon's most important communal rituals occurred. The city's annual liturgical processions, which ensured divine protection of the community, began and ended there, and it was where extraordinary ceremonies commemorating important events associated with the papacy or the French monarchy took place. The cathedral was built on the southern slope of a large stone outcropping overlooking the Rhône River called the *Rocher des Doms* which was the nucleus of the original Roman town (see Figure 15.1). This site had been a ritual site since long before the Christian era. Archaeological evidence found on the *Rocher* suggests that it had been a religious site as far back as the Neolithic era, and the cathedral itself was originally built in the fourth century over the site of a temple to Hercules.[9]

---

[8] The literature on the secularization of French political ideology in the eighteenth century is immense, but some of the works that are particularly relevant to this paper include: M. Vovelle, *Piété baroque et déchristianisation en Provence au XVIIIe siècle* (Paris, 1973); D. Bell, *The Cult of the Nation in France: Inventing Nationalism, 1680–1800* (Cambridge, MA, 2001); J. Merrick, *The Desacralization of the French Monarchy in the Eighteenth Century* (Baton Rouge, LA, 1990); B. Cousin, *Le Miracle et le quotidien: les ex-voto provençaux images d'une société* (Aix-en-Provence, 1983); M.-H. Froeschlé-Chopard, *La Religion populaire en Provence Orientale au XVIIIe siècle* (Paris, 1980).
[9] C. and J.-M. Spill, *Les Villes françaises: Avignon* (Paris, 1977).

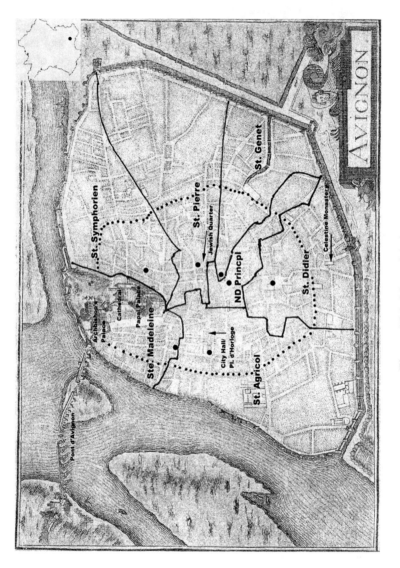

Figure 15.1 Map of Avignon.

Because Avignon had been the capital of the Western Church for most of the fourteenth century, the cathedral enjoyed a number of special privileges that underscored the city's history and relationship with Rome. The cathedral chapter had the unusual privilege of wearing red at religious rituals, while the beneficed clergy wore purple.[10] These colours were normally reserved for the upper echelons of the church hierarchy, a fact that was not lost on one visitor from the 1770s who attended Easter Mass in the cathedral and 'almost thought that the whole Sacred College [of cardinals] had come from Rome on that day'.[11] On certain days of the liturgical year one could visit the *Métropolitaine* and pray at seven of its altars to gain the same indulgences as one earned by making a pilgrimage to Rome and praying at the seven designated altars in basilica of Saint Peter.[12] In this way Avignon was truly an 'other Rome', being a surrogate pilgrimage site where one could acquire the same spiritual benefits as going to Rome, but without making the long journey.

The *Métropolitaine*'s privileges and rituals reaffirmed Avignon's ties with Rome and its identity as a papal city. This was especially important because the archdiocese of Avignon, which the cathedral was the seat of, included territories in the French provinces of Languedoc and Provence. Of the forty parishes under the archbishop's direct authority, twenty-nine were situated in royal domain. Thus while Avignon was a papal city, a significant portion of the archbishop's constituents were royal subjects. Because the cathedral played a dual role as the primary ritual centre for the papal city of Avignon, and the seat of an archdiocese that was mostly situated in royal territory, it had two separate functions as a sacred space with two distinct protocols for commemorating events associated with France: one for its parishes in royal territory, and another for the city of Avignon itself. For example, when the Dauphin was born in 1781, Archbishop Giovio ordered a *Te Deum* to be sung 'in all the churches in our diocese in the parts that are in Languedoc and Provence'.[13] More than a week elapsed before he ordered a second *Te Deum* to be sung in the *Métropolitaine* so that the papal subjects in Avignon could also pay their respects to the French monarchy.[14]

---

[10] H. Trouillet, 'Cérémonial du Chapitre Métropolitan d'Avignon au XVIIIe s.', *Mémoires de l'Académie de Vaucluse* (1912), 277–301.

[11] M. Van de Brande, *Voyage de Languedoc, Provence, et Comtat d'Avignon* (Paris, 1774), p. 26.

[12] *Journal Spirituel. Où sont annoncées les Fêtes solemnelles & particuleres qui se célébrent dans toutes les Eglises d'Avignon* (Avignon, 1781), introduction.

[13] ADV 1G298, f. 111.

[14] Ibid., f. 139.

Adjacent to the cathedral was the massive palace that was built to house the papacy in the fourteenth century and served thereafter as the residence of the vice-legates who governed Avignon in the pope's name. The palace was by far the largest structure in the city, and, when it was built, the largest fortified palace in Europe. Even in the eighteenth century, it remained a formidable symbol of papal authority that dwarfed the cathedral and dominated the urban skyline from every vantage point.[15] Every urban procession in Avignon originated in the cathedral and passed by the western façade of the palace before beginning its circuit through the rest of the city. Thus the vice-legate's residence was the first threshold between the sacred space of the cathedral and the rest of the city.

In front of the palace and cathedral was the *Place du Palais*, which was the largest public square in the city. This plaza functioned as a sort of public foyer for the cathedral, where the general populace of Avignon gathered during communal festivals while the vice-legate, magistrates, and urban elite attended ceremonies inside. After the rituals inside the cathedral were concluded, the ceremony moved into the *Place du Palais* to include the participation of the rest of the townspeople.

Although the plaza was not a consecrated place or sacred site as such, at times of certain religious festivals it became the focus for celebrations and quasi-sacred customs associated with popular folk beliefs in the city. The most important of these was the eve of the Feast of Saint John the Baptist, or Midsummer's Night, on 23 June. This festival, which fell near the summer solstice, originated in pre-Christian times and is a classic example of how Christian rituals were grafted onto pagan agrarian rites.[16] Like other communities throughout Europe, Avignon celebrated the longest day of the year with a communal bonfire that was only loosely Christian but was nevertheless imbued with sacred properties. According to Provençal tradition, children who breathed the smoke from this fire grew faster and stronger, and leading livestock over the warm ashes the following morning protected them from disease.[17]

Furthermore in Avignon the *Feu Saint Jean* carried an important political symbolic meaning because the vice-legate's leading role in it linked sovereign authority to the passage of liturgical and cosmological time through urban geography and ritual. After attending a high Mass in the cathedral with the magistrates, the vice-legate would light the bonfire in the plaza using a candle made of white wax. He would then toss the candle, which was supposed to bring

---

[15] On urban skylines as indicators of authority, see W. Braunfels, *Urban Design in Western Europe: Regime and Architecture, 900–1900*, trans. K. J. Norcott (Chicago, 1988).

[16] F. Benoit, *La Provence et le Comtat Venaissin: arts et traditions populaires* (Avignon, 1945).

[17] A. van Gennep, *Manuel de folklore français contemporain* (Paris, 1937).

good luck, into the crowd and then retire to the palace.[18] Festivals such as this were among the rare occasions in which the vice-legate left the palace and was seen in public. The absence of the vice-legate from the vast majority of Avignon's religious rituals (he only participated in fifteen of the forty-seven rituals that the magistrates attended)[19] added to the importance of the rituals he attended. At the same time it created an aura of dignity and prestige around him because it set him apart from the everyday and mundane.

The Hôtel-de-Ville and the Place d'Horloge

A hundred metres to the south of the *Place du Palais* was the Hôtel-de-Ville, the centre of municipal government. The magistracy of Avignon was closely associated with several neighbouring sacred sites. These included public spaces such as the parish church of Saint Agricol and the square in front of the Hôtel-de-Ville, and private spaces such as the chapel inside the town hall itself. The uses of these sacred sites in and around the Hôtel-de-Ville reveal some of the tensions between the municipal, papal, and royal authorities that were continuously negotiated throughout the *ancien régime*. While the local magistrates gave all the expected signs of the fidelity they owed to their papal sovereign, they augmented their independent authority in the city and the surrounding countryside by creating an affiliation between the Hôtel-de-Ville and the cult of Avignon's patronal saint, Saint Agricol. At the same time, both the papacy and the monarchy competed for political representation at the Hôtel-de-Ville through the placement of their own sacred objects.

The church of Saint Agricol was the most important sacred space associated with municipal authority. It was adjacent to the Hôtel-de-Ville, and the most frequently used ritual centre in the city (see Figure 15.1). One hundred and thirty religious rituals took place in Saint Agricol every year; this was almost four times the number as at the cathedral. This church was the official parish of the city magistrates, who appeared with the parish chapter during religious processions, and were buried inside whenever they died in office.[20] Avignon's coat of arms was

---

[18] This echoes a medieval tradition in which the pope would distribute lambs moulded from white wax on Easter that were also supposed to bring good luck. A. Paravicini-Bagliani, *The Pope's Body*, trans. D.S. Peterson (Chicago, 2000), pp. 75–81.

[19] ADV AA153.

[20] When M. Aubert, the second consul, died in 1785, he was buried in Saint Agricol even though he was not from that parish. ADV AA153.

painted on the façade of the church, thereby creating a visual link between it and the Hôtel-de-Ville.

The church of Saint Agricol was one of Avignon's oldest and was named after the city's patron saint. Saint Agricol (*c.*630–700) was a native of Avignon who was descended from a noble Roman family. He succeeded his father Saint Magne as bishop of Avignon in the late seventh century, and was named as Avignon's patron saint in 1647.[21] He supposedly established the church that bears his name himself when he donated his ancestral estate to the diocese. Its main altar contained the relics of Saint Agricol and his father, which were originally in the cathedral, but were translated to the church from the cathedral during the reign of Pope John XXII (1316–34). John XXII was the first pope to spend his entire reign in Avignon. He would have known about Saint Agricol because he was bishop of Avignon before he was elected to the papal throne.

The cult of Saint Agricol was of minor importance until the mid-fifteenth century, when the papacy definitively returned to Rome and established a legation to administer the city in its name. As the papal legation became a permanent fixture in the city's political landscape, the magistrates moved the city hall in 1471 from its original location adjacent to the papal palace to a new location next to the church of Saint Agricol. The cult of Saint Agricol experienced a revival during this period because it offered the city a divine protector whose local affiliations were a counterbalance to the growing influence of foreign authority in Avignon. In the final decades of the *ancien régime*, the city magistrates were still great patrons of this church and its titular cult. In 1763 they used city funds to refurbish a statue of Saint Agricol at the north entrance of the city,[22] and in 1783 they gave 150 livres to whitewash the church interior.[23] Every year they disbursed 60 livres from the city budget to pay for fireworks for Saint Agricol's Feast Day on 2 September.[24] No other religious institution in the city benefited so much from the magistrates' largesse.

While the church of Saint Agricol provided a sacred space which reflected the independent authority of the municipality, within the Hôtel-de-Ville itself there was another locus of the sacred but one over which the political influence was contested. Although the Hôtel-de-Ville was a secular building in which the day-to-day administration and governance of Avignon was conducted, on the uppermost floor of the building was a private chapel. This chapel constituted not only a sacred space, but it was also a place in which the authority of the papacy challenged that

---

[21] Deliberations of Avignon's city council, 10 December 1647. BMA MS 3334, no. 51.

[22] BMA MS 1516.

[23] BMA MS 2937, no. 1.

[24] BMA MS 2936–2937.

of the city magistrates. Dedicated to St Clement, whose relics had been presented to the magistrates in 1703 by Pope Clement XI (1700–1721), it symbolized the supremacy of Papal authority over the city.

Saint Clement was a first-century pope and martyr (92–101?) and, like the cult of Saint Louis in France, his cult was by proxy a cult of the eighteenth-century papacy.[25] Four of the eight popes of the eighteenth century were named Clement, and their combined reign lasted forty-six years.[26] Clement was a common name for popes from this time because Saint Clement's letter to the church in Corinth was the first documented example of a bishop of Rome asserting his authority in the affairs of another diocese, and thus served as a reminder of papal supremacy over the Catholic Church at a time when the papacy was contending with the challenges of Gallicanism and Febronianism.[27]

Every year on the feast of Saint Clement (23 November) the magistrates assembled in the chapel to hear Mass, which was concluded with exclamations of *vive le pape*. This was the only official ceremony that took place in the chapel during the year. This ritual of submission became especially pertinent in the midst of a quarrel in 1764–65 between the papal government and the consuls. The dispute began when the *viguier* (the most senior member of the town council) adorned his balcony at the opera house with a tapestry, a sumptuary privilege that was reserved exclusively for the vice-legate. In the ensuing row Vice-Legate Salviati dismissed both the *viguier* and the first consul from office, although they were eventually reinstated after making a lengthy appeal to Rome.

On the feast of Saint Clement in 1764, Vice-Legate Salviati informed the consuls that he would attend Mass in the chapel of the Hôtel-de-Ville 'in consideration of the pope our sovereign, who carries his name'.[28] This was highly unusual because no vice-legate had ever attended this ceremony before, and the vice-legate never entered the Hôtel-de-Ville except on the most extraordinary of occasions, such as the inauguration of a portrait of Pope Pius VI in 1778. On the evening of the 23 November, Salviati arrived at the Hôtel-de-Ville by carriage to the sound of a trumpet fanfare and escorted by his Swiss Guards and cavalry. The consuls met him at the door (a standard gesture of deference) and accompanied him to the chapel where he was placed on a throne between the magistrates and the altar where the relics of Saint Clement were kept. Salviati celebrated the Feast of Saint

---

[25] On the cult of Saint Louis in early modern France, see P. Burke, *The Fabrication of Louis XIV* (New Haven, 1984), pp. 28, 115.

[26] Clement XI (1700–1721), Clement XII (1730–40), Clement XIII (1758–69), and Clement XIV (1769–74).

[27] O. Chadwick, *The Popes and the European Revolution* (Oxford, 1981).

[28] BMA MS 2564, f. 66.

Clement at the Hôtel-de-Ville the following year as well, and the ceremony was even more lavish. Having had more time to anticipate the vice-legate's arrival, the magistrates adorned the halls with tapestries and chandeliers, and hung the papal arms on the façade of the building. At the elevation of the Eucharist there was an artillery salvo, and that night the façade of the city hall was illuminated with candles and lamps.[29]

This seating arrangement was a change from how the magistrates and vice-legate were seated for ceremonies in the cathedral, where they sat across from each other on opposite sides of the main altar. It was a visual lesson for the consuls of the political order in Avignon, with the vice-legate posited as the intermediary between their sovereign the pope (symbolized by Saint Clement's relics) and the magistrates.[30] Salviati was also placed between the Eucharist and the magistrates when the host was consecrated at the height of the Mass. This reassertion of the vice-legate's authority was an especially humiliating reproof for the consuls because it occurred in their own centre of power.

A third major ritual site associated with the Hôtel-de-Ville was the public square in front of the building which was called the *Place d'Horloge* because of the clock tower that crowned the city hall. This public square was a counterpart to the *Place du Palais*, and was where urban festivals moved to after the vice-legate had retired from the ceremonies. Continuing with the earlier example from the Feast of Saint John, it was customary for the consuls and magistrates to return to the Hôtel-de-Ville after escorting the vice-legate back to his palace to light a second bonfire in the plaza using a candle of yellow wax.[31] This inaugurated the more raucous portion of the festival that Avignon was famous for, when the night was given over to drinking, music and dancing.

The *Place d'Horloge* was where the sacred and profane overlapped on the outer threshold of the city's primary ritual centre. In as much as religious festivals were, to borrow from the terminology of Mircea Eliade, a departure from 'historical time', which is devoid of spiritual significance, and a recovery of 'primordial time' or an 'eternal present' that is contemporaneous with the divine, the *Place d'Horloge* marked the points of entry and exit between the two.[32] The assembly of the magistrates in the *Place d'Horloge* formally began the festival, and their return from the *Place du Palais* and lighting the fire in front of the Hôtel-de-Ville marked the start of the merry-making.. The relationship between urban hierarchy and

---

[29] Ibid., f. 74.

[30] The design of the royal chapel at Versailles had a similar effect, where the seating was arranged so that one could not see the altar without seeing the king.

[31] ADV AA153, f. 5.

[32] Eliade, *The Sacred and the Profane*, pp. 85–91.

sacred geography is further evident with the respective decorum observed at the two sites; musicians and fountains of wine could be found in the *Place d'Horloge*, but not in the *Place du Palais*.[33]

The Royal Convent of the Celestines

The third sacred space in Avignon that had important political implications was the royal monastery of the Celestines, which was located on the southern periphery of the city at a distance from the *Place du Palais* and *Place d'Horloge* (see Figure 15.1). It was built in the late fourteenth century during the Papal Schism to house the tomb of the Blessed Peter of Luxembourg (1369–87), a cardinal at the court of the schismatic pope Clement VII (1378–94). Although it was primarily a royal site, the papal government also co-opted it to represent its authority and to counter royal influence in the city. Through this dual affiliation, the monastery of the Celestines provided a means for the townspeople of Avignon to articulate their loyalty to both the papacy and the monarchy without giving the appearance of favouring one over the other.

Peter of Luxembourg's career and the monastery of the Celestines were both outcomes of the relationship between the papacy and the French monarchy during the Avignon papacy and the Schism.[34] Peter was from an aristocratic family that was allied with the French king during the Hundred Years' War (his father Gui de Luxembourg was killed fighting for the French at the Battle of Bastvillers in 1371), and with the help of royal patronage, he rose quickly through the church ranks. In 1384, at the age of fourteen, he became the bishop of Metz, and later that same year he was elevated to the College of Cardinals. During his brief life he acquired a great reputation for holiness, and when he died in Avignon in 1387, his grave at the paupers' cemetery of Saint Michel on the south side of the city immediately became a pilgrimage site for thousands of people who came seeking miraculous cures.[35]

Construction of the monastery began in 1393, and the king's uncle and former regent, the duke of Berry, was there to lay the first stone along with the king's

---

[33] For the festival held for the election Pope Pius VI, wine fountains were set up in the *Place d'Horloge*, the *Place Pie*, the *Place Carmes*, and the *Place St. Didier*. ADV 1J668 no. 27.

[34] S. Comte, 'Les Celestines, le roi et le pape: les monastères d'Avignon et de Gentilly et le pouvoir', *Provence Historique* 184 (1996), 229–51.

[35] D. Carru and S. Gagnière, 'Notes sur quelques objets de devotion populaire: ampoules et enseignes de pèlerinage du Moyen Age tardif provenant d'Avignon', *Mémoires de l'Academie de Vaucluse* 7:12 (1992), 55–92.

brother, the duke of Orleans, and the duke of Burgundy. The Celestines in Avignon enjoyed 'all the privileges and honours attached to other royal convents situated in Rome and other Ecclesiastical States; [including] the right to post the royal arms above all their doors'.[36] The Celestine order, which the king had chosen to occupy the monastery, was likewise affiliated with the French monarchy. It was founded in 1264 by Pietro da Morrone, a hermit who was elected as Pope Celestine V, and then abdicated after only five months. He was subsequently imprisoned by his successor Boniface VIII and died in his custody. Philip IV patronized the Celestine order when it was introduced in France in 1300 as a way of humiliating his political adversary Boniface VIII, and his successors continued to patronize it as well. King Charles V established a Celestine convent in Paris in 1352, and several of his Valois successors had their hearts interred there.[37]

Royal patronage of the monastery and the cult of Peter of Luxembourg continued into the seventeenth century. In 1659 Louis XIV made a request to Pope Alexander VII for Peter's feast day on 15 July to be celebrated in every Celestine monastery in France.[38] In 1673 it became necessary to remove the relics of Saint Benezet, the legendary builder of Avignon's famous bridge, from their original location in a chapel on the bridge when it was in danger of collapsing. Louis XIV intervened to have them transferred to the Celestines, even though there were several other religious institutions in Avignon with a better claim to them.[39] Louis himself was descended from the House of Luxembourg, and so by patronizing the cult of Peter of Luxembourg and augmenting the role of the monastery of the Celestines as a sacred site, he made papal Avignon into a centre of the state cult of the French monarchy.

Royal patronage of the cult of Peter of Luxembourg declined after the reign of Louis XIV, and the Celestine order waned in France during the eighteenth century until it was dissolved in the 1780s. However, the monastery in Avignon, which lay outside the control of the Gallican Church, remained active until the Revolution and continued to be affiliated with the monarchy. When the Dauphin was born in 1781, members of the Royal Order of Saint Louis residing in Avignon sang a *Te Deum* at the Celestines church in a separate ceremony from the official urban celebrations held in the cathedral.[40] The Feast of Saint Louis, which was observed

---

[36] ADV H Celestines.

[37] Among the Valois monarchs whose hearts were buried at the Celestines in Paris were Louis XII, Henry III, Francis II, and Charles IX. Catherine de Medici also had her heart buried there. Vanessa Harding, *The Dead and the Living in Paris and London, 1500–1670* (Cambridge, 2002), p. 126.

[38] BMA MS 2816.

[39] BMA MS 2817, f. 180.

[40] ADV 1G298, f. 140.

every year on 25 August, was not, however, celebrated at the Celestines, but in the Chapel of Saint Louis in the former College of the Jesuits. This diluted the affiliation of the Celestines with the monarchy and prevented it from being a space for exclusively royal representation.

The vice-legates also associated themselves with the Celestines and the cult of Peter of Luxembourg. There were many affinities between the vice-legates and Peter of Luxembourg because they were both members of the papal court and prominent figures in Avignon's political history who came from outside the city. There was also the mutual affiliation with the College of Cardinals, since serving as vice-legate was typically followed by one's elevation to the Sacred College. Because Peter of Luxembourg was a cardinal, many cardinals chose to build their tombs at the Celestines, which contemporaries described as a 'veritable necropolis' of the College.[41]

The vice-legates actively promoted the cult of Peter of Luxembourg in Avignon as the magistrates did that of Saint Agricol. They attended the ceremonies at the Celestines for the Feast of Peter of Luxembourg on 15 July which, apart from the annual processions, was the only religious observance they participated in outside the immediate vicinity of the palace. They also promoted his role as a divine protector of Avignon. During an outbreak of the plague in 1640, for example, Vice-Legate Sforza placed the city under Peter of Luxembourg's protection.[42]

In a speech inaugurating the portrait of Louis XVI in the Hôtel-de-Ville in 1783, Avignon's municipal assessor asserted that 'To serve the King, and to be Subjects of the Pope, has always been the object of our primary vow. To cherish the two, but to cherish them in a way that our attachment for one never harms the fidelity that we owe to the other, this is our primary duty'.[43] The dual affiliation of the cult of Peter of Luxembourg made it an ideal medium for the magistrates in Avignon to demonstrate simultaneously their loyalty to the papacy and the French monarchy without overtly showing a preference for one or the other. This cult represented foreign sovereignty over Avignon in a way that was ambiguous enough to be both royal and papal at the same time.

Even though Peter of Luxembourg was never formally canonized as a saint (he was beatified but his canonization proceedings were disrupted by the political turmoil of the Great Schism), his dual association with the monarchy and the papal

---

[41] BMA MS 3063.

[42] A painting by Nicholas Mignard commemorating the event, now in the Musée Calvet in Avignon, shows Sforza standing in the foreground with Peter of Luxembourg appearing through the clouds above him and the papal palace in the background. On the floor in front of Sforza there is a cardinal's red berretta that both he and Peter are motioning towards, adding emphasis to their mutual affiliation.

[43] BMA MS 2936, no. 38.

government gave him an elevated status that is reflected in Avignon's sacred geography. The magistrates played a subordinate role on his feast day, thereby reinforcing the political hierarchy in Avignon, by carrying the dais containing his relics in procession around the cloister of the monastery.[44]

The interaction of the cult of Peter of Luxembourg and the cult of Saint Agricol further underscores how the urban political hierarchy was articulated and reinforced through respective affiliations with the sacred objects and spaces. Whenever the city was threatened by storm or drought, the townspeople made a communal appeal to Saint Agricol for his intercession by exposing his relics in the church for three days, and then carrying them in procession on a route which linked the three principal sacred sites within the city. First they were taken to the cathedral where they were placed on the archbishop's throne.[45] Afterwards the relics were carried in procession to the Celestines and placed on Peter of Luxembourg's tomb. Even though Saint Agricol was technically higher in the celestial hierarchy because he was recognized as a saint while Peter of Luxembourg was only beatified, Saint Agricol played a supplicatory role in this ritual.

Peter of Luxembourg's relics never left the monastery of the Celestines, and rituals involving his intercession always required the act of going to him, much as the magistrates were accustomed to meeting the vice-legate in his palace at the beginning of urban rituals, or persons seeking a royal favour went to Versailles. Eighteenth-century rulers no longer went to their subjects as their predecessors had done during the Middle Ages and Renaissance, rather, their subjects came to them. This was in contrast with Saint Agricol who was more mobile and immediately accessible to the townspeople. His relics were physically present in Avignon's public spaces when they were carried through the streets during public rituals and annual processions while the Avignonnais sang hymns in his honour. The fact that many of these songs were in Provençal rather than French or Latin suggests that this cult had a lot of popular appeal, and was not just a cult for the urban elite.

The location of the Celestine monastery on the periphery of the city likewise reflected its special status as an urban cult centre. Situated on the extreme southern side of the city, a location that was not even within the city limits until the second half of the fourteenth century, it lay far from Avignon's ritual axis of the *Place du Palais* and the *Place d'Horloge*. The rituals that took place there involved a departure from the normal radius of Avignon's sacred geography, which echoed the local tradition of the *roumavage* or 'miniature pilgrimage' in which individuals or communities visited a sacred space that lay outside the confines of their

---

[44] BMA MS 3063.
[45] BMA 2829, f. 290.

everyday lives either as part of an annual ritual, or during special circumstances when they sought divine intervention.[46]

Conclusion

The use of Avignon's sacred spaces remained an important medium for articulating urban authority on the eve of the French Revolution. Their continued political importance was not simply a matter of conserving religious custom for its own sake, although tradition was indeed important to the Avignonnais. The cosmology behind religious rituals and sacred spaces retained much of its vitality in the age of enlightenment and was continuously co-opted and reinterpreted to facilitate changes in the structure of urban authority.

For example, in 1768 Louis XV temporarily annexed the papal states in France to force Clement XIII to dissolve the Jesuit order. The Marquis de Rochechouard, who governed the city in the king's name, made several changes to the ritual practices associated with Avignon's sacred spaces in order to bolster royal authority. He moved the celebrations of the Feast of Saint Louis from the former college of the Jesuits to the Celestines, and opened the festival by ringing a special silver bell in the *Place du Palais*, which was previously used only to announce the death of a pope and the election of his successor.[47] He also instituted a new annual procession for the Feast of the Assumption of the Virgin on 15 August, which had been observed in the royal domain since the seventeenth century. In this procession, the magistrates were made to carry the dais of the Virgin rather than march with the chapter of Saint Agricol as was the custom in other processions.[48]

Avignon was eventually restored to the papacy in 1774, and everything went back largely to the way it had been before. However, when the French Revolution began fifteen years later, the city's sacred geography was again deployed to reflect political change. When local patriots expelled papal officials and declared themselves united with France in 1790, they moved the Feast of Saint Louis to the cathedral. The silver bell in the *Place du Palais* was co-opted once again for royal representation and was rung continuously for twenty-four hours on the feast day, as

---

[46] M.-H. Froeschlé-Chopard, *Espace et sacré en Provence (XVIe–Xxe siècle): cultes, images, confréries* (Paris, 1994); J.-P. Clébert, *Les Fêtes en Provence* (Avignon, 1982).

[47] A contemporary description of the Feast of Saint Louis in 1768 is in a diary by Joseph-Agricol Arnavon, BMA MS 1520, 152–4.

[48] The procession for the Feast of the Assumption was a votive festival established by Louis XIII in 1638; therefore, by instituting this procession in Avignon, Rochechouard was bringing the city in conformity with the rest of France. K. Krause, *Der "Voeu de Louis XIII": Die Chorausstrattung von Notre-Dame in Paris unter Ludwig XIV* (Munich, 1989).

if to rechristen it and the city as part of the French Nation.[49] This new location for the Feast of Saint Louis moved royal representation from the periphery to the centre of Avignon's ritual geography in a way that reflected the changing physical relationship between the monarchy and the French people, since the king had recently been moved from his palace at Versailles miles outside of Paris to the Tuileries in the heart of the capital. Entering into the royal presence, either symbolically or literally, was no longer akin to making a pilgrimage.

As political power in Avignon began to originate from a more local level during the Revolution, the cult of Saint Agricol also became more prominent, and there was a dramatic increase in the frequency with which his relics were displayed to invoke his intercession. In the twenty-five-year period between 1768 and 1792 his relics were exposed only seventeen times, five of which were during the revolutionary years of 1790–92.[50] They were brought out three times in 1791 alone, which was the most turbulent year of the Revolution in Avignon, when factional violence was at its height. This was more than in any comparable period. Except for the brief period in 1794 when the Catholic faith was suppressed in Avignon, the church of Saint Agricol remained a sacred space and survived the Revolution largely intact. It became the seat of the Diocese of Vaucluse in 1793, was closed and converted into a forge in 1794, but was then reconsecrated the following year.[51] The cathedral, which was closed in 1791, was not restored to the Catholic faith until 1822.

The cult of Peter of Luxembourg, on the other hand, fell out of use when it was no longer imperative to balance papal and royal representation in the city. The convent of the Celestines was closed in 1791 and converted into barracks and a storage depot for books and hay. In 1794 it became a military hospital. The relics of Peter of Luxemburg were moved to the parish church of Saint Didier in February 1793, and were badly damaged the following year when the church was closed and used as a prison.[52] During the nineteenth century a shrine was erected in the chapel in Saint Didier where Peter of Luxembourg's relics were transferred and

---

[49] *Courrier d'Avignon*, 26 August 1790. BMA P1000, T5.

[50] ADV 1G298 and 1G299. There is no data on exposition of Saint Agricol's relics after May 1792, when the registers of the archbishop end.

[51] B. Thomas, 'Monuments et oeuvres d'art avignonnais à l'épreuve de la Révolution', *Mémoires de l'Académie de Vaucluse* 7:9 (1989), 113–52.

[52] S. Gagnière, 'Les reliques de Saint Benezet: notes historiques et récolement', *Mémoires de l'Académie de Vaucluse* (1984), 161–73. The relics of Saint Benezet had also been transferred to Saint Didier. It is generally believed that the relics were damaged not by anti-clerical vandals, but by religious prisoners who were seeking to gain a piece of the saint for themselves. Many of the stolen relics were returned to the church in the early nineteenth century.

are still kept; while this re-established a sacred focus for the cult, it never regained the importance it had had in Avignon under the *ancien régime*.

Avignon is an example of how traditional notions of sacred space endured during this period of dechristianization, secularization, and enlightenment; when the spiritual and physical worlds were supposedly growing more distant from each other. For many historians, this period marks a decisive shift in European society and culture from Mircea Eliade's '*homo religiosus*' to modern man, for whom 'the sense of the religiousness of the cosmos becomes lost'.[53] David Bell summarizes this trend in France in his recent work when he remarks about how intellectuals of the eighteenth century 'replaced a transcendent vision in which human existence derived its structure and purpose from external, supernatural forces with a political vision in which this structure and purpose arose out of humanity itself'.[54] While Bell is certainly right in as much as he speaks of a political culture of France as a whole, provincial studies such as Avignon on the eve of the French Revolution remind us that the transition from a sacred to a secular cosmology was a gradual process that did not occur uniformly, and that change and continuity frequently overlapped.

---

[53] Eliade, *The Sacred and the Profane*, p. 107.
[54] D.A. Bell, *The Cult of the Nation in France, Inventing Nationalism, 1680–1800* (Cambridge, MA, 2001), p. 39.

Index

The numbers in italics refer to plates in the volume.